CIVIL WAR RECOLLECTIONS

Ellis Spear in 1863

THE CIVIL WAR RECOLLECTIONS
OF GENERAL ELLIS SPEAR

Co-edited by ABBOTT SPEAR,
ANDREA C. HAWKES, MARIE H. MCCOSH,
CRAIG L. SYMONDS *and* MICHAEL H. ALPERT

THE UNIVERSITY OF MAINE PRESS
ORONO, MAINE 1997

Copyright © 1997 by the University of Maine Press. All rights reserved under International and Pan-American Copyright Conventions. No part of this book may be reproduced, in whole or in part, by any means whatsoever, whether photomechanical, electronic, or otherwise, without permission in writing from the publisher, except by a reviewer who may quote brief passages in a review to be printed in a magazine or newspaper.

ISBN: 0-89101-094-7

This book has been smyth-sewn for permanence. The paper used in this publication meets the minimum requirements of the American National Standard for Information Sciences—Permanence of Paper for Printed Library Materials, ANSI Z39.48-1984.

DEDICATION

My objective was to preserve General Ellis Spear's Recollections *for his many descendants, among them my sons Edward and James, and my grandchildren Alan, Mark, Suzanne, Jason, Jeffrey and Gregory.*

—Abbott Spear

CONTENTS

PREFACE / TEXTUAL INTRODUCTION ix

THE CIVIL WAR RECOLLECTIONS
[*circa* 1904-1918]
Introduction 3
From Wiscasset to Washington 4
Shepherdstown and Fredericksburg 12
The Retreat from Fredericksburg 21
Winter Quarters and "The Mud March" 23
The Battle of Chancellorsville 27
The Battle of Gettysburg 32
Following Lee's Retreat 41
"Playing for Position" 52
Rappahannock Station 61
Mine Run 67
Winter Quarters 76
The Wilderness 92
Spotsylvania Court House 103
Bethesda Church 116
Petersburg 123
The Weldon Railroad 140
Peebles Farm and Pegram's Farm 148
Destruction of the Weldon Railroad 158
Lewis Farm, Gravelly Run and Five Forks 166
Appomattox 175
The Return Home 184

ADDENDA

CIVIL WAR DIARIES, 1863 — 1865
1863   197
1864   235
1865   265

THE PERSONAL MEMORANDA
[1896]
Introduction   289
From Wiscasset to Washington   289
Shepherdstown and Fredericksburg   294
Winter Quarters and "The Mud March"   303
The Battle of Chancellorsville   308
The Battle of Gettysburg   309
Following Lee's Retreat   319
"Playing for Position"   324
Rappahannock Station   327
Mine Run   330
Winter Quarters   335
The Wilderness   337
Spotsylvania Court House   345

ENDNOTES   351

INDEX   385

ILLUSTRATIONS

FRONTISPIECE: Ellis Spear in 1863

PHOTOGRAPHS FOLLOWING PAGE 194
I. Ellis Spear
II. Samuel T. Keene
III. Ellis Spear
IV. Susan Wilde Spear
V. Sarah F. and Samuel T. Keene
VI. William W. Morrell
VII. Adelbert Ames
VIII. Joshua L. Chamberlain
IX. A. W. Clark
X. Walter G. Morrill
XI. Rappahannock Station in 1863
XII. Officers of the Twentieth Maine, *late 1863-early 1864*
XIII. Officers and wives of the Twentieth Maine,
photograph taken March 21, 1864
XIV. Ellis Spear, *undated, late nineteenth-century photograph*
XV. Sarah F. Keene Spear, *undated, late nineteenth-century photograph*
XVI. Ellis Spear, *undated, turn-of-the-century photograph*
XVII. Ellis Spear, *undated, early twentieth-century photograph*

FLOOR PLAN OF SHELTER,
drawing reproduced from Personal Memoranda *manuscript*   305

PREFACE

General Ellis Spear was born in Warren, Maine, on October 15, 1834. He graduated from Bowdoin College in 1858. After the Civil War, he returned to civilian life and was first employed by the United States Patent Office. He then practiced Patent Law privately in Washington, D. C., until shortly before his death on April 3, 1918. (He was appointed Commissioner of Patents in 1876 and interrupted his private practice to serve two years in that office.)

During the Civil War, Ellis Spear first served as Captain of Company G of the 20th Maine Regiment of volunteers which was assigned to the Third Brigade, First Division of the Fifth Corps. After May, 1863, he served as Major, but he did not receive his commission as Major until August of that year. He was in command of the regiment much of the time after Gettysburg until almost the end of the war. He was commissioned Lieutenant Colonel on July 11, 1864, and was mustered in as Colonel in March, 1865. He then served on General Bartlett's staff until, during the Appomattox Campaign, he was placed in command of the 198th Pennsylvania Regiment.

He was breveted Lieutenant Colonel for "gallant and distinguished service" at the battle of Peebles Farm and breveted Colonel for "gallant and meritorious service" at the engagement at Lewis Farm. Finally, he was breveted Brigadier General for his "faithful and meritorious service" during the campaign which led to the surrender of the Army of Northern Virginia.

About 1896, General Spear was assigned the task of preparing an historical sketch of the regiment for use in the forthcoming *Maine at Gettysburg* (Portland, Maine, Lakeside Press, 1898) in which each unit had a section. Each section had a photograph of its monument, an account of its activities, a listing of participants, a listing of casualties, an historical sketch and a roster. In *Maine at Gettysburg* the account of the fighting, "The Regiment Engaged," was written by Captain Howard L. Prince. Prince's article became the generally accepted account of the action at Little Round Top. The account of

PREFACE

that action in Spear's *Civil War Recollections* differs markedly from Prince's and provides new information by a front-line participant.

Spear was active in the Twentieth Maine Association. A 1911 clipping from a Boston newspaper notes that General Spear was again chosen head of the organization. He was also on the committee of the Association that was charged with designing the Gettysburg monument and selecting a site for it. In fact, General Spear designed the monument himself.

Ellis Spear spent as much time as he could at "The Farm" in Warren where he was born; his home in Washington was named "Mt. Pleasant" after one of the Camden Hills best seen from his property. He was respected by many people in Warren, and in 1882 he gave the Memorial Day address there. In 1913 he gave the address on the occasion of the dedication of the monument at the Old Settlers Cemetery. Always attentive to his upbringing and education, he served for many years on the Board of Overseers of Bowdoin College.

Susan Wilde, who Ellis Spear married on March 18, 1863, died in 1873. As described in the *Civil War Recollections*, Captain Samuel T. Keene was killed at Petersburg. In 1875 the widower Spear married the widow Sarah Keene; co-editor Abbott Spear was a grandson of that marriage.

—revised from a preface written by Abbott Spear in 1992

EDITORS' INTRODUCTION

The main textual matter of this volume consists of three original documents: Ellis Spear's 1863-65 *Diaries*, his 1896 *Personal Memoranda*, and his *Civil War Recollections*, dating from the early decades of the twentieth century.

Spear's 1862 Civil War diary, if it ever existed, has been lost; the 1863-65 diary volumes are presented in this edition on pages 197-285. The three diaries are comprised of brief daily entries written into small (1863: 2½" x 4"; 1864: 3" x 3¾"; 1865: 3" x 5¾") leather-covered volumes that have lined pages with preprinted dates.

Many readers will undoubtedly be struck by the immediacy of Spear's concerns, especially the attention he pays to his daily routine and to his correspondence, which served as a life-line to and from the safe harbor of Spear's home in Maine. The daily list of correspondence, along with other personal concerns, is notated with an air of matter-of-factness that obscures the brutal condition in which Spear found himself. Harrowing experiences, such as the night spent on the field at the Second Bull Run battlefield, on October, 19, 1863 (page 228), are recounted without elaboration.

These diary entries collectively form an historical account of the war as experienced on the field of battle. Kept as a record of personal experience, they were not necessarily intended to serve as source material for an extended memoir. In their own unassuming way, the entries offer a thorough testimonial to the immediate world of a soldier's life; the broader horizon of Spear's later memoirs required having his highly-charged emotional experiences "recollected in tranquility," to use Wordsworth's well-known formula. Only, in Spear's case, the tranquility was tempered by his fierce insistence on truth-telling, without self-aggrandizement or histrionic stance-taking. In this sense, the experiential focus of the later writing grows deliberately from the *Diaries*.

Spear's 1896 *Personal Memoranda* is printed on pages 289-350. The *Personal Memoranda* manuscript is a carefully written final draft in a

INTRODUCTION

leather-covered volume with lined 7½" x 9¾" paper. The surviving manuscript is clearly intended as a volume for Spear's descendants to keep *in memoriam*. The manuscript does not appear to be a working draft intended for eventual publication.

In style, the *Personal Memoranda* develops at times in a stream-of-consciousness modality that reveals the intricate process of salvaging events from memory. The manuscript volume ends abruptly at and around Spotslyvania Court House. Presumably there was a second volume, now lost, that brought the *Personal Memoranda* to the war's conclusion. Although dated 1896, there is no way to determine what length of time was required to bring the memoir to its extant state of completion. It may very well have been worked on sporadically over a period of many years.

In this edition, Spear's *Civil War Recollections* is placed first. It is treated in a privileged manner since it is as close as we can come to the author's account in its final intended form. Of the three documents, it provides the most detailed articulation of the actual lived experience of a Civil War soldier, with historical information on Gettysburg and other important battles that may alter the "official" history of the war. Based on the *Personal Memoranda* and on the *Diaries* (as well as on Spear's post-war research), the *Civil War Recollections*, with its fuller presentation of events and persons, was possibly intended for eventual publication, though the author continues to state that his descendants constitute his intended audience.

Ellis Spear never brought his *Civil War Recollections* into fully copy-edited form. The manuscript consists of unbound 8½" x 11" sheets that show much revision and stylistic fine-tuning. The first quarter of the manuscript is typed, with hand-written corrections and changes; and the remainder of the manuscript is handwritten. Spear's lack of closure may have been due to age or ill-health or perfectionism or loss of interest. In any case, it seems reasonable to assume that the manuscript was worked on intermittently during the period between 1905 and 1914/1918: on page 3 Spear dates the manuscript to 40 years after the Civil War, whereas the reference on page

INTRODUCTION

186 to the tactical use of airplanes dates work on the manuscript to World War I, at the very end of Spear's long life.

Whatever the compositional time-frame, Spear carried the manuscript to a point where it is *essentially* complete, with an articulate description of the broad sweep of events from the beginning of his engagement in the Civil War to the end of his involvement, and with everything in the *Personal Memoranda* included and often significantly augmented. One loses the feeling of immediacy that is very much evident in the earlier documents, but the flow of Spear's experience is presented with a richness of detail and integrity of sequence that reads without disruption or absurdity; and, importantly, the voice of the writer as a skilled literary author is also wonderfully evident in the *Civil War Recollections* as extant.

Following the *Personal Memoranda* readers will find 30 pages of endnotes to literary and historical references and to factual information on individuals and events. Since this book is a personal memoir, and not intended to serve as an introduction to Civil War history, the endnotes are limited in scope. The aim throughout is to present the manuscripts accurately in an unimpeded format while providing the reader with an intelligible text.

Though this edition gives prominence to the later *Civil War Recollections*, each version of Ellis Spear's personal account is important; and in some significant ways the earlier accounts bring to the foreground the emotional core of Spear's concerns. The editors believe that the presentation of these three manuscripts together makes this volume a rich source for raising and studying intriguing issues concerning historical memory. Taken together, the manuscripts let us see how history (understood as both factual account and private "legend") was conceived and revisited by a highly-articulate private citizen thrown into the chaos of the Civil War.

★ ★ ★ ★ ★

INTRODUCTION

This edition follows the author's final intended wording, which, with a bit of effort, is almost always decipherable in the original manuscripts. The spelling and punctuation of the manuscripts are followed closely. Idiosyncratic and inconsistent usage is unaltered throughout, including the use of nonstandard contractions and abbreviations. Readers will undoubtedly notice Spear's spelling irregularities and inconsistencies. Whenever clarifying words, letters or punctuation marks are added, they are enclosed in square brackets. Words that cannot be read due to damage to the manuscript-page are referred to as *illegible*; words that cannot be understood due to Ellis Spear's handwriting are referred to as *indecipherable*. Since the entries in the *Diaries* are compact and are especially irregular in punctuation, capitalization and spelling, they are presented without significant emendation; in this way the reader does not need to confront a relentless (and unnecessary) thicket of editorial additions. The main body of this book is typeset in a "ragged right" format in order to suggest the informal character of the manuscripts.

★ ★ ★ ★ ★

The editorial work for this book involved many people. Among them, Abbott Spear was the most important. Abbott gathered the manuscripts and photographs and did the initial editorial work so that his grandfather's memoir could be intelligently considered for publication. Using Abbott's effort as a foundation, Marie H. McCosh transcribed the *Civil War Recollections*. In a similar vein, Andrea C. Hawkes transcribed the *Personal Memoranda* and the *Diaries*. Craig Symonds offered much necessary insight and provided most of the endnotes which put Ellis Spear's experiences into a larger context and provide clarification for moments when Spear was unsure of his military superiors' motivation. Michael H. Alpert acted as general editor of the book. He, with Andrea C. Hawkes, made the final editorial decisions for this volume. This book was indexed by Mary E. Lawrence.

THE CIVIL WAR RECOLLECTIONS
OF GENERAL ELLIS SPEAR

THE CIVIL WAR RECOLLECTIONS OF GENERAL ELLIS SPEAR

[INTRODUCTION]

I propose herein as occasion may offer, to put into effect a long cherished plan of writing my personal recollections of the Civil War. I do not for a moment suppose that this will be of any public interest but that it may possibly be interesting to some of my descendents.

As I have not the time to make searches for verifying statements (excepting those of my own diary) I may some times be in error as to places and dates, but it will be understood that for the greater part at least, I write only of my personal recollections and of what I personally saw and of what I took part; and I shall write as truthfully as I am able and as fully as my time and memory, impaired perhaps by the lapse of forty years, will permit. As my first service was in command of a Company and afterwards and for the greater part in command of a regiment, and only for a brief period in command of a Brigade, my observations relate to subordinate matters and are concerned chiefly with the march, the camp, and the fighting line. The general movements, the strategy and tactics of the Army of the Potomac in which I served are matters of history, which is not always accurate in details since it is made up of reports, or based on reports colored sometimes, more or less, by personal interest. These general matters my family and descendents can read about in the published records, but I caution them not to believe all they read. Those of which I write are the smaller details, often not without importance to a just and accurate understanding of general movements and of the results of those movements.

It appears to me that the actors in these affairs owe to posterity a just and truthful account of what they saw without unjust disparag[e]ment to others and without boasting or misrepresentations of one[']s own services.

CIVIL WAR RECOLLECTIONS

[FROM WISCASSET TO WASHINGTON]

During the first year of the war I was teaching school in the village of Wiscasset in Maine. I remember well the strain of the war in that first year, upon those who remained at home, the eager interest for news from the front, the vague rumors, the false reports[,] the hopes fondly cherished too often on unsufficient foundation, the blundering and reverses; the jealousies and resentments with which we watched the "Copper Heads" and all the dull and constant pain and anxiety for the fate of the country.[1] It was as if the skies were always clouded. I had for my own part (and I think this was not uncommon) a feeling which I could not always suppress, that the confederates (rebels we then called them) were better commanded and better fitted for war. I feared they were on the whole of superior material for soldiers. We had the impression that the southern people were as a class fighting men with a strain of domineering, of overbearing insolence, bred of a slave-holding state of society. The northern people had not the military spirit[.] The Militia of the State of Maine had been for so long a time disbanded that I only could faintly remember the last "General Muster" which I saw, in which perhaps there were 150 men and one old piece of artillery, to me at that time a tremendous display. So I [more] feared disaster than hoped for success for the National Armies, even before the Battle of Bull Run, and when the news came of that disaster it seemed for a little while like the beginning of the end. The disaster at Balls Bluff was a severe blow also.[2]

The battle of Fort Donelson was a light in the darkness and gave us some ground for hope. Here was not only victory certain and important, but what was of more importance, here was also a man at last discovered who could win victories, and I remember also what was highly encouraging, he appeared to be modest and to be making truthful reports.[3]

My school dragged tediously on and I have since noticed in the old copy of the Aeneid which I was using in school, memoranda relating to the war which reminded me that my mind was not at that time wholly upon the book.

At the close of the first year of the war it seemed easier to go to the front than to stay at home. There was a call, which followed the disasterous Peninsula Campaign, for "300,000 more" troops, and it was a relief to take part in the struggle after the bitter disappointment and grief caused by that great and disasterous campaign.[4] Although we were reluctant to admit that the disaster was due to any fault of the Army and deeply resented the criticisms made by the "Copper Heads", there was nothing in the campaign to inspire confidence in the leader, although there was nothing discreditable to the troops whose fighting qualities, developed in the campaign, could not fail to inspire confidence in the quality of the Northern soldiers.

I think it was early in July of 1862 when I began to raise a Company. I procured the necessary authority from the Governor of the State, the necessary blanks and other papers, and made a beginning in the business which was altogether new and unlike anything I had ever undertaken before. I was utterly ignorant of the business and I knew nobody any better informed in the matter than I was. As a matter of course I commenced enlistment in the town where I lived. It was slow work and I had very little money, but explored, as well as I could[,] the country round about the village. I obtained some recruits from the village and more from the farming country in the vicinity of the village. For a while it seemed as if I should fail and I contemplated enlisting as a private soldier. Fortunately however, there were two other men in neighboring towns engaged in the same business of endeavoring to raise Companies and these had not men sufficient in numbers to form a Company and were not yet assigned to any organization. One of these men was Joseph F. Land in Edgecomb just across the river from Wiscasset, and the other was J. J. A. Hoffses of Jefferson.[5] We consolidated our respective enlistments and formed a Company of 87 men, not a full Company but above the minimum[,] and this Company was assigned by the Governor to the 20th Regiment[,] the last regiment of the State troops enlisted under that call. I collected our men and took them to Portland, the rendezvous of the Regiment. The understanding was (as proposed by them) that I should be Captain, Land First Lieutenant, and Hoffses Second Lieutenant. The regiment was made up of men enlisted in widely separated parts of the State and had comparatively few from the larger centers. But the men were almost wholly of the original New England stock, all sturdy, reliable characters, self-respecting and as good as any that had been organized into regiments. Of course there were some (as afterwards appeared) unfitted morally and physically to make good soldiers. As we had had no military experience and knew nothing of the qualifications necessary for a soldier beyond mere physical conditions (and not always those,) we were poorly qualified to serve as recruiting officers. Besides that[,] we were over eager to get recruits, the temptation was to take anything we could get. One stout little fellow [Henry Pero, of Wiscasset] who wanted to enlist was a trifle too short and I had an extra pair of taps put on his boots, a pious fraud I fear, but it caused him to pass unchallenged. He served until the close of the war and became an excellent soldier. I remember another fraud, not perpetrated by the enlisting officer, and not discovered by him, until after organization of the regiment. This was a man with a very black beard, which turned gray by degrees after we got into camp. He was not of my Company and I was not responsible for him. Of the enlisted men there was not one who had any military training or drill whatever. In the military sense they did not know their right hands from their left.

All of the officers, with few exceptions, were good men, but almost all of them were without military experience or training. One Captain had served in the Mexican war and was supposed therefore to know all that was necessary to be known; but he had forgotten much and proved to be too old to bear the hardships of active service. There was also another Captain who had served in an earlier regiment in 1861 as a Lieutenant and whose experience was of some value in the organization of the regiment.[6]

The Major of the regiment [Charles D. Gilmore, of Bangor] had served as a Captain in the 6th Maine and had procured a transfer from that regiment and appointment to a Major in the 20th. He appeared to have some political influence but I do not remember that he rendered any material aid in the organization or instruction of the regiment; but I do remember that he afterwards proved to be a most untrustworthy, worthless skulker.

The Lieutenant Colonel (Chamberlain) was fresh from a Professorship in Bowdoin College where I had known him when I was a student there. He was (and is) a gentleman and a scholar and although he was also without military knowledge or experience[,] he was a man of such intelligence and urbanity and kindliness of feeling that he exerted a useful influence even in the organization of the regiment.[7] The Colonel assigned to the regiment was Adelbert Ames a young man who had graduated from West Point early in 1861 and had served as a Lieutenant in Griffin[']s Regular Battery from the beginning of the war, an able man, of great energy and courage and a trained soldier, but at that time, without great experience in dealing with men and (like many of the West Pointers) understanding very little the character of the volunteers.[8]

The camp was provided with comfortable quarters for the men, with plain camp rations, good and wholesome, with a competent cook for each Company. There was no difficulty in finding cooks amongst the enlisted men and some of them were fairly skillful. We had mainly beef and vegetables and good appetites. Officers and men were served from the same rations and so far as food was concerned there was no difficulty whatever. That part of the duty of the soldier which consisted in cooking rations was all learned; but in every thing else there was confusion. At first there was no quartermaster, and one of the officers [Moses W. Brown, of Brownsville] was temporarily detailed for that service. Although a very able man and a lawyer, of some experience, he had to learn the duties of his office with the instant performance of them pressing upon him. He had to learn how to keep the books, how to fill out blanks, how to make requisites and to prepare vouchers while distributing the uniforms and clothing.

However, in some way order was gradually evolved out of confusion and the men were put into uniform and provided with suitable underclothing, shoes and caps. Only two Companies were armed and they served as guards, although knowledge of guard mounting and guard service was limited. However[,] the men were orderly, as they had always been accustomed to be, and we did not need any guard house or the use of force in preserving order. My remembrance of the occurences at that camp is very dim, but I am positive that we did not have there any regimental drill. We had Company drill to a small extent but it was not in the Manual in Arms, and the men learned only to get into line, to count off and to go from line into column[s] of fours, and from column[s] back into line. We held one regimental parade of which I have a distinct recollection. To say that it was a crude affair is to state the matter very mildly. The Battalion[,] with no other drilling excepting that which I have indicated, with only two Companies armed, and without sufficient skill to enable it to get into straight line, must have presented the appearance of a very large awkward squad. The Drum Corps was equally new to itself and to the business. The Colonel took his position in front of the battalion and the band began to play, if that could be called playing in which every instrument had its own key and time. It made a noise and interrupted the instructions and exhortations of the Colonel. Deafened by its own uproar the band began to move along the line, in defiance of the order to "stop that (condemned) drumming." Finally, as a last resort the Colonel advanced, sword in hand, & drove the drum corps to the rear of the Battalion. Thereafter [the] dress parade proceeded and was of the nature of a school in which there was no reciting but only instruction adapted to the need of the regiment, and of the most primitive sort. The Colonel addressed individuals of whom he knew only the officers by name and not all of them. Some he designated by name, and some by designation or location. The terms he used were rather those of West Point than of a Sunday School. The criticisms, for which there was abundant occasion, were insistent and severe, and one exceptionally awkward Lieutenant, was ordered into the rear of the Regiment, because after repeated requests that officer would not draw up his bowels.[9]

I remember my first service as Officer of the day, I had not yet received my uniform or sword. In the dress of an ordinary citizen and armed with a ram rod I was endeavoring to perform duties of which I knew nothing. Fortunately there was little occasion for an Officer of the day. There was nothing to do and I did not know how to do it. In the evening I was summoned to the tent of the Colonel who had just arrived in camp. This was the day before the memorable Dress Parade. I found that Officer in his tent with Lieutenant Colonel Chamberlain. I do not remember what was said on my entrance, but I do recall that my greeting was strictly military, in that it was not civil. The Colonel proceeded to express his opinion of the conditions of affairs in which the only thing clear to my mind was that that condition was [a] highly unsatisfactory one. He summed the matter up by saying that it was a "hell of a regiment." I was uncertain whether he was talking to me, for my benefit or for the benefit of the Lieutenant Colonel. I am inclined to think it was the latter, and as soon as it was proper, excused myself and went out.

Fortunately, our uniforms arrived, and I procured my sword and belt and the regulation sash and the shoulder straps. How I got the sword and belt and the sash I do not know. The uniform, a patriotic friend furnished on credit, and my old friend Wales Hubbard of Wiscasset loaned me $10 wherewith to start in the undertaking of putting down the rebellion. The men had more money than the officers for they received each a bounty of $100 as an inducement to enlist, the officers of course got nothing, excepting such as were shrewd enough to enlist first and get their commissions afterwards. Our commissions were dated back to the 9th of August 1862 and we were mustered in on the 29th of the same month, and on the next day mostly without arms but with drill enough to be able to get into line and to march by the flank, we took the train for Boston, the exigencies of the service permitting no delay. At Boston we took [a] steam ship in company with the 36th Massachusetts for Washington.[10] The ship was crowded. There was not space in the state rooms for all the officers; and the men, (nearly 2,000 in all), were crowded in the hold. On the voyage Colonel Ames kept school for the officers. We studied Casey's Tactics, and so incessantly that there was no time for sea sickness; and I have no recollection whatever of any incidents of the voyage, excepting that when going up the Potomac River there was a brief vacation in the schools.[11] We arrived at Alexandria just in time to see the wharves of that City and a number of river steamers crowded the river near the wharves, occupied largely by wounded men; and then we heard first of the disastrous battle of Second Bull Run.[12] The ghastly sights at Alexandria were not at all cheering nor was the news which accompanied and explained those sights. Apparently we were going to butt in at the worst of it. Above Alexandria we were transferred to smaller steamers and soon were landed in Washington, and spent our first night in a spacious and well ventilated hotel which consisted of an open lot on 6th Street above the Arsenal, well furnished with old bottles and dead cats[.] The next day we moved down into the Arsenal grounds and the eight unarmed companies were then armed and equipped. After this and near night fall we moved to join our Brigade, which was the Third Brigade of the First Division of the 5th Army Corps to which we had been assigned. We crossed the original "Long Bridge", since demolished, and moved into Virginia for the first time, the distance I now know must have been seven or eight miles.[13] The evening was warm, the men just disembarked from a wearisome ocean voyage in which they had been cramped and without exercise and many of them weakened by sea sickness. Further, they were utterly unaccustomed to marching in column and unused to the burden of the knap sack, ammunition and gun, which, under the most favorable circumstances annoyed the soldier and impeded his movement. The Colonel had been accustomed to march with a battery and had no idea of the condition and present capacity of the men for marching on foot, and he moved at such a pace and without halting to rest, that the regiment straggled badly. I did not myself suffer as I was not heavily loaded and had been accustomed to long walks. Unfortunately, when we reached the camp of the Brigade the Colonel, annoyed by the straggling, upbraided the men and as those only heard the reproaches who had kept up, and therefor[e] deserved praise instead of blame, the impression was not very favorable, and a very unfortunate prejudice arose against the commanding officer by an incident apparently trivial. I saw these men afterwards, indeed I had them follow me many times, on marches more prolonged and painful, without a murmur; but this first march rankled in their minds a long time, and prevented them from giving just credit to the Commanding Officer to whose discipline and instruction they were to owe so much.

We arrived at this camp after dark and could not see even the ground we lay on, but we slept soundly. My recollection of this camp, although it was the first, is very dim. But we [were] on the front, with pickets out. I remember I had not enough to eat, and the work of studying tactics, caring for the men and perfecting the organization was insistent. The enemy were some where in our front and the rumors of an attack on our front all false, but natural enough in view of our recent defeat and the presence of the enemy in the country near. A camp is always a hot bed of rumors. Soon after joining the Brigade, I do not remember how long, but it must have been only a few days, we moved on the Antietam Campaign[.] The men had rations, but some of the Officers, I among the number, did not have time or opportunity or did not know enough, to provide themselves with rations for the march. We crossed the Potomac by the old Aqueduct Bridge the column moving in the empty canal aqueduct underneath the wagon way. At Frederick City we came upon traces of the enemy showing signs of sudden evacuation. There were cattle killed and half dressed and abandoned.

[SHEPHERDSTOWN AND FREDERICKSBURG SEPTEMBER—DECEMBER, 1862]

Thence after delays we moved to South Mountain, the march was a hard one and I have no recollection of the details of it.[14] My whole thought and energy were absorbed and expended in keeping up the men, who thus put into the field and into a hard campaign without preparation, suffered severely, many fell out by the way, and I remember one night when we halted for bivouac only twelve of my men were in line. But the others soon came up. At South Mountain we first saw a battle field with the dead lying upon it. We came to the field of Antietam on the evening of the 16th of September. Every body knows the history of that battle so far as the general movements are concerned, and the disputes concerning it. The 5th corps lay in the rear in reserve, and so far as I know, did not fire a gun. Our regiment was in rear of a battery and had the experience of a few hostile shells, but nobody was hurt on our side, and we did not hurt anybody. Our innocence was rewarded with safety but not with praise.

Later however, we got into trouble. The battle of Antietam was fought on Wednesday[,] and on Saturday a part of the 5th Corps crossed the Potomac and we were for the first time under musketry fire. The 3rd Brigade consisting of the 44th New York and 83rd Pennsylvania 16th Michigan and 20th Maine crossed at Shepherdstown Ford; another Brigade crossed at the dam above. We waded in water two or three feet deep and upon the right

12

bank formed line of battle under cover of the bluff. As soon as we had formed it was discovered, (I presume for the first time,) that the enemy were on that side of the river, and in force. Whether or not this might not have been ascertained without sending over two Brigades I am unable to say, and being at that time not yet very learned in military matters, I assumed that it was all right. As soon as we were fairly into the river on our hasty return the enemy opened fire from the bluffs, but fortunately for us they were held back by a battery on the north side and we escaped with slight loss; I believe only one man wounded, although we came back with more water than glory and not much elated by the adventure. The retreat, under fire, was rather trying to raw recruits but the regiment behaved well. Whether the steadiness of the men was due to steadiness of nerve, or to the difficulty of running in three feet of water, I am unable to say; but although still under fire when we regained the north bank, there was no disorder. The troops at the dam above fared worse[,] the dead and wounded were in the river and on the other side at the lime kilns. We moved up there and endeavored to rescue them. I found a flat boat and put some men in it who paddled across. The enemy very considerately did not fire upon them. They opened fire afterwards and occupied an old brick-kiln from which their sharp shooters annoyed us during the rest of the day. The water had been drawn from the canal and this made a very good intrenchment. We established pickets along the bank and slept in the canal, rather I should say, I attempted to sleep there, but found it so uncomfortable that I preferred to run the risk of sleeping on the bank. In the morning one of our batteries opened [fire] upon the brick building and speedily drove out the sharp shooters. Why this battery could not have been put into position to hold back the enemy on the day before, was another mystery, which in my ignorance of military matters I could not explain. I noticed it did the work very effectively on the next morning, knocked great holes in the brick wall at the first fire and promptly scattered the enemy's sharp shooters.

After this affair we moved down the river and came on Antietam Creek near the mouth and on a low malarial ground. We remained there during the rest of September and all the greater part of October. I do not now know of any more unhealthy malarial location, or any more unhealthy malarial season of the year, than the place and the season of encampment at that time, but there seemed to be either no consideration of such matters, or some supposed military necessity yet unknown to me, which compelled our encampment there. The other regiments of the Brigade were of more seasoned men, but our men were absolutely unacclimated. Further, we were not provided with tents and had no protection against dew or rain excepting rubber blankets, and as a matter of course slept on the bare ground. Inevitably very many of the men were sick. Strange to say, there was neither shelter nor proper food provided for the sick. Fortunately there were some old deserted houses near by and in this the sick were placed lying on the bare floor, suffering chiefly from malarial poisoning and diarrhea, there was no food for them excepting the regular marching rations and not sufficient medical attention. [*deleted:* The sick lay upon the bare floor.] Many of them died, and I believe we lost about 300 men there. Of these, the greater number were sent to hospitals, but very many of them, originally perhaps less fit for service, never returned to the regiment. During all this time we were almost incessantly at work. The Colonel drilled the officers part of the day and the officers drilled their Companies the remainder of the day, and studied tactics by night. It will not seem wonderful that some of the officers broke down. One Captain died [Timothy F. Andrews, of Harmony] and some other officers went to the hospital and did not return. During all this also, so far as my recollection goes, we had nothing but marching rations, that is to say, coffee, salt pork and the regular arm[y] cracker, the worst thing ever invented for feeding men.[15] How all this happened when we were less than seventy miles from Washington with a railroad running to that place is another of the puzzles chargeable[,] I suppose, to military necessity, or the incompetency of the head of the Army. I remember very distinctly one young man by the name of [Xenophon] Heath in my Company who died there lying upon the floor and for whom I was able to do nothing except to give him what little I could of my personal attention. He had come to Portland with a younger brother both of them under 20 years of age[,] the only sons of a widowed mother. I would not allow the younger brother to be mustered in, but sent him back to his mother, and this when the older brother died, was a great consolation to me.

I should say in relation to the shelter, that for my self I was fortunate enough to get a tent fly which formed a fair covering, although when pitched it was open at both ends. I slept on the ground however, rolled in a blanket like all the rest. October closed our first six weeks in the field, but it had not been very encouraging. The enemy had captured 10,000 men at Harpers Ferry and falling back into Virginia with all their plunder and with no more loss in killed and wounded than they had inflicted upon us.[16]

Early in November we moved across the river. Tramping on foot as an Infantry Captain must, and trying to keep his men in column and prevent straggling, my outlook was narrow. [[*deleted:* Somewhere on the march, the exact place I do not remember, I was in [the] rear of my Company, as was proper in such a march[,] for the purpose of preventing straggling, when the Adjutant rode back with orders from the Colonel [Ames] putting me in arrest. Of course this was something of a surprise and I inquired the cause[.] [T]he Adjutant informed that one of my men had straggled to the front, an incident of course which I could not be aware of and for which I was not responsible. I attributed the arrest to the fact that I had some words with the Colonel a few days before, in which I had resented some profanity addressed to myself and other officers by the Colonel and had advised him [that] while I was ready and anxious to do my duty as an officer, I had always been accustomed to be treated as a gentleman and thought it not unreasonable to expect that. However, he a few days later revoked the order on some lame excuse. I never had any reason however to complain of anything from him afterwards, indeed rather the reverse.]]

We moved down to Harpers Ferry passing the old rendezvous of John Brown. We crossed the Potomac on pontoons above the ruins of the railroad bridge, and moving through the lower part of the ruined old town of Harpers Ferry[,] crossed the Shenandoah and thence followed the road near the river. As we filed down the wooded hilly slope we saw the gate way made by the river in the mountain[s], and in the distance the thread of a pontoon bridge stretched across the river and men like a column of flies walking across it. Below was the ruined bridge and on the right the ruins of the old arsenal, a scene quite striking, the picturesque mountains, the river, the wrecks of the war, and the moving army seen from the hills above. Mixed with my remembrance of this unusual scenery is an incident quite as distinctly impressed upon my memory which illustrated the vividness of the impressions made by the stomach. I was in perpetual hunger and by some accident came into possession, just at that time, of a tin can of lobster of which I ate as we marched down the road. I think my recollection of that is quite as vivid as my remembrance of the scenery. We passed the northern end of the high ridge of the mountain lying east of the Shenandoah, then turned to the right and moved into Virginia. I have no recollection of the march excepting our camp at Snickers Gap where we were drenched by rain in the night. [*deleted:* At another camp near Warrenton we were in the woods and there were two or three inches of snow.] While we were in camp near Warrenton[,] McClelland was relieved of command of the Army of the Potomac.[17] Our men had seen but little of him and did not share in the attachment to his person which many of the men who had served longer under him seemed to have. We had had no reason to cherish any high opinion of his military abilities and had not fallen under the charms of his personal qualities. We looked on with indifference while he made his last military flourish, and indeed I do not remember that there was any great demonstration of regret in that part of the Army which we saw on that occasion. Burnside took command and this incident occasioned no enthusiasm.[18] There was one incident at White Plains which I recall, as illustrating the manner in which we marched. [*deleted:* The provision trains moved with us and] We had recently been provided with shelter tents. These the Company Officers left with the regimental wagons when we started on the march. When we halted that night at White Plains in a snow storm[,] I sent my Second Lieutenant to find the wagons and get our shelter tents and to procure rations, if possible, for we had nothing to eat. Neither the Second Lieutenant, nor the First who followed him, could find the wagons, and the prospect was dismal, cold, hunger and an unsheltered snow bank for a bed; but it was not yet dark and after a long tramp I found the wagon, recovered the shelter tent pieces and procured some hard tack. When I returned to the regiment[,] matters looked more cheerful. A fire had been kindled and the snow around it brushed away down to the dead leaves. One of our men had brought us part of the hind quarter of a captured sheep, and we had the luxurious prospect of fried mutton with our hard tack. We put up our shelter tent while the mutton was in the frying pan and spread our blankets on the leaves in front of the fire. We dined sumptuously[,] and after a smoke before the fire, slept soundly and comfortably. We had some hard marching on the way to Fredericksburg and a three days['] bivouac on a level clay field in the mud and rain, but our shelter tent kept off the rain and by diligent attention to the ditch outside of the tent we kept out the water.[19] There were three of us in the tent and as we had no reading matter, but only a pack of cards[,] we played "cut throat euchre" as long as we could endure it.[20] The tent was not high enough to stand in and one of us had to lie across the end and one on each side, each resting upon one elbow and handling the cards as best we could. When we got tired of that position we would exchange places so as to bring the other elbow into action, and when we were utterly weary of the game we went out and stood in the rain. At last we came down to the vicinity of Fredericksburg and the 5th Corps went into camp near Stoneman's Switch, on the railroad from Fredericksburg to Acquia Creek. There we resumed drilling and the study of tactics, matters to which we gave constant attention when not on the march and when the weather permitted. I think we were in camp at that place about three weeks, incidentally giving notice to the enemy of our intention to cross the river and attack them, and as a matter of course they had ample time for making preparations to resist us. They certainly could not complain of surprise.[21]

On the morning of December 11th the monotony of the camp was broken, and the long expected battle announced with roar of Artillery. If the enemy were not fully prepared, it was not from lack of notice. The whole Army of the Potomac had been encamped in their front, three weeks or more. Their line of defence was upon a ridge, which, of elongated S. shape projected at the northwest or Falmouth End close to the river, and extended in rear of the City of Fredericksburg. The[ir] line of intrenchments followed this ridge, & on their right was refused.[22] A broad open space lay between their lines and the town, which was close to the river. A low ridge intervened, parallel with the main ridge, but nearer to the City. Our corps did not move with the advance, and, during the morning nothing of the battle which roared on our front was visible to us. But as later in the day, we came out upon the hill which formed the north bank of the river we could see the line of works of the enemy and our long line of battle, apparently clinging to the intervening ridge, in long musket range of the Confederates, but not advancing.[23] Evidently the line of the enemy over the main ridge was intact, and nothing was yet accomplished. The enemy's line was clouded with white smoke, a line of angry puffs apparently half way between the town and the crest held by the enemy, marked our line, and the roar of battle was over all the field. Evidently the charge had failed, and the backward rush had caught on the intermediate ridge and was clinging there. Some of our artillery had crossed on the pontoons and other batteries were moving forward to cross as we came up. The clay roads were wet and slippery, and in crossing one of the gullies[,] the horses of one gun near us, on the gallop to gain the opposite hill, slipped and all fell in a heap. It was plainly evident that the guns of the enemy could reach across the river and that they had accurate knowledge of the location of the bridge on which we were to cross. As we turned to the right to enter the bridge, a cannon shot fell into the mud in line with the bridge, but a little to our left. No other fell near us and we crossed without loss, climbed the bank, and filed to the right and moved, by the flank, along the street parallel with & nearest to the river. The city was deserted by the inhabitants and full of troops. Many of the houses showed marks of artillery shots, and a bank building near the river, had been smashed.[24]

The men were passing bankbills (supposed to be worthless) from hand to hand. There were no people in the town other than the soldiers, and as we passed this bank [*deleted:* some fellow who had been looting handed me a roll of bills with the remark that he would pay me off before we went into the fight. I assumed they were worthless, as he evidently assumed, and handed them along to the men as a curiosity. They were of some Virginia State Bank, and I found out afterwards they were worth about thirty cents on the dollar.] They were those of a [Virginia] state bank, the building of which, near the river, and on the street on which we were passing, had been smashed by our artillery fire. The run on the bank had been a disorderly one and not made by depositors.

Farther along we filed to the left and took a road leading obliquely towards the enemy.

I recall some of my sensations, or rather lack of sensations, in this first battle. After we had moved out on the road near a hay stack, orders came for the men to lie down. I recollect that in the act of sitting down one of my men in some way, perhaps by his knee, struck the hammer of his gun and shot himself in the hand.

It was a curious illustration of the action of a recruit in the uproar and danger of battle. He supposed he was struck by a missile of the enemy and notwithstanding my shouting for him to stay in his place, he dropped his gun and ran to the rear. He was not badly hurt.[25] While we waited [*deleted:* in the rear of the battle], I walked to the center of the line where Ames and Chamberlain were. Ames said "this is earnest work": the remark struck me as a very reasonable one and appropriate to the occasion. I went back to my Company and set upon a rock in front of my men. A little dog came along whimpering with fright, evidently some body's house pet, and I took him in my arms and held him while I remained there. There was a tremendous uproar of artillery, batteries all about us, some scarcely visible through the smoke, firing or galloping into position. I saw one of our batteries rapidly moving into position on our right. It was our first serious work in battle. The 3rd Brigade bugle sounded the charge. I put down the poor dog and abandoned him to his fate. I could not charge with a little dog under my arm. We moved forward into line of battle and advanced over the field towards the enemy chiefly I believe under fire of artillery. Further on, my Company ran up against a board fence part of which we quickly pulled down, and I moved the Company by the right flank through the gap and then came forward into line. I have no distinct recollection of the movement of the troops to our right or left. A captain of a Company has no extensive range of vision in battle. I remember on the advance that we passed some cows which seemed to be grazing undisturbed, and probably under the impression that it was a bad thunder storm. We advanced to the crest of the ridge and there halted under long range musketry fire. The troops in front of us had been unsuccessful in their charge and had fallen back, at least there were none in our immediate front. The ridge afforded us some shelter and we lay just beneath the crest of it fairly well protected. We seemed to be simply holding the line, as close as possible to the enemy, without attempting another charge upon his intrenchments.

We had lost but few men. I remember but two dead men in our vicinity. The field of the real charge of the Center grand division was far to the front of us. Evidently we were not sent in to make a second charge, but simply to hold as much as possible of the ground gained. There we lay all night. I had no blanket, but fortunately found a bit of board on which to lie. I recall one circumstance which much impressed me at the time. During the night there was [a] brilliant Aurora in the northern sky and much of the sky was blood red, not a very cheering sight even to a man who did not believe in omens. We were lying on the battle field, unsuccessful so far and with a confident enemy in our front, and a bloody sky over us, but we were undisturbed during the night though there was some scattering musketry fire. We lay there all day under fire, but partially sheltered by the ridge, and at night were relieved and moved back into the town where we were supplied with rations and remained one [day] and until the next night. Then we moved the next evening back to the front and occupied the line bivouacing in the streets we had left. Some rude intrenchments had been made in our absence and these we occupied.

The Retreat from Fredericksburg[26]

It was apparent that the battle was over, and that the part assigned to us was that of covering the rear of the corps, in the retreat. We therefore simply occupied the line and waited. The sky was obscured by black and wildly flying clouds, driven by a southwest wind, and through the rifts were occasional weird glimpses of the moon, too brief to light up the landscape. We could not see the lines of the enemy in front, nor the movement of the army in our rear, falling back to the north side of the river. While we waited, with another officer I went out, under cover of the darkness, towards the lines of the enemy. We could see nothing, distinctly, but could hear the sound of picks and shovels, as of men digging.

The clouds became more dense, and the night blacker. Some

general officer came along the line on foot. About midnight, or an hour later, the road being clear, and the main body of the army across the river, we filed silently by the left towards the river. The burial of Sir John Moore was not more doleful.[27] Not a drum was heard nor a note of any kind, though funeral notes might appropriately have been sounded; we had lost from the army about 13,000 men, in killed and wounded, and had inflicted little damage upon the enemy. In fact, we went back discouraged and left the enemy more confident.[28]

It had been reported that Burnside, in the tumult of his mortification and rages when his army was driven back, on left and front, had made foolish talk about putting himself at the head of his old corps, the Ninth, and making a desperate charge upon the works, but that, if true, must have been mere vaporing. He might as well have charged alone, and better, for with less loss. He had wasted too much already.[29]

At the river we found men of the Engineer Corps ready to take up the bridge of boats, as soon as we should have crossed.

On the other bank, we struck the clay bed of a road soaked and soaking in the rain, trampled and stirred by thousands of feet, of horses and men, and plowed deep by wheels of batteries and wagons.

We wallowed along in silence, and in the stupidity of exhaustion, which served to dull our sense of shame and humiliation.

After a while we filed to the right, and found ourselves in a field of stumps of trees. The mud was not so deep, but the ground was amply wet, and the rain still falling copiously. The men contrived to prop their shelter tents upon their guns, and to rest as well as they could on the wet ground. This was in the middle of December, and no summer picnic. My Lieutenant Land and I, being without shelter, or rations, sat dolefully upon stumps. We had not life enough remaining to talk; indeed there was nothing pleasant to talk about, and nothing remained but doggedly oppose and wear out the night and the storm.

Suddenly a happy idea struck me. Our man Vinal, who carried our rations, blankets and shelter, had been missing since we crossed the river, on the advance.[30] The climate on the south side had not agreed with him, and, wiser than Burnside he had withdrawn before suffering great loss. It occurred to me that we must be near the spot where we rested before crossing to the battle, and that Vinal would be likely to return to that spot. Land had a voice adapted to carry, and at my suggestion he stood upon the stump and lifted up his voice, and crashed into the silence of night.

Amongst the returning echoes we heard the squeak of Vinal, not two rods distant.

We soon found him, a shelter tent, dry inside & floored with straw, and with rations. Even-handed justice appeared to us to require that he should stand in the rain during the remainder of the night while we slept.

[WINTER QUARTERS & "THE MUD MARCH" JANUARY—APRIL, 1863]

We went back the next day to our old camp. It seemed probable that we should remain here the rest of the winter and we made what rude preparations we could to be comfortable, or to be as little uncomfortable, as possible. Of course the study of tactics and the drilling went on as occasion permitted, but we made our men as comfortable as possible. There were small pine trees in the vicinity which we used to help out the meagerness of the covering afforded by the shelter tents. These were composed of pieces about six feet square, and formed with button holes and buttons so that three men combining could button their pieces together to form the two sides and one end[,] and with small logs or poles to form walls underneath, a fairly comfortable shelter could be made, and with small poles a bed could be raised from the ground. We also built a Company cook house with logs, and Vinal was assigned as cook for the Company. I was luxuriously provided for as I had an old tent "fly," and built a shelter partly by excavation, and partly by walls of the small logs, this house being about six feet wide and eight feet long. A chimney and fireplace were built of stones sticks and mud, the chimney being topped out with a barrel. This elaborate structure of chimney was on the outside and at the front end, and occupied more than half of the end; but space enough was allowed for the door. Inside a bed, at the end opposite the fireplace, was made of poles resting on cross pieces. There was space enough remaining for one chair made from a barrel half cut away and with pine boughs stuffed into the bottom for a seat. The remaining half formed the back of this luxurious chair. As there was but one we occupied it alternately, the other member of the firm resorting to the bed. However, we were very comfortable; we had enough to eat, and at one time even advanced temporarily to the luxury of soft bread sent down from Washington by the way of Acquia Creek. It was brought up loosely in the cars and thrown about like so many bricks, and finally in the lack of baskets, delivered to us in blankets. The blankets were doubtless infested with that troublesome army insect [lice] which never forsook us; but the bread was soft and was considered the height of luxury. It gave us a new view of life; even the Colonel seemed to mellow.

I had reason to be satisfied as after the battle he had sent for me and complimented me [on] the "handsome manner" in which I had brought up my Company in the battle. We had some but not very much picket duty. Otherwise we were confined closely to the camp and lived in little space and in the little round of camp duties.

Before the battle I had been ill of the jaundice, a disease not likely to be benefited by a regular diet of fried pork and dry bread or by sleeping on the ground without a blanket in the middle of December; and after the battle I was worse. It occurred to me finally to apply to the Surgeon [Nathum P. Munrow, of Belfast] who gave me powdered rhubarb with such an ill effect, that I realized plainly the truth of the adage that the remedy is sometimes

WINTER QUARTERS AND "THE MUD MARCH"

worse than disease. I applied to him for further remedy[,] and either by reason of the scantiness of his supply of medicine, or failure in his diagnosis, or his lack of medical skill, he gave me the same dose. That did me no harm as I threw it away. Fortunately for myself and the men of my Company, there happened to be a supply of wheat flour, half a barrel of which [was] issued to me. I kept it for medicinal purposes, and took it myself in the form of flour gruel and put my men upon the same diet when they were sick, with excellent results. We lost, as I remember, about 40 men by disease that winter from the regiment and not one from my Company. I visited the same ground about thirty years afterwards and recognized the contour of hill and valley, the old spring, where we procured water, bubbling from beneath the roots of trees. The line of officer[']s tents was recognizable by the piles of stones marking the position of the chimneys.

Our stay at that camp was interrupted by the unfortunate movement in which, apparently[,] General Burnside sought to retrieve his fortune, known amongst the men as the "Mud March". We started from camp on the 1st day of January (I think it was the first day) and moved to the right of Falmouth up the river.[31] The march was rapid at first and the men straggled somewhat. Men just out of camp are liable to over load themselves at first. I remember one incident that amused me at the time. Pero the short fellow, whose shoes I had "tapped" in order to increase his height for enlistment, was wabbling under a load apparently larger than those of the others, [f]or on the top of his knap sack he had some extra article of large size wrapped in a tent piece. He came up while we were resting, unslung his knap-sack and proceeded to untie the bundle. It contained his violin, the solace of himself and comrades, many a long evening, but his load had been heavy and he evidently was a tired boy. He grasped the fiddle by the neck and holding it up gazed upon it with a last lingering look of affection, and then smashed it upon the top of the stump upon which he had been sitting. How much it lightened his load I do not know but it reduced the dimensions. I remember a similar instance when a little Frenchman in the regiment on a hard march gave away neck ties to reduce his burden.

We were moving on the road to the U.S. Ford and about noon it began to rain. Anybody fairly weatherwise might have expected foul weather, especially at that season of the year. It soon settled down into a cold wintry driving rain. The roads were clay and scarcely needed the thorough stirring which the batteries in advance of us had given them. Of course the column in front was soon stuck, and that evening we did not advance more than half a mile. Two or three hours before dark we halted before the side of a heavily timbered wood. Everywhere was mud. I saw two battery teams struggling to pull a single gun. There was no dry place whereupon to sit and the standing was far from comfortable. The men stood leaning upon their guns and patiently received the pelting rain. I say patiently, but of course there was the customary grumbling. About dark we moved to the right into the wood and the men took care of themselves as well as they could. For my part I wrapped my blanket around me and sat down with my back to a tree with my rubber blanket over my head. I slept fairly well I think, considering my cramped position. Next morning we moved slowly on but not far, and the next night camped in the woods. The rain had ceased but there was a low fog, aggravated by smoke from green wood fires kindled by the men. The smoke became finally almost insufferable and we lay with our heads wrapped in blankets close as possible to the ground. The whole movement (an attempt to pass the left flank of the enemy) was a failure of course; the delay gave the enemy ample notice and the head of the column did not succeed even in crossing the river.[32]

We went back into the same camp and remained there until early in April without material loss, but still more discouraged. Then we had a case of small pox in the regiment and we were put in quarantine on a hill half a mile south of the railroad, where we remained undisturbed until the battle of Chancellorsville. We were visited there by the Governor of the State [Maine Governor Abner Coburn], who explored the quarters of the men, and tasted their hard tack. I do not think he therefore ordered any for his private table. He was the guest of course of the Colonel[,] but I had the honor to escort him through the camp of my company. As the small pox cases were all removed to hospitals he ran no risk of catching that disease, whatever popularity the honor of the visit might afford him.

[THE BATTLE OF CHANCELLORSVILLE
MAY—JUNE, 1863]

At the battle of Chancellorsville, we were not permitted to join our brigade. Ames went upon some temporary staff duty and Chamberlain on his own request was sent with the regiment to guard the telegraph line from the Head quarters near Falmouth to the vicinity of the battle ground above.[33] I was upon the extreme left and fortunately occupied high ground from which I plainly saw the charge of the 6th Corps at the Marye['s] Heights.[34]

Of course the enemy occupied the strongly fortified line which they occupied at the time of the first battle of Fredericksburg in December of the year before. But as the main army of Lee had been drawn up at Chance[llo]r[s]ville to meet Hooker, a comparatively small body of men was left to command the works.[35] The charge was a fine one and I could distinctly see the lines charging over the green slopes under fire of artillery and musketry from the crest, until the men had plunged into the smoke; then the fugitive infantry and batteries could be seen escaping to the rear.

As everybody knows the battle was a failure on the right and Sedgwick was compelled to withdraw.[36] As soon as the battle was over we returned to our camp. Up to this time we had lost but few men in battle; but we had lost heavily by disease, and I do not think that the regiment numbered on the 1st of May in 1863 more than 500 men present for duty. Up to this time the line officers had been somewhat changed, one (a Captain) had died and five had resigned, all but two of them were my superiors in rank, and this left me the 2nd Captain. Land had been appointed Captain of the Company H, and [Thomas] Chamberlain had been promoted from the ranks to first Lieutenant, through the intermediate grade of Sargent, and 2nd Lieutenant.[37] Lieutenant Warren [Kendall] was afterwards assigned to my Company. While we were yet at what we called Camp Small Pox, one evening I was in Keene's tent with some other officers and Gilmore was present.[38] He was still Major, and as all danger had passed he was present. On the evening specified an orderly came and brought a message from Ames to the effect that he wished to see us, (myself and Keene) at his head quarters. We went up immediately and found him alone. He told us that he had received his promotion as Brigadier General, and would soon leave; that as a matter of course [Joshua] Chamberlain would be made Colonel. Further he said as a matter of compliment Gilmore would be made Lieutenant Colonel, but would immediately resign and then I should be Lieutenant Colonel and Keene [Major]. The plan was carried out as far as the first appointments were concerned, promptly as to Chamberlain and Gilmore. I had no friends at Court and did not get my commission as Major until August, by reason, as I heard, of the contention of [Atherton W.] Clark, senior Captain. The plan outlined by Colonel Ames that Gilmore should resign immediately upon his being mustered, and then I should be promoted to be Lieutenant Colonel and Keene to be Major failed. Gilmore evidently, had no intention of resigning. I did not receive my commission until August following and poor Keene never saw his.

 Later in May we rejoined the Brigade and moved further up the river. We lay for some days in the valley of the Rappahannock in a malarial location where I contracted further malarial poisoning. We had drawn for clothing before we left the small pox camp. We had been drilling whenever the opportunity offered. We had also some picket duty. On the 19th day of May we were reviewed, some English Lord being present. On the 25th day of May I received an assignment of nine new men for my Company, and I find also in my memorandum frequent reference to drilling. On the 28th day of May we moved up the river further and encamped near the ford, and on the 29th I was in command of the detachment digging rifle pits on the hill. On the 4th day of June we broke camp and marched further up the river, about eight miles and bivouac[ed] about two miles from another ford on the Rappahannock. On the 5th day of June we moved about three miles further up and camped near Ellis Ford. Pickets of the enemy appeared on the other side of the river. We heard cannonading, and there were rumors of movements of the troops. On the 5th day of June orders for inspection were countermanded, and marching orders received. At that time some of the sick had returned and with these and other attendants of my Company I had 52 rifles. The enem[y's] pickets were withdrawn on the 9th.[39] During these days there were reports of the movements of the enemy across the Orange and Alexandria Railroad. On the 13th day of June we moved about 7 P. M. marching until 11 where we bivouaced until noon of the 14th, and then marched until sunset bivouacing in the open field near the Orange and Alexandria Railroad. On the 16th day of June we marched about 5 A.M.[;] the day was exceedingly hot and many men fell out[,] two of my Company suffering sun stroke. We halted near Manasses Junction and about dark our regiment moved down the Brentsville wood where we picketed. We were relieved in the morning by the 16th Michigan and in the evening we rejoined the Corps, marching towards Centerville where we turned northward on the Leesburg road.[40] The day was exceedingly hot but the column was frequently halted for rest. The dust was thick and enveloped the column. In the evening of the 16th we crossed Broad Run and encamped near Gum Springs to which place we marched on the 17th and heard firing in front apparently in direction of Leesburg.[41] On the 17th Chamberlain was sick and went to a neighboring house. In the evening, there was heavy rain fall with thunder and lightning and reports came of the fighting of the day before [at] Aldie, that the cavalry had driven the enemy through the gap. On the 18th we were on picket and in the evening moved to Aldie, here I was detailed to act as field officer. Chamberlain was still ill. On the night of the 20th of June we were aroused at three o'clock with orders to be ready to move. We marched through Aldie to Middleburg where we encountered a thin line of the enemy posted behind stone walls to the north of Middleburg and in the direction of Goose Creek. I was on the left and threw forward a line of skirmishers. We drove the enemy from their position in the edge of the wood and advanced under artillery fire through the wood. Sargent [John P.] West was killed near me by a solid shot, or unexploded shell[,] and several others of the Company wounded. Col. Chamberlain was still on the sick list and just before the fighting commenced Gilmore was taken sick as usual. We crossed Goose Creek by the bridge below the position to which we had advanced and followed the enemy towards Snickersville. The enemy in our front I believe were mainly mounted men. The Cavalry which had moved up on our right took the advance and followed the enemy to Snickersville and beyond. We moved back on the 22nd and during the halt I took a squad and buried West. He lies near the stream above the stone bridge on Goose Creek and about two miles from Middleburg. On the 26th of June we marched through Leesburg across the Potomac [and it was] late in the evening when we bivouaced.[42]

    I had acquired more malarial poisoning on the Rappahannock and was suffering severely, but as I had procured a horse and was still acting as Major of the regiment, and was entitled to ride, I was able to keep up. My malarial fever was accompanied by diarrhea and [I] was barely able to ride[;] and after dismounting to rest[,] it was almost impossible to remount, but going to the hospital in such an emergency was not to be thought of [as] Gilmore had monopolized that resort as usual, and rendered it impossible for a really sick man to go to the hospital without discredit. It was known that Lee had crossed the Potomac and was with a powerful and confident army. He might strike anywhere and we all appreciated the gravity of the situation. It was no small element also in the anxious situation that the army Commanders had been changed during the movement. The greater part of the army did not know General Meade and felt no special confidence in him.[43] My diary records that we crossed the Monocacy at the ford and marched through Buckeystown and marched to about six miles from Frederick.

The country was fresh and beautiful, but we were on no picnic, but on the very serious business of hunting for the enemy, with the reasonable certainty that they would make themselves very disagreeable to us when found. We marched through Frederick on the 29th, the same old Maryland town which we had visited in September of 1862. As we had made no acquaintances on the former visit, we had no social duties here on this. There was no time even to pay a visit to the poultry houses, where we might claim acquaintance with more reason. Occasionally, with deep regret, we passed a cherry tree, but no straggling was permitted. The wheat was ripe and some fields were in sheaf, inviting to repose on luxurious straw beds, but, unfortunately for us, wheatfields and bivouacs did not coincide.

On the 30th we passed through Unionville where the rebel cavalry seemed to have preceded us, and to be prowling around the country strangely. They were formidable only by ordinarily indicating the presence of infantry but as we found, did not in this instance. It was found that Stuart, with the Confederate cavalry, had detached himself from the main body of his army, and was looking for trouble in our rear or on our flanks. This was a new and surprising bit of strategy, as we had no vulnerable line of communicating to be cut, & the infantry of the army could take care of its own trains.[44]

We moved to Hanover on the first day of July, and turned toward the sound of cannon in the west. There was no time for loitering. It was enough for us to know from this sound, that some part of our army had struck the enemy.[45] It was curious afterwards to remember how ignorant we were (I mean, we of the regiments) of the position, or movements, of the other corps of the army. Even Army Head Qrs. were not swift in finding out the positions & movements of the enemy. We knew only that Lee's army had crossed the Potomac and was hurrying up the valley behind the mountains. They could threaten Harrisburg, ravage the country, but where they would break through, we did not know. The sound of cannon indicated Gettysburg, and the passes in that vicinity.

We marched about 8 miles from the vicinity of Hanover, moving rapidly. The night was warm, but in some respects the experience was unusual. We were in a friendly country. People cheered as the columns passed, and men[,] women and children, mostly women and children, stood by the roadside with buckets of water and cups, and gave the men drink. This was a small matter, but I think it had great effect in raising the spirits of the men. We were now marching to battle in defence of our own.

At one time, as we were hurrying along in the darkness, a wave of cheering swept along from the head of the column, with the report that McLellan was again in command.

We halted and went into bivouac about 11 P. M. of the 1st. It appeared certain that there was a battle in the vicinity of Gettysburg, but the troops could safely be pushed no further without rest.

[THE BATTLE OF GETTYSBURG
2—5 JULY, 1863]

By the light of the early summer day of July 2, and to the sound of increasing cannonade, we pushed on again, all the time with the sound of battle in front developing more and more and sharper and clearer, as we came on the rear of the field in the afternoon. The white puffs of exploding shells appeared over the hill. About 4, while the sun was still high in the west, we moved by the flank to the left. Shells were coming over, and one exploded in our column just in front of us. Stragglers and wounded men coming to rear, indicated a severe struggle. Then the head of our columns turned directly to the front, and the sound of battle, just over the ridge, in and about the wheatfield, where the enemy were pushing back Sickles.[46] We had passed the northern end of the ridge of Little Round Top, and apparently would soon be in the midst of the battle[,] [in] support of Sickles corps, but in a moment the head of our brigade was turned to the left, & rear, and we marched around the north end of Little Round Top and, with the three right regiments, occupied the crest.[47] The front was open and rocky and the western face like a broken down wall of boulders, large & small.

The crest and the eastern slope were covered with open woods, and scattered over with boulders. The ridge seemed to terminate in a slope to the south. So the 83[r]d Pennsylvania, on our right, bent around, with its left refused, and the 20th joining it, faced the south, at right angles to what appeared to be the main line of battle. From our position, the ground sloped to the south. I could see through the trees, the steep and thickly wooded side of Big Round Top, two or three hundred yards distant. Towards the rear the same open forest and beyond was a fenced field not visible from our position. Our line thus formed on the higher part of the slope partly amongst boulders, and with boulders and trees on the sloping front, faced squarely to the left. We were then placed to guard against flank attack, but the battle had not then extended so far. Company "B" was sent forward as a skirmish line, under command of its Captain Morrill.[48] It disappeared in the woods on front and left, but did not connect with the skirmishes on the right.

As Major, I was in my position on the left. The first indication of the presence of the enemy was the sudden appearance of their line of battle.[49] Emerging from the woody side of Big Round Top, they burst through the bushes down the steep slope. I saw their legs first. They were so far to the left that they seemed about to overlap and flank us. They had not opened fire, and evidently had missed our skirmish line, which had gone too far to the left. Nor, when the right of the enemy's line emerged from the thicket had they struck any skirmishers on our right, as there had been no firing there. Chamberlain was on the right, and not visible from my position, but I went quickly over to him and advised him of the situation, suggesting that it seemed best to bend back two companies to meet the threat upon that flank. He assented and I did so.[50] I cannot remember which side opened fire first. Indeed, it is possible that the first volleys were practically simultaneous; perhaps we were a trifle ahead, as the enemy was moving and we were standing on the defense and ready. Then uproar of musketry, the cloud and smell of battle smoke, tense excitement but no shouting but men loading and firing as fast as possible.

The enemy, or many of them, crept forward & took shelter behind boulders, and fired on us from some partial covering, but I think these fellows overshot us generally. I have no idea how long the fight continued. At one time the left swayed back a few steps, but only for a moment. Then their fire slackened a little on the left. I walked along to the center. It seemed to me most of the color guard were knocked out. I recall that [James A.] Knight of my company was on the ground.[51] I bent over him and asked him where he was hit. "Right through me", he feebly answered. What I most distinctly remember there, besides Knight, was the Color Sergeant [Andrew J.] Tozier, who had picked up a musket dropped by one of the killed or wounded, and with his left arm about the colors, stood loading and firing, and chewing a bit of cartridge paper. Then I went back to the left. The line all the way was steady, though men were dropping out, as they were struck, but none beside [me]. I saw John Kennedy limping to the rear, but do not now recall any other man, distinctly, excepting Knight & Tozier.[52] Suddenly, in the midst of the noise of musketry, I heard a shout on the center, of "Forward," & saw the line & colors begin to move. I had received no orders, other than to hold the left and guard the flank and did not understand the meaning of the movement. But there was no time to seek explanation. The center was going ahead, apparently charging the enemy, if any, then all of course, and we all joined in the shouts and movement, and went in a rush down the slope and over the boulders. Behind one boulder, on the slope, over which I went, were two Confederates, who rose up, evidently with empty muskets. By reason of soreness of the bowels I had left my belt & revolver on my saddle, & had my sword only in hand, but there was no contest with them. They went to the rear without resistance, and those in front ran, not so many towards the Round Top as to the rear, and many ran and corralled themselves in a worm fence lane. Some of these, attempting to escape, were shot down, as they climbed the fence, and the others surrendered.

Then we discovered that Morrill and Company B had been behind a stone wall at the edge of the field behind the line of the enemy, and had been firing upon them from the rear. This probably accounts for the readiness with which they yielded to our charge. Morrill finding that the enemy had, in their advance through the woods from the right, had cut him off, withdrew his men and with a squad of Berdan's sharpshooters, who deployed on our left, took up this position behind the stone wall, in the rear of the enemy. Many years afterward I talked with Col. [William Calvin] Oates, who commanded the 15th Alabama, the regiment assailing us in the battle of Gettysburg. He was then a Representative in Congress. He told us, Capt. [Howard L.] Prince and myself, that during the fight he had the impression that he was fired upon from the rear, that he saw one of his men fall struck in the back.[53]

We gathered in the prisoners, and were caring for the wounded when orders came for the regiment to take possession of[,] when we received orders to advance[,] Big Round Top.

But before describing that affair, I will refer to the incident of the charge.

I am aware of the report that we were out of ammunition. That was not the case on the left. It has also been reported that the charge was ordered, because of that, but of this I have no knowledge. I received no such orders. Sergeant [Ruel] Thomas of Co. I, was at that time acting as a sort of messenger for the Colonel [Chamberlain] and has subsequently told me that he knew no such orders.

The story told by the men, at the time, that is to say, immediately after the battle is this. Immediately on the left of the colors, the line thinned by the fire had readjusted itself amongst the boulders, and this left wounded men in front of the line and still exposed to the fire.

These were calling on their comrades to take them to the rear, a task which would require cessation in firing. A brave fellow [Lieutenant Holman S. Melcher] in the company on the left of the colors, proposed to his fellows, to "advance and cover them["]. This, as was said of the charge of Balaklaver, was "fine but not war".[54] That is to say, it could not be done as he meant it; but as it turned out, better than he meant it. For the cry once started, went along the line with the movement which accompanied the cry. A few files away from the point where the cry and movement started, the men heard only ["]advance["] and took it for a charge, and acted accordingly.

Amongst good men like these, it was easy to start, but nothing but the enemy could stop the movement, and in this case the enemy could not, but were swept away by it. This story, though in the highest degree creditable to the men, has, so far as I am aware, never been told in print. I cannot assert of my own knowledge, that the charge was so started. I can only record that I, though acting as Major, and therefore in command of the left wing, received no orders to charge, nor any of them, excepting as to the bending back of the two left companies, as I have before related. All that I saw or heard, as to the inception of the charge, was the shout on the center, and the advance of the men commencing apparently on the center [and] following rapidly to the left. I could not see the right which was over the ridge or, at least, my whole attention was directed to the left.[55]

The center suffered most. Captain Keene, in command of the Color Company, was disabled by a bullet early in the fight, and lost in killed and wounded about 50 per cent of his Company, the total loss in the regiment being about 40 per cent. I believe there were only two hundred men remaining.[56]

The order to advance upon Big Round Top left us no time in which to bury our own dead, and we were compelled to leave them to other hands.

It was nearly dark when, unsupported, the 20th started up the hill. The slopes were too steep and rough for riding, and we, officers as well as men, climbed laboriously on foot. There was a more level space on the top, but both top and sides were heavily wooded, and strewn with boulders, some of which were of enormous size. We formed [a] line on the summit and in the darkness threw forward a picket line. Soon the sound of footsteps was heard in front. One of our men called out, "Who goes there?" Some stupid man answered "Fourth Texas". More quick-witted[,] our men replied, "All right, come on. We're Fourth Texas", and they came on, until, close at hand, they heard the clicking of muskets cocking and were confronted with the muzzles. The first fire is recognized always as an important advantage, and they surrendered & dropped their muskets. The squad of about thirty men was under command of a Lieutenant Christian.

As they were brought up, one of them inquired, as men usually did, the name of the regiment, and he good naturedly commented on the fact that men from the two ends of the country should so meet, in the woods & dark.

We were separated by a large space from the left of our line, and, so far as we knew, were entirely without support. We kept up our picket and got what sleep we could. As for myself I was weak from the dull continual malarial fever, and diarhea, lack of food and sleep, and had no blanket. My man [John Vinal] and blanket had kept out of the zone of fire.

So thinking it imprudent to lie down upon the ground, I

selected the softest seat I could find at the foot of a tree, and seated myself, using the tree as a chair back. I presume that I fell asleep immediately. I woke sometime in the night, shaking with a chill. My teeth were chattering and every bone in my body apparently in rebellion. It was dark, but I discovered one of the men lying near me, wrapped in his blanket which he shared with me, when sufficiently awake. After awhile the shelter of the blanket[,] and the warmth of his body, subdued the chill, and in the morning the hospital steward came up and gave me a flask of whisky saturated with quinine pills. This, frequently sipped, braced me for further exertion.

In the morning we were relieved and moving to the right, went into position somewhere in rear of the left of the center. The ground we occupied was the rocky eastern slope, (a gentle slope) of the ridge extending from Cemetery Ridge, now the main line. We were not in position to see the field in front of us, but it was evident that the battle was not over.

We had repulsed the enemy on the left, and at the close of the second day, it was evident that he had been driven back on the right, since that was partly in our rear, and if not held, would have made our position untenable. But official information as to positions, success or failure, on parts of the field distant from us, did not reach down so far as regimental headquarters while the battle continued.[57]

There was some cannonading on the morning of the 3rd, apparently desultory and manifestly intermittent. Something was brewing. About noon, the mischief meditated by the enemy, broke out, in cannonading apparently from every battery they had which bore on or about the center of our line.[58] Not much of the shelling reached us, but the air in front was full of bursting shells, and the uproar was immense. Our batteries were replying, and an occasional cheer told that they had made an unusually good hit. I have no definite idea how long the cannonading lasted, an hour maybe; then it suddenly ceased for the greater part. There was comparative stillness and then musketry, over the hill, and then cheers. Evidently the enemy had been driven back again, and so it proved. This was the repulse of the famous Picket[t's] Charge.

About sunset it was reported that part of the Sixth Corps, which was on the left, had charged the enemy and captured a battery, but there was no movement in any part of the line visible to us. We did not move from the position occupied in the morning.

During the day Capt. Clarke had picked up a blanket, the relic on the field of some man wounded or killed, and when night came, we selected a spot apparently most favorable for a bed. It was level and grassy, and clear of stones, though rather low.

There, when darkness came, we spread the blanket, and lay down. Sound sleep is the usual companion of a soldier's bivouac. Of fresh air there is no lack; no overloading of the stomach breeds bad dreams, and sleep favoring fatigue generally makes amends for the hardness of the bed. But mishaps are liable to occur even under these favorable hygenic conditions. In this case a heavy shower in the night interrupted sleep. We endured this until our bed became a puddle and we found ourselves in soak. Then we got up, and being already dressed, pulled on, with some difficulty, our wet boots and sat upon a wall through the remainder of the night.

Morning came none too soon. It was not the "saffron morn with early blushes spread" of Pope's Iliad, but misty oppressive and hot.[59] We were soaked from head to feet, and not much refreshed by sleep. The top of a stone wall is no luxurious couch. Although it was the "Glorious Fourth", the celebration had been premature and was over. No sound or movement or order to move indicated a renewal of the battle.

What was to be done? Were the enemy to be allowed to pick up their wounded at their leisure, gather their wagons and wrecked batteries and move off, unmolested? As to all this we were in profound ignorance. We did not know enough of General Meade, to form a basis of conjecture. Subsequently, under Grant we soon learned that battle of one day was a stepping stone to battle of the next day. But that order of things had not been established in 1863.

I find in my diary that we lay on the same ground on the Fourth. I wrote a letter on that day, and (novel experience) sent it to mail by a citizen, some Gettysburger exploring the battlefield on the heels of the battle.

In the afternoon it rained again.

On the morning of the fifth our brigade moved out, over the battle field, across the Emmetsburg pike, and went into line upon the ground occupied on the 3rd by batteries of the enemy.

The field over which we moved and where we halted, was a sad illustration of the havoc of war.

All the slope up to the pike was strewn with muskets, haversacks, soldiers' caps, dead horses and dead men, killed during the second or third day. In one place there were seventeen dead horses in one group. Dead bodies of men lay here and there, just as they fell, some lying on the back, & with clenched hands, and others lying as if advancing when struck and fallen forward. All were black in the face and distorted and swollen until their clothes were tight upon them. These were our men. Beyond the pike and along the line occupied on the 3rd by the artillery of the enemy, were scattered bodies of confederate dead, in like condition. At one point was a small barn which had hay upon the floor, and was burned down to the hay. On the charred surface lay half burned bodies, evidently of wounded men placed there and too much hurt to move. There they were half burned and ghostly. Near the barn, on the outside were other bodies of confederates, among whom I noticed the body of what seemed an officer, distinguishable by his fine boots. But his head and shoulders, towards the fire, had been scorched to a shapeless mass. Behind the barn were the bodies of battery horses, half roasted and burst open, and putrifying in the moist heat.[60]

Over all the field, in the damp hot July air was a subtle, penetrating deadly smell, of which no friendly horse dispelled.

While we lay here waiting orders, we did what we could to give decent high burial alike to friend and enemy. Also we ate what dinner we had, of dry hardtack, for to horrors men may become accustomed, but not to hunger.

Toward night, on the fifth, we moved back, rejoined the Corps, and in darkness and mud marched southward. Near midnight we bivouaced as best we could.

[FOLLOWING LEE'S RETREAT 6 JULY—9 OCTOBER, 1863]

On the sixth we marched in the same direction, about one mile, then moved back a short distance and went into bivouac for the night. What was the object of this? I have never ascertained. We moved according to orders, at which men sometimes grumbled, but never questioned.

All that was clear to me was that we were following Lee by a very circuitous route. He had fallen back from Gettysburg directly into the valley west of the range, and we were moving southward on the east side of the range. It was a safe route, both for us and the enemy. Perhaps this was necessary.[61]

On the seventh we moved early, in cloud and rain and deep mud, and halted for the night at a point said to be about seven miles above Frederick. Rations were not abundant, but, strange to say, our mail followed and found us. My diary shows that I received three letters on that day, from my wife, dear anxious girl, hearing little except of battles, and writing every day, and the mail service, apparently better organized than the commissary, brought all these letters through mud and darkness, over fields & streams, and never lost any, so far as I am aware. We bivouaced in rain and mud, on the seventh and marched early on the eighth. The unwelcome rain followed us.

We halted on the night of the 5th as before stated and on the 6th we moved forward about one mile[,] halted awhile[,] and then moved back a short distance and bivouacked for the night. On the 7th we marched again and bivouacked about seven miles from

Frederick, there was rain and the roads were muddy and heavy. On the 9th we crossed a mountain[.][62] [I]n the distance it was a beautiful sight, the country lay like a map below us. There were broad fields divided by fences, roads, groves of trees in full leaf, wheat fields and corn fields, farm houses, the ordinary country landscape, but one thing more was quite extraordinary[:] columns of troops, batteries in long order, and long columns of trains were moving on different roads. Here and there was also a mass of troops in bivouac and beyond[,] a little town.

On the 10th of July, we moved down to the Sharpsburg Pike in the movement following Lee to the Potomac and for the first time since the evening of the 3rd of July came in contact with the enemy. We threw forward a skirmish line in the woods beyond the pike but the skirmishing was not heavy though by incautious exposure of part of our skirmish line, we lost eight men captured by the enemy. I was not on the line myself but was with the reserve. There was a cavalry scout in advance of us[,] and I find by my notes that we lost several killed or wounded in the skirmish. I remember more distinctly the capture for the reason that these men suffered severely in Andersonville. I believe this was near a place called Tighlmanville [*spelled correctly*: Tilghmanville], as faintly recorded in my book.[63]

On the 11th day of July we moved up the pike and halted near Antietam Creek, the 44th [New York] being in our rear. I see by my notes that I had time to take a bath in the stream. We moved forward in line of regiments in column double on the center[,] and subsequently we moved by the left flank while the other troops moved forward. Movement was slow and cautious. On the next day on the 12th we continued the same movement and the same order, sometimes moving to the front and sometimes by the flank to the left. We of course knew the enemy were in our front and making for the river[,] and we appeared to be going on very deliberately and with great caution. In the afternoon we had a heavy shower and moved into a clump of woods. I heard a sound of slight skirmishing and in the evening about sunset we moved back into an open field and bivouaced for the night. The business was not very strenuous as my notes indicated that a mail was distributed. On the 13th of July we moved in the afternoon towards the front. The 6th Corps on the right we found to be throwing up breast works of rocks and earth. We halted in front of these breast works and threw out pickets under Lieutenant Colonel [Freeman] Conner of the 44th New York. Up to this time we had been on this campaign without a Surgeon but on this day a new Surgeon [Dr. Abner O. Shaw] came recently appointed to the service. Some prisoners were brought in on the 14th and there was some picket firing but the report was circulating that Lee had escaped across the river. We moved forward on the same day and the news was confirmed that Lee had crossed on the 13th. There were earth works on prominent places and there were obstructions in the road. Some 200 prisoners went to the rear. We bivouacked on the night of the 14th. Pursuit had not been so hot that the sutler could not come up. There was rain that night and on Wednesday the 15th we broke camp about 2 A.M. and marched in the rain. The sun came out very hot[,] and with the heat and moisture the march over South Mountain was exceedingly painful and laborious. The men were straggling and half our regiment was in the rear. I remember distinctly the batteries were straggling worse than the infantry, the horses were broken down and there was scarcely a whole line to be seen. We went into bivouac about 5 P. M. Marched early on Thursday the 16th and bivouaced about noon near Burksville. The teams were sent for and tents put up and we went into the business of making repairs. On Friday the 17th of July we received a mail and moved early in the forenoon in the rain. We crossed the Potomac on pontoons and marched three or four miles southward. We bivouacked at night in a wheat field. I recollect at this point that Gen. [George] Sykes who was in command of the Corps compelled the regimental commanders to return the bundles of wheat which the men had picked up in the wheat field for use as beds to protect them from the ground.[64] It was of course a disagreeable duty to compel the men to return the bundles so that duty was developed on me. I personally saw that the wheat was all returned and piled up on the field and a sentinel placed over it. I took pains to withdraw the sentinel at dark conspicuously, and I noticed that the next morning when we broke camp the men had comfortable beds of wheat to sleep on. We marched on Saturday until about 11 A.M. and on Sunday the 19th moved about five miles. We were going very deliberately but on Monday we moved 14 miles down to Goose Creek.

On the 22nd we moved suddenly at 11 A.M. near Upperville and bivouacked near Rectortown, and on the next day, the 23rd moved towards Manassas Gap a march about 12 miles over bad roads. Somewhere in the gap we relieved the 3rd Corps and went to the front and had some skirmishing with the enemy during the day. Our rations failed here, the teams not being able to follow us. Cannonading further down the mountain was just audible, possibly at Chester Gap. We moved forward into the woods during the day and got possession of the crest of the hill with some skirmishing. We were recalled quite suddenly and moved back.[65] On the 25th we continued the movement down the gap without rations. As we marched from the gap into the open fields we found them thickly strewn with low growing black berries, commonly called dew berries[.] [T]he men had been without rations for two days and it was impossible to keep them in the ranks. They scattered over the grounds picking dew berries. Towards evening[,] however[,] we halted and got possession of a lean steer which the men speedily turned into fresh beef and economically cooked it before the animal heat was out thereby saving fuel. I went with Chamberlain and got a small piece of this beef partially cooked and carried it in my hands. We moved to the front with the division pickets[;] a tempest was threatening but we made haste to get the pickets out before the storm and darkness should come upon us[.] [I]n this we were partially successful and we finished establishing the pickets in the midst of a heavy tempest, in which the almost incessant lightening served to disclose the situation. We[,] however[,] succeeded in establishing a line although the country was new and partly wooded and the fields were gullied and obstructed with fences. About nine o'clock the rain ceased. Chamberlain went to the right and I to the left. For a while I guided myself by a light towards the left which I found to be from a shelter tent in which some of our men had lighted a candle[;] upon my call they came out bringing a piece of honey comb from a bee hive which they had captured in the rain from a neighboring house. The rain had beaten down the bees and they had secured the honey without harm to themselves. With a two days hunger upon me very slightly mitigated by the small bit of beef[,] I ate the honey without any close inspection[,] comb and all. I was in some doubt afterwards whether bees wax was digestible or not, but I suffered no inconvenience. My digestion[,] I have no doubt, was in excellent working order. I found my orderly and blankets and laid down and slept the remainder of the night very comfortably although the ground was as wet as my clothing. I woke early in the morning and found the weather clear, I had some difficulty in getting in the pickets. My horse was pretty well used up and I walked until the middle of the afternoon when we halted near Warrenton where I took a horse of the Head Quarter orderly until I could get another. On the 27th, we marched early in the morning and passed through Warrenton and encamped that evening near the Orange & Alexandria Railroad[;] we remained in camp there until the 2nd day of August when I was detailed in command of 100 men for fatigue duty. We had a hundred men from each brigade and marched down to the railroad on the morning of the 3rd of August. We halted for orders on the way at Meade's headquarters and soon began working on a corduroy wagon road.[66] This work was continued until the 10th day of August. We corduroyed the roads by cutting young oak trees and laying them directly upon the earth and as we were supplied with dull axes the work was very tedious and the weather was excessively hot. We continued to work down to the junction at Warrenton I do not know how many miles, but on the 10th of August we had completed the work and returned to camp. We had battalion drill that afternoon. I find in my notebook in August the 13th the unusual item that the paymaster came to the regiment. We were paid at long intervals. I think that was the second time since we had entered the service. Of course the enlisted men were well provided for since everything they needed was furnished directly by the Government[,] but nothing was so furnished to the officers[,] and their rations were bought from the Commissary for cash. How much the Government might be in our debt[,] there was no credit at the Commissary[,] and of course clothing and horses, equipment of all sorts had to be bought wherever they could be procured. Fortunately the Quartermaster [Alden Litchfield] was an expert thief and we could buy our horses of him cheaper, consoling ourselves for sharing in the plunder, with the reflection that they were stolen from the enemy. As for clothing we could go in shabby uniforms as there were no ladies in the party. A dress coat and a pair of white cotton gloves for parade was all that was required in addition to the every day fatigue suit. Upon my promotion to the majority I was of course compelled to have a new coat which was of a different construction than that of a line officers. This was a heavy strain upon my finances as it cost $60[,] nearly one-half the pay of the month. Fortunately, the commission came not long after pay day and I was thereby able to have the coat. That coat lasted through the remainder of the war, but it was not worn except upon occasions of parade, not very frequent after 1863. I may as well say here that in the matter of rations the expense was not heavy. Ordinarily it consisted of salt pork, usually more or less rusty, hard tack, a small rectangular cracker of about the texture and hardness of a piece of sand stone and in addition to this we had coffee from which was usually extracted by long continued boiling all of the substance and as much flavor as remained after the boiling process. On rare occasions we had dried beans which after the boiling with a piece of salt pork we baked in a hole in the ground previously heated and with a cover of hot ashes and earth over the covered iron kettle. This was a luxury of which it is impossible to form a conception without the previous training of months of the fried pork and hard tack diet. The country around about was too thoroughly exhausted to afford any variation whatever of the diet. I recall at this moment that there had been one brief variation in the winter of 1863 and 64 when we procured from the sutler a few loaves of soft bread.

During all this time even upon the march we received frequent mails and wrote frequent letters.

I find no entry in my note book from August 16 to Sunday August 23 on which day I have noted that services were held.

On the 24th Col. Chamberlain who had been absent returned to the army and he took command on the 25th.[67] On this day I find an entry that I had sent for the coat heretofore mentioned, so I assume that I had received my commission as Major at that time. I had waited for it since May previous. It was understood that although I had been recommended by Ames in that month, the appointment had been delayed by the opposition of the friends of Capt. Clark who was also an aspirant for that place and who, as he was senior Captain, regarded himself as entitled to it. On the 28th day of August Gilmore returned, he having influential friends, had promptly received his commission of Lieutenant Colonel, but had not resigned as he had contemplated. He had promptly absented himself [on a] plea of sickness in the latter part of June before fighting came on at Middletown and Goose Creek and had remained until after the battle of Gettysburg and all the subsequent skirmishing[;] in fact he came back at the expiration of 60 days after which time he was liable to be mustered out under existing orders on account of such absences. Saturday the 29th day of August was the anniversary of our first muster into the service and we celebrated the occasion by working upon muster rolls and by attending a military execution. Five deserters were shot, the corps was formed on the slope of the hill in compact order and upon the opposite slope directly in front were five graves and by the side of each a coffin of rough pine boards. The men were brought up under guard each with his arms pinioned behind him marching in slow procession with a band playing the Dead March, a most melancholy sight. The men were placed each sitting upon the end of his own coffin and blind folded, the squad was brought up in front of the prisoners and at the order there was a volley and the poor fellows tumbled from their seats all dead. We immediately marched off returning to camp. This was the only military execution which I saw with one exception. We were all this time in camp near the Rappahannock. I drilled the regiment and attended to the regimental duties. The study of tactics and regimental and parade drill filled the intervals between regular camp duties. We were in such accessible position that an occasional army nurse appeared, I recollect visits of Mrs. [Isabella] Fogg and Mrs. [Ruth] Mayhew.

Quiet was broken on the 12th day of September by an order to be ready to move and to support the 2nd Corps which was making a reconnaissance towards Culpepper Court House and cannonading began about 10 A.M. and gradually receded.[68] We had brigade drill on the 15th of September, orders were repeated to have the teams up and to be ready to move at once. On the 16th we had reveille at 3 A.M. and moved across the Rappahannock about 6 o'clock going into camp about 4 in the afternoon near to Culpepper. On the 17th of September we moved through Culpepper with another Corps in advance and encamped in the afternoon near the road leading to Rappahannock about two miles beyond Culpepper[.] Some cannonading was heard towards the front and left, presumably at the ford. I should not forget to mention that before the movement which was to be in the direction of the enemy, Gilmore had again absented himself and left me in command of the regiment.[69] He went, as usual, to Washington, and for the benefit of his health. After the heavy rain which began soon after we were comfortably in camp, we had delightful September weather, the country was pleasant and we had camp rations which means the addition of beans to the ordinary fare of coffee[,] salt-pork and hard-tack. But this luxurious diet was some agreeably enlarged. One morning the cook surprised my needs by bringing in fresh boiled eggs, and sweet potatoes. This was before the invention of cold storage. So unexpected a luxury in the wilderness demanded explanation, and we were advised that these provisions were supplied by the Quartermaster with his compliments. Next morning came the same supply from the same source, and later in the day I interviewed that officer. He informed me that he got them from countrymen in the neighborhood of the camp, and I said, we appreciate the luxury highly and I should be glad to share in the expence and continue the supply. "No expense; cost me nothing"—"But I don't want any raiding or robbery of the peaceful farmers[,"] I said, and thereupon he explained the high financing of the Quartermaster's department in the field. It appeared that enterprising patriots in New York, in order to make a little money and further depreciate the Confederate currency, were printing counterfeit Confederate bills, and selling them to the army, and, I suppose, wherever they could on the border. It was a game certainly safe as it did not fall within the laws of the U.S. against counterfeiting, and the makers and users were not within reach of the Confederate authorities. Further as the counterfeit bills were mechanically better than the genuine, everybody concerned appeared to be satisfied. Nobody in the South ever suspected that a Confederate bill (even in 63 woefully depreciated) would be counterfeited, and, in any event the purchases with them as an equivalent, was better than the ordinary military plundering. So occasionally we had eggs and sweet potatoes; the weather was delightful; only the labor of drilling & picketing was upon us. We forgot the hardships & woes, and borrowed no trouble from the future.

 Even picketing was not without interest. The frontier was new to us; we explored and kept our eyes open and were necessarily on the alert. There was a fine old farmer mansion on the north of the line, where only the colored inhabitants remained. At the door once when I rode to that part of the line, was an old colored "Mammy", neatly dressed & not very dark, and speaking in as good English as anybody. Evidently she was a houseservant, & accustomed to good treatment and was contented. But the colored men had all run away. She said that some of them were afraid of the Yankees at first, and she related with much detail the stories which she said the white people told the negroes, of the terrible treatment they would receive if they fell into the hands of the Yankees[;] how in one instance these devils had loaded a ship with colored people, and then sunk it in the Potomac. She did not appear to be at all alarmed herself, and whether she was telling the truth, or indulging her imagination I was uncertain; nor was it material. The colored people were coming through our lines in numbers greater than we needed. It would of course have been imprudent, and contrary to orders, to allow them to return, and, for convenience in guarding them we loaded them into the wagons which had brought our rations [and] were otherwise returning empty. Many of these were women and children, but one morning before break of day, there came in, creeping stealthily up to the picket-line and there halted, a party of three fugitives from an adjacent plantation, frightened, but eager to "go North". There were two women and one man, one the wife of the man and the third her sister. They were very robust and decent looking colored people. The sister had a touch of ornament in her dress, an army blanket, folded diagonally and carefully arranged so that the large initials "U. S." appeared centrally on her back, these being evidently regarded as for ornament purposes solely. As they had been taken on my part of the line, they were brought directly to me. I ordered that food be given them and, when a wagon came along the line, the man, (a stout fellow) put first his wife and then her sister, head first over the high tailboard, and underneath the canvas covering, into the wagon. Their big plantation shoes disappeared last from view.

On the line I found an old familiar acquaintance, a copy of a Greek lexicon. Some fellow had doubtless stolen it from the home, and, finding it in all respects too heavy, had dropped it. I sympathized with him. I had myself felt like dropping a copy of the same edition, though not there on the march.

Our picket lines were undisturbed, with the mild exception of the invading negroes. But we kept strict watch. I rode over every part of the line once in every two hours. If one has not been roused from healthy and well earned sleep, every two hours, all night long, he cannot imagine the unserene and even impenitent spirit with which a man first receives such summons.

I tightened my belt, and mounted my horse, from force of habit, and because "it was the orders"—but if I had consulted my own feelings the country might have gone to the devil, if I could have continued my nap. A hot beef steak might have appealed more immediately to my drowsy faculties, but patriotism was at a low ebb, just then.

But our three days['] tour on pickets was over and we marched into camp. In the pleasant September weather, I drilled the regiment sufficiently for exercise, & kept the camp grounds policed. The only incident which broke the monotony and gave material for camp gossip, was the episode of the Surgeon's horse. This was a fine animal[,] the pride and comfort of the Doctor, a beautiful Sorrell with white mane and tail. He had been stolen during the last march, and the Doctor had offered a reward of fifty dollars for the recovery of the animal. In the absence of other occupation, the Quartermaster, himself an expert horse thief of large experience, had been searching, mainly for the fifty dollars and incidentally for the horse, and one day rode into camp and presented to the Doctor, simultaneously, horse and his claim for services. Great interest in the camp and officers gathering about the horse and Litchfield! It appeared that he had taken the horse forcibly, from a private soldier, at Rappahannock Station twelve miles away; and it further appeared that he had committed robbery, as the horse proved not to be the Doctor[']s, though closely resembling that animal. The man had undoubtedly stolen the horse, and gave him up to the first claimant.

The story of the Doctor[']s horse does not end here. As the horse captured by the Qrm. could not be returned[,] nothing remained for the Doctor but to mount the animal, when we moved, and ride him as if nothing had happened in the line of horse stealing, in the whole army. A week later we were on the march and near Centerville. The doctor was in his place, in rear of the regiment, when we passed the First Connecticut heavy Artillery. Officers of the battery with enlisted men were standing by the roadside, and when the hitherto unidentified animal came along, one of the battery officers recognized the steed and claimed him.

The Doctor explained the situation, and not being able to put in any strong claim surrendered the animal, borrowing in return a sorry nag for immediate use, without requirement to return.

But the Surgeon finally came to his own, and evenhanded justice prevailing, the Q.M. did not get the reward. A few days later, on the march, I saw the doctor's horse ridden by one of the cattle drivers, who undoubtedly had stolen him to save his own legs. I sent a corporal with a file of men, who dismounted the fellow and brought in the horse. Thus was the particular complication of horse thefts unravelled. This story illustrates the morals of the Army, and teaches that the way of the transgressor is not so hard in time of war, when the worst punishment likely to occur is loss of the stolen horse, but not the prior use of him.

["PLAYING FOR POSITION"
OCTOBER—NOVEMBER, 1863]

The movements of the Army, which followed our encampment beyond the Rappahannock, I did not understand at the time, and they seemed to be without purpose or plan. Indeed I have never seen in them any high degree of strategic skill. Both armies were playing for position. On the morning of the 10th of October we broke camp before daylight, and, after some delay moved towards the Rapidan, about five or six miles, where we remained during the day and at night returned to the same camp.[70]

The teams were ordered to the rear, and early on the morning of the 11th we passed through Culpepper. The streets were narrow, and part of the column was on the sidewalk. At one place the thin pale face of a woman appeared at the window, above our heads, uttering imprecations upon us. Cassandra or a fury—she might have been—"Do you know where Bull Run is" she shrieked. She yelled it again as Major [Augustus P.] Martin of the Artillery was riding by, on the walk, just beneath her. "Sister" he said, "you ought to have your head shaved". But excepting this, and the witty answer of our Irishman, nobody noticed her. Bitter losses in the war had perhaps half crazed her.

But such things always reminded us that we were in the enemy country; and indeed we were not fully assured that another Bull Run was not possible, except that we could not be stampeded as in the first. We had exceptional confidence in ourselves, perhaps more than in our Army Commanders, so often changed, and so frequently unsuccessful, and we felt that we were then in a game of strategy.

We fell back to a line a little north of Brandy Station, our brigade being rear guard; and later struck back at the enemy hanging on our rear, the same old tactics which Xenophon practiced against the Persians, in the retreat of the Ten Thousand. Xenophon had no cavalry at first, and no artillery, but the principle was the same.[71]

We crossed the river about 8 o'clock next morning, rested, and then moved on and went into camp between Bealton and Warrenton Junction. Cannonading on our rear & left. It was evident that the enemy had crossed the river above us, and was endeavoring to take us on the flank, or to force battle on conditions unfavorable to us. This might have been an affair not unlike the Second Bull Run.[72]

I find in my note book very meager memoranda of these days. What was known of the general movement, at brigade and division Head Quarters, I do not know. There were always rumors flying around. We formed part of the greater part of the army machine, nearest the bottom, and the friction came chiefly before us, and the machine having some intelligence, even at the bottom, we were curious to know what might be going on outside of our immediate vicinity. We were reasonably assured that the 2nd Corps, (then under Warren), was in our rear. The sound of firing on Oct. 14th seemed to indicate that the enemy were on our rear and perhaps partly overlapping the 2nd Corps. On that day we moved at 3 A.M. towards Manassas Junction, and halted in a high hill 4 or 5 miles west of the Junction, and at 4 P. M. were at the Junction with the Corps batteries in position. The firing on the rear increased in volume, indicating some earnest work, and later our brigade was hurried back on the double quick, apparently to reinforce the battle of the 2nd Corps.[73] Participation in the battle was apparent enough at least, to cause the Lt. Col. [Gilmore] to halt and let me take the regiment. This was not done with any formality. He simply sneaked back and I went on with the regiment.[74] In the dusk with 2nd Corps troops and a captured battery, with some infantry business, we formed lines on the railway, on which the battle had been fought, but the enemy showed no inclination to renew the contest. About 8 P. M. we withdrew, crossed Bull Run, and halted about 2 o'clock in the morning on the ridge near Centerville.[75] It was a hard march that night, and many of the men, wearied by the long continuance of it, and dulled by loss of sleep, stumbled about & straggled in the darkness, so that, when the brigade lines had been determined upon the ridge, brigade bugle calls were continuously sounded, to guide the stragglers to their regiments. We had been moving since 3 in the morning, not marching all the time, but always on the alert, and everybody was exhausted. But the 5th Corps was the last in; the others [were] all in line, and all seemed to be in favorable position to give battle if the enemy should offer it.

But, on the 15th we moved again, to the rear. Whether we were running away or skillfully maneuvering for position, or both, we did not know, nor do I know now.[76] We passed through the old earthworks at Centerville and in the afternoon halted near Fairfax, having left the 1st and 6th Corps at Centerville. The excitement occasioned by recent movements, and constant menace of battle, had affected the health of the Lt. Col. as usual, and he reported himself sick in camp. In the rainy afternoon, I was ordered with 300 men to picket on the right, relieving the details of the 1st and 2nd brigades, but before my line was firmly established[,] the bugle sounded, and a staff officer came with orders to call in the pickets and report to the brigade immediately. With difficulty, in the unknown woods, I extricated the pickets, formed them and started in pursuit, for the brigade was on the march before I could reach the place where it had encamped. What this marching, picketing, and counter marching meant none of us knew, and the uncertainty nowise tended to lessen the misery of fatigue and drenching. The rain flooded the road and we stumbled on in the darkness. Some time in the night the rain ceased, and we went into bivouac near the Centerville earthworks again in an open field. I tied my horse to a sassafras bush, and wrapping my wet self in a wet blanket, lay down on the wet ground unsheltered.

The hardships of the day had been unusual even in those days of weariness, discomfort, and short rations. The men had been carrying 7 days['] rations of bread in their haversacks and blankets. So much hard tack however carried on the persons of the men, or on horseback, crumbled and wasted, and ultimately hunger was added to weariness.

But this does not necessarily imply any acute suffering. Fatigue and lack of sleep, and wet and cold, dull the senses.

The mind retreats into itself and hibernates. As I rode tired and sometimes[,] perhaps, discouraged by the apparent lack of plans or results, I dozed. The men plodded on doggedly, generally silent after they become wearied, but with an occasional outbreak of damnations, general or particular[,] sometimes including the Colonel commanding, and sometimes the Corps or Division Commander, or whomsoever might be more reasonably charged with the badness of the roads, or the length of the march.

Thus I had celebrated my 29th birthday anniversary. The unprofitable carcass of the Lt. Col. was in the ambulance[,] dry, and comfortable. The discomfort of the place for the rest of us, was so great that we remained there all day of the 16th and consoled ourselves with the reflection that standing was as advantageous as moving under present conditions and involved less wear and tear.

The patience of a soldier is generally under cultivation, though often at the expense of profanity. Experiences in those days were abundantly promotive of the vice, at least, for at 5 A.M. on the 18th we moved back again towards Centerville over the same road but with less moisture. The movement seemed hardly necessary to our health, nor justified by the scenery or the conditions of the roads after a heavy rain; but one theory was as good as another. The brigade moved back to the junction of the Centerville and Little River roads, near Fairfax. There were rumors flying about that the enemy pickets were on our front and right, they might have been—at a distance of ten or fifteen miles. At any rate we went into bivouac and the teams were sent for, but while the men were unpacking[,] the bugle sounded, and in a few minutes we were on the march on an obscure wood road, and came out on Ox Creek. It was a beautiful place. A clear stream rippled over pebbles, and the hillsides were thick with oak and chestnut, water and wood and sheltered, but open to the sun. There were[,] as usual in those times, no orders, but rumor, comforting and therefore easily credible, had it that we were going into camp. Gilmore manifested his belief in the report, by coming up and getting into a neighboring shanty. The regiments readjusted themselves, and took ample ground for camp. This was the second time we had unpacked on that day (Oct 18), but the second time we really rested. The men promptly appropriated the chestnut crop; and, having not permanent or future interest in the trees, cut some of them down to save climbing, as the trees were tall. Additions of chestnuts to the marching ration was a matter of great interest.

We were so much settled in place, that we got a mail, and we seemed to be much at home.

It may seem that, at such a time of the war, such an appreciation of rest smacked of the ignoble. But it must be remembered that we seemed to have been exerting ourselves without results. We had marched back and forth aimlessly, as it seemed to us outside of headquarters, and on short rations, wearing out for nothing. Rest, though ignoble, seemed better for awhile at least, until some profitable strategy could be thought out. I slept that night under a shelter tent, dreaming of freshly baked beans, rest, washing in the stream & clean clothes.

At least I could sleep late. Alas, it was all a dream.

On the morning of the 19th, early, without other warning, the sound of the Division bugle indicated immediate movement.

The clear pebbly stream and possible bathing, the ungathered chestnuts, the wealth of fuel, all these vanished at the sound of the bugle. I thought of my great Grandmother Eve "Must I thus leave thee Paradise".[77] But Eve did not have to see that her horse was properly saddled, her tooth and hair brush[ed], and towel packed, and her regiment in line, and that she had her proper place in column.

Of course we turned into the old road to Centerville. Our feet knew it well. The very skies sympathized with the occasion, and although it was morning, and no proper time for thunder, it thundered loud and shook down rain copiously.

The road and the weather seemed familiar, and Centerville our place of residence.

However, we passed through and beyond [Centerville], and

about three p.m. we succeeded on a part of the second Bull Run battlefield, & whether by design or ill chance, our Division was placed in bivouac on the ground where it fought in '62, a little more than a year before. As the Division had suffered severely there, and to no purpose, the coincidence was not enlivening to men already drenched and thundered at.

It seemed like a hint of fate, and a case of *Jove non probante*.[78] The dead had never been buried, only imperfectly covered, as they lay, by sods or thin earth thrown upon them. This covering had partly washed off, and the grinning skeletons appeared all about the field. One Company of the Pennsylvania Reserves recognized the body of their Captain by the gold fillings in his front teeth. We completed these burials as well as we could.

Long before daylight the reveille sounded, and the customary scramble for coffee ensued. Little time was required for dressing. We lived Indian fashion. Water enough in the canteens for the coffee was an appreciated luxury. What extravagant fellow, on whom it had not rained for 18 hours, could afford to wash his face?

We were ready and attempted to move at 3 A.M. on the 20th, but the road was blocked, a not unusual incident in night marching, due to lack of staff officers or of intelligence in staff officers. Surely the army had been moving over these roads long enough to know them well, and the condition of them. "Three o'clock in the morning courage" may be rare, but the same may be said of appetite. Rising at that abnormal hour adds no juices to hardtack, and detracts nothing from the crust of the ancient bacon. There remains only the dregs of coffee. This enlivens for the start, and adds to the subsequent semi-comfortable stupidity of the later & more weary hours. As a starter[,] however[,] coffee is a success, and the most valuable element of the rations. It was more nearly true of the soldier in the field that he could live & work without the necessities of life, but the luxury of coffee he must. Many causes have been assigned, many answers to the question, what or who put down the rebellion. I have heard of the Army Mule and known some claimants. But, in my opinion it was due mainly to coffee. It was this palatable drug which enabled us to wait till daylight on the morning of the 20th of October, to march on the muddy Warrenton road, to wade Broad Run, and to march to the vicinity of "New Baltimore". I find in my diary the unnecessary record that here I slept well. Of course I slept well. I had risen early, had taken ample exercise, and I appeal to Caesar that I had not overeaten.

But here is an important entry. On the 21st the teams came up! And Mails! The people at home were always thinking of us. My dear wife was writing reams of paper to me, and though suffering a world more of anxiety than I did, and thereby more than fatigue or wet cold or hunger, was keeping up courage and showing a braver and more cheerful front than did any of our Army. And there were other old friends who cheered us with their letters. (Alas most of them are dead now.)

The arrival of the teams meant also the palatial residence of a wall tent. That may appear a trifling incident, but it was not. You could stand up in a wall tent; with a shelter tent you can stand up out of doors. Moreover, when you get your wall tent your valise comes also, & possibly clean underclothing; but it was not certain in those days, and probably (I blush to write it) I had worn the same underclothing continuously three weeks. But then, in those days, we did not go much with society, and, as all fared alike, in the matter of uncleanliness there was no occasion for reproach.

In order to prevent effeminacy we moved again next day to a neighboring hill, and for further exercise, the brigade moved again, on the 23rd to a new camping ground.

Mail came again, and a cold rain, and having reerected my luxurious quarters and borrow[ed] a tree from a neighbor I had a glowing fire in front of my tent. I remember that fire well. Stakes were driven down across the space in front of the tent, and against these a wall of logs was filed. In front of this wall a fire of smaller stuff was built, and this when well inflamed, made the front of the log wall a mass of glowing coal, the heat of which could be felt in the tent. But we got out our camp chairs, and sat as near as the glow would permit, as near perhaps as the King of Spain sat, when he called to have the fire removed. What solid comfort! And there was coal wherewith to light our pipes. The glow of the fire and a smoke at last.

What was it we were grumbling about yesterday? Oh yes we were wet then; but we are dry now; we were hungry then; now we have eaten not luxuriously, but sufficiently to furnish foundation for a smoke; luxury enough. We were cold then & weary, but we are hot enough now, and rested, & the memory of past suffering formed only an agreeable background & emphasized present comforts.

Forsan et haec olim meminisse juvabit.[79]

All this was good, while it lasted. We had no occasion to rebuild the fire, or to settle the bill for the fuel, though we had burned enough to last an economical family, or a lazy wood cutter a month. We left our home and fireside in the morning (much more moving than fighting) and made slow and tedious progress, as usual in the dark, and especially where there were bad crossings. Bivouacked about 8 P. M. It was reported that Head Quarters were at Auburn. This was in Virginia, and not the "loveliest village of the plain".[80] Dust and mud alternated; cold continued, the country was sparsely & poorly inhabited. It was the meanest part of the country, and we therefore remained there until the 30th when we moved and encamped near Three Mile Station on the Warrenton branch of the railroad. This was a comfortable place, when, after two or three days['] delay, we got our tents up. Evidently we were settled for a few days, and the Lt. Col. left the Ambulance, but did not interfere with the ordinary duties. I mustered the regiment, worked on the payrolls, and drilled occasionally to keep the men in exercise. Mail came with sweet letters from home and one day I rode to the Second Corps & called on acquaintances. We remained in this camp one full week. We had been three weeks on the back

RAPPAHANNOCK STATION

and forth movement, which I have described. Now, being on the line of railroad direct to Washington, we had supplies. But sutlers had been excluded from the Army for so long a time that the men were quite out of tobacco, and the Lt. Col. saw his opportunity. He had evidently some friend in Washington, who could effectively aid him, and so confidently applied for permission to have a package of tobacco brought in the Govt transportation, to supply the urgent need of the men of the regiment. The "package" which came was a huge drygoods box, of perhaps 500 weight, and this was placed in the Hd. Qrs. tent, and retailed to whomsoever had the cash, by a civilian retainer, whom the Lt. Col. kept along with him.

[RAPPAHANNOCK STATION NOVEMBER, 1863]

On the eve of the 6th of Nov. there were indications of movement. To our experienced eyes such indications often appeared in advance of orders.

The order on this occasion came in the evening.

We could not be far from the outposts of the enemy, since we were within a few miles of the Rappanhannock, and Lee must be holding that as a line, at least at the railroad crossing.

The road had been torn up by the enemy on the advance in October.

Bugles sounded early on the morning of the 7th and, although we were ready, there was the usual bustle.

Loading of the wagons was completed, the unsold remainder of the Lt. Cols. tobacco went into the Headquarter's wagon. I "fell in" the regiment and moved it up to the front where Gilmore was sitting on his horse, and was then turning to my place in the rear of the column, when he asked me to ride with him at the head of the column. We turned towards the enemy, and understood what that meant. Soon he began to complain of his leg, and an acute attack of neuralgia, and the pains and these complaints grew more frequent, as we went on. At last we came to a fence, the men threw off the top bars; I jumped my horse over it, and went on, but, looking back I saw that the Lt. Col. could not get over the fence, and then I knew that I was in command, and recognized the hypochondric soul of the gentleman who had asked me to ride with him at the head of the column. He again took refuge in the Ambulance.

We moved on and went into line of battle, in the woods which bordered the fields about Rappahannock Station, where an outpost of the enemy was intrenched, on the north side of the river.[81] Apparently there was a brigade of them, & a battery of artillery, with some going on the other side. The R.R. bridge had been destroyed, but the enemy, (as we afterwards learned) had placed a pontoon across the river in their rear. Their works were on a ridge which bordered the river, and between their and our positions was an open field. The Sixth Corps troops were in line on the right of the railroad, and our brigade, commanded now by Col. Chamberlain, was on the left.[82] We advanced in a line of columns doubled on the center, to the edge of the wood, and I put out Co. B as a skirmish line. I was soon advised that we were not to advance further, at present, as a railroad embankment intervened and a cut in the ridge beyond, were between us & the enemy's position, while the field was unobstructed in front of the Sixth Corps troops. They therefore were to charge and they were formed for that purpose with a strong skirmish line in front.

Before the charge, however, Capt. Morrill, in command of Co. B. advanced as far as the line of the Sixth Corps skirmishers, and, finding that the Sixth Maine was on his right, took his company over the embankment, and joined that regiment on their left, in a neighborly way, as they advanced.

The line moved forward steadily with the bayonets, and unchecked by the fire of musketry and cannister went over the works. Morrill, on the left, swept around the right of the enemy, and as they broke and rushed upon the bridge, fired down upon the crowd. A slight bend in the river, and the diagonal position of the troops, brought it directly within Morrill's position, and his fire was directly down upon the crowded position. Many were crowded into the river, (at that time swollen) and the retreat of the enemy was cut off. The main part of the work[,] of course, was done by the Sixth Corps. Eight stands of colors, 4 guns with caissons & horses, and 1200 prisoners were taken. But the little battle left here a large grave yard[,] for the charging line across the open field was cut by musketry & slaughter. After the fight I rode along the line. There was a squad of my men curiously interested in something held in the hand of one. He held it up to me, smiling. It was a "denture" of which the gold plate shone brightly. I said ["]you rascal. Where did you get that?["] "Out of the mouth of a dead Reb. His mouth was open, and I saw the gold and thought he did not want it any more".

We bivouacked that night in the woods. Some of the men gathering, with the prisoners taken by Morrill, around a camp fire.

Next day, Nov. 8, was cold. I guarded the flank of the regiment and crossed the river with them. There was a slight fall of snow, and the weather was cold. By reason of the waste of rations due to carrying so much on the person, we were short, and hunger was added to the discomforts of cold and fatigue, and the men were not in cheerful mood. As the Division Commander ([Joseph J.] Bartlett) rode past us, the men called out "Hardtack". This he took as an affront, and ordered that the Commanders of the regiments so offending should drill their men. As my regiment was understood to be one of the offenders, I was so ordered, and put them through a battalion drill, on the double quick, for the sake of warmth. Lack of bread in the midst of such exposure and hardship, was no small matter, and the call should have been taken good naturedly, and not as insubordination, as it plainly was not so intended. But there was one advantage in the drill. It kept the men warm during the exercise, though taken on an empty stomach.

But this illustrates the subordination of the volunteer. They bore everything patiently, which was in the line of legitimate orders. It was competent for a Division Commander to order a battalion drill at any time. Obedience to such an order was unquestioned and immediate; and generally good natured, whatever may have been the reasonableness of the order. The men never have privately expressed their opinion of the order, but they, later, always referred to the affair, humorously, as the "Hardtack Drill".

In the afternoon of the 9th we moved back and recrossed the river without finding out why we went over there. No indications appeared of the presence of the enemy, and, if he had appeared in force, we should have been in bad conditions, with no rations and the river at our back. No food but too much to drink.[83]

On the 10th of November and, in November weather, we moved up the river towards Rappahannock Station and encamped. I had my tent put up, and made as comfortable as conditions permitted, and evidently more comfortable than the ambulance, for Gilmore returned to the regiment. This was also an indication that we were no longer in the immediate presence of the enemy. He made a wild disturbance, having discovered that cavalrymen had raided the wagons of the regiment and carried off all his valuable tobacco. It was an affair not clear of suspicion of treachery, if it be assumed that any loyalty were due to the Lt. Col. in the matter of private tobacco in a Government wagon. Apparently, some one about the teams had advised the First Maine Cavalry, that there were valuable and contraband goods in the headquarters wagon of the Twentieth Maine. The quartermaster was suspected, who had reasonable grudges and no scruples; and the teamsters were suspected, excepting one, a henchman of the Lt. Col. These teamsters alone were unprotected and the Lt. Col. assumed command and directed that the teamsters, less one, should report to their Companies. As this involved substitution of inexpert for expert men, I objected, and assured my superior officer that I should send these men back to the teams, as soon as I was again in command, which would probably be in season for the next movement. The argument was effectual. He remained with the regiment long enough to write a letter to the Bangor newspaper, giving an account of the battle of Rappahannock Station, and to sign it "C. D. Gilmore, Lt. Col. Commanding", and then disappeared for the winter, & took refuge in Washington, under the protection of some mysterious, but powerful friend.[84]

We remained in this camp until the 19th of November. The Division was reviewed. My classmate, Major [Jonathan P.] Cilley, of the 1st Maine Cavalry visited me, and rain came, less welcome.[85]

The question of the bread ration was still acute. I have mentioned the fact that during the marches and counter marches between Culpepper and Centerville and Fairfax, the men had been required to carry on their persons, seven days['] rations of hard bread. This was in apprehension of failure of the trains to supply at the regular three days['] interval. In fact, they did not so fail, but delivered regularly and without failure. This kept the seven days['] issue constant, that is to say, the men had always, in theory at least from three to seven days of bread ration on hand. But as a part of this had to be carried rolled in the blanket, it wasted, and finally there was three days['] lack. They were charged with three days['] ration of bread which they did not have, and very excusably were they lacking. If you will consider the difficulty of carrying and caring for several pounds of crackers, two hundred miles, in wet and dry, and in a blanket which must be unrolled and used as a bed every night, and, in the morning, wet or dry, again used as a bread receptacle.

But the "Regulations" did not permit of the issue of a duplicate ration. It appeared that this rule was as fixed as that of the Medes and Persians [Daniel 6:12], and perhaps belonged, like those, all to the military class—unless indeed it were awkward to explain the improvident reason of the lack to the War Departments.

But, there was a military way out of the difficulty. I did not discover or invent this, but I learned it, as I was temporarily serving as Division Inspector.

I had authority vested in me alone of the Division, by authority of the Congress of the United States, and the Army Regulations, but before unknown and unsuspected, to condemn bad bread and order its destruction or burial. There was always bad bread. It was, in fact[,] all bad. It was conceived in iniquity. But, of course there were degrees of badness, though none of excellence, and sometimes a box or part thereof, more than usually exposed to the weather appeared ornamented with green mould. I was informed that there was such bad bread offered by the Commissary of the Division, damned, but not yet condemned, and my mysterious powers were invoked. I was conducted to the Cereal Cemetery & there arranged in a row were the bread boxes open, and mouldy crackers in plain view, on the top of each box. I straightaway condemned them all and ordered them buried, but the Regulations did not require me to see that order was executed. Indeed, it might reasonably be supposed that an order from such mighty authority would execute this. However, the bread famine was exorcised, the vouchers of condemnation given, & the missing three days['] rations reappeared. It was said that the men ate the bread & found it less mouldy under the top layer. As with the cakes used first as plates and then eaten, by the companions of Aeneas, this may have been a good omen. The Government was not cheated by that act, and if "somebody blundered" in the original issue of too much for the tran sportation facilities, the evidence was suppressed and it was not mentioned in the bulletin, and never got into history, and we took a fresh start.

We moved at 8 A.M. on the 19th, crossed the Rappahannock & encamped 2 miles beyond the road. Although the weather was not agreeable, we were comfortably encamped. My headquarters were on the top of a bluff, wooded to the edge.

I introduced a new construction of fireplace and chimney, for which the materials available were suited. A hole was dug within the tent, near the wall, and a trench therefrom, to the outside. A large flat stone covered this hole, excepting on one edge, and smaller flat stones covered the trench excepting at its outer end, where two headless barrels were set one on the other, to serve as a chimney. This was sufficient to give draft to the fire in the hole, and the tent was comfortably warmed and place was afforded for drying one[']s feet. I here prepared reports, and in afternoons drilled the battalion.

This was too comfortable to last, and the military fates, guarding us from the evil effects of such luxuries, sounded order to move in the morning. So we did. The reveille sounded at 4 A.M. & we marched out at 6 in a lively rain. Moved about a mile, towards the Rapidan, and then turned back to the camp, or rather to the place where the camp had been, unpacked and put up our tents again. This clearly seemed to be a waste of time and labor; but it should be remembered that we were employed by the month and in spite of the drudgery of details, and many disappointments, we sometimes remembered the main point in the business [was] to "put down the Rebellion". Fortunately the daily demands upon a regimental commander kept his mind fully occupied and prevented useless forebodings as to the final result.

[MINE RUN
NOVEMBER—DECEMBER, 1863]

Although the 25th was a clear day, we did not move again until the 26th. We understood that this was Thanksgiving Day, and, as we trudged on towards the Rapidan[,] the wilderness, and the enemy, on a winter campaign, we thought affectionately of our friends and mince pie and turkey. The day, not the surroundings, prompted the suggestions, though I have distinct recollection of dining, (as I rode) on two doughnuts and a drink of water from my canteen.

Such a luxury was not unknown in a camp of Maine soldiers. If we happened, by hook or crook, to become the happy possessors of flour, salt pork afforded the fat and our cooks understood the doughnut business. To that extent, occasionally, a table was set for us in the wilderness, but our cup did not run over.

But this is a digression from this history of the campaign occasioned by the humble incident of the two doughnuts, now apparently trivial, but not then.

The march continued notwithstanding, and we came to the Rapidan, a stream insignificant from a purely geographical point of view, but considerably and inextricably mixed with high strategy, in 1863 and 1864, and becoming historical. The humble stream and the frogs and water snakes therein were unconscious of their growing importance, but must have been startled by the laying of the pontoon bridge, where only the ancient and muddy Culpepper Ford had been before.

On the right, at the entrance to the ford, was a cotton field, the first I had ever seen. Its dry and withered stalks and leaves rustled in the wind, and the balls of cotton, ungathered and ragged, were soiled and forlorn. Two brass field pieces stood in the field threatening the thick woods of the opposite bank. This was the border of the Wilderness and Chancellorsville, the scene of the disaster to the right of Hooker, in May; and the memory of that unfortunate affair was rather too fresh in our minds to lend any charm to the region.

Prior to the crossing, some companies of the 44th N.Y. were assigned to me, and with these and my own regiment, I was directed to guard the right flank of the column, on its way through the wilderness. The road was a narrow dirt road, and the continuous forest was of thickly growing small pines, interspersed with a tangle of scrub oaks, in many places, nearly impassable. At irregular intervals there were cross roads, leading apparently from nowhere to nowhere.

Our Division wagons moved with the infantry, in the rear of the larger part of the division, and it was possible for a squad of the enemy's cavalry, to waylay the train at any of these cross roads, if unprotected, and to snatch out some of the wagons before troops could be brought to the point of attack. This in fact was what happened on the left. We flanked on the right, and fortunately, without

MINE RUN

mishap. The flanking was in this wise[:] My men were in single file, following each other closely enough to keep every front man in sight of the man following, and this column of single file was guided by a deployed line of men reaching laterally from the head of the column to be guarded to the head of the flanking column. It was a laborious, clothes-rending and skin scratching business. My anxiety to keep the line continuous and at a sufficient distance away from the road, made necessary many excursions up and down, in and out, through the branches and tangles of branches, the frictional resistance of which greatly reduced the speed. Occasionally in front of one of these clumps of "frizzled hair implicit," I went as fast as I could and putting my head by the side of the neck of my horse, spurred him through.

The best part of me got through. But the business, prolonged until midnight, was an anxious and laborious task, and with a keen sense of relief, we emerged from the tangled thickets into the open fields and bright moonlight about the celler house.[86] But there was no rest even for the Saints, and we, who had torn our distressed way through the underbrush, were ordered to picket and stand guard over those who had marched in the unobstructed road, and no greater distance.

But, as with the Six Hundred, it was not for us to reason why.[87] The enlisted men could fall back on the everlasting resource of grumbling.

I got a nap however; *sub Jove frigido*; and with my feet to the fire it was sweet, well earned and refreshing, but all too brief.[88]

In the morning we moved on to an unfinished railway in the woods. The carbines of the cavalry, uttering the low growl of skirmishing, were indicating the position of the enemy in our front, and as it happened in the development of the infantry line behind the cavalry; I moved up to the rear of First Maine Cavalry then comanded by my classmate Cilley, and met him with his reserve. We chatted of friends and old times as if no tragedies were going on in front, so commonplace do tragedies become in war. The cavalry moved off, and we bivouaced there not uncomfortably and undisturbed.

In the morning of the 28th, a heavy rain was falling, with the chill of November in the air, and we shifted our uneasy position, near the cross roads and Robertson Tavern to the right and encamped with mud for downy beds of ease.[89] The "Tavern" was not entertaining guests. Evidently, there was work to be done in that neighborhood. There was sound of cannon in front and popping of the skirmish fire on the left, but the country was largely covered with forest. And, as yet we had knowledge of them only by sound. Fortunately the rain ceased, and a cold northwest wind gave promise of clear weather and cold. But the cold was tolerable and if it froze the mud, facilitated rather than impeded our movements.

We pushed on next day, always to the sound of cannon, and over ground yet unfrozen, and soon emerged into open fields.

In the distance, beyond the valley, on rising ground appeared a line of strong intrenchments of the enemy, extending to left and right, as far as we could see.[90]

Intermediate was a large farm house, with barns and outbuildings, far to the left open fields, and on the right timber land. It thus appeared that we were to relieve a part of the Sixth Corps, which had been holding an intrenched picket line on the eastern slope of the valley. I deployed my regiment under scattering fire of musketry to that part of the line in my front, & placed my men in the slightly built picket intrenchments, and made my connections on right and left.[91]

The farm house was a little in the rear of my lines on the slope towards the enemy, and the half underground basement was open in the rear. After the line was established I went into the house. The living room was a large plain room, with a fireplace & fire burning on the hearth, and in it was a citizen, a man perhaps 50 years old, and a young lady of 18 or 20. They were greatly agitated, for besides the occasional shots that passed by or over the house, there was a thief, in the uniform of a battery man, who was rummaging in the drawers of a bureau in the room, and utterly regardless of the owner's present, was helping himself to anything he might fancy, and the fancy of a fellow of that class has a wide range. I ordered the rascal to leave & when he demurred I persuaded him at the muzzle of my revolver. This, apparently reassured the people, and they asked me to go into the basement and calm the nerves of the people there. Here was a crowd, mostly women & children, but also two fat old men, all non-combatants and scared. They had come from the neighboring houses, where yesterday they found themselves suddenly shut in between two armies. The house with a basement appeared the safest. I comforted them as well as I could & assured them that I would place a sentinel at the door to prevent annoyance from intruders, and that I did not think that either army would fire upon the house. No shots struck the house that day, but an occasional bullet whizzed past. Either by a shell or accident one of the slave shanties took fire. The colored women were lamenting the loss of their bedding, but did not dare to go and rescue it.

Finally Capt. [Atherton] Clark, with some conventional expression of his opinion as to the little value of their "old duds", went down, through musketry fire, and brought them to a place of safety, and so, for them, the country was saved for awhile. But later the Captain of the battery on the higher ground in our rear, came down and advised me that he had orders to open fire at 8 next morning, and as he would be compelled to fire directly over the house, the people must be turned out before that hour. We decided to let them remain undisturbed overnight, as it would be necessary to send them to the rear, and we knew of no houses in that direction, where they could find shelter.[92]

In the evening General Sykes (then commanding the Fifth Corps) came down in person to inspect that part of the line, I understood to determine whether or not the ground was suitable for an advance at that point. As the character of the ground in front of my line was not apparent therefrom, in accordance with orders to ascertain whether or not it was suitable for crossing troops, I sent, after dark, two men and a sergeant from Co. B. with orders to explore the ground, within the enemy's picket line if necessary, and report at once. I waited anxiously an hour or two. They were not to fire, if they could avoid it. One hour went by and no sound and I was beginning to be anxious, when they returned much elated. They had slipped through the pickets of the enemy and explored all the way across the stream [Mine Run] and valley beyond. The ground was wet and marshy, and I so reported. The sergeant begged me to let them go back and capture some of the enemy's pickets, whose position they had ascertained, but I thought it better to stick to my instructions and permit no demonstrations, which might indicate that we were exploring that part of the line.

The next morning, at daybreak, I called out the man of the house and explained to him the unpleasant necessity of moving. There was no time for waiting. Eight o'clock came early in the morning on the 30th day of November. The women and children gathered such belongings as they could carry and wrapped themselves, as the weather was now bitterly cold. One, a very old lady, was unable to walk, and her I sent upon a stretcher, comfortably bolstered with pillows and covered with blankets. Amply before eight o'clock the doleful procession, in single file, was on its way to the rear, and disappeared over the hill. As soon as this charge was disposed of I went on the line in order to be ready for anything which might happen. The cannonading opened, on schedule time, and in abundance. What harm it was doing to the enemy I could not see. All their guns were well protected by what seemed to be substantial works.

After much of this ineffectual pounding, [James Clay] Rice's brigade of the First Corps, next on my left advanced.

I had no orders, and understood that Warren had been sent to turn the enemy's right and that the charge on the main front, at whatever point made, would depend on Warren's success.[93]

But I went to the left of my line, to aid Rice if I could. There was a squad of the enemy on a knoll in my front, well advanced, but still a long shot off, and these began firing into the right of Rice and his brigade. I called [Daniel A.] Jackson of Co. B. who was a good marksman, but, of course, carried only a Springfield musket, good for not much over three hundred yards. I told him to put in an extra cartridge of powder and fire at the squad aforesaid. One man fell and the rest ran, and the brigade was relieved from that annoyance.

There was fresh scattering fire along the line between the pickets, though the cold was severe. The men built fires and shifted[,] as best they could[,] not to keep warm, as that was impossible, but to avoid freezing. It was reported to me that in some of the canteens the water froze. I had my head quarters in the house, and slept on the floor with my feet to the fire on the hearth. Occasionally in the night I went along the line and in the alternating of warmings and chillings I caught a severe cold.

During the day there was some movement of the Sixth Corps troops in the woods on my right, and a flock of sheep ran out and came down in front of my line. One fell, shot by accident or design in front of Co. E. The captain's stomach moving him to mutton and heroic deeds, he climbed over the redoubt, and choosing risk of death by bullets rather than the slow starvation of hardtack, ran for the animal.[94] The Confederates, appreciating his dash, and perhaps deeply sympathizing with his hunger, stopped firing and yelled at him until he had dragged the carcass over the works. During the affair of the 29th, while I was on the line, and sentinels withdrawn, the unguarded house was thoroughly plundered, probably by the battery [artillery] men. They had also taken all the wheat and corn from the granaries for their horses. Some one found in the house two pistols and a bowie knife with a sheath and shoulder strap. These we confiscated. I also confiscated a Libbey tent, of the U. S. pattern, probably picked up or captured in the Wilderness battle in May. The fortunes of war restored it.

On the evening of the Dec. 1st we received orders to fall back, the movement to be made during the night.⁹⁵ This was no difficult matter for the main body of troops in the rear. These were mostly concealed by the woody country; but for us, in the open field, and full moonlight, in the immediate vicinity of the enemy, it was not such a simple matter.

The picket line was to begin its movement to follow the corps, at 3 A.M. of the second. The sentinel waked me at two o'clock, and as I went forward to the line I heard the bugles of the Confederates, indicating their attention to our matters. By that hour all of our corps was on the way, and, I understood that, we like other regiments forming the picket line, about 1000 men, in all, and two guns, constituted the rear guard. It was sufficiently light for them at least, to see the glitter of our gun barrel[s], and perhaps the men moving, and if they should throw forward a brigade or two or a few squadrons of cavalry, they might make it a very awkward affair for us, though some of them would also get hurt. I went along the line and cautioned the men to keep up the fires, and to put on a supply of wood just before we left, and to wrap their muskets in their blankets. We also arranged the order in which the companies should fall back[,] as they must go up the slope in full view of the pickets of the enemy, if not of those in the earthworks. Precisely at the hour I started the movement. I had left one of the lieutenants in the rear, behind the crest of the slope, to indicate the point where the regiment would reform. The company went quickly back, following bushy ravines, and in thirty minutes we had formed behind the crest and were ready to move.

It seemed to me probable that our withdrawal was not unknown to the enemy, but evidently Lee was not anxious to bring on a battle. Longstreet's corps was absent, and he was not in condition to fight a battle, excepting within his intrenchments.⁹⁶

And it seemed to me that we were in no position, so far from our base of supplies, in such weather and condition of roads, to assail the Confederate army, still formidable, and firmly intrenched.

Indeed the whole enterprise appeared to have been made to turn on the anticipated success of Warren in finding a weak place on their right. Of course that he did not find, and we had march[ed] up the hill, like the King's men, only to march down again.

The march back to the Rapidan was appropriately rapid. I think the consciousness that we were in the enemy's country, and in the rear of the column, and that their cavalry had intimate knowledge of all the cross roads, tended to keep the column well closed up. I heard some grumbling, but that was a common occurrence, often the sole luxury, for relief and not for insubordination.

We covered the twelve miles, to the ford, in five hours, and crossing, marched three or four miles beyond. There we gave the weary men rest and a chance to make coffee. The temperature for the previous three days had been low, & the ground as hard as cast iron. My cold had become worse, and the prospect of a long ride in the northwest wind, and at the slow pace of an infantry column, did not seem encouraging. I feared that I might be condemned to the hospital. When we halted for the day, however, I was so utterly worn out, weariness and lack of sleep, that I wrapped myself in my blanket and lay down on the ground. I slept three hours and when I awoke was entirely free from the cold. So in army life, in the field, conditions were reversed. The cold had been caught by sleeping in a house and cured by exposure to the inclement air.

Further movement brought us on the 3rd day of December again to the Rappahannock. We had been eight days on this expedition, and during that time, in most inclement weather, the men had been either on the march or on picket, for three days on picket in the immediate front of the enemy. They were weary and hungry and had not had sufficient sleep.

Orders received to move my regiment to the hill near the railroad bridge, seemed to indicate more than temporary occupancy; but lest the transition should [be too] sudden, this order was quickly followed by another to be ready to move. We were ready to move, excepting in the matter of legs and stomach. We had not unpacked, had put up no shelters, only we were unrested and unfed, and to the sense of weariness was added the more oppressive sense of labor in vain, which gave no encouragement for the future.

But the orders to be ready to move on the 4th meant nothing on the 5th and were countermanded on the 6th. They must have been issued out of a very great abundance of caution, and there seemed generally to be a great abundance of that unprofitable virtue. The Fabian strategy had been overworked.[97] There was no probability that Lee, with his two remaining corps, and at that season, would leave his intrenchments and near base of supplies, and follow us beyond the Rapidan, and he did not.

[WINTER QUARTERS
DECEMBER—APRIL, 1864]

The positive countermanding of the order and the general conditions, to my mind, indicated a permanent encampment and as the regiments of the brigade were widely separated and I had been directed to this point, at the bridge[,] I understood it to mean winter quarters and the responsibility of guarding the bridge. The main part of the Army was about Culpepper and part of our Corps were on the line of the Orange & Alexandria R.R. in the rear. The railway had been repaired and the bridge rebuilt, and our communications established with Washington and Headquarters. This was highly satisfactory. The base, but highly important question of rations was never lost sight of in our minds. Our patriotism was doubtless abiding, but appetite loud in its demands, & much in evidence.

We were in a business purely animal and even brutal, and we ate like savages, and, reversing the moral code, dwelt most upon the question—what shall we eat? But shelter was, at that season[,] of next importance, for the season continued excessively cold. The position assigned me for camping ground included the earthworks we had taken from the enemy on the 7th of November. These I first levelled, and then laid out my camp. I formed the camp facing the river, and almost at the bank, the streets running at right angles to the river, with parade ground in front, line officers tents in rear, and Hd. Qrs. on the left. As there was good pine timber in this neighborhood and the men needed exercise and were skillful with the axe, I determined to put up more substantial quarters than the little shelter tents afforded.

Pine logs were hauled up, and split into slabs, and these were notched and fitted, set on edge and interlocked at the corners, and, for a roof, covered by the tent pieces, stretched over a ridge pole and rafters, afforded comfortable quarters. Axes we had with us always and that useful tool, an adze[,] was procured. With this, the wall was smoothed. The boards for doors were, I fear, partly at least borrowed; but the cloth covering served for roof and window.

The houses for the captains were built in like manner[,] and between the captain's & the company's quarters were located the kitchens, one for each company. All the combined ingenuity of the regiment was lavished on these. No range, no gas or coal, no elaborate ovens[—]these were [not] then in that part of the country. But wood was plenty both for construction and fuel, and there was clay, as useful and used for the same purpose as that suggested for "Great Caesar". Also his *Alum igniferous* remaining might serve to flatten the cobbled sticks of wood which camouflaged the chimneys.[98]

Such chimneys, with ample fireplaces, and smoke flues, their kitchen had. Every one of them built to the plan of one master mind, genius theretofor unknown, and carrying a gun, now alas also forgotten to this historian. These cheerful fire places faced the door, which fronted on the quarters of the men, and the cook[']s bunk had an humble lateral situation, and served for bed by night and seat by day.

But the crowning achievement of the genius of this architect now also passed into the class of the builders of Babel, and the builder of the Pyramid of Cheops, and the other great and unknown before Vitruvius, the crowning achievement related to the bean-hole.[99] Beanholes had been known and, (where conditions permitted) used before in our campaigns. They were of the greatest invention of that age, discovered, strange to say, many ages after the invention of beans. The Egyptian and Pythagorian bean eaters, with all their wisdom and familiarity with beans as a diet and for inspiration missed this hole. They were too much occupied with such trivial matters as the invention of calendars, and the revolution of the earth on its axis, whereby that disciple of Pythagoras laid the foundation of polar expedition and bred the Dr. Cook controversy, disturbed all Copenhagen and even got into Congress.[100]

Bean holes as I have said, were old. We had used them, but out of doors, exposed to the inclemency of the skies, and to predatory comrades. This genius hit upon the idea of locating the bean hole in the immediate front of the fire place! It seemed simple when once thought of, but it was of immense importance, and commanded universal admiration. Every fellow would ask as usual, "How he to be the inventor missed."

It solved the whole problem. It was usable by day or night. It was sheltered from the rain; the smoke could escape up [the] chimney, and the coals from the fireplace could be raked over the buried bean pot. Finally, it could not be stolen. The closed door, and the anxious cook, doubly guaranteed safety, and one could sleep in peace, secure of beans for breakfast, and not wake up, as I did once, beanless and compelled to breakfast instead on the usual dish of hard tack, and fried salt pork.

But one company was unfortunate in its location of their kitchen[,] and the invention there failed. It appeared that the poor Confederates who fought and fell at the station on the 7th of November, were buried in the trenches in graves unmarked, as is often the sad lot of soldiers; and one of them, unfortunately happened to be just at the front of the kitchen fire place and was discovered in the digging of the hole. He was left to sleep in peace, beneath a hearth stone and with names not his own. Soldiers, though unmindful too often of the rights of civilians, respected a soldier's prior right, in the matter of burial.

The work upon these rude houses went briskly on, interrupted only by occasional drills, guard mountings and the daily dress parade. My headquarters were placed on the left, by reason of the more convenient nature of the ground on that flank, & the unfavorable slopes to rear and right. My lodgings were palatial. A wall tent formed office, reception room and living room. A floor of smooth boards, borrowed I know not where[,] raised me above the mud, and the masons of the regiment built a chimney of bricks likewise borrowed, and of clay easily procured in that region. The chimney was built close to the tent, with the fireplace opening against the canvas, which was slitted and rolled up to disclose the cavity. Bricks set on edge served to support the sticks of wood and a small fire was sufficient to warm the small apartment, (about 7 feet square) even in cold weather. That fire however needed watching, and a bucket of water stood ready for emergencies. On one occasion prompt application alone saved the mansion from the flames. In the rear, an "A" tent formed my bed room.[101] About the whole on the outside[,] stakes and interwoven pine boughs, reinforced the walls. The bed was built of small elastic poles and soft boughs of pine or cedar. A pylon in front, of rough poles and interwoven evergreen, rather less imposing and less durable, than the Egyptian, bore the legend, "Head Quarters" ["]20th Maine".

A parade ground, in front of the camp was made smooth, and, when the weather permitted, I held "dress parade", so called in the regulations; but as to dress, beyond the blacking of well worn shoes and the brushing of their old clothes, changed only when worn out, and others could be obtained, there was no pretense among the enlisted men. The company officers generally wore blouses, but the commanding officer, as became his rank and conspicuous position, arrayed himself, when on parade, with a long blue coat of the general Prince Albert style, double breasted and with a double row of shining brass buttons in front. A red sash (or once red) rendered more effective as an ornament by distance, encircled his backbone, and hung its frayed tassels on the left. The men in line, the Colonel (or rather Major acting as Colonel,) in place so many paces in front & facing the men, the Adjutant let out the drum corps, and with drums beating and fifes squeaking[,] the corps marched along the front. Then came the presenting of arms, and the various salutings, which at the beginning of our military service, appeared to me absurd; now had became a very serious business, neglect of which, or of the proper performance of which, had become a serious offense, practically criminal.

Military life tends to make an animal of a man. As a matter of course, the work of an active campaign is of an animal nature.

Fighting is animalism fine and simple, and all the extreme effort, and endurance of physical hardship, involved in march and bivouac, involves muscular effort and endurance, in the highest degree, however much also, it may involve exercise of higher qualities.

But in a winter encampment the greatest care and effort must be exercised to keep the men in good physical condition, and under good discipline. The habit of obedience to orders must not be permitted to relax, since this habit is essential in the presence of hardship and danger.

So the strict guard was established and maintained. A guard house was built of logs where, the reserve of the guard always kept, and where, on "Port Number One" the sentinel stood perpetually. The Guard House was in military life, more necessary than the jail in civil life. This confinement (as a punishment) for offenses against "good order and military discipline" was inflicted. On one occasion, during the winter, I received, amongst other recruits, six Irishmen, material for good soldiers, but also involving an element of disorder. They had not been in camp twenty-four hours before there was a row and the "Officer of the Day" found them all drunk, more or less, and the valuable quality of fighting was prematurely developed. The case, of course, was brought before me. The procedure was simpler than the proceedings of a Police Court even. The culprits brought the evidence of their own persons against themselves, though the word of the Officer of the Day, was sufficient, for a prompt sentence to the guard house, for the most flagrant offender. Although the camp was a prohibition State, and drinking was not in favor, simple and unoffending hilarity was not deemed a guardhouse offense; but when the hilarity developed into practical pugnacity, the "Good Order" of the Regulations, (the practical Ten Commandments of the Army) was enforceable, and the guard house intervened. So the worst culprit went thereto, without right of habeas corpus or appeal. But even there his fighting ardor was not cooled, and complaint soon came that the prisoner could not be kept quiet, even in the guard house. The book of "Army Regulations" is not large enough and could not be large enough, to contain a list of all possible offenses, of which a soldier may conceive, nor are all the punishments defined. Much power is given, in small offenses, to the ingenuity of the Regimental Commander, and the punishment must meet—not only the offense but the environment and conditions. The man needed to be cooled off; the turbulent offender could not be kept in the guard house, without discomfort to the guard, for even if tied he would yell. Fortunately, the weather was cold, and I ordered, as a remedy & punishment, that the fellow should be tied on the outside to the projecting logs of the corner of the house. He soon cooled off, and I was advised of the fact by the appearance of one of his fine friends, who appeared at my head quarters. He drew himself up in military fashion, and with his hand to his cap, said, "And may I speak with you?" "Yes, what have you to say?" He admitted that he was one of the "Wild Irishmen", (Someone had given them the name) and said that it was his particular friend who was in bonds and undergoing the cooling process at the guard house. He professed that his friend was penitent, and promised to behave if released. I accepted his statement and put my interviewer also under pledge of his honor, called the Officer of the Day, and ordered release of the prisoner. I believe there was no other guard house offense during the winter. The other men had too much character and self respect, to get into the guard house. Where the Wild Irishmen procured their drink I never ascertained. Probably they brought it with them, concealed in their knapsacks.

There were, however, offenses of various kinds known, in general terms, to the Regulations in the brigade, and for the trial of petty offenses, we had a brigade Court Martial of which I was President and Capt[.] Sam T. Keene, Judge Advocate. Only one of the offenses I now remember. One particular sin the private soldier was inclined to, and this was not of the nature of *mala in se*.[102] On the march, particularly if it were a hard one, he would pick up an abandoned and dilapidated horse, perhaps with a sore back, or not too lame, and on him would be loaded his knapsack, and all that the beast could carry of his friends in the Company. This was a sin which the officers winked at, as it favored the march & helped lame & sick, but when we got in camp, good order and military discipline favored the abandonment of the animal. But the prudent soldier, unadvised as to the imminence of the next march, whether next day or next week, generally hid the horse in the bushes, and nourished him, if there were no grass, on the Quartermaster's hay, and so had him ready & refreshed for transportation, unsupplied & unauthorized by the Regulations. Stealing the hay of the Q.M. if that official discovered it, was a serious crime in his eyes, and promptly & loudly proclaimed. Of course such a complaint could not be ignored, not only would the loss of valuable hay, hauled along at great expense, be involved, but what would become of the dragon guarded "Good order & Military discipline", if this stealing were permitted[?]

One such offense came before us, and the specifications, in phrase carefully copied from the Regulations, stated at full length with all the apparently superfluous but really necessary [language] that the fellow stole the Government hay. His defense was worthy of a larger cause and a civil court. He admitted that fact alleged in the specification, but not the charge. He stole nothing. He stated the case briefly. The hay belonged to the Government, the horse belonged to the Government, and he belonged to the Government, and he took the Government hay and put it into the Government horse. There was simply a transfer of the Government hay from one Government storehouse, to another; and in fact the latter was the final and destined receptacle. The fellow might have pleaded humanity, to the horse, but he left that to be inferred and stood on his strict legal argument.

In these court martials there was a fair knowledge of the inevitable *vade mecum* of the blue covered Army Regulations, somewhere in the court, not much legal training, but an earnest intention to do justice.[103]

The Judge Advocate examined the witnesses, though of course, any member of the court could ask questions. In voting, the member lowest in rank voted first, and so on in order. Manifestly in order that the junior might not be influenced by the vote of his superior.

In one case, there was a single charge and a single specification, that is to say a single act was alleged in the specification, and this was the basis of a single regulation charge. Vote was first taken to ascertain, whether, in the opinion of the Court, the commission of the act was proved; then, if that were found, vote on the charge would show the opinion of the court on the question whether that act constituted the specified offense. The junior member, a second lieutenant, an energetic commander of a squad, but not equipped for nice questions, voted "No", on the specification. In his opinion[,] therefore[,] there was no evidence that the defendant did anything. But when it came to his turn to vote on the charge, he voted "Yes". I explained to him that I could not dictate his vote, and did not wish to influence him either way, but asked him to consider how the man could have committed an offense if he had not been guilty [of] the act alleged—and had in fact done nothing. Next time, therefore, in order to be certain, he voted "No" on both.

The winter of 1863-4 was bitterly cold but our connections

were established with Washington, sixty miles away, & we had soft bread. Only an old soldier after a campaign of six or seven months on "hardtack", knows the full meaning of soft bread.

Of course, with the soft bread came beans, herein before mentioned, and at intervals there was fresh beef. The sutler also brought cakes and cigars and other minor luxuries, though these were rather expensive and not to be indulged in, at the prices then prevailing, even by officers. The pay of an officer was materially less then, in dollars, and the dollars were greatly depreciated in value.[104]

The temperature was so low that the ice on the Rappahannock would sustain a horse, and continued low through December, spurring us all the while to the task of perfecting our quarters. The first of January was celebrated in at Brigade Hd. Qrs. in a way most remarkable to us.

The brigade commander invited all the Regimental Commanders, and members of the Division Staff to dine with him.[105] Two tents and a log house, warmed by a fireplace, constituted his apartments, and the menu included roast turkey and soft [bread,] followed by brandy and water, and cigars, luxuries unknown before in the campaign. Surely a table was spread for us in the wilderness, and our cups ran over. It is wonderful how warm even a tent may be, with an open fire glowing into it, though the northwest wind forced through the canvas air at the near zero temperature. Perhaps the brandy aided the fire. But about midnight we plunged into the cold northwest stream, we mounted our shivering horses and rode to our regiments. I had my horse put into the Mine River Sibley tent, and Capt. Clark and I doubled our blankets and slept together, for mutual warmth.[106]

With drills, guard mountings, dress parades, policing of the camps (the military phrase for cleaning up), study of tactics and Regulations, the Military bible, playing euchre in the evenings and holding religious service on Sundays, the cold month of January wore away. Some leaves of absence were granted to captains and lieutenants. The regiment was in excellent condition, and were kept so by care as to their food & the sanitary conditions, and exercise of the men. Idleness in camp as elsewhere, breeds trouble. In camp & away from the immediate presence of the enemy, it is always more difficult to maintain strict discipline, but our officers and men, were, with very few exceptions, of an order much higher than the average. But, as we had little picket duty, the routine of camp duty had to be strictly maintained. We watched closely the rations delivered, and their distribution. It will be understood that rations were issued to the men without charge, but were sold to the officers at fixed rates. Rations issued to the men consisted of bread, hard or soft, salt pork, at stated intervals, [and] where practicable fresh beef, sugar & coffee, and candles, in small amounts. These were the ordinary rations, and, excepting the soft bread, alike for camp and march. But for camp, in addition, were beans, occasionally cucumber pickles, and desiccated potatoes, an unappreciated article, regarded as a burlesque on the original, and called by the men "desecrated potatoes".[107]

The Commissary also issued flour, at times, in lieu of bread, and kept smoked hams, but the latter only for the officers of higher rank and pay, who could afford such luxuries. Cigars also & tobacco were in the sutler's stores, the latter within reach of the men and officers, who had cash or credit.[108] In camp every man[']s credit was good with the sutler, while we were in camp, as the man could not run away, & was not likely to be killed, but that mercenary person[,] vigilant on pay day, closed up his accounts, and betook himself to the rear, in good season before bullets began to fly. The cigars of the sutler had no suspicion of Havana, but even these that seemed to consist of cabbage leaf, and an interior of dust and stems, were bought only by those reckless officers who had no families at home to provide for.

In the supervision of the issuing of rations to the men it [was] necessary to have some care, in order that the full amount should be given, especially in respect of those articles which especially were sold to the officers. Most officers could afford soft bread &

some the luxury of ham and all bought sugar, so that if these were issued to the men in short measure, while receipts of full measure were obtained, there would be a margin favorable preferably in balancing the Brigade Commissary's accounts with the government. So when in camp I had all the issued rations weighed, and receipted according to my Commissary Sergeant's account. Whether from this or from the greater saving arising from having the rations of every Company cooked together in the single Company kitchen, probably from both, and perhaps also in part from appetites dulled by Sutler's stuff, there was an accumulated saving before we broke camp for the spring campaign. I had unwisely expected to turn this in & get an amount of cash credited to a regimental fund, available to purchase instruments for a band, or other matters of general interest. But after all my care I found that I had reckoned without my host. The Commissary would not thus formally take the surplus; thus formally I say! I have no doubt his teams came over, after I had left, and he doubtless got my surplus, as his surplus. However, we were no worse off. The men had had enough, & of wholesome well cooked food. Only there was the reflection that if I had been wiser the surplus rations might have gone freely to the officers, though that might have been contrary to the "Regulations".

We were able to buy flour in my head quarter mess; and had a cook expert in biscuits, and they were a part of the daily fare. I am ashamed to write, (so gross did Army life make us) that these biscuits constitute a bright and important memory of camp life. Such biscuits, light, flaky in texture, equally done above & below, and such effetes, are not of civil life. Let not the incredulous reader raise questions about ovens, & cook stoves. Of course we had none of these such as he thinks of. We had better, simpler, more effective, and suited perfectly to the environment, the "Dutch Oven." If its name correctly indicates its origins I say God bless the Dutch! The apparatus seems to[o] simple for the culinary miracle it habitually accomplished. It was a three legged iron pan, (called in New

England a "spider,") but provided with a cover which had an upper [*illegible word*] rim, capable of holding coals, as in a cup. In the modus operandi, the kneaded & well shaped biscuits were placed in the spider, the spider placed on hot coals, and more hot coals put upon the [*text missing*] and so "twixt upper nether and surrounding fire" our biscuits were baked.[109] Of course, over the oven, the hopeful cook doubtful stood lest on the Dutch oven his hopeful dough prove cinder, and he snatched off the cover for frequent inspections, and always brought the biscuits "done to a turn". Then & there etiquette permitted the spider to rest on the table and served better than hot plates to keep the biscuits warm, during the short process of eating them. [*illegible word*] wanted what seemed butter, in which there was no suspicion of oleomargarine, fat fried from the salt pork. It was salt and fat, and hot, and while it could be applied with a spoon, there was an easier and more even way, of inverting the half biscuit in the fat pan. A bit of pork fried crisp, was not a bad accompaniment, if not too rusty, and I think we became accustomed and immune to that kind of rust. In three days microbes, unless large and highly original[,] did not infect us.[110]

But as to the Dutch ovens, we had many. I think one for each officer[']s mess. Where we got them it was better not to inquire. There were plenty in the Country and supplemented the apparatus of the Southern country kitchen, at that time nearly as primitive as ours of the camp.

I saw, during our fall campaign in 1863, one fine specimen of such a country kitchen. It was part of the equipment of a rather substantial farm house, which stood in ample grounds, surrounded by oak trees sturdy and with wide spreading branches. Vines and climbing roses adorned the porches, and all about was an air of amplitude and comfort, and of magnificence rather than neatness.

In the rear, also among the trees, was the kitchen, fifty paces distant from the house.

It was a rough frame structure, which apparently, had never known paint.

It contained a simple room, and had an incombustible floor of the order of [*illegible word*] rather than decadence. It could be swept but not washed. A simple table and a bench furnished the room, and on one side was a most primitive breadth of fireplace, with huge cast iron fire dogs, the feet & legs of which were imbedded in an accumulation of ashes. Spurs on the dogs were arranged to hold the spits for the roasts, and long handled iron pans were evidently for frying.

There was room for Dutch ovens, and, in cold weather a battalion of people could warm themselves by the fire. No covered way connected the kitchen with the house, and in cold weather, haste and covered dishes must have [been] necessary in order that the cooked food should reach the house in warm condition. One thing was manifest. There was nothing about the room or its furniture or outerside that a colored servant could mar or break, and the mistress of the house was thus relieved of one of the vexations of modern housekeeping. Doubtless also, until the coming on of the war, the mistress was not troubled by frequent change of servants, or the desertion of the cook when invitations were out for a dinner party.

Early in January came a remarkable innovation, unknown to us before in the history of the war. Ladies were permitted to come to a regimental camp. This was practicable with us, as we were encamped comfortably and on the line of the railroad three hours from Washington.

Also, furloughs for the men, and leaves of absence for the officers were permitted to a reasonable percentage of the number present and for short periods. I obtained a leave for two weeks, and met my wife in Washington. Together we took a flying trip to Maine, and then returned to the camp. Two or three other ladies, wives of officers, came also and later Capt[.] Keene, who had been on recruiting service in Portland, returned with his wife.

For the first time[,] therefore, camp seemed like a home, and grim visaged war smoothed his wrinkled front.[111] There were no accommodations for large parties. No room in the whole camp, excepting the Sibley tent used for sheltering horses, could accommodate six persons at one time. But we were neighborly and sociable. Distinctions of rank were laid aside, hardships forgotten. The future fortunately unknown & unthought of. We knew that we were still in the midst of the war, grown more earnest and destructive, that the Government was raising and putting into the field more troops and preparing for a more vigorous struggle, that Grant[,] a determined fighter and uniformly successful in the West, was coming to the East to take command, and that meant no occasional battle, but a campaign of battles; and finally we knew that before us lay an enemy, compact and of brave men absolutely disciplined and drilled and led by able and experienced officers, an army which heretofore we had on only few occasions been able to defeat.[112] The campaign impending must also be fought out on their own ground and aggressively on our part. Enough was there known of General Grant to assure us that the fight would be persistent. Yet curiously we thought little of all this and borrowed no trouble. We went about our work as if it were the regular business of life, and were as cheerful and unapprehensive as if the shadow of doom for some of us was in the far future, and indefinitely uncertain instead of near.

Fortunately, we did not know, and little apprehended that it was the last winter for many of the party, and that the wreck of families would be included in the wrecks of war. I think that the generally animalizing tendency of military life, of which I have before written, tended logically also, to make us unapprehensive, and inclined, like an animal, to live only in the present, and to bask in the sunshine of whatever comforts & pleasures we might have, and not to think of the morrow.

The great social event of the winter was a ball given at Corps Head Quarters which occupied a house a mile or two away from my camp. The compliment of an invitation was extended to some at least of the officers of my regiments, & included their wives. I went with Susie and Captain Keene with Sara. I remember no others. The ladies rode in an ambulance and we on horseback. We had no party rigs, neither officers nor ladies, but we brushed our clothes, and the ladies wore their best, intending only to be observers. The weather was cold, and the house colder, and we made no long stay. We could act only as wall flowers, and had no special qualifications or costumes successfully to act even that very subordinate part. So after having paid our respects, and remained long enough to satisfy our curiosity and the requirements of courtesy we left, by the same conveyances, and returned to our own camp better satisfied with the ordinary lot of the soldier.

I have little data of the routine of duty during the winter. The duties of Brigade Court Martial occupied much of my time, and administrative duties required some part of every day. Men in camp must be kept in drill and discipline and there are frequent reports to be made. Capt[.] Clark was on detail in Portland, endeavoring without much success, to recruit men for the regiment. I had less than 400 men present for duty, excluding teamsters and men detailed for various duties at brigade division and corps headquarters.

We had one excitement in the latter part of the winter. It was reported that a considerable body of the cavalry of the enemy had crossed the Rappahannock above us, apparently with the intention of cutting our communications with the rear. As this river was the largest, the bridge which I was guarding would be the most important to destroy, and we were on the alert. This alarm occurred while the ladies were in camp, and for awhile it seemed possible that they might see real war near at hand. Fortunately there was an old bomb-proof on the other side of the river, built by the Confederates when they occupied this point in 1863, and I made arrangements to send the ladies under the care of that other non-combatant, the quartermaster, to this shelter. Happily, the threatened attack never came. We had no doubt of our ability to hold the position and indeed it is probable that no attack was intended. It was probably only a scouting expedition, perhaps to keep the enemy's cavalry in exercise. We saw nothing of our own cavalry, excepting the details at Army Hd. Qrs during the winter, as they were encamped on front and flanks.

There was a small affair at Germanna Ford, on the Rapidan about 12 miles distant, so that the atmospheric conditions being favorable[,] the ladies heard the sounds of musketry and artillery of actual battle.

We were happy enough with our own daily assembling, and contented with our daily duties & without the functioning of society.

But these too soon came to an end. Orders to make immediate preparations for the spring campaign brought no distress excepting as they included as a preliminary measure the sending of non-combatants away from camp. The ladies would have remained, I have no doubt, until the bullets began to fly and later, but the orders were peremptory, and we were not even permitted to accompany them to Washington. So in a snow storm on the 23rd day of March we put them on the car for Washington & home. Our home went with them, and nothing but cold bare hard duty remained with us. We did not realize the effect of their departure until they had left us and were out of our sight, and then it was as if thick cloud had suddenly obscured the sun.

But, with the coming of spring came the usual preparations for active operations. The weather and the conditions of the ground were more favorable for the drilling of the men. We had also instruction of the company officers, a considerable number of whom had been promoted from the list of non-commissioned officers.

I was occupied largely in closing up the business of the brigade court martial and in fitting out the men for the ensuing campaign of the nature of which we had no idea. The corps was reorganized and a fourth division, formed out of the old First Corps, was added.[113] Our brigade was greatly increased, and in addition to the original regiments, (the 16th Michigan, 44 N.Y., 83rd Pa. & 20th Maine) which had constituted the brigade since we joined it in Sept[.] of 1862, there were added the 118th Pa., the 18th & 22d Mass.

Col. Chamberlain was absent, I believe in Washington, and Gilmore as a matter of course.[114] As Clarke, the senior captain[,] was also absent on recruiting service, I had Captain Keene detailed to act as Major as soon as we should move. Such a detail was not necessary in camp, and indeed was unadvisable, since under the army regulations, it would deprive the captain so detailed, of ten dollars per month, allowed him for the care of arms. But in active campaign, with all its probable casualties, it was necessary that there should be at least two field officers present, even if one had to be detailed from the line.

The Army regulations seemed in other respects antiquated and unequal for an army in the field. Officers were paid according to their muster, and not according to their command and duties. As Major my pay was about $150 per month, (half that of a Colonel) although I was under the same expense for servants and equipment, and cost of maintaining headquarters. Indeed it was only by closest economy, with the depreciated currency, that we could pay expenses.

But under a new Army Commander, we had new hopes, and thought little of our personal privations.

[THE WILDERNESS
MAY, 1864]

On the morning of May 1st, I was relieved by the 57th Mass., part of the 9th Corps, a new regiment, which with its full numbers, seemed to us like a brigade.[115] This regiment was to assume guard of the bridge, and I was under orders to join the brigade on the march.

On the bright and warm morning of the 1st of May, 1864, I moved out, from a camp which had seemed like home. The men evidently shared in this feeling, and grudged turning over their laboriously built and comfortable quarters to a swarm of raw recruits, who, as they supposed, were to have the easy task of guarding the line of communications in the rear, and I had some difficulty in preventing them from burning the whole camp. Fires broke out in several places, and the raw recruits of the 57th had valuable experience in extinguishing fires.

We moved at 9 A.M. and marched to Ingalls Station on the railway.

Here we had a brigade parade, I suppose for the reason that Bartlett wished to see his whole brigade in line, before going into battle.

He saw it only for a brief period. Just as we had all moved into position, a storm, black and threatening from the south, broke upon us and we went on the double quick for the shelter of our tents.

On the 3rd we moved again, at 1 P. M.[,] and bivouaced about 4 miles from Culpepper. We were now near the Rapidan, and there was no doubt of the direction of the movement, or of the object of it. Lee's Army had wintered South of the Rapidan, and near Madison.

At midnight the brigade struck out straight for Germanna Ford, where we crossed a little after sunrise. The march that forenoon was oppressive. The men were fresh from winter camp, and not yet inured to marching. The road led almost directly south, and through the woods, and the sun shone hot upon the column, which no breeze could fan, and the men, as usually happens when moving out from a camp occupied any considerable time, were overloaded.

There was a general throwing away of superfluities, and in some instances, of things necessary. The people of the county, if there were any, could have supplied themselves with a miscellaneous lot of goods, amongst which there were not a few blankets. But we had brought no overcoats. The necessary things were Springfield rifle musket and bayonet, forty rounds of ammunition and caps, three days['] rations, a canteen of water, an extra suit of underclothing, and one tent piece. For most men a pipe and tobacco were essential. I had an extra horse, led by a man, my rations, three pieces of tent, (forming an entire shelter,) & an extra suit of underclothing. All other goods were in the wagon, which we never saw but once, (and that was in June,) until we were settled down at the siege of Petersburg.

We marched on the 4th, along the [*space left for road name*] pike [the Germanna Plank Road], crossed the plank road [that is, the Orange Turnpike], and about noon went into line of battle, facing westward. I was in the second line, with the 83[r]d in my front, and with the right resting on the plank road. It was understood by us, that the Sixth Corps [Sedgwick] was on our right, and the Second [Hancock] on our left, whether our immediate left or not, I was not certain. In those times a regimental commander was not advised as to the position of the other divisions of the Corps in which he belonged, nor even of the other brigades of his division, unless by accident, or his own efforts, and in the campaign of 1864, conducted so largely in the woods, was there opportunity to learn. When we formed our line, on the 5th of May, I know that I was in the 2d line, supporting the 83[r]d and on the right of the brigade, and was to move guiding my right on the road. I was not advised what was on our right, and only assumed that the rest of the brigade was on the left, though it was reported that the 44th N.Y. was in reserve. Though the woods were not dense[,] I could see only my own regiment.

It was reported on the morning of the 5th that the enemy was in our front, and advancing. Apparently the expectation was that he would attack us, and we cleared our front of the bushes which obstructed our view, and threw up some slight breastworks and there rested in line.

I rode out on the plank road [Orange Turnpike] and saw a cloud of dust, as if the enemy were moving towards us.[116] At 12:30 P. M. we received orders to advance, without specific directions. As we advanced two or three hundred yards[,] the woods became thicker, and then we broke out suddenly into an open field. A volley of musketry greeted us, from the woods on the other side of the field, a hundred and fifty or two hundred yards distant. On this the two lines struck into a double quick gait, and we went across the field with a rush. A ditch midway, & parallel with our line, broke us up somewhat, but did not materially retard the advance. The enemy broke and ran after the first volley, and we pursued them several hundred yards further until we came into another cleared space, with rising ground.

At no time could I see more than my own regiment, and the 83[r]d at my front; but as we emerged into the second clearing I caught the sound of scattering musketry on my right & rear, and apparently a considerable distance in the rear. As this indicated that their line on the right of the road had not come up and that there was no support on our right, and we were liable to be flanked. No field officers of the 83[r]d appeared, & I was advised that the Col. had been severely wounded in the advance.[117] I therefore assumed command of the 83[r]d to the extent of ordering them to halt, and to let my men pass to the front. I at once also deployed my right company in skirmish order into the woods across the road. The captain reported that none of our troops could be seen, but that he saw what appeared to be a skirmish line of the enemy crossing the road and passing into our rear.

I thereupon wheeled the 83[r]d to the right and formed them along the road, making a right angle with my line. Just then Col [Joseph] Hayes of the 18th Mass. on my left, came up. He had halted also, and wished to know the condition on the right. After a brief consultation, we determined to hold on and see what might happen. It will be understood that there was no brigade or staff officer, in sight. I had seen none in all the advance & we appeared to have been turned loose on the enemy, without orders or supervision, or support, or provision for any exigency.[118]

In a few moments Hayes left me and went back to his regiment. He had scarcely disappeared among the low bushes, when a heavy volley broke out, on his front, and I caught glimpses of his men going rapidly & in disorder to the rear.[119] This left two regiments in the woods, entirely isolated, and with an enemy of force to me unknown, in my rear, and with a force on my left sufficient to break Hayes. It seemed best to fall back, and I so ordered. I attempted to form a line before reaching the first clearing, but could not in the woods form but a few companies, & so fell back to our original line. On the way back we captured the enemy's skirmishers some thirty or forty, who had pocketed themselves, with more valor than prudence, in our rear.

I had lost 90 officers and men, killed or wounded. Some of the wounded perhaps we had not been able to bring off. Only one man, so far as I was ever able to ascertain, was captured unwounded. He had gone forward, while I was holding in the second opening, and reconnoitering on the right, and had taken shelter behind a stump, and was firing on some of the enemy appearing in an opening in the woods. He was so occupied that he did not observe when we fell back

The experience of this first day of the campaign was not especially encouraging. We had lost 25 percent of the regiment, and, on our front, had gained nothing.[120]

Further[,] our experience was not calculated to inspire more confidence in brigade and division officers. I think the chief defect was in the staff. Of these there was a lack in numbers and experience. There were no means of communication, and no proper coordination of movement, and apparently no reserve to repair defects, in the line or, if there were, such reserves were not used.

But we slept soundly, we had done the best we could, and my regiment had moved back without disorder. The battle of the second day (May 6) was of a puzzling sort. We "fell in" at 3 A.M. and our brigade moved forward and relieved troops on the right of the road, with the understanding that an attack of the enemy was expected. There was considerable heavy firing both of musketry and artillery in the woods on our right, and some desultory firing on our front, but nothing decisive. We were in two lines of battle, and at one time, the enemy appeared to be gaining ground on the right, their cannon shots were crashing through the treetops in line to enfilade us, & our rear line faced to the rear—the guns sounding to right & rear. After the hullabaloo of a day in which we accomplished nothing, the brigade fell back after dark to our original position. The enemy had attempted to break down the right & strike our line of communications.[121]

In the night, the Colonel of the 155th Pa., brought his regiment back, and went into position in rear of mine. He said he had been left, without notice, when his brigade fell back. In the morning his brigade commander rode along and accused him of deserting his brigade. He heard the charge with evident wrath, and replied that he had not deserted the brigade; the brigade had deserted him, and that "if it had not been for a drunken brigadier he would not have lost so many men yesterday." He was put in arrest, and rode along without his sword for several days, and then released and with his regiment was transferred to our brigade for awhile.[122]

A forest fire broke out on that part of the field over which we charged on the 5th, and burned extensively.[123]

During these two days there had been the sound of heavy musketry on our left, but the forest hid everything from our view, and we heard only the rumor that Hancock had thrown back the enemy on his front, but that nothing decisive had been accomplished.[124]

Our wounded had been all sent to the rear, but our dead were in the woods, & unburied, perhaps consumed by the fire, but I believe we left no wounded.

On the morning of the seventh, the third day of the battle, my regiment with the 118th Pa. and the 11th & 12th regulars, was ordered forward to reconnoiter, in order to ascertain the position and force of the enemy. I suppose it was suspected that they had withdrawn in whole or part, and were moving to their right. Our advance was further to the left of the road and not over the ground of our charge of the first day.

I was on the right of the line, the 118th next and the other small regiments on our left, but concealed by the woods. Col. [Charles P.] Herring had command of the line & I was next in command. We advanced into an opening, Herring and I in advance, when we were met by a volley of musketry, and some artillery.

Instinctively looking back I saw a cannon shot strike a corporal of Co. A. & cut him in two, so that the upper part of his body seemed to fall, doubling on the lower. The enemy, however, were concealed from us by the bushes. I thought there was but one gun. No artillery had before been brought into action, either by the enemy or ourselves, in the encounters of the first two days, with the single exception of one gun, which had been run out on the plank road and lost. I thought it possible that this was the gun which the enemy was using. We halted, however, and after consultation, Herring concluded his report. The result was that we were ordered to hold the line we occupied. This we established and reinforced by the 16th Michigan remained undisturbed the remainder of the day.

It occurred to me afterwards that we should have pushed further. But the musketry seemed to indicate a considerable line of the enemy, at least a very strong skirmish line, and the presence of artillery, unless it were only the captured gun, indicated more. Further[,] the instructions given Herring were oral, and only to fire if the enemy were still in our front. This was evident enough, and, when Herring asked for my opinion, I thought we had fulfilled our orders & should report. A further advance would probably have cost us much more, but we should have learned more and perhaps gone to Andersonville.

It was understood by us that the Army was to move to the right [that is, northward] and that we were simply to remain as a picket line, and to follow in the morning. Indeed we had received orders in the night of the 6th or 7th, to be ready to move, and specifying the order. This was a customary order, but it meant more than usual. On marches the regiments of a brigade moved in prescribed order, and that which led one day, had its place in the rear on the next. This was for the reason that marching was ordinarily easiest at the head, & hardest in the rear, and to avoid possibility of confusion[,] the order of regiments in column was prescribed. And this also determined, ordinarily, the order in line, and when there was no special reason for forming line quickly. Ordinarily, the column moved right in front. At this time the rear (towards the Rapidan) was on our right; the enemy in our front, and the direction of Richmond on our left. After the uncertain battles of the 5th & 6th, the great question occupying our minds was, what is to be done next? The Army of the Potomac had rarely fought more than two days, only I think in the Richmond campaign of 1862, and at Gettysburg. In the first it went back, and in the second the enemy went back. There was no expectation now that the enemy were on the run. Will we fall back? This would seem like giving up the whole thing, in the East. With these feelings, I heard after dark, the orderly calling "Where's the 20th Maine?" and lighting my candle end[,] I read the order. The brigade [was to] be ready to move in the following order, specifying the regiments and adding "left in front".

It was a pregnant clause. It meant go ahead! The greater part of our brigade moved in the early part of the night, and, at one o'clock on the morning of the 8th we fell back quietly and marched, following the corps, on the road towards Spotsylvania Court House.

We marched following the Corps, on the Brock road, at a brisk step, as rapidly as practicable, in the dark passing in rear of Hancock. There was only one serious obstruction, that of a brook flowing across the road, not bridged but easily passable, though muddy and[,] unless with care[,] overshoes deep. One would not suppose this a material obstruction, but upon reflection[,] he can perceive that it might inflict considerable delay, depending, in amount, upon the length of the column. Men on a march soon learn how important it is to keep the feet dry, and over such a wet & muddy place, will hesitate & pick their way. Each set of forces is therefore delayed, and this, though only of a fraction of a minute, is to be multiplied by the number of sets of fours in the column. The whole column of the Corps had passed on this road ahead of us, and the [trouble] lies in the fact that the enemy reach[ed] the line of ridge, to be occupied, and commanding the situation, only a little in advance of the head of our Corps. I met Col[.] Freeman [Conner] of the 44[th New York], coming back wounded as we came up, and he told me that part of the enemy were on the crest when he attacked, & he could see others coming rapidly up. Apparently a half hour would have given us the ridge without firing a gun.[125]

What would have been the result had there been intelligent staff officers, to see that the road was in good condition and to hasten the march, can be easily conjectured. Had our Corps occupied the ridge first, they could doubtless have held it.

Soon after we reached the ground occupied by the corps, we were detached from our brigade and sent to [Samuel W.] Crawford, much to our discontent, such detachments being generally unpleasant, and in this case especially so, as we did not like Crawford.[126]

However, we went according to orders. Our detachment reporting to Crawford, consisted of the 20th Maine, 118th Pa. the 16th Mich. and, I believe some companies of the 18th or 22d Mass. Our men had been on picket till one A.M. and on the march till about 8 A.M. and had had no time to make coffee. Herring [of the 118th Pa.] being unwilling[,] I took the detachment a little to the rear, and, watching carefully[,] gave them opportunity for coffee & hard tack.

Later, Crawford placed us in an oak forest, where we were subjected to heavy shelling, a most unpleasant experience always, and trying to the nerves; for although the danger is not great[,] the fragments of shells are buzzing about maliciously, and, until each strikes somewhere else, there is an unpleasant possibility that it may hit you. However, I lost only one man.

Near dusk and too late, we were ordered forward, & placed in the 2d line, to support the Penn[sylvani]a Reserves. (Crawford[']s brigade).[127] We moved first through broken forest, and over mossy ground, following closely the Reserves; then into thick second growth pines, where we could see but little distance. We advanced under fire, until the line of the reserves halted, and opened fire. We halted also, and remained a few minutes, when the Reserves broke, and came back with a rush through our line. I caught hold of the colors of one regiment, and attempted to rally the Reserves on our line, but with little success. Quickly following the Reserves came the line of the enemy. The light was then so dim in the woods that blue was hardly distinguishable from grey, but the Confederates were recognizable by their short jackets. For awhile (I have no idea how long) there was a most disorderly contest; clubbed muskets mixing with bayonets, and shooting. Near me one tall fellow, an officer apparently, clenched with one puny man, grasping his musket, and each trying to shake the other off, till a comrade put his musket under the fellow[']s arm and against the officer[']s breast, and fired[,] killing him, of course[,] instantly.

It was a pandemonium for awhile, but [it] suddenly ceased. We gathered some prisoners, and one battle flag. I got two line officer swords, one of which I have yet.

As soon as we felt assured that the fight was over, we (Herring and I,) went to the right and left, and found nothing. Our line had not yielded any ground, and we were evidently near the enemy and unsupported. Nor did we know how far to the rear their Reserves had gone, only we were certain that none were left with us.

Nor did we know what was in our rear, nor if troops in our rear knew of our position in front. Curiously, [not] in all this affair after the first order, did we see or hear from Crawford, or any of his staff, and no pains were taken by them to ascertain where we were, to rally us if we had gone back, or to give us orders if we had remained. Apparently again, as on the 5th in the Wilderness, the two lines were let loose against the enemy by the brigade commander, and at random, and he knew of failure only by their disorderly return. What had become of us apparently did not concern him.

We were left to extricate ourselves. It was dangerous to remain in that position, with both flanks unprotected, and near the enemy, and further, on the coming of daylight, we were liable to be fired on by our own troops in the rear. In these dense woods it was soon absolutely dark, and one[']s hand before his face could not be seen. Our only guide was the direction of our line, which in all parts had stubbornly held its place. So we knew the directions of front rear & flank. At first after consultation, [Rufus W.] Jacklin[,] adjutant of the 16th Mich.[,] volunteered to go to the rear and ascertain what was there, & if possible get orders. He did not return in reasonable time (in fact not in that month) and we sent out two more men, as Noah sent his doves.

Impatient at the long delay of these, I took a sergeant [William B. Greenwood], and started myself. In my boyhood I had been accustomed to the woods and felt confident that I could go in a straight line. This was necessary, for the reason, that, though taking the direction from our line, which we were reasonably certain had not changed position, and still faced the enemy, one could start directly towards the rear, where some part of the army must be located[;] there was absolutely no guide. I could not see my hand held before my face. If I diverged from the straight line I might curve around and run into the enemy, as Jacklin did. So placing myself with back to our line, & facing the rear, and with the sergeant behind me, I started.

The woods of small pine were thick, with many small dead branches, and it was necessary to keep my hand before my face, & feel my way, brushing aside the boughs. After awhile I felt, underfoot, the mossy ground over which we had advanced in the first part of the present movement. This assured me, and I was conscious that I had not materially turned aside.

The sergeant, following, called occasionally to be sure that he was not losing his way, and, at last in response to his call, some one answered in front. We had found the picket line of Neal's brigade [Thomas H. Neill] of the Sixth Corps, and by remarkable coincidence a captain of the Sixth Maine with whom I was acquainted. There was only one other officer in that Corps whom I knew, and in the utter darkness, and by mere chance I had come straight upon him. But the two men sent out after Jacklin, had preceded us, & found the same line. We brought the regiments back about three A.M. and went into line in rear, with the assent of the brigade commander [Bartlett], who had not been aware that we were in his front.

We did not see Crawford until the next morning, when on our way to our brigade, we met him. He complained that we had not supported him, and claimed and took possession of the battle flag which we had captured. How he could know that we had not supported him was not clear, as he had not appeared on our line at any time, during the whole affair, nor indeed any of his staff. The complaint was especially exasperating, as his own brigade had broken and left us to fight the battle, and we had captured the flag and the only prisoners taken. I have now the "C.S." sword of the line officer killed by my men. We got no credit however from Crawford. I lost three officers, Capt. [William W.] Morrell killed, and lieutenants Melcher and Prince wounded. How many of the men I do not remember, and there is no report of this battle, so far as I am aware.[128]

[SPOTSYLVANIA COURT HOUSE
MAY, 1864]

On the 9th we lay in the same place, in front of the enemy, with the Sixth Corps on our left & the 2d on our right. We threw up earth works for infantry and the batteries were posted at various points. The enemy made a rush upon part of the line, but were driven back. In my diary for that day[,] I find mention of a letter from my wife (dated Apr. 29th) which illustrates the care and energy with which the mails were forwarded. Letters from home followed us to the firing line, and the postal messenger (usually an enlisted man) often delivered the mail to the regiments at the peril of his life. We sometimes read our letters under like conditions.

We were under orders on the morning of the 10th of May, to be ready at daybreak, to move against the enemy, or to repel attack, but daybreak passed without movement on our front. What occurred outside of our immediate vicinity we could not see by reason of the woods. The country was for the greater part covered by forests, with here & there an opening or field.

Various rumors flew about. Butler was within ten miles of Richmond, and Sherman had pushed Joe Johnston back from Dalton. This was encouraging on the whole, though Butler within ten miles of Richmond did not mean much.[129] Later in the day, our brigade moved out in front of our works. At this point the ground was open. We moved with the 16th Michigan in front, as a skirmish line, into a shallow ravine, in front of our batteries. Beyond us, in front, an open field, a little higher, but fairly level, was bordered by a forest of tall pines, in which the enemy were supposed to be, and our orders were to charge across this field. I was on the extreme left of the brigade. We lay an hour perhaps, but sheltered from the fire of the enemy, by the bank of the ravine, while our batteries in the rear were throwing solid shot over our heads.

We were momentarily expecting orders to advance, when "Old Fields", (the cook of my men) appeared, with coffee & hardtack and his invariable grin. The prospect of immediate death is not sharpening to the appetite, but to encourage the audacity and enterprise of Field, I worried down the viands. The coffee was (as usual) easier than the hardtack.

The success of the charge appeared to depend largely on celerity.

At any rate the sooner we got to the works of the enemy, the less exposure to the fire of the enemy, & this concerned me, as my special orders were to partially wheel to the left, & go for a clump of taller pines. So I had my men unload themselves from their knapsacks, these being the greatest impediment to running. After some delay it was announced that the charge would be led by the troops, part of the corps which was in the woods, on our right. Only the regular brigade was visible to us, and we were to be guided on them. While I waited intently watching for their movement, there was a crash of musketry in the woods, the regulars rose, I ordered my men up; the regulars advanced a few paces & then halted, and as the orders required us to guide on the right I halted. Nothing came of the affair, excepting a severe loss to our right. It was reported that our right charged into an opening in which was a line of the enemy behind works, and our line at short range, received their fire and were crushed by it. The dead were found there, after the close of the war, a line of skeletons, in uniform, unburied.

It was reported, on this day, that the 2d Corps were more successful.[130]

We fell back, in rear of the batteries, & bivouaced for the night.

I note down these details, partly from my diary. They are perhaps of no interest excepting as they indicate that the sessions at this time were that of steady unintermittent pressure upon the enemy. The pressure was more or less severe at different times & points on the line, but it was constant, and the enemy was under constant supervision.

They occupied a ridge, or line of more elevated ground extending to Spotsylvania Court House.

During the 11th there was constant artillery fire, and, on our front some skirmishing. My regiment, on that day was under artillery fire only, and I lost but one man, a sergeant [David M. Overlock, of Waldoboro]. We rested in the afternoon, and during the night there was rain, with thunder and lightning.

On the 12th the brigade moved to the right & front, and occupied works with an open field in front. It was reported that Hancock or Burnside at 5 A.M. were to assault the right of the enemy at the salient, but Burnside was to the left of Hancock, and as a matter of fact, Hancock charged the salient, later supported by Wright.

The work of the day was to break the enemy[']s center & our part, it was understood, was to put pressure upon that part of the enemy[']s line in our front, and on the right of Hancock.[131]

We were all ready at daybreak, awaiting anxiously for the sound of Hancock's battle. There had been rain, and the woods were full of mist.

According to my diary, the attack did not begin until 5 A.M. but my recollection is that it was earlier.[132] The sound of battle came suddenly, through the intervening woods and misty air, first a patter of musketry, as of a skirmish or picket line, immediately followed by a roar, of immense volume. It was (to compare such things with small [events]) like a summer shower on the roof, first a few scattering drops, the sound of which changed into an undistinguishable roar. But, watching intently, I could only faintly hear the artillery throbbing through the vast volume of musketry.

We waited, intent, & ready ourselves to strike, but eager to catch from the sound, whether the assault was successful or not—whether the "Yankee hurra" or the "Rebel yell". The sound of battle seemed to subside a little or recede, and, suddenly came the "hurra"—and we knew that Hancock had carried the works. Very soon a staff officer came tearing through the woods, shouting that Hancock had carried the Angle and captured [Edward] Johnson and his whole division.[133] The sound of battle continued intermittently, during the day, part of our corps sharing in it, but our division took no part, excepting to be present & ready. Although on the very margin of that severe and important action at what was called the Bloody Angle, we took no part in it, except to hold the enemy in our front, and thus to prevent them from acting against the 2nd Corps & other troops engaged during the unavailing efforts of the enemy to recapture that part of their line. Towards evening we moved to the left, and massed in column of regiments in the woods.[134]

There was light rain. A straggler of the 9th Corps, with the legend "57th Mass." on his knapsack, supposed to have been left in the rear, in our camp, to guard the railway all summer, strayed past my regiment. Rain, fatigue, hunger & ever present danger, could not repress the sense of humor in the men, and they jeered unfeelingly at the disappointed & forlorn looking fellow, a recruit of not a month on the field, expecting to have been guarding railroads, & now in this worst of messes.

He reminded me of another man seen of a new Maine regiment, seen also straggling about that time. One of my men, recognizing him as an old neighbor, accosted him. He admitted his discontent and discomfort, & said he wished he were "in Pa's barn"— Why do you wish to be in "your Pa's barn?"— "I would go in the house damned quick." It was too much to wish however for the house directly. The rain was falling gently, and the bullets striking spitefully in the trees, when I went to sleep, lying in my blanket on the ground, but I slept soundly, but woke early, perforce, for we moved before day break, to the front line, and intrenched, or strengthened former works. My recollection is that the whole division was in line but we could not see far in the woods, and a regimental commander had no time to explore to right or left. The enemy held our attention also, by shelling. Sergeant [William] Griffin, a valuable man, was wounded, but my losses were slight, & [there was] more or less artillery fire all day, and some musketry about 5 P. M. During the days in the Wilderness and Spotsylvania C[ourt] H[ouse,] we always expected severe fighting early in the morning, or about sunset; so that the men were accustomed to say that if they lived till after eight o'clock in the morning, or six in the evening, they were safe for the day or night. I see by my diary that I had time on the 13th to write a letter to my wife and one to the father of Capt[.] Morrell, who was killed on the 8th.

We bivouaced, as we supposed, for the night, in a gentle rain, a little before dark. I had sent my horse to the rear, to be out of the fire, and had lain down, when suddenly orders came, to be ready to move at once, left in front. This indicated a sudden movement around the enemy[']s right, and we assumed that the breaking of the center on the 12th had so weakened him as to make such a movement promising of success. This was encouraging, though a night march, in wet weather, is always a severe trial of the men and this came after the work of a day.[135]

Personally I was most concerned on account of the absence of my horse. But I called to the adjutant to fall in the regiment, and to my orderly to bring the horse as quickly as he could; and waited with as much composure as I could for the appearance of my beast, and the disappearance of the regiment next on my left, which I was to follow. Fortunately the horse appeared and I took my feet from the ground, and was in the saddle before the 44th [New York] moved. It was a dreary march. The night was cloudy. It was with difficulty that I could see the forms of men in the rear of the Forty-fourth which I followed. The road[,] cut by wheels and trampled by thousands of men in front of me, soon became deep mire, evidently of clay, or very soft soil. Constant difficulty confronted me to keep in touch with the regiment in front, & at the same time to keep in touch with my own, so as not to break the column, and divert and mislead the rear, in the darkness. Consideration of the men, struggling in the darkness & mud, to keep up, could not be thought of. We must keep up. Added to this was the constant recurrence of sudden & unexpected stoppings and startings, caused probably by batteries ahead sticking temporarily in the mud. There was practically no rest for the men, as no place of rest could be found. The only approach to rest was leaning upon the musket. Night and march dragged along painfully, & it was a relief when we came around in the chilly raw gray morning, in front of the enemy, at the Court House.[136]

They promptly opened upon us with artillery, probably to

warm our chilled bones. But soon our batteries got up, and discouraged their industry. They had our range, rather closely, and the shells flew uncomfortably close over our heads. The indomitable Fields soon appeared with his customary viands[:] the succulent hardtack, and hot coffee, miraculously evolved out of an environment of dampness. It was indeed a warming and comforting drink, and renewed our courage and patriotism, seriously tried by the march. Just as I was lifting the tin cup to my lips[,] a vicious shell screamed low and suddenly over my head. Not yet braced up by the coffee, & lacking sleep for 24 hours, I ducked, & part of the coffee was spilled. Fields enlarged his customary grin, and added more coffee. I believed in the doctrine of Horace that it is pleasant to drink from a full cup.[137] The pleasure was modified by the conditions, but I succeeded and rested, if that could be called rest, during which I ground up a few obdurate crackers. As we afterwards found we were directly east of the Court House & near the road to Fredericksburg. The country was uneven, of low hills, & valleys, partly wooded & partly clear. Neither the little town nor the works of the enemy were visible, but they frequently assured us of their direction, by means of a shell, which had very little or no effect. We had passed through part of the 9th Corps, and part of the sixth appeared moving to the left. Evidently we were enveloping the right of the enemy, to force him from his works.

There were heavy showers in the forenoon, but the sky thereafter became fair, but occasional showers came in the afternoon. Battery D. was posted near us, and at night I relieved the pickets, on our front.

We remained on the 15th in the same place. There were anticipations of an attack; indeed we were always against them & under fire, always ready to attack or repel attack.

That evening Chamberlain returned, but as Bartlett, the brigade commander was ill, Chamberlain, as senior Colonel, took command of the brigade.[138]

We occupied substantially the same ground on the 16th with

the same preparations for attack, more accentuated at right but not culminating, and the weather continued showery keeping us in a condition of moisture, with moist beds at night.

There was one mitigation in this long continued exposure and great effort. The senses became dulled; we dozed, and did not much care what happened.

On the 17th of May, with the regimental commanders, Bartlett explored the front. We crawled out looking over the ground, as much as possible, without showing ourselves in any group. At night, after dark we advanced, under cover of the darkness, and crossed a branch of the Mattapony, a small stream, but swollen by the recent rains[,] and rushing over a rocky bed. Crossing at the head of the regiment[,] I slipped in and came out with high boots full of water. We occupied a hill, selected during the reconnaissance, and intrenched.

Daylight of the 18th disclosed to our view the scattered houses of the town and the line of the enemy, and brought about our ears the usual liberal donation of shells, which had no effect except to kill a man here & there. My center & left were on the hill, the right extending into lower ground. A mail came up, and reports of reinforcements.

The same conditions continued through the 19th and 20th. On the 19th there was sound of battle on the right, and camp rumor reported that the enemy had attempted to break through our line and gain the road & trains, but that they were repulsed with loss of prisoners, by the heavy artillery.[139]

Saturday the 21st found us in the same position, facing the works of the enemy, on the opposite hills, and under orders to be ready to repel his attack. I suppose there was no definite expectation that they would attack us, only, as we were constantly stretching around his right, and, I suppose, shifting our base, that was opportunity for them so to strike us, with chance of success, but we were in good position & would have been glad to see them in the role of charging, which we had so long been compelled to act.

But there was no advance of the enemy, only some skirmishing[;] and suddenly, while also there seemed to be some movement in their lines, we were ordered to fall back. This was about midday. We marched that afternoon about 12 miles following the enemy; crossed a railway and the Ny river[,] another small branch of the Mattapony.[140] At one point the enemy, on another road a mile or more to the west, put a light gun into position and threw a shell or two at us.

We crossed the Ta [River] on the 22nd. A slight mounted force with a single light gun, evidently a rear guard of the enemy, opposed us at one point, after we had crossed the stream. The shots from the gun sounded small, as of small guns. The 16th Mich.[,] 118th Pa[.] & my regiment moved forward into line, and rather slowly (too slowly) pushing their rear guard back. There was little resistance; in fact they ran as soon as we appeared through the bushes, and apparently they were there only for the purpose of compelling us to go into line, & to lose a little time for their advantage. We ought to have smashed right on with only a skirmish line ahead. We picked up some stragglers of the 38th Va.[,] doubtless fellows not much averse to being captured. We went into bivouac at 6 P. M. having been sufficiently exercised for sleep and with increasing confidence arising from the fact that the enemy, for that day at least, had been on the run. There were rumors concerning Butler, this time that he had been driven back. Rumors with us had not at this time much weight. They ran about camps or through troops in the fields with astonishing rapidity and inaccuracy. What an orderly heard or half heard at Corps or Army Hd. Qrs, flew with the speed of the wind and as lonely; it is not so much a matter of exaggeration as inaccuracy. Verily, Rumor is truly an exaggeration. But in this particular case of Butler being driven back, the report had distressing earmarks of truth, and tallied with the probability, as if one should report that a man fell out of a tree, this being in accord with the law of gravitation.[141]

On the morning of the 23rd of May the bugle sounded at

4:30. It was a busy time. So far as I was concerned[,] or any in my neighborhood, we were all at sea in a fog. The country was mostly wooded and the roads of dirt and narrow. We were moving south in general directions and towards the right and picked up some stragglers of the enemy, which indicated, if any indications were needed, that the enemy were in our front, a necessary consequence arising from the fact that we were following them. We had been advised by Goldsmith that:

> "The King himself hath followed her,
> When she has gone before."[142]

That we were going in the direction of Richmond as well as of the Confederate Army, was evident enough, but whereabouts in the country we were[,] or how large a part of Lee's army was in our front, or where they were going to stop, or what other corps was following us or marching about in some other part of the woods, of all this we were in utter ignorance. There were rumors that the Sixth Corps was in our rear, and this probably came by wireless word of mouth along the column. If anybody had a map of this uninhabited wilderness, it was not published or in general circulation. We lived and moved by faith or in obedience to orders and not so much by sight, and got orders and information only as, and to the extent, we needed. But we were not unreasonably interested to know where we were, and when, and under what conditions we were going to run up against the enemy. We had not been under fire now for 24 hours, and had marched not rapidly, and slept soundly and if not on downy beds of earth, at least fairly dry, so that we were in good condition, and ready for anything which might turn up.

In the afternoon, we passed an old frame unpainted church, in the woods on the left of the road. It was evidently of the class described by the Italian cab drivers, as a church for religion, not for show. At least it was not for show. I believe it was called Mount Cassod Church; why I can not perceive, certainly not for any similarity in country, for the whole region here was flat & wooded. In front of the church by the roadside were some large logs, and on one of them sat Grant. A snapshot of him as he was pictured, and still is, in my eye, would be interesting I am sure. But alas snapshots (of the modern kind,) were not there. He was not an imposing, nor even of the conventional figure, compared with the late General Corbin in full uniform and ornaments of medals and badges.[143] He was an insignificant looking figure. A fatigue uniform, much worse for wear, a crushed soft felt hat, with only a black & gold cord to indicate that it was a military hat, without sword or belt, or shoulder strap, or star, and holding the stump of a cigar in his teeth, he sat in a half curled up fashion, as we passed near him. I watched him closely. There was a curiously calm expression on his face, and a faraway look in his eyes, and I doubt if he saw us. Probably the 5th Corps, and the rest of the army were marching in his head.

Although it was Sunday it is needless to say that there were no services in that church when we passed. The congregation, if any had gathered earlier in the day, had taken refuge in the woods, on our approach, warned doubtless by the confederate cavalry squad in our fronts.

We trudged on, stirring the dust and making more, and not discovering why this was called the telegraph road.

The monotony was broken when we came to the [North Anna] river. That feature in the country indicating the probability that the enemy would make a stand on one side or the other. But no enemy appeared on the north side.

That point in the river was called Jericho Ford.[144] It was a good omen. We had just passed Gideon with the sword of the Lord, if none of his own and Jericho must be near, to be overthrown, if not by the tooting of ram's horns, surely by some other kind of a noise. Our brigade (Bartlett's) waded the stream.

The pontoons of canvas boats were soon down, and the light batteries crossed[,] the rifle guns going into position on the north bank. No Jericho or other town was in sight, but open fields and forest surrounding at a quarter of a mile in front and much further on either flank.

Our division formed near the river, and the fourth on our right, the Iron Brigade being next to us.[145]

It was perfectly quiet for awhile; our skirmishing pushed forward into the woods. I think there had been some slight musketry before we crossed, probably as the guard watching at the ford had been driven off. I rode out to the front, and saw far out to front & left, through an opening in the woods, cattle driven rapidly in a distant open field.

On a sudden however, the enemy, far behind the woods in front of us, opened with artillery. The shells seemed to come over the tree tops, & to burst in the open. We moved quickly forward. A shell bursting too near disturbed my horse & he began to rear & plunge, and I dismounted & gave the reins to my orderly. Soon another burst near me & apparently over my head. I was struck in the groin and whirled around & fell. My first impression was that a bullet had hit me, but I found I was not bleeding, and with help, got up. It proved to be only a severe bruise, but I could not walk.

I sat on a stump and watched the fight. The attack of the enemy fell upon our right on the iron brigade, & was repulsed with severe loss to the enemy. I sat upon a stump and watched the artillery in our rear, firing over our heads. It was then dark and the blaze from the guns showed curiously in great puff of light.

One of the men helped me upon my horse, and, as Chamberlain was now present, I rode to the rear, to nurse my bruises. There was no further fighting that night, and I lay by a fire, with others, and we were entertained by Father Eagan, a Catholic priest and Chaplain of the Division, who talked pleasantly, until late.

I kept a wet towel on my bruised groin, and was fairly comfortable, though it was difficult for me to move around.

After I left the regiment, the corps remained near the river, but the next day advanced and on the 25th and 26th pushed to the [Virginia Central] railroad and cut it, taking some 500 prisoners. The object of the movement apparently was to cut this road, and to make such a formidable threat, as to move the enemy from their right. These objects accomplished, the corps fell back rapidly on the evening of the 26th. The corps passed us straggling badly, which indicated the severity of the march. I mounted, with some help, next morning, though suffering from the wound and a cold. The night had been chilly with rain but the 27th was exceedingly hot and the march rapid.

This movement to the right across the North Anna turned out to be only a demonstration. In fact I believe the enemy were found to be strongly intrenched and nothing was gained excepting the destruction of the railway, and the drawing of a large part of Lee's Army to that flank.[146] We were pushing now, we supposed, to get on the other flank of the enemy, in sectors to take advantage of this depletion of the enemy's right.

We marched all day in excessive heat. As I was suffering from my wound, and half sick, I picked my way along in rear.

A curious incident occurring on May 27th, illustrates the distress brought upon the poor country people, within the sphere of movement of the armies. As I was riding past a house by the roadside, an old man in front of the house appealed to me to order the men out of his garden. I rode into the garden, and found stragglers digging up the newly planted sweet potatoes, and drove them out. The old man said they were the only thing he had been able to plant, and all the vegetables he and his two little grandchildren had to rely upon.

Although they left the garden I have no doubt they or others returned later to the plunder.

Vegetables, even in the form of newly planted sweet potatoes, offered a temptation too strong to men who had been a month on a diet of hardtack and fried pork.

The march of the 27th and 28th brought us to the Pamunkey

[River], far to the left, and about midday we crossed the river on a pontoon bridge. I believe the Sixth Corps had crossed earlier and were on our right. Notwithstanding all the pushing and the shifting of base and difficulty of keeping up supplies of food and forage and ammunition for so large an army over bad roads, we got our mail as usual and [I received] a letter from Susie dated on the 17th of May. Her anxious thoughts and her letters followed me incessantly. It was worse for the anxious ones at home, waiting in the dark as to our movements, than it was for us, who were in the midst of the campaign.

[BETHESDA CHURCH MAY—JUNE, 1864]

The retreat of Lee's Army from the line south of the North Anna, to a line nearer Richmond, made necessary slow and complicated movements in following him. During those movements in the last days of May, and early part of June, which culminated in the battle of Cold Harbor, our corps were near the right of the line. We were pushing slowly through the woods and woody swamps, driving the enemy's skirmishers before us, and working our way to Bethesda Church. The Ninth Corps [Burnside's] had been on our right. We had some sharp fighting in which our Division was engaged with [Robert] Rode's Division of Early's Corps.

On the second day of June we were involved in an ugly situation. Burnside on our right, in the act of withdrawing to move to the left, was attacked, or rather the enemy advanced with little resistance and extended his skirmish line in rear of part of the 5th Corps skirmishers.[147]

While we were readjusting our line on the woody slope, a battery of the enemy on our right, got an enfilading fire on us, and were cutting through our line severely. I went to one poor fellow who had been hit by a solid shot, which crushed his hip, and left his bowels exposed. A comrade was wiping, with a rough towel, the great drops of perspiration, which in his agony formed on his forehead. Strange to say, he was still conscious, but of course, died soon afterward. The higher ground on which we were, bordered a ravine in front which curved to the right into open fields. The enemy's battery, which was cutting us obliquely, was on the other side of this valley, and on the thinly wooded, rocky slope. We should not have been able to hold the ground if this battery had been allowed to continue its fire upon us. Fortunately [Charles A.] Phillips['] battery was rushed to the open ridge bordering the valley on our side and opened fire with his usual deliberation and accuracy, firing single guns, in regular and quick succession. His shots sounded as regular as the ticking of a clock, and, in a few moments the fire of the enemy ceased.

On this day [June third] I was placed in command of the Division pickets, a long line extending almost wholly through the woods and across ravines and swampy lands. Most of the line was intrenched. In part the intrenchments were held by the reserves, with the skirmishers or pickets well out in the woods. In fact the whole body was in front of the works. At one point, on the second day, the enemy drove in our pickets, and a volley of bullets rattled amongst the trees in a lively way. But we drove the attacking party promptly back. It was evidently an attempt only to discover our presence and force.[148]

On Sunday the 5th, the main part of the regiment being in reserve, amongst some tall pines, the Chaplain [Luther P. French] held services while a battery of the enemy, on the other side of the ravine, and beyond the woods, were sending shot through the tree tops, by way of responses.

I was present at the service but a few moments, having urgent business along the picket line; but the Chaplain seemed to be sticking well to his text, notwithstanding the disagreeable nature of the music.

Riding to the right[,] my attention was attracted to unusual, but not rapid firing at one point on my line, where the pickets were in the open, on the edge of a steep part of the wooded ravine. When I came in sight, the firing ceased, and I ascertained, after some cross examination, that the men were firing ramrods, through or over the tree tops, into what they called a camp-meeting on the other side. They had collected the ramrods from muskets left in the action of the previous day or days. I disapproved of this form of amusement, & rode on.

I was congratulating myself that this was the last of my three days['] tour as Officer of the Division picket; but on reporting, in obedience to orders, to the Division headquarters, I was told that Gen[.] Warren wished me to remain on duty until the pickets were withdrawn, assuring me that the extra day would be counted as a tour. The order was couched in that form, but it was an order, and weariness and sleeplessness were never to be pleaded. I was directed to report to Gen. Warren's Hd. Qrs., and under his orders I was to remain there until directed to withdraw the pickets. My picket reserves were stationed at the Church, in rear of the center of the line. There was a little opening at the Church, and I directed the officers commanding the brigade pickets to remain there with the reserves until further orders from me, and then returned to Warren. The movement of the troops began soon after dark, but was slow. The column was of course, moving to the left. The road was a narrow country cart trail, and, I suppose[,] the batteries stuck. I found a resting place on the bench of a stoop outside of the house, while my orderly held my horse and his own, on the greensward below. In the intervals of dozing I heard the coming and going of Divisions and brigade officers and, as it seemed to me, a continuous torrent of profane swearing of the most emphatic kind. Complaints were made that the way was blocked, and everybody, excepting the complainant, seemed to be in fault. The nights were short at that season and the troops must be out of the way and the pickets withdrawn before daylight, and Warren was exhausting the West Point vocabulary, in his exhortations. I, of course, had no share in the conversations. I was only awaiting orders. But my reflections were not cheerful. I had no desire to be caught with a thin picket line, strung out a half mile or more through the woods in front of our enterprising enemy, of what force nobody knew, but surely suspicious and alert. Indeed their picket fire did not wholly cease all night. The night was wearing away, and a faint light was showing in the east, when Warren called me and ordered me to withdraw the pickets. Bartlett, whose brigade was in the rear and still sticking in the woods, was present when the order was given, and threatened that if I withdrew back on him he would fire into the pickets. This of course was mere bluffing. I was much more concerned about daylight and the enemy.

Hurrying down I found my orderly in sound sleep on the grass and no horse, and walking would be too slow, for this business, even if I could drag heavy riding boots. Fortunately the horse was found, grazing not far off, and I mounted and rode rapidly as possible to the reserves at the church. The picket-line faced south, the right being curved straight back.

I directed the officer commanding the brigade pickets on the right to bring in his pickets at once, quietly and rapidly as possible, & to form on the right of the reserve at the church, facing the enemy.

Giving him what time I thought sufficient to start his men, I sent the officer commanding the brigade picket, and, as I had no mounted officers for the 3rd brigade on the left, I rode out myself for them, picking my way through the woods, in the dim light. When I had brought them back I found greatly to my relief the other detachments in line, formed the Third with the others, and started them off, to follow the main body. A squad of cavalry had been assigned me, and with these I remained until the rear of my column had disappeared. It was then fairly day light, but a low fog had risen in the woods and this favored us. When [I] left I directed the cavalry to remain twenty minutes longer, unless attacked, in which case they were to make as much resistance and noise as possible and fall back. Scattering and random shots were coming over, as I rode away. I am confident that the enemy, on that part of the line at least, were unaware of our withdrawal. I did not lose a man.

We marched in heat, and about noon overtook the division, and halted, in rear of the 18th Corps. Our only thought was of rest. I had been under stress nearly four days, with little sleep or rest, the fourth day terminating in a severe march.

I found that Chamberlain had been relieved, and assigned to command of the first brigade. This left me in command of the regiment again. He had been with the army since the 16th of May, though part of that time on special duty at Corps Hd. Qrs.

We got but little rest, for at 2 in the morning of the 7th of June, we rec[eive]d sudden orders to move, & advanced four or five miles down to the Chickahoiminy, along the north branch of which I picketed. I had my reserve in tall pine timbers, & the pickets along the bank of the stream. The enemy amused themselves by throwing shells at us, but they failed to get our range and did no damage excepting to the tops of the trees, in which we had no property interest.

We remained here doing picket duty until the 12th day of June, without special incident. The enemy shelled at intervals and was [*indecipherable word*] their ammunition. The pickets reported that one of their shells burst over the river and killed a large copperhead snake, which was regarded as a good omen. During one of these intervals of shelling Mrs. Fogg the old army nurse, with a pair of Christian Commission men new to the business, came up in an ambulance. An unfortunate shell burst over them. The old lady, not inexperienced, was undisturbed, but her clerical escort took too personal view of the matter, and seemed to think that that particular shell [was] intended for them. Apparently, they attributed their escape to a special intervention of Providence. Several mails came up, and our Division wagons, and here an event of unusual importance occurred. We had a change of clean underwear. This may seem a very commonplace matter, and is, in the piping times of peace, but was quite otherwise to men who had been sweating in the dirt six weeks, with only one change of clothing, and no bathroom or its equivalent. Sufficient water to drink was not always in abundance. A clean shirt, two or three weeks belated, becomes a pronounced luxury. Laundry facilities were at a very low ebb, that summer.

We made a night march down the left bank of the Chickahominy starting at 8 o'clock, through wooded country, and with many haltings. At one of these, occurring in a deep ravine, there was singular discomfort. In a cavalry fight a few days before, some horses had been killed and, aided by the heat and dampness, had filled the air with vapors too foul to conceive of in time of peace. The very air was rotten, the wretched distillations settling down, in the still damp night air, to the bottom of the valley. Unfortunately some unseen obstruction in the road ahead had blocked the column, and my regiment was compelled to stand there, half hour, in the darkness, and breathe dead and decaying horse flesh. It may appear like a joke in the relation, but it was a serious and sickening matter at the time.

We crossed the Chickahominy, at the Long bridge, early on the morning of the 13th, halted at 7:30 and threw out pickets in the direction of Richmond, but at dusk called them in and marched ten miles. Much of the country seemed low, and the greater part of the way the road was a narrow country by-way, bordered by bushes. The swamp magnolia was in bloom, and the scent of it filled the damp night air. It was still and warm, and the men trudged on, patiently, but in the silence of weariness. We halted about 2 o'clock in the morning, and felt about us for a place to lie down for a brief rest, for we moved again at 5, and marched till nine, when we halted for breakfast. This meant that the men made coffee (if they could find fuel) and nibbled hardtack. It was evident that we were forcing the march, to get ahead of the enemy. But in what direction, or what place or particular movement, we were in utter ignorance, although a part of it.[149] But we came out into open country. Across the fields we could see, over the low hills, the topmasts of vessels. We were near the James, and the river was full of shipping.

This meant supplies or crossing or both. It proved to be both. We were about five miles below Harrison's Landing where McClellan fell back in 1862. But this was a very different situation.

We were the pursuers now. The sound of our cannon must have been heard, growing nearer for some days, in Richmond.

We had been marching several days, & not under fire. Even the sound of artillery was distant, and showed only that we [had] not lost touch of the enemy. We had had a finger on him constantly since the 5th of May.

But what days in June these were, the 14th and 15th. We were almost literally in clover, in green fields, with plenty of water, the broad James, and plenty of fuel from the rail fences, rations and rest, the smell of green fields instead of the fumes of gun powder. We washed our faces and hands, ate and slept, and borrowed no trouble. The 2nd Corps began crossing on the 14th and finished on the 15th, followed by teams and batteries. The bridge of boats was long, but it was steadied by large schooners anchored at different points, and the days were calm. Like Xerxes, we were "bridging our way,["] but with no occasion [to] ["]discourage the indignant waves."[150]

Sometime in the night of the 15th-16th the inevitable orderly hunted out & wakened each regimental commander, with orders to move at daybreak. Disturbed in the midst of a sound and well earned sleep, one's patriotism does not cheerfully or promptly respond, and it is only by force of habit and under pressure that sleep is thrown off. It is something of a relief and shifting of the burden, to wake up the adjutant and have the sentinels instructed. The days now were hot, we crossed on the 16th, rested an hour and then moved on, in no doubt now, as to the direction. With little rest and as rapidly as possible we marched until nine P. M. and gave the tired men an hour for supper and rest. The reader will understand that the only difference between breakfast[,] dinner and supper was in the hour of the day, and the time required was the same, excepting that in the dark it was more difficult to procure wood & the making of coffee was omitted. While we were halting, the sound of artillery could be heard in front, and we understood well that it was the old problem of "getting there first with the most men".

Before we halted I had a misfortune. Like Achilles I was wounded in the heel. Big horseflies infested the column, and one or more paid particular attention to the belly of my horse. In his frantic striking he hit my heel, and inflicted a most painful bruise, and I had the combination of heat, dust, weariness, an aching heel and a restive horse, a condition of misery worse than the presence of the enemy.

[PETERSBURG
JUNE—AUGUST, 1864]

Next morning we were confronted by the enemy, intrenched at Petersburg. They were there first, and if not with the most men, yet with men enough to man the formidable works which they had prudently built long before.[151]

As we were coming up reports spread that the second Corps and the colored troops had captured works and prisoners. These proved to be only outworks, some of which were taken by the colored brigades.[152]

Our division pressed the enemy back & then the 1st & 2nd brigades charged. Chamberlain commanding the first, moved to the left, but the charge was ineffectual, & Chamberlain was severely wounded.[153] After dark, when I could leave the regiment, I went back to the hospital to see him. I found him sitting up, and taking nourishment in the form of soup, rather clumsily administered by the Chaplain. He was severely wounded, but talked cheerfully. The extemporized hospital was well filled. Col. [Hiram Lincoln] Prescott of the 32nd Mass. sat opposite[,] bolstered up, and writing his farewell letter to his family. He was shot through the bowels, and such a wound, at that time[,] was necessarily fatal.

Nothing decisive was accomplished on the 19th. Our batteries

& skirmishes were pushed well to the front, apparently with the object of holding the ground as closely as possible to the works of the enemy. We were that day on the left, and there were negro troops in our rear. On the edge of a deep ravine near the line of intrenchments captured on the 16th, lay a long row of our dead. Evidently the charging line had risen out of the ravine, and caught the fire of the enemy, at short range, directly in their faces, and apparently, half the line or more, had fallen at one volley. But the second line, directly behind the first, had caught the enemy before they could reload, and revenged the first. A line of the enemy lay dead in the intrenchment.

It was a curious illustration of the hardening effect of war, that our men were looking over the dead bodies, and exchanging muskets, where they could find a better [weapon].

That day John Marshall Brown, then Col. of the 32nd Maine, and formerly adjutant of the 20th, was severely wounded. Chamberlain was taken back to City Point.[154] That night I had 125 men on picket, a large detail for a regiment so much reduced, more than half.

In the morning we moved to the left, across the railroad leading to Norfolk [the Norfolk and Petersburg Railroad], and near heavy earth works. We rested in one edge of a wood and at sunset moved forward in column, five regiments of the brigade, the 118th Pa., 20th Maine, 18th Mass., First and Sixteenth Michigan. I was in the advance and we halted under the slope of the hill. Major Keene, who was in his place in the rear, came forward, where I lay at the head of the column. He seemed depressed, and thought we were going to make a useless charge. It was unusual with him, but I thought little of it as we were all pretty well worn out. We had been forty-seven days in active campaign, by far the greater part of the time, in the presence of the enemy, holding and watching or pressing them, or shifting for position in dirt or mud, with the unwholesome fare of salt pork and hardbread rightly named hard bread, often marching by night & skirmishing by day, with nine serious battles interposed. It was all that any man could endure, and more than many could endure, although our men, at the beginning of the campaign, were seasoned soldiers. I would not like to give the impression that anybody grumbled or was disposed to shirk. I remember to have heard none. But the "spoiling for a fight" temper sometimes talked of by our late President, was gone.[155] The elasticity of the men was gone, and their feeling was well expressed about that time by one of the men (a good soldier), when a charge was expected. He said he would "like to lose a day," pay & rations included. But no man flinched.

But as we lay resting and waiting on the slope, I assured Keene that, in my opinion, the conditions indicated only a change of position.

So it proved, and soon, for soon Bartlett came up with orders to that effect, and details of the position to be occupied, as close as possible to the intended positions of the enemy.

He took several of us regimental commanders with him, and we picked our way out, in the dusk of evening, and selected a line to be taken. I procured for markers a bundle of green sassafras sticks, which grew abundantly in the old fields about Petersburg and had the bark peeled off to render them more easily distinguishable. We were to be guided by a clump of tall pines on the left, visible against the sky. The men who carried the sticks following me, stuck them in the ground at intervals and when this was completed we went back and brought up the regiments.

Spades had been distributed and men told off from the first relief of the spades, & others to picket in front. All marched with fixed bayonets, so undercover of the darkness we occupied ground open & unprotected from the enemy, and in plain sight of them in daylight. The spade men, when in position, inverted their muskets and stuck the bayonets in the ground, while the detailed pickets stepped a few paces to the front, and stood at guard. Keene & I went along the line cautioning the men to keep quiet and impressing upon them the necessity of diligence, since we must have cover before the moon arose, which would be about one in the morning, or at least before daylight. The line was manifestly for permanent occupation, but works sufficient for temporary shelter, must be built that night, as we were in easy range of the enemy's artillery and in range of sharpshooters in strongly fortified positions in our front. They would not be likely to permit us to dig unmolested by day. We made that night only temporary intrenchments which consisted of a ditch, in forming which the earth removed was thrown to the front, to form a bank, & to increase the protection with the least amount of digging.

The night was calm and hot, but the men worked diligently, relieving each other at intervals. The still air was soon saturated with the odor of sassafras root, cut & thrown out by the spades. The soil was sandy and easily worked, and before the appearance of the moon, substantial protection had been effected, from which we could not have been forced.

While this work was going on, I suggested to Keene that he take a detail of men and put up a little shelter of branches, just back of the line, where we could establish headquarters unexposed to the blaze of the sun. Alas for him, we did not take the same care to avoid exposure to the enemy.

In the morning they discovered us and opened fire of artillery and scattering musketry.

But the men were fairly well sheltered, lying in the trench. The artillery fire soon slackened, and subsequently, was generally only at intervals, and the musketry seemed a negligible quantity.

During the night our quartermaster had brought up a can of peaches, a luxury theretofore unheard of in that campaign, and it constituted the dessert of our noonday meal of hardtack. We sat in the shade. About three o'clock it was reported that one of Capt. [Prentiss M.] Fogler's men was severely wounded by a piece of shell, and Keene and I walked to that company and gave directions to have him taken back to the field hospital.

That attended to, and a survey taken of the line at that point we walked back, and at our shelter, stopped a moment to look at the enemy. I had turned aside, & stooped to pick up some article I had dropped, when I heard the stroke of the bullet, and Keene reeled against me, exclaiming, "I am killed, write to my wife". I caught him as he was falling, and he added, "Its all right I die for the country"; and as he sank in my arms, he murmured faintly, "the doctor". His ears were then white, and the blood was rapidly leaving his body, and he was evidently losing consciousness. I sat down with his head on my knee, but he was dead. He had been acting as Major, all that campaign, and we had been intimately associated nearly two years.

The loss to me was a severe one, and overwhelming to her, to whom he had sent the message in his last hurried breath.

"Nothing was here for tears, nothing to wail or beat the breast."[156]

I sent the body to the rear, and it was, by the kind services of Hon. E. B. French, then Second Auditor of the Treasury, embalmed and sent to Thomaston for burial. More to relieve my lonesomeness, than because at this time I needed assistance, I detailed the Captain, next in rank, ([Joseph B.] Fitch of Co. D.) to act as Major. He came up and hung his coat on a post of the shelter, the same sharpshooter probably who had killed Keene, soon sent a bullet through the coat, and was evidently watching us with care. The sharpshooters also killed on that day [Fred Roscoe] Wright of Co. G. one of my old men, and a fine fellow, and wounded severely another man in Co. I. It was evidently unsafe to be standing around. The distance of the enemy's line rendered the ordinary Springfield musket of little account, and we were practically defenseless against these rebel sharpshooters. The artillery fire was annoying, but did little harm. Our sentinels were on the alert, and on the instant of the appearance of a puff of cannon smoke, shouted "Down", and there was a prompt and general ducking. But the men were often careless, and in this, as in other things, familiarity bred contempt terrible.

[*At this point Spear rewrites and expands the previous paragraph.*]

We sent poor Keene's body back, and notice to his relative E. B. French, then Second Auditor of the Treasury, who had the body embalmed, and sent to Thomaston for burial. A letter lay under the shelter, unsealed, and directed to his wife. I suppose he had intended to add more. I felt we had lost many officers and men in the campaign but none with whom I had been so intimate.

He was a noble fellow, of unusual ability and culture. He had college and legal education, was happily married, and had, or seemed to have, a brilliant future before him. The exclamation of his last breath showed the poise and attitude of his mind. Life was precious to him, but he had deliberately put it into the balance. We were dulled by reason of fatigue and exposure and hard fare and familiarity with death, and everything had become more or less commonplace. Our nearest and dearest comrades fell, but the gaps were filled and the unrelenting and inevitable business went on, and that business was to kill.

But many times since I have thought of Keene and time has lifted his heroic death out of the commonplace, and set him amongst the heroes of the past.[157]

> Nothing is here for tears, nothing to wail
> Or knock the breast; no weakness, no contempt,
> Dispraise or blame, nothing but well & fair,
> And what may quiet us in a death so noble.

It was apparent now that we had settled down to a siege of Petersburg, and the routine every day was substantially the same.[158] The enemy appeared to be well supplied with artillery, and were using it liberally, but without serious effect upon us. There was constant picket firing on our right, along the front of the Ninth Corps, and occasionally scattering fire of pickets merged with the longer range and more certain shots of the enemy's sharpshooters.

With the permission of the proper authorities I set about forming a detail of sharpshooters in my regiment. Of good material there was abundance. Very many of the men were expert marksmen, accustomed to hunting from boyhood. The majority in Co. B were such.

I was allowed to detail at the rate of two men from each company, and at the expense of the Government, we sent for their sporting rifles. These came in a few days. They were, of course, all muzzle loaders. Some little time was required to clean and put them in order, but the next morning early, I put them out on the vidette line.[159] Everything was favorable for their work, and we had a good opportunity to impress upon the enemy that the murderous game of picking off officers and men, at safe distances, was one which could be played by two. The air was still that morning, and the sun on the backs of my men. They had scores to pay, and were accustomed to shoot squirrels and partridges in the head. Soon the crack of their rifles, easily distinguished, could be heard along the line, and they soon made things even, for the enemy were not expecting long range and accurate shooting from us. One of my rifles was telescopic, a heavy barrel surmounted by a telescope with the crossed threads for sighting. The man was as good as the gun, and, under such favorable conditions, certain at the distance between the lines.

We were not required, however, to continue this kind of assassination. I think it was the next day, at any rate, very soon, that their pickets shouted to ours, proposing that they would not fire any more, if we would not, and the truce was agreed to by the picket lines, and was scrupulously observed on my front, so long as my regiment held that part of the line.

But this agreement did not include the artillery. Of that we had abundance in position, and with good range, and probably we had ammunition supplies more abundant than they. I do not know why their desultory artillery fire was kept up. It settled and could settle nothing.

One night only it subjected us to serious annoyance. On the early part of the siege we were building pits, and one was just on the right of my regiment. The men worked in the night, under cover of the darkness; but one gun of the enemy had their range pretty accurately, and to impede the work threw a shell every three or four minutes, which exploded over us with a sharp and very wakeful bang. Under ordinary circumstances, in those days, I needed no anodyne. Sleep came unsought, day or night, and needed only opportunity.

But this night, as soon as I was fairly asleep, came the execrable bang, and I was awake again. I slept at last, but whether from exhaustion, or because the firing ceased, I do not know. It had ceased when I awoke in the early morning.

After a few days the enemy brought into use a coehorn mortar, which dropped amongst us a shell entirely unadvertised and more amusing than destructive.[160] I saw but one man killed by it. The shell dropped apparently between his feet and instantly exploded, literally blowing him up.

I saw another as I was standing on the parapet, fall near a man going to the vidette line. It fell near him, but beyond suddenly quickening his pace it had no effect.

With only such interruptions, dull routine possessed us. Rations were abundant but not luxurious, and cooking was under difficulties. The heat was excessive, and water not abundant and brought from a distance in the rear. We had pickled cucumbers once, & once peaches brought up by the Sanitary Commission, and distributed to the enlisted men, so many to each.[161] Flies, of the biting sort, rivaled in numbers, and surpassed in viciousness the swarm of a Nile village.

One evening as we sat smoking our pipes, my adjutant amused himself by scorching some thousands of them, by flashing gunpowder around the bait of sprinkled sugar. But what was thousands in such a swarm!

A corpulent toad also made our acquaintance. In the abundance of leisure and muscle[,] our orderly blacked our boots frequently, and the blackening mixed with molasses drew the flies, and the flies drew the toad. As we were generally quiet in these after supper smokes, he would hop into view, and then tiptoe to a boot. There was a flash of his red tongue and a fly disappeared. He was a well fed toad, for his game was abundant. Such small matters served to break the dull monotony. Even the shelling was monotonous.

On calm evenings, we sat sometimes on the parapet and watched the picket firing at Fort Hill, where the lines were near together, and the firing constant.[162] It was not a mile away, across the valley, yet often the flashes were plainly visible and we heard no sound. I conjectured that the air waves rebounded from the heavier air in the valley, and passed over our heads.

There was an eleven inch mortar on the right far off, which made nightly exhibitions in a flash as of low summer lightning, a crinkling line of fire curving through the sky and another flash, a flash at both ends of the curve. Then came the sounds, first the dull roar of the mortar, and after the visual exhibition was over, the sharper sound of the exploding shell. It was curious to note the line of light of the flying shell revolving with its burning fuse, decreasing in speed at the apex of the curve, then toppling down with increasing speed.

As my men had plenty of time I set them to the task of digging a well, without great expectations, for we were on a sandy ridge. We found no water but at a depth of about 12 feet, shells large and partly fossilized, as if that level had been once an ancient shore or sand spit.

I find in my diary of that time mention of occasional visits to Hd. Qrs., to other regiments and once to City Point, almost daily receipt of letters, most of all from my wife, the dear girl always anxious, I knew, but not from her letters, and writing incessantly. Our friends did not neglect us. No daily paper, excepting at one time those of Richmond smuggled through the picket lines, but that leak was eventually discovered, and stopped. We could see the newsboy on horseback, within the confederate lines, selling papers. The Army, anticipating the later newspaper reporters, could manufacture its own news, and once made[,] it was self moving, and by wireless.

Rumors multiplied and spread especially when Early went into Maryland, and there were mysterious movements in our army, as if electrically affected.163

The Second Corps was going to the right, as if to wrap around the enemy's left, threats to prevent reinforcements to Early, or to draw him back. We had now such confidence in Grant, that we did not worry about the safety of Washington. He was plainly master of the game.164

Returns and reports had to be made & this was distasteful and laborious. Mental habits are too much disturbed by war, and the conditions were not favorable to literary effort. Besides, I was not well. I had forgotten it, but I find in my notes mention of nausea and lassitude. Two months and a half of active service in immediate front of the enemy most of the time, has little of the elements of a vacation, and we had been, from the North Anna to the James exposed to malarial atmospheres.

Simultaneously, with the reports of Early's advance into Maryland came another more active shelling from the enemy, and occasional outbursts of musketry, apparently to encourage us in the belief that they were still there, and ready for business.

About the middle of July we strengthened our works on the left. We had been working on the whole line, and had greatly changed from the simple ditch and bank which we first made.

After mortar shelling had been commenced by the enemy we built bomb proof. We brought up rough logs cut from the abundant second growth pines in the rear, and built a frame work in rear of our breastworks, and on a covering of logs piled earth. This afforded safe shelter in time of mortar shelling, but the whole was uncomfortable and the men would not stay in it preferring to take their chances outside.

About this time I was ordered to advance the vidette line in my front, so that from it the bottom of the valley could be seen. The valley slopes were gentle, and, apparently there was no stream intervening. But directly in front was a spring, a little nearer to their lines than to ours. Here the Confederates had been obtaining water.

It was reported that the object of this advance was to guard against mining on the part of the Confederates, but I have no idea that this was the true object. We were mining opposite the Confederate fort on the right, and an advance on our front might be advantageous under some circumstances, and for that as well as other reasons it was desirable that our advance line should bear far out as possible. However[,] with the reasons I had nothing to do. My orders were to advance the line of the vidette. This we occupied at dusk and withdrew the vidette at daylight. I obtained spades and added a man with a spade to the detail for each vidette post, and prepared to move them a little earlier than usual, so as to first get possession, as advantageous to war as in law, though not always to the one out of nine points.

We did get there first, and passing over our old line of posts, advanced beyond the line of the rebel videttes. I went out on the center, & halted when I thought we were far enough. There was light enough to permit the men, on right & left, to align on me. The men lost no time in beginning to dig the crescent shaped little forts. Soon sounds of footsteps advancing from the enemy, and a low voice said "There's the Yanks". Then some fellow began to remonstrate. "Get back. You are on our ground." A sergeant with us replied "Can't help it, we were ordered out here". Logically he fell back on the old excuse of orders, which justified anything. There was more of these remonstrances, and then the confederate pickets threw some clods and subsided and left us in peace. I had instructed my men not to fire unless fired upon. But the truce proposed by the Rebs was kept by them and of course by us, as we were the intruders.

I think that the ludicrousness of two lines of pickets, between two hostile armies, seriously arguing, on legal or moral grounds, their respective rights to a strip of land did not occur to any of us at the time. I was prepared for a fight and the absurdity of the affair did not appear until later.

In the morning of July 22nd Gen[.] Warren rode along our lines and later Generals Grant and Meade, and kept us full of expectation, as to what was going to be done. But we were quiet until July 30[th], notwithstanding orders to be ready to move, rec[eive]d on the 27[th]. The same cramped quarters, the same intense heat, no fewer flies & no less dirt.

Water for drinking was brought in canteens from far in the rear. A wet towel for the face and hands was an extravagance. There was no oasis in that Sahara. On the eve of the 29[th] I sent back for my horse, and rode over to see Gen[.] Ames. He informed me that the mine in front of his division was to be exploded at daylight next morning, and (I think) he had orders to charge. The lines there were the closest. A big well had been sunk inside of our works, and a tunnel run terminating in a chamber, under the center of the rebel fort. Then lateral branches, each including four other chambers, and in every chamber a ton of gun powder. This work had been performed by coal miners detailed from Pennsylvania regiments. The fuses were laid ready for firing.[165]

I rode back to my regiments, expecting general orders. These came in the evening & we were to be under arms at daybreak. So [we] were[,] promptly before dawn. The "Reservoir" hill, where were the enemy's earthworks and batteries[,] was still shrouded in darkness. The first faint flush of dawn low down in the eastern sky was visible, while all about us was in shade. It moved up the sky and began to disclose the landscape. All eyes were fixed on the hill now fairly visible. It was still, excepting a few shots in that direction. I turned my head to [Captain Joseph] Fitch to say "Adjourned", when I saw his face light up and turning my eyes again to the hill[,] I saw the explosion begin—great rolling domes of white smoke, dense & low, with black objects shooting up through the mass. I could never recall that I heard any sound. My eyes absorbed all my available senses. Immediately the turbulent masses of smoke began to roll down the slope, pressed low & not rising in the air. For an instant, for some seconds, there was or seemed to be, absolute silence. Then a single cannon sounded and another & another, until every gun and mortar bearing on Petersburg and the works of the enemy took some part. The din and roar were immense. But what was to be done? The enemy seemed stunned. A great gap had been made in their line, and at the very point where our troops were nearest. Will they charge; shall we be ordered forward also? There seemed never to be a better time. But all our attention was held upon the scene of the explosion.

Soon, with my glasses I could see the legs of men as they charged through the smoke, now a little lifted from the ground. That was encouraging. They seemed to be going directly into the gap or crater as it was afterwards called, and the Confederate batteries, waking up, began to throw shells into the infernal cauldron. Then emerging from the smoke, a line of our flags rose into the light.

But the uproar continued; more rebel guns were brought into play, and nothing decisive [happened]. No more of our troops advanced, so far as we could see. After awhile men seemed to be running for the hill (still smoke covered), towards the Confederate rear. "They are breaking, they are running," Fitch exclaimed. But I turned my glass in that direction. "Those men running to the rebel rear wear blue uniforms, Captain." They did, under cover of the smoke[,] the Confederates had charged in and broken the line, recaptured the blown up fort, and captured many of the men who had taken it. It was disheartening, but that was the end of it. How did it happen? Burnside was in command there, and he was relieved soon afterwards, but not soon enough. I saw nothing more than this which I have related.[166]

It may not be amiss to add that, prior to the day of the explosion, a battery of eleven inch mortars had been put in position, in our rear, and, immediately after the explosion, they joined in the bombardment, at first in the inexperience of the gunners, bursting shells over our heads.

The next day was quiet, and the following. Indeed, the spasm of firing of the 30th seemed to have satisfied or exhausted the combatants. The miserable part of the business was the exposure of the killed and wounded, on that slope, in the heat of July and August. It was, as I remember, some twenty-four hours or more, before a truce was patched up, and the poor fellows, who survived, were removed.

Curiously, in the midst of all this murder and distress, the civil part of the military business went on. The machine in all its parts continued in uninterrupted movements. On the Second day of August the paymaster appeared, and the regiments of our brigade were paid for two months. Alas, there was a much smaller number to pay, and the value also of the pay was materially lessened. The currency was so depreciated that our dollar was worth only about forty (40) cents, and, excepting the Commissary supplies, which were bought at wholesale rates, everything was at high prices. Fortunately we absolutely needed little excepting food & clothing, and of clothing not much, as we were not much in society, not even holding dress parades, and the fatigue suits were durable. The severest pinch came upon those of us who had dear ones at home dependent upon us.

Our appetites were not keen; we suffered from feverishness and nausea, and the cost of the regular ration of salt pork, coffee and sugar and hardtack was not great. Nor was the amount expended for pipes and tobacco very large, though we smoked excessively— or what would have been excessively had we not been living in the open air.

Recurring to the payment, it was significant of the financial condition of the country, it was significant that part of the currency there disbursed consisted of United States coupon notes called seven thirties. My recollection is that there were three interest coupons attached. I do not know if anybody benefitted, unless it were the Government, by this disbursement, for no one of us could keep them long enough to take advantage of the coupons. I paid mine out at face value. One of the men cut his coupons off, as of no value, and detracting from the symmetry of the note.[167]

About this time reports were flying about that the enemy were in Alexandria, and that Chambersburg had been burned. It was sufficiently clear to us that the enemy were not all in Alexandria, & our interest in Chambersburg was faint.[168]

There was a general desire in the Corps that we should be sent to look after Early, but we had entire confidence in the ability of the Sixth Corps.[169]

During the early part of August deserters from the enemy not unfrequently came in. The first one came soon after the advance of my vidette line, and in the open day. I was sitting under the shade, at my headquarters, when one of my videttes appeared with a man under guard. The guard saluted and said that he had brought this man in. I looked at him and inquired why, for the man, though unknown to me, had on our uniform. "Oh" said the guard, "He is from the other side"—the innate politeness of the man not permitting him, under the circumstances, to call the deserter a "Reb". Upon inquiry I found that he belonged in Finnegan's Florida Brigade, then opposite our front; that his home, in Florida, by reason of advance, was now in the Federal lines; & that under pretence of getting water from the spring he had crawled in a bushy ravine, from the spring into one of my vidette posts. As it would have been dangerous to walk thence, in the open, back to our main lines, my men had disguised him, in borrowed uniform, & then he came safely in unrecognized & safe from his own picket line, under the general but informal truce of which I have before made mention. I directed that he be treated well, and sent to the Provost Guard. The fellow wanted to be sent to his home in Florida, & the safety of the Federal flag. Many men came straggling in afterwards.[170]

About this time occurred an incident which illustrates the more humane side of war, and the not bitter feelings between lines. One morning a Confederate came out in plain view, between the lines, with some white object in his hand, waved the branch of a tree, and stuck it in the earth, and placing the white object beside it, [he] left. I sent a man out, who found a letter in an unsealed envelope, directed to some person in Pennsylvania. I found that the letter within had been written by a Union Soldier, wounded & in a Confederate hospital near Petersburg.

In expectation of death he had written this to his friends. A note on the bottom, written by a nurse, stated that the poor fellow died the next day after writing the letter. As there was no firing on my line, the letter was sent to me. It was out of pure kindness that the Confederates had taken all this trouble. I sealed the letter, put on a stamp and placed it in the mail, regretting afterwards that I had not kept the address of the parties to whom it was directed.

On the 14th of August we received orders to move to the rear when relieved, and rumor added to this that we should be relieved by troops of the Ninth Corps during the night. It proved true in the main part. We were relieved, & by the Ninth Corps troops, but in broad day light, the next morning, for the edification of the enemy, I suppose, more probably by reason of delay on the part of that corps.

We had been butting against Petersburg, nearly two months, and so far as direct advance was concerned we had not gained an inch. But we had fortified formidably, and securely. Our works could be held firmly by a thin line, and [a] covered way, for safe approach of supplies, had been built with great labor.

Indications of movement had not been wanting, since the reported detachment of Early's corps, and his advance into Maryland. The Sixth Corps had gone, and part of the cavalry, and we had exercised constant vigilance, and had extended our lines to the left, and, on the left, had fortified against flank & rear attacks. Before our relief from the works it was reported that the Second Corps had gone to the right.

Evidently, for us, the dull monotony of the siege was broken—two months of comparative inaction and positive and continued discomfort in the hot trenches. The battery men could practice, but infantry could not, nor even drill or hold dress parade.

After being relieved our brigade moved into the woods in the rear. The weather was excessively hot, the region was malarial, and no breeze caught even the tree tops.

Vigilance and readiness were enjoined as it was reported that the enemy were moving heavy masses of infantry to our left. This, I believe, was a humbug. But in the early part of the night of the 16th we were supplied with spades, and moved to the right, to the railroad, where we halted, and after some hours, during which we used neither spades nor guns, but only patience, we marched back, to the camp from which we started, and remained during the 17th, under orders to move on the morning of the 18th. Why we should have gone there and why with spades, I could never ascertain. If it were a ruse, it is not clear how the enemy should know it.

Under these orders and wearied by the marching of the previous night we slept soundly as usual, having nothing but orders on our minds.

But in the night I had a vision of the same class, I fancy, as the chariots of fire and horses of fire, seen by the prophet [Elijah, II Kings, 2:11]. A huge ball began to roll from the higher ground of the works we had left, moving a little way it burst, and a smaller emerging, went on in the same line, towards us. That burst, and a smaller appeared, and so on. I was conscious of hearing no sound but awakened in an uproar of cannonading. Instantly I shouted to the Adjutant to "fall in the regiment" and we stood under arms. Soon an order came from Division Headquarters to the effect that the firing was wholly from the enemy, and that we were to hold our men in readiness to move. Such orders were not countermanded, but generally lapsed by lapse of time. After an hour or so, I think, every man was stretched on the ground and asleep, with his musket by his side. What all this uproar and waste of ammunition meant, none of us could guess, unless the enemy apprehended some movement or attack, on our part, an apprehension caused by the movements of Grant's army on the right, where there had been some firing. I have never seen any explanation of this midnight cannonade.

[THE WELDON RAILROAD
AUGUST — SEPTEMBER, 1864]

We moved at 5 A.M. on the 18th of August. The orders which a regimental commander receives, usually indicate what he is to do next, and on this occasion it was to move at 5 A.M. I knew my place, that is to say, what regiment I was to follow, and the time. Under the circumstances we had a lively curiosity. Was it to the right or left? The Second Corps were undoubtedly on the right, and had been for two or more days. Were we to turn the left of the enemy and strike in between Petersburg and Richmond, & thus cut the Rebel army in two? Or were we to use the now extended and well fortified left, which was across the Jerusalem Plank Road, but did not extend to the Weldon Railroad. This was one of the two lines connecting Petersburg and Richmond with the south and southwest. The Weldon ran directly to the seacoast and Wilmington, the main point of supplies from Southern Virginia and the Carolinas, and for supplies brought in from abroad by blockade runners.[171]

The movements and demonstrations made by Grant on the [Federal] right should have tended to draw the Confederate troops to that point, and thus leave their [own] right inadequately defended. We were soon to know. As I drew upon the head of my regiment I saw the Division staff & orderlies mounted, at a distance to the left, and soon saw the Division flag moved off, in that direction. We followed with our Division leading the Corps.

Towards noon, we came upon a mounted outpost, which after a

few shots, fled. Our Division moved down to the [Weldon] railroad, keeping to the left, and the other Divisions to the right. In the afternoon there was sharp fighting mostly on our right, and it was reported that the Maryland brigade broke & lost prisoners.[172]

We held our ground, tore up the track, and began a line of earthworks on the west side of the road, under no fire, excepting that of artillery.

I was obliged to send back Captains Morrill and Fitch. Morrill had not fully recovered from the wound received on the first day in the Wilderness, and both, exhausted by the long siege, broke down on the first day's march. I could not well spare them, as they were experienced officers, and such officers were not numerous at that time.

Fighting grew heavier on the right (which was nearest Petersburg) in the afternoon of the 19th, and part of our Corps, which was across the railroad[,] was broken and lost prisoners; and we of the first Division reinforced them, and drove the enemy back. It had been raining & there was difficulty in moving the batteries.

It was evident that Lee had rushed troops from his left, but too late to regain the railroad, which he had left unguarded to meet the supposed attack on his left. Here I saw two men, the front & rear rank men, killed by the same cannon ball, which went directly through the bodies of both.

Next day, the 20th of August, we were undisturbed, and we made the best possible use of the time in building a line of intrenchments along and on the west of the railroad.

Our line was divided by a diagonal ravine, on the left of which was my regiment, with the 118th Pa. on my left.

Our other divisions were intrenched across the road, and had made connections on their right.

Some artillery shots were coming over, but doing little damage, when suddenly the enemy appeared in a cornfield on the north side of the ravine, drove in our pickets, and charged the brigade on the north side of the ravine. This gave them an effective fire, while I fired into them diagonally. They soon broke, and our men, unmindful of orders, ran after them. We obtained some prisoners, about 300. The heaviest part of the attack fell upon the 4th Div. next to ours on the right. Our assailants were North Carolina troops, and their belts and cartridge boxes evidently of foreign make. The paper of their cartridges was white and fine, and such as was not at that time procured in the South. This was the first time my regiment had ever fought behind breastworks, and the men became unusually excited. It was with difficulty that I could keep them in line, and when the enemy broke they lost all control of themselves, and with wild yells, rushed after them.[173]

This day's fight settled the question of the Weldon railroad, and no trains passed on that road after the 18th. All schedules were abolished on that part of the line at least, though our work on the road was not then completed.

Our division thereafter went into camp along the road, in low level ground, and in unwholesome regions.

Anywhere we could get water by digging three or four feet, and, although this water seemed clear, it could not be wholesome, or at least could not long remain so, in the vicinity of a camp. In these days we paid little attention to such matters, and, in the matter of selecting camp grounds, could not. The line of battle, and military, not sanitary, considerations, determined the position of the camp.

However, some precautions were used, and our unfailing resources, quinine and whiskey, were at hand. A military drill, unknown to Casey's tactics, was resumed. At proper intervals the companies were formed and the sergeant went down the line, with canteen and a big iron spoon, and delivered to the open mouth of each man the regulation dose of commissary whiskey, with as much quinine as it could be made to soak up. We did not trust the men to take their dose, and there is a certain advantage in military discipline, even in the administering of medicine. Left to themselves men might take none, or too much. In fact, one morning a detachment of one company was on detail duty and the sergeant of that company reserved, in their canteen, the doses assigned to those men.

This[,] consisting of a dozen doses, both of whiskey & quinine, was stolen by one of the men not on detail, and possessed of an original thirst for whiskey, which did not balk at the quinine mixed therewith. The trouble with stolen whiskey is the difficulty of concealment. The whiskey was missing and the man furnished evidence that he was the thief. The goods were found in hiding, audibly and visibly as well as usually manifest[,] and he was exceeding the bounds of good order and military discipline. He was immune doubtless to malaria, but not to the discipline[,] and I subdued his excitement by compelling him to cut up the pine stumps which abounded in the camp ground. He and the remedy worked well and he recovered from both overdoses.

We were in this camp during the remainder of August and the whole of September. It was a new experience not to be under fire. Not once for five or six weeks did a shot of any kind or caliber whizz over our heads.

We were in the rear, so to speak, or rather we were making a new front from which the enemy had disappeared.

We built a heavy line of intrenchments on the western side of the railroad and slashed the trees in front. These trees formed a thick forest of second growth pines, five or six inches in diameter, the overgrowth of an abandoned field. Men from each regiment were detailed without regard to skill as axemen and each regiment slashed its own front. On most regimental fronts there were unskilled men in confusion and at cross purposes.

Trees were falling in all directions, at haphazard, and as it was absolutely uncertain where any particular tree would fall, no man was safe; nor could he pursue his occupation of cutting with undivided attention. One eye at least, must be on the tree of his neighbor, and there was a perpetual yelling of "look out", and more "looking out" than cutting. Then, as trees fell without intelligent direction, and by gravitation only, one fell against others still standing, and there was tangle and confusion and the work was impeded by its own doing.

Meantime, while such disorder reigned on the other fronts, a wonder of skill was on mine. It happened that I had just received a hundred recruits from the Eastern or lumber region of Maine. I had not received arms for them and so directed that they be detailed for the work. With the air of experts they examined the axes furnished by the Quartermaster. They were not of the best but they would do for sapling pines; besides the men [were] working by the month, and it did not matter to them whether they cut much or little. So these men marched out to perform their first military service, with axes on shoulder, instead of guns, and in the familiar work of cutting down trees. An expert foreman selected himself. They deployed themselves along the regimental front, and the sound of blows began all along the line; and soon disappeared, still cutting, in the forest. But not a tree fell. After an hour or two, or perhaps more, during which the confused cutting and falling, and yelling went on on either side, the sound of their axes ceased, and soon thereafter there was a dull roar, and the whole section of the forest assigned to them, & covering my front, came down like a wave, beginning at the front where they last cut, & curving to the rear. Every tree lay flat, and all fell in the same direction.

The trick was in the cutting. These men cut one kerf in each tree and that facing to the rear. But they left uncut wood enough to hold the tree upright, if not pressed. When they had cut the last row[,] they arranged themselves in line against their trees on the sides opposite kerfs, and gave simultaneous pressure, throwing down towards the rear, the first row of trees. These, falling against the next, with momentum, overthrew them, and so on with ever increasing force, as children tumble down a row of bricks.

The slashing left the front clear for range of artillery and musketry & also made approach of troops well nigh impossible by reason of the tangle of fallen trees.

Thus, the works might be held by a very thin line, while the main body of the troops operated further to the left. The difficulty and cost of direct assault on these strongly fortified lines, had reduced the game to a matter of stretching. Around the original Petersburg front the lines were curved, & we had the outside & therefore longer curve, requiring for the holding of it more troops, but we had now reached that point on the flank where the task of the enemy was to protect a straight line of railroad, the "South Side"—and here the lines were parallel, excepting where we made flank guarding works, which could be abandoned in case of further advance.

Our lines were extended in the latter part of August, along the railroad, and redoubts built. I moved further to the left. Grant, Meade and Warren rode along the line on the 27th day of August, and, on the 28th we were ordered to be ready to move at a moment's notice. We did not move, and, of course, no explanation was vouchsafed for this disturbance of our peace of mind. In fact it was not a great disturbance, for about any change would have been better than to stagnate in that marsh. Many were sick. Several of my officers had gone to the hospital, and Herring also of the 118th Pa.

As for myself, I was worn and with low fever, down to such a degree that the resistance was equal to the pressure, and kept me in low equilibrium. I made very little entry in my diary, in the six weeks residence on the Weldon Railroad

The enemy occasionally made vain disturbance on our front. On the 15th of September we were under arms until dark, the enemy being reported as moving in our front. What they wanted on our front was difficult to conceive, since we were in such position that we would cheerfully have entertained them, and paid old scores begun in the Wilderness. But their movements on our front were all a farce masking another movement by which they raided the Army cattle in the rear of the army. It was reported that forty-seven hundred beef cattle with a part of the First District

Cavalry guarding the cattle had been driven off, but rumor may have exaggerated the number of the cattle. So large a part of our best cavalry were with Sheridan in the Valley, that this arm with us was greatly weakened doubtless. The report troubled us little. We got not much fresh beef any way, & had small appetites in this malarial swamp.[174]

One day Gen. Bartlett sent for me. He had a new musket, which somebody wished to get into use in the Army. Samples of it were in Bartlett's tent. It was an ordinary Springfield rifled musket, but with two nipples and hammers. On one side the ordinary nipple and hammer, and on the other a nipple (for the cap) with its hammer, the nipple having a passage leading to a second firing chamber above the first; so that one cartridge could be loaded upon the other. The soldier was expected to fire the top cartridge first. I had had experience enough to know that such nice calculations could not be depended on in the heat of battle, and that it sometimes happened that the first and only cartridge did not explode, and the man continued to load utterly unaware that he had not fired. I had seen muskets after a battle, half full of cartridges. I inquired if the request was an order, and as it was not I declined. [Colonel Norval] Welch (of the 16th [Michigan]) took them; and, in the next battle, (in which he was killed) his men threw them all away & replaced them from arms left by the killed and wounded. The puzzle was that such worthless inventions should have been permitted to come to us, when the repeating arms, such as the Spencer and Henry's Winchester, doing good service in the hands of the cavalry, were withheld from us.[175]

For the latter part of the month I was in charge of the pickets, and unusual vigilance was enjoined. Indeed we were constantly on vigilant picket. I do not think there was ever any considerable body of the enemy on our front, since we faced to the flank, that is to say, to the West, and not towards Petersburg. The country in front, beyond our slashing was wooded, and we could see nothing, further than the edge of the slashings. On one occasion, on this front, there had been some indication, or report, of a scouting party of the enemy, & we were on the alert.

It was a drizzly day. There were some thin bushes on my left, and through them I saw the commanding officer of the regiment next on my left (of another brigade) riding slowly towards me with a bunch of buttons on his coat. He was much given to grumbling, and broke out in complaints.

"That d—d old fool" (referring to his superior officer of the brigade) "has stretched me out in the woods until I cannot see three men at one time, and I have come to give you notice [that] if the enemy attack me I shall fight like hell for about five minutes and then run; so look out for your own flank". This was not the usual way of speaking of a superior officer, but it was not unknown, and indeed bickering between officers of high rank was not unheard of.

I had no apprehension that his regiment would run, however, and if it did mine was well in hand.

It was not an original discovery in the Army, that scolding was a relief to the feelings of a man in distress, but it seemed never an indication of strength. Nobody ever heard Grant swear or even raise his voice above the ordinary conversational pitch. Nor did this seem to be studied, or from training, but consisted in the massiveness of the man, and the momentum with which he moved.

Although we were in comparative quiet on our front, and only impatient in the idle detention, in unwholesome and disagreeable surroundings, with many officers and men sick, we were encouraged by the activity reported on the right. These reports were in the form of camp rumors only, both as to the right of our line, and as to the operations of Sheridan in the valley, and we were in anticipation of another advance for the extension of our lines, similar to that of August which had brought us across, and effected the destruction of the Weldon railroad, so far as we could reach. It was understood that the enemy were still using that road and were wagoning from the vicinity of Reams['] Station below us, around our lines, into connection with the South Side road. Our ultimate aim must be some point on the road last named.

We were awakened one night in September by the sudden roar of artillery which seemed to be coming from our side. It broke the stillness of the night & roused all the camp. We could hear more plainly the guns on our immediate right, but, as we had received no orders, we were utterly unable to explain the meaning of it. There seemed to be no reply from the enemy. While we were thus wondering[,] an orderly came, with an order from Army Hd. Qrs announcing Sheridan's victory at Winchester, and directing that a salute of shotted guns should be fired from all the artillery bearing upon the enemy.[176]

It was something of the nature of a grim joke, but not without moral effect on us, and probably not without effect on the enemy. We were greatly encouraged. Disaster had fallen upon the effort to create a diversion in Maryland and the valley, and we had not relaxed an inch of our grip upon Petersburg, but had rather increased and extended it. The control of the game was in our hands, and we imagined the enemy cowering in the shelter of their work, fully in as much wonder, and more apprehension.

[PEEBLES FARM AND PEGRAM'S FARM SEPTEMBER — DECEMBER, 1864]

Orders of the 29th of September stirred the sluggishness of our malarial blood. These came in the night, and were to the effect that we should be ready to move at 4 o'clock on the morning of the 30th. We were easily ready. There was not much to pack. My tent could be pulled down, packed and put into the wagon in ten minutes, and the throwing in of the little regimental desk, of eighteen inches in its greatest dimension, and one small valise was the work of a moment. Each soldier always had his rations, and canteen of water, his musket, equipment, & ammunition. We could always be ready to move in ten minutes

The storm seem[ed] to be brewing. There was unusual musketry and artillery firing on our right and a brigade of cavalry, (I believe it was [Samuel Perkins] Spear's Pennsylvania), moved to the left. Further to the right some infantry pickets were advanced. But we remained on our ground till morning. I believe it was about 9 A.M. when the head of our column started. The First Division, with our brigade (the 3[r]d) leading, moved through the slashing directly westward. Every body knew that the enemy must be in that direction, but in what force, or exactly where, we had no information. We anticipated no long march that day. But, by whose orders, or for what purpose, I can't tell, we marched with the Division brass band, in full blast, at the head of the Division. I was at or near the head of the column, and watched these fellows, with some interest. No doubt this was more than a mere military parade. The game had been going on upon the right, and no demonstration had been made on the left since we siezed the Weldon Railroad in August.[177]

Suddenly the game began. There was outbreak of musketry from the bushes, and as sudden scurrying to rear of the brass band. Drums, which had rolled all the way out, now ran, and trusted to the legs of the drummers rather than to the plea of noncombatance.

Fifes ceased to squeak, and horns to blow, and all kept accurate time, for once, in ceasing, and the musketry had the field. Not long, however, for as soon as we opened [fire], the enemy, not there in force, retired as rapidly as our band.

In the distance, beyond the trees, a battery of the enemy began prematurely to let us know where it was. We moved on past the Shady Grove Church, and the Squirrel Level Road, keeping to the west, in the edge of the woods, with fields occasionally visible on our right, and finally formed under a slight rise of ground at the edge of the field. I think we went into position on the right by file into line. At any rate I was on the right of the line, with the 16th Michigan (Col. Welch) on my left. The artillery of the enemy continued to pay warm regards to us but without great effect. While we were waiting the expected order to advance, a staff officer came from the left, with orders from Gen. [Simon G.] Griffin, that the 20th Maine should be put on the skirmish line, which was to lead the charge, and had not shown promptness in starting, probably by reason of the difficulty in making the order heard & the necessity that all should start at once. The officer, as an encouragement, I suppose, reported Gen[.] Griffin as saying that the "Twentieth Maine would wake them up".

Notwithstanding all that was said during the Spanish War and afterwards, by distinguished soldiers, about "men anxious to fight", as the kind the U. S. wanted, I believe I am safe in saying that the Twentieth Maine was not clamoring for that job. As I moved to the left I passed Welch, and he said "Goodbye, I will meet you on the other side of the water." I never saw him again. Of course, we obeyed orders and I formed my men on the skirmish line putting them in one line so as to suffer less from casualties. But as I looked over the clear sweep of six or seven hundred yards, I thought, as Col. [Hiram] Burnham said to the Sixth Maine at the Marye Heights [in the Battle of Fredericksburg] "It[']s not much like matrimony, but it[']s got to be done". As I could not make myself heard all along the line, I dismounted and went upon the highest ground in front of the men, took off my hat and waved it, as a signal to start. The sight of that line, rising as one man and coming on was enough, and I knew that if I got to the works of the enemy they would be there too. We rushed to and past an intervening [Peeble's] house and grounds, under a shower of canister, which rattled on the ground, being fired at too great a distance to be of much effect. One struck me on the leg above the knee and knocked me down, but did no great harm. It was as if a stone had been thrown by hand. There was a slight hollow between this point and the works of the enemy and I think much of their next fire went over our heads. I remember only the white puffs of the musketry over their breastworks, as we rushed up. In a moment we were over. There was a rush to the rear of Confederate infantry and artillery. The rear gun was a minute too late. One of the horses [pulling the gun] fell, and it was anchored there. Their guns had the start, and one halted further back at a gap in the woods, and intimated as if to renew the fight; but the men, without formation or orders, rushed pell mell towards it. The gunners did not wait for them, or to reload, but fled following the others.

We gathered up our prisoners and reformed our lines. Soon it was ascertained that I was the only field officer remaining in the brigade, which then consisted of five completely organized (though small) regiments and two battalions of four or five companies. Poor Welch, my senior, was killed while mounting the works. Gen. Bartlett was absent sick and the Col. commanding the brigade [James A. Gwyn], disabled in the charge.

Quite unexpectedly to myself, I was put in command of the brigade; unexpectedly because I had then only the mustered rank of Major, the commission of Lt[.] Colonel not being counted since I had not been able to muster upon it as the regiment had fallen, by reason of its severe losses, below the minimum. Gilmore had the commission of Col. & I of Lt. Col. However I had the unique honor of being a major commanding a brigade. My horse came up quickly.

Meantime, while we were reforming and getting our regiments into line, a Division of the Ninth Corps was moving past our left, to push the enemy further and I was directed to move out and protect their right flank. It required a few moments to get up the Eighty-third [Pennsylvania] (separated from us on the right) but I moved out promptly, and, half way, heard in front & on the left, the sound of musketry and soon artillery, began. I "double-quicked", and soon came out into a field open to the left but with woods in front. To the left, as I came on the field at the head of the brigade I saw the Ninth Corps troops breaking and beginning to run, infantry and batteries. I sent a staff officer at once to the Division Commander, with this information, and went at once into line of battle. I was compelled to take position too near the edge of the wood on the center and right, but this was the crest of the ridge and the only available line, and the nearness of the wood could be compensated for by greater watchfulness, and the woods especially on the right, were open.

I was developing my line towards the open field on the left, where the Ninth Corps troops were falling back rapidly and in confusion, and to add to the difficulty[,] the enemy shelled the left as it was deploying. I sent [Captain] Prince, who had received his horse or had a captured one, and he most handsomely steadied the line and extended it straight and firm in near view of the fugitives.

The enemy kept up a sharp musketry fire all along the line, but it stood firm. Only one man, I suppose a recruit, attempted to run, but I swung my horse across his path, and gave him a blow with the flat of my sword and he ran back into the ranks. On the right the enemy advanced in an attempt to turn it, but were driven back by a well directed fire of Capt. Brent's Companies of the 18th Mass.

Meantime the other two brigades of the Division came up and went into position, one in rear of my right & one in rear of my left, and a New York battery went into position in my rear, and were throwing shells over our heads.

I persuaded [Captain Charles E. Mink] the Lieutenant commanding to bring up his guns, and put them on the line, and took out the 118th Pa. next to the Twentieth Maine, to give him room.

These guns soon cleared our front. One curious incident occurred on the left. Looking to the left, I saw Major [I. Harris] Hopper [of the 15th Massachusetts] sitting on his horse in front of his regiment. Shells of the enemy were coming over, and generally bursting in the air. Suddenly, and while I was looking at Hopper, one broke directly over his head, and he instantly disappeared in a cloud of white smoke. In a moment this drifted away, and he and his horse reappeared, in quite another attitude, the horse rearing and Hopper standing on the ground in front of him, and pulling on the reins. It was a[s] wonderful piece of kaleidoscopic or shifting picture [as] I ever saw. Fortunately for Hopper[,] the fragments of the shell, as is usual in such cases, went forward, & not laterally or downward and neither he nor the horse was hurt.

It was dark before the enemy left our front. We had fired sixty rounds of ammunition. Our losses had not been very heavy, and of the few officers only one was killed, West Keene, whom I had promoted to the vacancy left by his Cousin Sam, killed on June 22. Poor fellow[,] he was killed in the same way, a bullet through the heart.

I was sorry also to lose there a man from my own town, Joe Libby, a good soldier.[178]

The men had borne the heat and burden of a hard day, and had charged well and resisted well, and we had gained and held the most of the line and the most advanced ground. But after dark I was directed to withdraw the brigade and to put it in behind the works of the enemy, which we had captured.

I slept with the brigade staff, in an old tobacco drying house, on the field, a queer old building, with a dirt floor, and poles at different stages, extending across from side to side, on which were suspended the sticks on which the tobacco was strung for drying.

In the morning, Gen[.] Bartlett came up, and, being thus relieved of the command of the brigade, I went to my regiment. In these days there were no compliments, but later, I received, on the recommendation of Gen. Griffin, the brevet Commission of Lt. Col. for gallant and distinguished services at the battle of the Peebles Farm. Unfortunately for me, it carried no additional pay, and was mere paper honor, though the highest compliment a brevet commission could give.

Next morning, (Oct. 1st) we moved forward and reoccupied the ground which we had held on the 30th. We pushed back the enemy's skirmish line, and occupied a peanut field, where, after dark, when the occupation was safe, the men gathered a crop where they had not planted. I ate that night for the first time, fresh roasted peanuts, and can recommend them, especially as a variation of the dish of rusty salt pork, and ancient hard bread. We lay on the ground, between the rows, that night, and slept soundly, lacking nothing in the matter of fresh air and exercise.

On the 2nd I walked over the ground with Generals Griffin and Bartlett, and in a narrow wood road, we met Gen. Meade with [Andrew A.] Humphreys, then his Chief of Staff, and a mounted orderly. We all halted. Griffin & Bartlett, (on foot), standing on the east side of the narrow wood road, Meade, on his horse, across the road and facing them, and Humphreys on the left of Meade his horse partly turned to the left, & not directly across the road. I was standing just behind the horses, when there came the whirr and crash of a cannon shot across the road. The horses sprang aside. I saw Griffin & Bartlett leap back, the shot struck between them. Meade exclaimed "That hit my leg". In a moment the excitement and the horses subsided. The shot had come from the left, (west) and grazed the rump of Humphrey's horse close enough to draw blood, had raised a groove across Meade's left bootleg, and gone into the ground between Griffin and Bartlett, fortunately without exploding. How near it had come to my head, I could not tell, but near enough. It broke up the party, and a little later I went back, on the same road, to the front. The enemy were throwing occasional shots from their artillery on the left, much at random apparently, and in a way that seemed to indicate plenty of ammunition. On the way back I passed one of our brigade staff, familiarly known as "Chet", a humorous fellow.[179] He was sitting there alone, in the woods, calmly smoking his pipe. "What are you doing here Chet"? I asked. He suspended the smoking long enough to explain, that he had been now three years or more in this business, and in all this time had never seen a cannon shot strike twice in the same place. One had just struck there, as he was walking along, and he thought it a good place to sit, rest and take a smoke. He assured me that he regarded the place as absolutely safe.

We had some skirmishing on the 2nd in the process of readjusting our lines, as far as practicable to the front, and in making connections with the other corps, the Ninth, and, I think, with part of the Second. While they did not give us the South Side railroad, it made a long stride towards possession of that coveted object, and the matter of its possession only a question of time.

By order of Gen. Bartlett I moved the brigade into proper position and [made] connections with the other parts of the line, and it was well understood that this line, now extending back to the left of our old works made before the movement of Sept. 30, would be [a] strong threat and when completed, hem the enemy still more closely in. Preliminary to building works we formed the lines, and permitted the regiments, not at the front, to stack arms. It happened that in front of the Third Brigade was a fine farm house, spacious and surrounded by trees, in ample grounds.

The house was of wood, but neat, and with green blinds, like a New England house, and was just in front of the line of stacks. This was in the early part of October, when the nights were beginning to be cool, and when rainy nights might be expected, and the men had thoroughly learned the value of board in the pitching of their shelters. A door to cover the ground & form a floor, meant much on a rainy night.

So the order to "break ranks" was the signal for a wild rush to the house, doubtless deserted during the fighting on the previous days. What I saw could happen only in time of war. The removal of the house was necessary, since it would obstruct the range of the guns, when the works were completed, and no effort was made to restrain the men. With yells and racing they ran by hundreds for the doomed house. As I looked doors and windows disappeared, then boards and covering of every sort, and in half an hour the house was reduced to a bare frame. Subsequently the trees were cut down, and every land mark obliterated by the building of the defence, and when I rode over there on our return from Appomatox, I could distinguish nothing of the original features of the place.

Thereafter we were quiet, and, undisturbed by the enemy, we

had nothing to do but to build earthworks. We had been so engaged on the Weldon Railroad for six weeks in August and September, and seemed likely to be as busy employed here. The region seemed much more favorable for troops than out along the Weldon road. It was higher, rolling country, with streams of clear water, and there was a fair prospect of rest and recuperation. I had been for five months under steady strain. I do not believe that there is a more laborious place in the whole army than the command of a regiment, and I had been under that burden there five months. I weighed less than 120 lbs. and was rarely free from low malarial fever. The Division Surgeon condemned me to the sick list, and my superior officers were kind enough to recommend me for leave of absence.

I was on some accounts reluctant to leave. One gets into an unreasoning habit of sticking to a thing, and this habit carries one a long and even painful way. Though I was never apprehensive about my health, it was not to be wholly left out of consideration. There were domestic reasons, and further I was anxious to go to Augusta, to see if something could not be done towards recruiting my regiment, so as to entitle us to all the field officers. It was agreed on all hands that new recruits were of vastly more value if put into an old regiment than if formed into new. In this I had a deep personal interest also. Gilmore had been promoted by the Governor to be Colonel, but, as he preferred to remain in Washington, and in some way, seemed able to do so, he had not so much interest in mustering as Colonel. It might make his retreat more difficult or uncertain. He was on the muster roll as Lt. Col. and blocked my way, though I had now served nearly a year as Major commanding a regiment, for Chamberlain's ability and standing kept him generally in command of a brigade, when he was in the field, even before his promotion to the grade of Brigadier General. This was also a pecuniary hardship, since I was obliged to bear all the expenses of Headquarters, on the small pay of Major, aggregating less than $150 per month.

Th[ough] drawn strongly to the home of my wife, at that time Stamford, N.Y., I determined to go directly to Maine. On my leave of absence I drew two months['] pay. The officials at Washington seemed to appreciate our long service at the front, and were very kind.

I reached Augusta on the 15th of Oct., my birthday anniversary.[180] But I find no mention of it in my notebook. I was too busy and anxious to think of birthdays and went at once to look after recruits. I had heard of a company called the Lewis Company, which had been recruited, and unassigned, but the Governor told me that it had first been assigned to the 19th Maine. This was a bitter disappointment, but he promised to approve my application for another. This company I never saw, but on paper it was assigned much later, to my regiment & so raised our members above the minimum. But this was much later indeed.

I reached home on the eve of the 22nd of Oct., and had there five weeks of rest, and recuperation. I found that a dear younger sister of my wife, had died while I was on the way, and the household was a sad one. But a great blessing came in the safe delivery, on the 9th of November, of our first born, Julia, a sweet babe, who grew to be a sweeter woman, so like her sainted mother, but now with her mother and among those loved long since and lost erstwhile.

The five (5) weeks I spent at Stamford seemed like a dream, from which the awakening was rude. I left on the 1st day of Dec. 1864, and reached the front on the 4th. It was a cold and cheerless evening, and the transition to the cold and dust and discomfort of a tent in winter would have been disagreeable, had there been time to think of it. But I had arrived just in the nick of time.

The Fifth Corps, and a division of Cavalry, had been ordered to move down and destroy the Weldon railroad, to such an extent that it could not be used at all, for bringing supplies to Petersburg.

[DESTRUCTION OF THE WELDON RAILROAD
DECEMBER, 1864—MARCH, 1865]

We moved down the Jerusalem Plank Road, and on the night of Dec. 7 bivouaced in a cornfield, in a gentle but not cheerful rain. The cornfield was of advantage, chiefly to our horses. We assisted in the gathering of the crop, to the extent of their needs, and were not niggardly in feeding. The owner has not to my knowledge, ever put in a claim for damages, and indeed, I do not think he was there.

I slept between two corn rows & the bed was more than usually soft, by reason of the rain, and there was no danger of falling out.

Orders to march came at two o'clock in the morning, and, as we turned out[,] down came a sudden and heavy downpour of rain, whereby our two o'clock in the morning courage was not a little quickened. The darkness was absolute, and we gathered up our blankets, each man for himself, in a hurry. How we found our men, or the men their places I can now hardly imagine. My orderly found my horse and me, and, in some way we got out upon the road.

That sudden shower was a signal for change of weather quite as sudden and pronounced. As we felt our way along the road, the wind shifted to the northwest, and blew as if we were seeking the Poles. Before daylight came, the ground began to freeze, and our damp clothing aided the cold by rapid evaporation. The process of drying was also of cooling. Towards evening we struck the railroad. This was on the 8th of Dec., an unprofitable day for the stockholders of that road. Indeed it could not have been on a paying basis for some time, since the Confederate Government probably did not pay freight, therein differing from ours, and passengers must have been few.

We were soon working for a further reduction of dividends. The track was of unusual construction, composed of rails, I judge, of English make, approximately of the shape of an inverted U in cross section, having flanges resting on the ties. The rails were connected by tongues of tough wrought iron inserted in the hollow ends and riveted therein. They were spiked to ties of oak or chestnut in the usual manner.

It was comparatively easy to separate rails from ties, but the tough splices gave trouble.

The method of operation was simple. We moved our line, with fixed bayonets, up to the roadside, sent forward skirmishes as pickets, a little beyond stacked arms, and the men grappling the structure by rail or tie ends turned the whole over. Then, with rails or whatever of levers the county supplied, pried the rails from the ties; then by swaying back & forth broke the splices, and so separated the rails. Meantime, others collected the ties and piled them loosely, but regularly, a layer on the ground, in one direction, & another layer across these, and so on, with ample spaces between. These piles were about five feet high. Combustible stuff, dry rails borrowed from fences, dry wood wherever found, was piled on the windward side of these piles, and the rails balanced on top, extending laterally to the wind, which blew keen and strong from the Northwest. When all was ready, fire was touched to the windward kindling, and soon each pile roared and glowed like a furnace, the wind drawing the flames through the interstices.

It was not long before the middle part of the rails resting on the fuel were at red heat, and sometimes the ends bent down automatically of their own weight. These ends were kept cool by the wind, and the men siezed them, took them to neighboring trees, and wrapped them thereon, one upon another.[181]

So we went on mile after mile. It was worthy of noting with what zeal the men worked.

There seemed to be a natural spirit of destruction. No man shirked, as he doubtless would have done had he been in the dull business of building a road.

Of course, there was the feeling present that we were damaging the enemy, and this was a material part in the scheme of hemming them in.

We worked and guarded alternately, and when darkness came we were at work in a cut. There was not time to tear up the track, and we piled therein all available fuel, whatever of wood could be found in the neighborhood and set it on fire to the windward end of the cut. The northwest wind, cold & strong, drove through the combustible mass, and made fierce heat.

It happened that there was a hedge of cedars on the east bank of the cut, & behind this I put the regiment in line, as behind a shelter which broke somewhat the force of the wind. The ground was frozen, and we lay down wrapped in our blankets, with some fires burning along the line. Sometime in the night I woke, thoroughly chilled. The men were up standing in groups around these fires. The wind had shifted and was taking us in flank. The hedge was no longer available as a windbreak, and we stood about, and stamped our feet, and so wore out the long December night.

Next day (the 9th) the business of destruction was resumed, we acting as guard and other troops of the corps doing the work.

That night we bivouaced in a thick wood of second growth pine.

A drizzle of rain, mixed with snow, fell during the night, but the temperature was milder. We were near the Hicksford and the North Carolina line. It was understood that the enemy, in some force, was in our front, but our cavalry was interposed between them and us, and we had no pickets out.

The morning of the 10th was sufficiently gloomy and brought also orders to move. We marched at 7 A.M., the weather becoming colder, and the trees frosted. Our brigade formed the rear guard, & I was in the rear of the brigade, for that day's march.

There was unusual difficulty in forming the regiment. Some of the men were scattered, and not in line. Riding about I discovered that many of them were half drunk, and some, perhaps a half dozen, were too drunk to march. This was a most astonishing condition. We carried no whiskey, and the country seemed nearly a

DESTRUCTION OF THE WELDON RAILROAD

wilderness. The necessities of life seemed scarce, and there had been before no suspicion of such luxuries as whiskey.

The column had moved off, and the incapacitated half dozen remained. Amongst them was an Irishman, a Corporal, promoted to that rank during the campaign. He was one of the two survivors of a squad of six, received as recruits, the winter before. He was on his feet, but had not the full use of them. It was effort wasted to scold a fellow more than half drunk, so I informed him that some of these men were drunk, and ordered him to see that they moved on to overtake the regiment. He cheerfully responded, and with a "Be Jabbers" he pledged his word of honor that he would do it. His zeal was better than his legs, and as we were falling back with the enemy in our rear, legs were the only resource. The wagons had gone ahead early, and not even an ambulance remained. I did all I could to urge on the disabled squad, and reluctantly left them, hoping that they would cool off and come up before the cavalry fell back. When I overtook the regiment it was halting for rest, and there was a tableau in the rear. The Adjutant sitting on his horse, two men of Company K, with fixed bayonets, guarding another Co. K man, whose gun was on the ground. He was one of the culprits, who had evidently shared in the mysterious drink, and, although able to keep up with the procession, was not able to constrain the joy he felt. As he would not obey orders of the Adjutant, who was leading the regiment, to keep still, that officer had put him under guard, a rather impracticable mode of punishment on a forced march and in the rear guard. The man had conceived a knowledge of the Army Regulations, and in response to my inquiry of the Adjutant as to the matter, informed me that he could not be compelled to carry his gun, when he was under arrest. I said "Bracket, pick up your gun". He saved his face by admitting that I had the authority, but insisted that the Adjutant could not make him carry his gun when under arrest. Of course, the main point was to keep the fellow in the ranks, and so long as he could march I was satisfied for the present. So I directed the guards to go to their Company and assumed responsibility for Bracket. Meantime, the column had moved off.

Bracket hung back, I noticed, and edged over to the side of my horse, pulled off his canteen, shaking it up to me, said that he had a little left. Though it was a cold day and I was wet, I assign as a reason why I took a drink, mere curiosity. It was fine old "Applejack"! Now Bracket, tell me where did you get this? "Well", he says—"But you won't give us away, will you"—and he proceeded to explain, prefacing his story with the inquiry if I knew the "Wild Irishmen." I professed acquaintance with the Division's good soldiers but, (to use a Virginia phrase), having a powerful weakness for whiskey. So he went on to tell me that these two survivors of [the squad of six] in whom one spirit rested; had gone out in the night, two miles, and found a house in the cellar of which were eight barrels of applejack. "And"—Bracket said in painful contrast—"They had only their two canteens".—But here, his voice rose—"They found a washtub". And they brought in a washtub full, and distributed it to their friends. It was fortunate that more men were not drunk in the morning.

Bracket kept up with his Company and gave no more trouble, and no further inquiry was made in the matter. Considering the conditions, a December night, and a storm, men sleeping unsheltered on the ground, and a sudden and free supply of whiskey, the incident was one of those unavoidable accidents of war. The Irish corporal and several other men were captured by the enemy. Under the regulations then existing, a prisoner of war was allowed a commutation of 30 cents per day, for rations, to be paid upon his release or exchange. The corporal was exchanged and applied for his own commutation stating that the Colonel of his regiment sent him to bring up stragglers on the Weldon railroad raid, and that he was captured in so doing. His paper came to me by regular reference, and regarding the experience of the Corporal as an unavoidable mistake, I certified that the statement was correct, and I suppose he got his ration money.

DESTRUCTION OF THE WELDON RAILROAD

The country through which we marched was sparsely settled, and wholly a farming region, where abandoned fields had grown up with pine, and the houses were distant from the road.

On the first day's march, I saw another instance of plundering, less alarming than the theft of the washtub of Applejack. A straggler of some other regiment of the corps, was in the rear, and carried, in addition to his regular burden of arms and ammunition, the large carcass of a turkey. I passed him as I was coming up to the regiment; and was certain that he would find that bird a heavy load before night, as the road was bad, and the march likely to be a hard and severe one. I therefore informed Captain Clark, who was acting as Major, and therefore was mounted, [and at the rear of the column] that if he kept that man under observation, he could probably buy the turkey later in the day. So Clark kept the man in view; saw him shift the heavy load from shoulder to shoulder and finally, on a halt, to drop it in a despairing way. This seemed to the hungry Major a critical moment, favorable to trade, and he purchased the bird for two dollars & it was transferred to our spare horse. It will be apparent that we had no available oven, nor did we halt for the night much before dark. Our culinary art on a march was limited chiefly to the use of the frying pan, and to that ignoble utensil was the noble bird consigned. Not entire & all at once, for the pan was too small; but sliced raw, and cooked with the customary slices of salt pork. But it was a revelation in turkey. We had been now more than two years in almost daily terms of intimacy with the Gentile hog, so that we had become fond of him. Any tendency of familiarity to breed contempt in his case was counteracted and entirely overcome by the necessity of nourishment, and this was furnished by the Hog. Indeed, I think it may be said with truth that salt pork had much to do with putting down the rebellion. But when to the familiar taste of salt and fatness was added the flavor of fried turkey breast, shades of Epicurus! The unfamiliar succulency of the bird blended with the familiar succulence of the beast in one delicious fry. Crispness was joined to tenderness, and fatness to juiciness. We supped that night on pork and turkey, and on pork and turkey we breakfasted, dined and supped next day, and, on the third day, his ruined carcass was broken up and stewed, with fragments of hardtack and probably bits of the inevitable pork. With the passing of the stew went all the consolation of the march.

One incident broke the monotony of the march. One day a staff officer, who had ridden too far from the flank of the column, was murdered by citizens or guerrillas lurking amongst the citizens. We had been pursuing our march peaceably and without molesting the people or their property, excepting the inevitable theft of eatables; but after the report as to the murder of this officer, the smoke of burning buildings blackened the December sky. This was of course, unauthorized, but it was impossible to restrain the men, when they were under such provocation. Unfortunately, such revenges are likely to fall upon the unoffending, and are wholly unjustifiable and I do not think that any of my men were implicated in these affairs.

We returned to cold and dismal camps. There was much grumbling[,] and this was not confined to the enlisted men. We had no shelter, excepting the ordinary tents, shelters carried on the march; fuel was scarce, and we shifted occasionally. It did not appear likely that anything of importance would be attempted before Spring.

The question of filling the regiment was still pressing. We were still below the minimum, and it concerned the service, and me personally. The law which permitted the muster of a Colonel, only when the regiment was above the minimum in number, was doubtless for the good of the service generally; yet in many cases it operated harshly, and with manifest injustice, as in this case. Chamberlain, with brief exceptions, had, when present, been in command of a brigade by assignment in the field, since August of 1863. Gilmore had been absent the greater part of the time, and in consequence, the labor, care and responsibility of command of the regiment had fallen on me, together with the expense of keeping up Headquarters, which I bore alone, on an allowance which amounted in all to less than 150 dollars per month. I was therefore personally interested in getting recruits. This was also manifestly better for the service, and the military policy altogether favored it, as against the raising of new regiments. A hundred new recruits mixed with veterans, and under veteran officers quickly learned the details of camp and march from their experienced comrades, and steadied in battle, fought like veterans. But, on the other hand, it was easier to raise new regiments and companies than to recruit the ranks of the old regiments in the field. New regiments and companies meant new officers, and aspirants for commissions would spend time and money to recruit new organizations with commissions in view, as compensation.

Every state and indeed every town from patriotic and other motives, desired to avoid the threatened draft, and all were inclined to take the easiest way to fill their quotas. Another condition adverse to recruiting for old regiments was the impression (not always correct) in the minds of men contemplating enlistment, that a new regiment was a safer place than an old. Indeed I heard, later, when endeavoring to get recruits, that enlistment in the Twentieth Maine, meant plenty of fighting and corresponding liability to be killed, while a new regiment might go into the defences of Washington, and drill for a long time, in perfect safety.

Willingness to go was all that was needed to secure an order, and on the 12th of January, (1865), I was sent with a detail of six enlisted men, including a sergeant, to Portland, on recruiting service. Fortunately this included also transportation for myself and transportation and supplies for the men.

I omit the details of my labors and cares in the disagreeable duty of getting recruits under these adverse circumstances. In these labors and cares I was cheered by the presence of Susie, who braved the difficulties of the winter journey from Stamford to Maine, and was, as always, my good angel.

Before the last of March I had secured recruits enough to fill the regiment above the minimum.

As soon as I received notice from the Governor of my commission, while in Portland, on my recommendation, Capt. Morrill was commissioned Lt. Col. To him I had written that he need not wait. The announcement that Gilmore had been mustered in as Colonel, though absent from the regiment, and resigned under charges and for alleged disability[,] left me still as Major, though having commission as Colonel. Morrill offered to resign, but I was not willing that the service should be deprived of so good an officer, in such a critical time. I was detailed to act as staff officer [on the division staff], and was thus relieved of the embarrassment of serving under one who had been my subordinate.

The winter had been a severe one. Our advances across the Hatcher[']s Run in Oct. and February had not been as successful as hoped, but had crowded the enemy on his right flank.[182] The condition of the Confederate Army was known to be weakened. His attack on Ford Stedman on the 27th day of March, was an indication of his desperate condition, and was disastrously unsuccessful, and must have dismayed the Army of Northern Virginia, at a time when they needed encouragement most. Of course we were correspondingly encouraged.[183]

[LEWIS FARM, GRAVELLY RUN & FIVE FORKS
MARCH—APRIL, 1865]

Sheridan and the Sixth Corps had returned to us, having accomplished the ruin of Early, and left his Corps but a fragment of that which left Petersburg in July of the year before.

So we moved out on the morning of the 29th of March with confidence[,] especially as it was known that Sheridan was to direct the movement against Lee's right. The Cavalry moved in advance, and our Division leading the infantry followed on the road to Dinwiddie Court House. About noon of that day we turned up the Quaker road, having crossed Hatcher[']s Run at Morrill's Neck bridge in the morning.

Chamberlain's (1st) brigade of three regiments was on the advance, and the 3[r]d, Bartlett's following. Suddenly, in the woods, Chamberlain struck what proved to be [Henry A.] Wise's brigade and had a rather sharp, though brief fight. I was then with Bartlett, and was supplying him with reinforcements for Chamberlain. His troops were in the woods, and I put the troops in there, and then rode to C. who was sitting on his horse in the open field.

He had been hit by a bullet, which, however, had done harm only to his coat.

Wise was soon driven from the field, with loss of some prisoners, among whom was one of his staff, a nephew, seriously wounded.

The next day, March 30, we moved slowly over towards Gravelly Run. The roads were bad and growing worse as it was raining, though not heavily. On the 31st we moved against the enemy intrenched beyond Gravelly Run. This "Run" was not much of a stream, but was wooded, throughout our front, and on our side. The forest was open, without much underbrush, and there were many tall trees. The other divisions were at first in the advance, and were checked. We were in line awaiting orders to advance. The artillery of the enemy kept up a desultory fire through the tree tops and there was an irregular fire of musketry. General Bartlett came along, and told me that [Benjamin F.] Partridge of the 16th Michigan was killed on the left; that he was killed just as Welch was, (the former commander of the 16th) by a bullet through the head. General Bartlett told me that he saw him laying on the ground, with the blood coming from his forehead. There was no time for lamentation on account of comrades killed. A little later Bartlett's brother "Chet", who was on his horse by my side was struck through the body by a bullet. I was near enough to catch him as he reeled in his saddle, and swing my leg over the neck of my horse, let him down, and lay him at the foot of a tree, just behind the line.

Later we advanced. The other two brigades of our Division

taking up the fight after the failure of the 3rd Division, by front & flank attack, drove the enemy from their intrenchments.[184]

Years afterwards, when I was Commissioner of Patents, General Hunton, then a member of the House of Representatives from the 7th Virginia District, was talking with me of this affair and said it was his brigade which occupied these works, and he supposed that the same division which he had driven back, reformed and drove him out. I was able to advise him that it was another division, and, as we thought, a better, which pushed him from the works.[185]

After we had advanced to the captured works, we rested. I dismounted and was lying on my back, resting my head on some prop, and looking listlessly to the rear, when I saw an officer approaching from the ravine, on what I recognized as Partridge's horse; and as he approached the man more and more resembled Partridge. Getting up, I went to meet him. It was undoubtedly Partridge, and as one rising from the dead. He had a handkerchief tied around his head, and his hat over that. He had been struck diagonally by the bullet, which had cut the flesh & stunned him. No close examination was needed and he was regarded as dead. But after a half hour had regained consciousness, and fully revived.

I will not attempt here to set down in detail all the movements of the Fifth Corps, on the 31st of March and the first of April. They are made clear (and I think accurately set forth) in "The Virginia Campaign of 64 & 65" by Gen. Humphreys.[186] I am not writing a history of the war, and those who may read this are referred to Humphrey's book for further information as to the several movements. I was then, and still am, of the opinion that General Sheridan was the main factor, of those on the ground and directing the details of the movement.

It was understood by me, after our affair of the 31st on the branch of the Gravelly Run, that the enemy had brought infantry to their right, and that this with their cavalry, had pushed back Sheridan's Cavalry from Five Forks towards Dinwiddie C[ourt] H[ouse]. Our brigade moved in that direction in the evening of the 31st and about 10 o'clock P. M. reached the house of Dr. [J.] Boisseau, a considerable plantation house, with ample fields and outbuildings. We massed in the vicinity of the house and placed our pickets.

Picket fires of the enemy could be seen in the distance but we did not come into contact with any of the outposts of the enemy.

We placed sentinels about the house and outbuildings, and introduced ourselves (the brigade officers, mainly) to the people of the house. It was occupied only by women. One lady of middle age, and three young ladies. There were, I think, no servants about, probably for the slaves, the sweep of the Yankee Cavalry, had brought a sense of freedom which their legs could not resist. The ladies all had the genuine Southern nerve, and appeared calm, though there had been some fighting about the house during the day & one of the ladies (the elder I believe) had been slightly wounded in the arm.

We were intruding visitors, callers not so much by courtesy as by force of arms; in fact enemies taking possession; yet I do not remember that there appeared to be any embarrassment, and the ladies treated us with the utmost courtesy. They sang songs to the accompaniment of the piano, old songs, of the commonplace sort, to a piano of the old sort; but after a little while the charming singers turned towards us, and said sweetly that the songs they were most accustomed to sing, were perhaps those we would not like to hear. Upon our protesting that these of all others we should like most to hear, they gave us of the rebel repertory, such as

"Here's to General Lee, drink him down
Here's to General Lee for he makes the Yankees flee"

and so on through the list. We applauded and possibly with more amusement and freedom than we should have done in 1863, or earlier.

During the evening I acted as candle bearer for one of the ladies, who wished to procure some article from one of the servant's houses, which seemed to be deserted.

I am afraid I was party to some plundering at this house, for later my cook treated me to a late supper of corn cake, and I know that corn meal formed no part of our regular rations.

Orders came recalling us, and before midnight we took leave. The ladies advised us that they did not regard the leave taking as final; that "Gen[.] Lee is up there" and they would probably see us coming back in the morning.

We took their bantering good naturedly & assured them that Gen[.] Sheridan was also "up there", and that we had not been "coming back" so much of late, as formerly.

We never saw Dr. Boisseau's house or family again. They did not have the pleasure of seeing us "coming back"; but rather instead heard anxiously the sound of battle the next day and probably saw their fugitive cavalry men and learned of the beginning of the end. In the satisfaction of triumph I fear that we gave them little thought; but I have since thought with some sadness, of their perverted enthusiasm, and of the bitterness of the defeat, which fell upon the women of the South, with probably more force than upon the men. It is a satisfaction to remember how courageously they bore themselves[;] and with what fine courtesy, on such trying circumstances they bore themselves and treated us their enemies.[187] The worst effect of war is the aftermath of sorrows and resentments and the worship of the false Gods which it creates.

Here were ladies of culture and high character, lovely doubtless to their family and friends, and worthy members of society; but fused into their souls by the white heat of war was a false patriotism, and unquenchable hate for their rightful government and the Northern people and besides this[,] admiration and devotion that amounted to worship of temporary military heroes. Lee, for conspicuous example, was undoubtedly an admirable man, in private life honorable, of dignity of character and agreeable in all the relations of life, but made a hero only by military skill, and military conditions, destructive in purpose and result of all that men prize in life.

In large measure, perhaps essentially, this worship of military heroes is of the character of the ancient worship of Moloch.

"Lonely King besmeared with blood".[188]

This worship was not all on one side, it infected both, and it must be said that military skill and force were not sometimes unaccompanied with high and noble qualities, justice and truth. But it was essentially the worship of Force and the Genius of destruction.

I do not remember the details of the earlier part of the next day. We marched during the night of the 31st and there was marching in different directions the next day, in this difficult country, with which fortunately we were becoming better acquainted. Sheridan's scouts were busy, and that tireless officer was forming his plans and gathering his forces. We were well beyond the old line of the intrenchments of Petersburg, but were well aware that the enemy would block the roads by which we must move towards the South side railroad, towards which, as the jugular vein of Petersburg & Richmond, we were striking.

Five Forks was the point where two roads, one from the Southwest and one from the Southeast, cross the White Oak road, (parallel with the South side) and at the point of the crossing unite in one leading therefrom to access that railroad. Undoubtedly the enemy would intrench along the White Oak road. All this region along the roads was wooded and neither the enemy nor their intrenchments could be seen.

As we moved up in these woods, evidences appeared of the difficulty and expense with which the infantry of the enemy had pushed back Sheridan from the Forks the day before. Their dead and wounded still lay amongst the trees.

The position of their intrenchments was understood, and our positions taken accordingly. The Cavalry under [George A.] Custer & [Thomas C.] Devin were deployed (it was said) in front of the works, and their task was to entertain the enemy on their front. The Fifth Corps was massed on the right and supposed to be in front of the left of the enemy's intrenchment.[189]

On our left was Ayers['] Division, next to him Crawford, and on the right and rear Griffin. Our orders were to swing to the left. As Bartlett's brigade comprised half or more of the Division, and consisted of nine battalions, I was sent to the right to take care of the movement.

It was near night before we were in position. Sheridan was chafing with the delay. Everything depended upon the crushing of the right of the enemy, at this point, and as we must be near the South Side road, success here would give us that essential line of communication. But the half hour before a battle is full of preparations and consultations and orders, and care of details. I do not remember any doubt as to the result. The infantry in this movement had pushed the enemy back at every point where we had struck and we expected to do the same thing here. The woods and the consequent uncertainty as to the position of the enemy and the nature of their defences, and even of their numbers, gave zest to the matter. Sheridan must have been pretty accurately advised by his scouts as to the position of the defences. I remember the conjecture talked about that Ayres, whose division was supposed to be in front of the left of the works, would "burst up".[190]

The order was given and we began to move. Our division at first went straight ahead. Soon I lost sight of the other divisions, and the noise of battle was wholly on our left at first. Indeed, it was mainly all the time on our left. As we wheeled in the woods, some cavalry of the enemy offered slight opposition firing slight volleys, and then falling back. We did not even open fire on them, but kept steadily on. I think they diverted the right regiments a little too much to the right, and interfered somewhat with the left swing, as we naturally went for the line firing on us.

The first notable thing I saw, as we emerged into an open field was Gen[.] [John A.] Rawlins['] Headquarter Wagon, plainly marked. We came suddenly upon it. But just then I saw two of our regiments detached from the line, and I rode rapidly to them, and was directing them towards the sound of battle in the woods, when

General Warren and his staff appeared, a little to the left. I rode to him and explained what I was doing. He countermanded my orders to these regiments and directed me to take these regiments and go back to the left, and drive back any flanking parties or guard I might meet, & prevent them from burning the bridge, over Hatcher's Run. The brief clash of sharp musketry seemed to be over when I left. I moved down the road from Dinwiddie towards Five Forks, a narrow road, for the greater part through thick pine forest. It was approaching dusk, and indeed the road was dimly lighted as we marched on. I had deployed a skirmish line and went on with that, the regiments following in column. Soon, on a rising ground ahead I saw a bright fire, on the road and caught a glimpse of a cavalry man, as he wheeled his horse and fled. We moved on till we came to the fire. It was a burning army wagon, stuck in the mud, with two mules, also down in the mud, and with their hinder parts roasting in the flame. They were groaning with pain. I directed the men nearest to bayonet the mules, not caring to notify the enemy of our position by shooting the animals. Then I moved on, and came, not to a bridge, but to a ford. There were troops on the other side, but dimly seen. Some shots were exchanged; I do not remember which side began the firing[,] but they called out to us to stop firing, that we were firing on our own men and in answer to our inquiry said that they were Fifth N.Y. cavalry. Captain Sawyer of the sharpshooters was acting as Adjutant, and, as it happened had a cousin who was adjutant of that regiment. So he inquired "who is your adjutant?" The fellow replied, "I am". "What is your name?" He gave the wrong name. Thereupon Sawyer expressed an opinion[,] altogether unfavorable, as to the veracity of the respondent, and in terms not quite fit to be here recorded. Thereupon came a volley, which left no doubt as to the unfriendly disposition of the people on that side of the stream. I was equally well advised however, that they would not burn the ford, and gave orders to picket the bank held by us, and to put the reserves in position, and then rode back to report.

When I reached the main body of the corps I found that Warren had been relieved, & Griffin was in command of the corps.[191] I reported what I had done, & by whose direction, and the conditions.

The enemy had surrendered, that is to say all who could not escape, I think some five or six thousand. All the batteries on their left were taken, and some thousands of small arms.[192] The confusion which follows even a successful battle, had not wholly subsided, and the new line had not been formed. Of course we must be now near the South Side Railroad, and would advance to it in the morning. Indeed that had been on Sheridan's mind during the fight. One brigade officer in the midst of the battle had ridden to him and shouted "We have carried the works". He got no answer except emphatic orders to go to his brigade and push on. He did not ["]care a d-mn about the works". He wanted the South Side railroad and he was going to have it. His exact language would require, for print, abundance of dashes and exclamation points. But he lacked nothing of the soldier. As I saw him in that campaign, I thought of the line of Milton,

"The strongest and the fiercest Spirit that fought[.]"[193]

But after the fight was over the tempest in him subsided. I was sent to bring over from the left, one of the smaller brigades and to put it in position on the new lines. It was dark, and in the woods, and the country was new. As I came along at the head of the column, I was a little uncertain of the position to be taken. Sheridan was sitting on his horse by the roadside and, in order to be certain, I asked him, rather expecting an explosive answer, but instead received assurance [that] I was going right, given in the most courteous of terms or manners and it was accompanied with explanation of the function and proposed future movement. This was the first conversation I had ever had with Sheridan, and as I had heard so much of his impatience and roughness, I rode away well satisfied.

I left him still sitting on his horse, by a little fire, near the works of the enemy just captured. I put the brigade in place, and then found the staff of the Division, now commanded by Bartlett. None of us needed opiates that night to induce sleep.

[APPOMATTOX
APRIL, 1865]

Next morning early we were astir. We were now ready to strike at the very vitals of the enemy. We thought we saw the beginning of the end, and that we were not to see our new acquaintances of Dr. Boisseau's nor to hear again their sweet voices singing "For he makes the Yankees flee". We were prepared for rough work, but were realizing the saying that he laughs best who laughs last, and our confidence in Sheridan was not at all shakened by the regrettable incident of the displacement of General Warren. That was, at the time, compensated for by the promotion of Griffin to the command of the corps. In him we had the utmost confidence, which was founded on long service in his division.

Our movement across the [South Side] railroad was unopposed, and apparently even unobserved, and we simply marched across the line of rails, which we had been so long fighting for. All the exultation manifested was on the part of the enlisted men. There was a dilapidated train of box cars and an engine, of rusty appearance on the track. Some men got upon this and as there was live steam, blew the whistle. But we did not delay there. We turned to the right and moved down within the extensions of the line of the enemy and towards the very heart of things. Of course we understood that if the enemy should let go the works, and fall upon us (the Fifth corps and the cavalry) we should have a serious affair. But, confronting the whole line of the enemy was the rest of the Army of the Potomac, and they were too near to permit the enemy to fall unhindered upon us. Indeed, as everybody knows, Grant, upon receipt of information of our success at Five Forks on the eve of the 1st[,] had ordered a charge upon the works of the enemy at daylight of the second.

The right of the enemy had been weakened by the detachments sent against us, and doubtless were further demoralized by knowledge that their extreme right was broken at Five Forks, and their rear endangered, so that the charge was successful. We did not share further in the active operations against the enemy at Petersburg, further than by our presence in their rear, threatening and modifying their action. Lee retreated on the night of the 2[n]d of April, abandoning the lines about Richmond and the east side of Petersburg without a struggle. We followed on the 3rd, keeping on the south side. What remained of Picket's and Bushrod Johnson's Divisions were understood to be in front of us, and we had evidences as we followed, that they were in swift flight.[194]

We halted on the first day[']s march, near a small house, one of the poor white class, which stood by the road, nearly surrounded by a second growth forest. It was a small unpainted frame building without cellar, and open underneath, and apparently containing two or three rooms, one below, and one or two on the second floor. It was of the plainest and most neglected kind, and the grounds about it were utterly unkempt and confused. But it was of a class not infrequent in Virginia at that time.

What attracted our attention, however, was a scene illustrative of the effects of war. While we were resting[,] a mounted enlisted man, said to have been one of Sheridan's scouts, though of that I have no knowledge, came along. He promptly explored the open space underneath the house & pulled out a small trunk. In it he found the uniform of a Confederate soldier, new and clean, and upon this he at once made claim as contraband of war, but not without dispute. The only apparent occupant of the house was a woman, plainly of the poor white class, of fifty or sixty years, but tall & strongly built, and like the ancient German women described by Tacitus, of fierce countenance.[195]

The Cavalry man had hold of one end of the trousers, and the old woman the other. She said the suit was her son's and was intended as his wedding suit. Soon the antagonists were pulling in opposite directions, and with equal vigor & determination, and not silently. The stuff of the trousers, and of the woman was well tested, and the man had no advantage. Some of us officers interferred and drove off the man. The uniform might be contraband, we did not undertake to settle that question of international law, but we did not think that in conditions then existing, possession of that rebel uniform would materially affect the contest. We felt so sure that we could afford to be magnanimous in the matter of a wedding uniform. We should probably soon have the bridegroom himself. Unfortunately for our entertainment the bride did not appear. She lived probably in some neighboring shanty. We soon moved on and left the poor woman and the trousers to the chances of war. I hope the fellow returned to his uniform and his girl, but as to all that, and how happily they were, this history is silent. There was nothing in the conditions imposed at Appomattox, which would prevent the man from marrying the girl, even in a Confederate uniform, though such funereal baked meats would coldly furnish the marriage table.

We pushed on rapidly. It was understood that we were making for Jetersville and that it was necessary to be there in season to obstruct the passage of Lee's Army, supposed to be moving in that direction. There were evidences that the enemy were in front of us and in distress. An occasional wagon, abandoned by them, was picked up by us, and disposed of in a systematic manner. There was no time to burn wagons, but we marched with a squad of axe men in front, and these promptly wheeled out of the column at the sight of an abandoned wagon, unslung axes and cut the spokes.

At one place we passed a battery stuck in the mud and burning, evidently the horses had given out, and the battery men had set the wheels and other woodwork on fire, that they might be useless to us. As we marched by[,] the ammunition chests were burning, and I could see the shot or shells through the burning walls. I favored the theory that they were solid shot, but was relieved when we had passed the burning wreck.

At other points on the road, we saw in the distance Confederate stragglers, apparently deserters, like rats leaving a sinking ship. We crossed a high bridge over a ravine, a rude structure and without guard rails. In the ravine below was piled the wreck of a wagon with the mule team, which must have run off from the bridge in the darkness of the night before.

It was late in the afternoon of the 4th of April when we reached the vicinity of Jetersville, after a brisk march. It was anticipated that Lee would move on the road passing that place, in his endeavor to reach Danville. The cavalry had preceded us, and the Sixth and Second Corps were following. But as we were the first infantry and we might be set upon by the whole of Lee's Army before the other corps could arrive, we began to build earthworks. It was a very chill April night, and the northwest wind swept the unprotected field where we lay.

Next day the cavalry brought in prisoners captured by them, a battery of artillery and some dismounted officers and men. The teams of the battery were all of mules with negro drivers, and presented a rather unmilitary appearance. Evidently the animals had been overworked and underfed in the hurried retreat and were jaded. The mules trotted on with their long ears low hung and flapping. The negro drivers were clad or rather half clad in what seemed a mixture of military and civil garb, ill fitting and evidently cast off garments. Yet they were jolly, and did not seem to regard their capture or the misfortunes of their confederates as of any concern to them.

Indeed capture was to them release and emancipation. Their arms and legs were flapping in unison with the ears of the mules, and their spacious grins were contrasted oddly with the dejected appearance of the captured officers and men, hurried along by the cavalry which guarded them.

With the battery had also been captured a wagon train which had been destroyed.

We were all day of the 5th near the junction of the Richmond and Danville railroad which I examined closely. It was a dilapidated road, and showed the poverty of the Confederacy in railway materials. At one point there was a switch in which the rails were of the old strip pattern, timbers with flat iron straps fixed thereon.[196]

While in the vicinity of Jetersville, our pickets captured a man mounted on a mule, who rode[,] unsuspecting trouble[,] into our line. On his person was found a dispatch from the Chief Commissary of Lee's Army, directed to the Commissary at Lynchburg, and ordering rations to be sent to Amelia Court House. The story was told that Sheridan sent two of his scouts, who were in half civilian, half confederate disguise, to take this dispatch and send it from the first station above the break in the telegraph line.

We expected on the morning of the sixth to move against Lee's Army at Amelia Court House. The movement began, but the enemy had escaped[,] passing our left.

On the sixth, seventh and eighth our corps marched to the intermittent sound of battle on the right and in front. We were pushing to get in front of Lee, while the other corps were attacking as opportunity offered. The principal contests were those on Sailors' Creek, these resulting so disastrously to the Confederates.[197] The march of the 8th of April was a severe one. During the afternoon and evening the distant sound of cannon in front, or rather to the right of the direction in which we were moving, notified every man that he was needed.

During the last week[,] or soon after Five Forks[,] I had been assigned to the temporary command of a new Pennsylvania regiment, lacking in field officers of experience, and rode at the head of that regiment [the 198th]. We marched till near midnight. How the men kept on their feet, I cannot imagine. I was so nearly overpowered by weariness that I alternately walked and rode to keep myself awake. I could hear the men behind me cursing their commanding officers indiscriminately, and hoping that we would come into the enemy, since fighting would be a relief to the pain of marching. I saw men reel out of the ranks and fall utterly unable to move farther.

About midnight we halted, and not receiving orders I rode forward to ascertain what was to be done. I was advised that we were to halt for the night and directed to put my men into bivouac by the side of the road. I returned picking my way amongst the men of the regiments in advance of mine, stretched out in the roadway. Mine had gone into bivouac, that is to say they had lain down[,] most of them in the woods by the roadside. Soon my orderly came up with my spare horse, and took that on which I had been riding. I lay down with my head in the saddle, too tired to pull off my boots. After awhile he aroused me, and notified me that my supper was ready. He had provided an unusual luxury. On the way he had found access to some farmer[']s meal bin, and borrowed therefrom a bucket of corn meal, and some of this hastily boiled, or rather stirred into hot water, constituted my supper.

At five o'clock on the 9th we moved again, the sound of cannon being renewed. We did not then know what severe losses had been inflicted upon the enemy at Sailors['] Creek, but we knew that Sheridan was on the advance, and the sound of cannon made it plain that he had been buffeting the enemy in flank. The sound of the 8th day seemed well in front, and no man needed urging. We moved out on the morning of the 9th well closed up[,] and about 8 A.M. turned to the right and crossing the railway track emerged from the woods into an open field which extended far to right and left. Four or five hundred yards to the front was a low wooded hill, extending to the right, or east, but curving around on our left towards the north, and facing west.

The only battle visible to us was far to the left & front, where along the western edge of the wooded slope was a line of white puffs, showing that the cavalry was across the road of Lee, blocking his way. We were just in time, for the cavalry alone could not long sustain the weight of infantry, which he might throw against them.

But we were there, and manifestly upon their flank, though they were concealed from us by the woods. The sun was showing feebly through the clouds just above the eastern tree tops, as the Fifth Corps swung out of the forest, into the open field and extended to right & left with wings thrown forward. The color bearers shook out the flags, and the skirmish line moved forward. From the skirmish line I could see the whole line of battle as it formed. There was a body of cavalry on the left, and just before we moved it passed our front, Sheridan leading on his Winchester horse, in full gallop. Next behind him was his color bearer with the broad swallow tail flag with its crossed swords fluttering in the wind. Behind this the staff and escort, moving to the right. He passed directly in front of us, as alert and eager as if just out of camp, though he had been incessantly upon the pursuit since the morning of the 29th of March, and, after the long chase and fierce buffetings; the prey was in his reach, and almost in his grasp. He seemed the embodiment of the fighting spirit, guided by the coolest calculation, and the sight of him affected us all. I think that there was not a man in the corps who was not eager to dash in upon the enemy. The only thought was to get at them. Our line of battle advanced across the open field, skirmishers in advance. I rode on the skirmish line, and could see the whole line advancing steadily, in good order, and without firing a shot over the level field.

Not since Gettysburg had we seen, in the open, such an extended line of battle. The shells thrown from a concealed battery of the enemy ricocheted on the ground, or burst with white puffs in the air, and gave a touch of battle effect to the scene.

We soon reached the woods which skirted the hill, and concealed the town and the enemy, and as the skirmish line entered it, I heard a shout a little to the left. "Lee surrenders". I spurred my horse in that direction and met a mounted Confederate officer, waving a white flag. He rode rapidly to the right and disappeared among the trees, the shout "Lee Surrenders" following him as he rode. This was at 9:30 A.M.[198]

It appears to me now that I did not at that moment appreciate the full meaning of that shout. Perhaps we were so dulled by fatigue and lack of sleep, or so keyed up to the fight that we could not quit at a moment's notice [or] apprehend the full effect of the flag of truce. At any rate we moved on, through the woods and into the open and in sight of part of the town. Then we halted. As we were advancing I noticed far to the right a crowd of cavalry on the hill in that direction and one or two of our batteries advancing for position. But we had not fired a shot. Nor had our artillery. I do not now remember hearing any firing on the right.

Soon orders came to remain in place, and to be ready to make or receive an attack. This was easy. We had been marching at rapid pace, since five A.M. not well rested at the starting, and breakfast had been not even a ceremony. The rest was well prolonged, and it probably dawned upon us that the war was over.

We lay near the McLain [McLean] house, afterwards so well known, but then only a small ordinary dwelling of a country village. It was a small brick house, with a high porch in front and door in the center. There Grant and Meade and Sheridan met Lee and Col. Marshall of his staff & I think Longstreet was there and some other general officers of both armies. On the morning of the 10th after the completion of the negotiations[,] I rode from our place of bivouac to the village & saw Grant and Lee sitting on their horses near the McLain house, side by side quietly chatting. I sat on my horse, with other subordinate officers, at a respectful distance, and watched them. It is a pity that "snap shot" cameras had not then been invented, but the picture is still in my mind[']s eyes. Lee was on the left of Grant, and nearer us. It was the first time I had ever seen him [Lee], and I was much impressed by his manly soldierly appearance. He had on what looked like a new uniform, the insignia of his rank, sword & belt, and a gray felt hat, and was well mounted. Grant wore the old fatigue suit of the campaign, a battered felt hat, & no belt or sword. They were looking straight ahead, but every now & then one would turn his head toward the other, apparently speaking, in a quiet, deliberate way. They sat there talking, as nearly as I can now remember, ten or fifteen minutes, and then, as quietly parted, with ordinary salute, and without any special demonstration, and rode each his own way.

Thereafter everything was free and easy—in a wholly unaccustomed way. There was "Lee's Army", within gunshot, and no firing. I think we had not even a picket line. At any rate I saw none. On our side were Griffin & Gibbon[']s Corps, and the cavalry, and beyond, on the east, the rest of the Army of the Potomac, which we had not seen since they left Petersburg.

Confederate officers came into our camp with more horses than money, and there was said to have been some horse trading, in which Confederate horses were exchanged for United States notes. Even the discount on Confederate money had disappeared on the 9th and whatever the Confederates may have had in their pockets at the waving of that white flag turned instantly to waste paper. Fortunately the officers and (I believe) many of the enlisted men, who were mounted, owned the horses they rode, and these became a valuable asset, and when sold relieved the unfortunate Confederates from the embarassment of going home penniless, as most of them probably did.

These men were indeed in bad plight, not only beaten and surrendered, most of them far from home, without transportation and without funds; but they were also without rations. We had only what the men carried in their haversacks, and a comparatively small supply in wagons which had been able to keep up with the rapid pursuit. All the unissued rations were given to the Confederates, and for two days we were on short rations or none. By the enterprise of some officers of our Division Head Quarters mess we made the acquaintance of a family near us in the village. They were very pleasant to us, and necessity, which is the mother of many things besides invention, brought about a combination of our supplies, and a dinner party in which the family entertained us, and we furnished the coffee and sugar, luxuries to them, and they furnished the bread and chicken. They effectually concealed their grief at the collapse of their cause and made everything pleasant for us. We left them with regret.

[THE RETURN HOME
APRIL—JULY, 1865]

On the fifteenth we moved. I rode ahead of the Division with an orderly, to select ground for the bivouac of the Division. On further, I saw a negro shanty by the roadside, where there was an old colored woman. I had had no breakfast or dinner, nothing since the compound banquet of the day before, and I was looking for provisions. The old woman had a hoe cake, four or five inches in diameter, and an inch thick, solid as a brick, and as dry and with very little dirt upon it. She parted with it cheerfully for twenty-five cents and probably did not know what a chance she had lost to drive a better bargain.[199]

I broke the cake into two parts, gave the orderly one, and as I rode along, ate the other. The orderly followed deeply interested in the same occupation, for he had probably had less nourishment than I during the two or three preceding days. We solved, so far as diet goes, the problems of the simple life, and I can recommend hoe cakes as a nourishing and sustaining food, and most palatable, if one has the proper appetite. As our horses walked along, we had time for thorough mastication, and thorough mastication developed the latent sweetness of the cake.

We marched at 6 A.M. from this bivouac, reached Farmville at 3 P. M. and went into camp.

Here were evidences of the recent occupation and passage of the rebel army in burned bridges and Confederate hospitals still occupied by their wounded. There were great stores of tobacco, evidently accumulated during the war, when there [was] no means of shipment. In one great storehouse were casks full of the dried leaf. It was broken into, and men from some Pennsylvania regiments skilled in cigar making, were busy at their trades and apparently their labor was as free as the material. Cigars, even of native leaf, were a luxury to us. I rode up to look and one man asked me to wait while he made a cigar for me. He selected a large leaf and the cigar was a big one. I smoked the larger part of it that evening after my supper of hardtack, and as I was not at that time sufficiently familiar with the real Havana to institute comparisons, it was a smoke satisfactory in quality as well as dimension.

Here the astounding news came of the assassination of President Lincoln, a stunning blow which marred all our rejoicing, and filled us with pain and resentment. In the absence of details we could, at that time, attribute the assassination only to the resentments of the South. But there was no open demonstration and the men were calm. What the effect would have been had these tidings come before the surrender, and during the campaign, I can't say. Doubtless increased bitterness & perhaps excesses. It was fortunate that the war had been practically finished.

The sad occasion afforded evidence of the strong hold which Mr. Lincoln had upon the affection of the Army, an affection deep and abiding, and won without the glamour of achievements in battle.

We were now moving at our leisure away from battles, and not towards them.

We had no front on which to skirmish and no flanks or rear to guard. The enemy had disappeared utterly, and we began to appreciate the saying of Grant, made a year before, that the Confederacy was but a shell. Once fairly broken it had fallen into pieces. It was a strange relief. The army of the Potomac was intact, but there was no war. Lee's Army, which we had been fighting for four years, was scattered to the winds and had ceased to exist. Military discipline was maintained, but with ease and relaxation. As we moved down the South Side railroad[,] fought for desperately three weeks before, the men marched on the track and the mounted officers on the wagon road. On the 19th of April we halted and held services appropriate for the day of the burial of the President, and here for the first time, we received the newspapers which gave the details of the assassination.

I was busy with my new duties as Inspector of Division, inspecting brigades and regiments and writing orders. During the last days of April we were encamped near Wilson[']s Station, and our chief care was exercised in putting "safe guard" on the houses in the neighborhood, to protect the people and property from depredations which might be committed by our own men straggling from camp. Of the people thus guarded we had no complaints, with a single exception, and I found, upon investigation, that this was without just foundation.

[In] spite of the previous cold weather[,] roses were in bloom, and the country was pleasant, although of generally shabby appearance, and not much cultivated. It was a pleasant Sunday in May, when we moved at the same easy pace, down to near Petersburg where now no hostile gun muzzle confronted us. We encamped near the Peebles Farm, the scene of our hard fighting on the 30th day of Sept. 1864. Camps and intrenchments and the destruction of houses and trees had obliterated all the original landmarks. Not far from the old line was an immense tower built in successive stories, of tall pine trees, from which, during the winter and spring campaign, our signal officers had observed the movements of the enemy. An aeroplane would serve the purpose now, but this, I believe was effective and good in the siege, though of course immovable.[200] It had gone out of use certainly, though the material might serve for rebuilding the houses of the people, unfortunately destroyed.

On the 3rd we marched through Petersburg inside of the works we had been so long assailing. It was all quiet then, strangely quiet. We bivouaced near the "Friend House", a substantial brick mansion in the midst of a grove of old oak trees. As usual we put guards on the property and pitched our tents on the lawn.

The people, an old clergyman and his daughters, were very

THE RETURN HOME

friendly. The troops of Gen[.] Butler had been about them in his advance from Bermuda Hundred, in 1864[,] and they were bitter against him. In the morning we, officers of the Division Head Quarters, were invited to join the family in morning prayers, and we filed into the great parlor, leaving our swords and belts in the hall. The venerable Parson read and expounded a chapter in the Bible, and we all knelt with the family while he made a long prayer. When we left to mount our horses, the ladies gave us flowers, acceptable doubly as an indication of returning peace and good will.

That night we encamped at Manchester near a fine old house which looked out over broad fields bordering upon the river. There was no sign that war had ever been near these people, though the famous Fort Drury [Fort Darling on Drewry's Bluff] was not far below.[201] Two pleasant days we spent there, pleasant for us, though not so agreeable to the owner of the plantation. It was impossible to prevent the men from burning his rails for fuel, and whole fields were unfenced when we left. I rode over to Richmond, and went into Libby Prison, a doleful looking building then unoccupied, excepting at one end, where some Confederates were confined, for what reason I do not know.[202] It had originally been a tobacco storage house, and was several stories in height, with floors unsubdivided, dirty and forbidding. It was very comfortable to think that its melancholy history as a military prison had closed. The miseries and deaths inflicted there had been to no good purpose, and the keepers, high & low had fled or were in hiding.

Next morning, May the sixth[,] we marched through the desolate city. A broad section, near the river, was blackened and ruined by the recent fire. The shutters of the houses were closed, and only negroes appeared on the streets, as we passed.

We bivouaced near the old battlefield of Hanover Court House, and thence by generally easy marches through Fredericksburg, to camp on the Columbia Pike, a highway leading to the city, and encamped on the north bank near the ruins of the old brick house, where were Burnside[']s Head Quarters during the battle of December 1862. We looked upon the river, the city and the distant hills, where in vain effort we had lost so many men, and where under leadership in which we had no confidence[,] all effort seemed hopeless, and it all seemed like a bad dream when one awakes. Restored confidence, and final success had put a different phase upon the matter.

Notwithstanding that we were not in haste[,] we had a hard march from Fredericksburg. The morning was pleasant, but a heavy tempest of thunder and lightning and rain came on in the forenoon, drenching us and continuing all day made the roads difficult and the march slow. The lightning struck one of our teams and killed a mule. We did not reach our camping ground until nine o'clock and later, and [I] had to turn the men into a soggy field, without rail fences, and therefore without fuel. Warm with marching and wet they had nothing better than to sleep on the ground.[203]

Our Division in advance, we came in sight of Washington early in the afternoon of the 12th of May. Over the low hills eastward[,] the white dome of the Capitol appeared like a huge bubble.[204] The city lay invisible behind the hills. The Army of the Potomac had been defending that bubble and the city [for] four years, in a hundred battles and skirmishes, and had won; but, even the sense of triumph & the sight of the dome of the Capitol, were not enough to raise a cheer. I fear that the prospect of fresh meat and a square meal occupied our minds quite as much as patriotic rejoicings. The Promised Land of abundance and soft-bread was before us, in sight, but not reached; and an order from Army Head Quarters came while the men were stacking arms, forbidding[,] under penalty, any man from leaving camp. We stood like Moses on Mount Nebo, though I hope Moses did not swear so much at the disappointment, as the men about me, on receipt of the order.[205]

However, the interdictum was soon modified, and in my position as chief of Division staff, I had no difficulty in getting the pass, which was necessary in the city when there seemed to be jealous watchfulness against even officers from the camp across the river. Whether or not [Secretary of War Edwin] Stanton feared that we would storm the city and overturn the Government, I am not assured. As a matter of fact our desires were much lower, and had relation solely to a dinner at the hotel. Lack of funds and pressing duties forbade daily visits, but we could live on camp fare three or four days and then wreck our appetites on the hotels, which were then (fortunately for us) conducted on the American plan.

We lay in this fly infested camp on the Columbia Pike, until the morning of the 17th day of July, busy in reorganizing, making our rolls, inspecting and a thousand and one camp duties including the fighting. Soon after we reached this camp and after so long a delay I was mustered as full Colonel of the regiment, which, with the rank and pay of Major, I had commanded most of the time since August of 1863.

Gilmore had been called to account for having himself mustered while under charges, or with pending resignation, but otherwise he got off scot free, I believe, and with the illgotten unearned pay. This did not restore to me the pay I had lost, but I had no interest in pensioning him.

The details of three weeks will not be of interest. The veterans of the 20th and of other regiments were mustered out as soon as practicable, after we reached Washington, and the remainder of the 16th & 20th Maine and the First Maine sharpshooters, were recombined with the 20th, of which I assumed command, though also in command of the brigade. I had completed my work as Division Inspector. These were busy days, but we were all looking forward to release.

The most interesting episode of this story in camp on the Pike was that of the "Grand Review" which took place on the 23[r]d and 24th days of May. Review of the Army of the Potomac was on the 23[r]d. The army moved during the latter part of the night or early in the morning, and massed on Capitol Hill, and about the Capitol, and at the signal the head of column moved out upon

Pennsylvania Avenue. The regiments were of unequal size, many very small, but they were formed in equal platoons, of twenty files front, made with regard to company, and the column extended nearly from curb to curb. The regiments carried their old battle flags, many of them faded and tattered, and cut by bullets. The batteries showed signs of use, and some the marks of bullets, in their woodwork. The whole column marched with that easy swing which only long habit can give. It was an army from the field, not a mere show army, and such as none now living may ever see again.

Sherman's army was reviewed next day, a splendid body of men.

After the review the mustering out of the troops went briskly on. It was deemed unpolitic, and probably was impracticable to muster out all the men at once. The questions of pay and transportation had to be considered, even after all questions as to the close of the fighting had been settled. But everybody, or at least a very large majority of officers and men were anxious to get out of the service and to go home. Service in camp was dull and tedious. Drilling, the only resource for exercise, had become a farce, and the men grew restless for lack of mental and physical occupation. At one time they organized torch light processions. It was not easy to maintain discipline. It was always more difficult in camp, than in active campaign, and now all campaigns were over.

It seemed just to muster out at first, men whose term of service had nearly expired, and to leave the later enlistments for later muster out, and this was done.[206] Those first enlisted were sent home under Lt. Col. Morrill. In the Maine regiments in Fifth Corps, after those from the 20th & 16th had been sent home, those of the 16th Maine, and the First Maine Sharpshooters who remained, were consolidated with what remained from my regiment, giving me about one thousand men, more than the regiment had ever before numbered on its rolls, even at the first muster in Portland. Most of the enlisted men, and even of the officers, were unknown or little known to me. The first task was to reorganize into companies, and to assign officers. I took two officers from the Sharpshooters, Major [George R.] Abbott as Major, and Capt. Sawyer as Adjutant and T. D. Chamberlain, brother of Gen. C., an excellent officer, as Lt. Col. The duties devolved upon me as brigade commander were slight, but those of the regiment were more serious. Complaints were made to me by some of the men of the Sharpshooters, that they had been defrauded by their officers, or rather by some of their officers. These men, enlisted in the latter part of 1864, and early in 1865, had received large bounties, amounting in some cases to $700 or $800 to a man. They now alleged fear that they would desert with the money. It was taken from them, after they were mustered in, and as the men asserted never had been returned to them. I examined these men, separately, and adjusted the matter as well as I could, for the men who remained. Some had been killed and some had justified the suspicions of the officers by deserting.

Having received order to that effect, on the 17th day of July I broke camp for the last time, and began the serious business of getting one thousand men from Virginia to Maine. It may seem absurd that this should have been considered a serious matter, when everybody desired to go. The trouble arose from the fact that some wished to go in their own way, and without the restraints of military discipline, and were impatient to plunge into the joys of civil life and civilized conditions, without any restraint, civil or military. The net of the recruiting officers catches all sorts of fish, and the examining surgeon does not examine the recruit in the matter of moral character. At any rate examining surgeons did not in the years of 1861 and 65, and between. The exigencies of the Government did not admit of such fine discriminations. Moral character did not fill the quota of the State, called for by the General Government. Only able bodied men could serve that purpose. The views of the recruit on the temperance question, or his ability or habits in making fine distinctions in matters of personal property, were not inquired into. And in fact, though good moral character was a substantial support, and backing, sound legs were of primary use in marching, & good arms and eyes for shooting. So we had men who were fairly good or even excellent soldiers, when under military discipline, but who did not reach a very high standard in civil life, and some got into the penitentiary after discharge from the Army. But only a few. A few men, however, unless restrained, can make a great disturbance. Further, men riotously inclined or with a tendency to thirst and with these inclinations and tendencies exasperated by long restraint, felt impelled to burst into unrestrained joy, and unlimited drink, as soon as they had recrossed the Potomac. They had served their country well, on rations always poor & sometimes short, and of what use was a return to plenty, if they could not have it all at once. Like the great Dr. Samuel Johnson, they could bear want, but not abundance.

They pictured themselves as going into a land flowing with milk and honey, and drinks, and greeted as conquering heroes. Of course, the majority took a more sober view of things; but they were all young fellows; many mere boys & for the benefit of the more exhilarant and excitable, I put the regiment into column so that I could make myself heard and from the saddle as from a pulpit, I exhorted them.

I informed them that reports of rioting and misbehavior of troops returning home had been published in the newspapers; that I had no doubt that most, if not all of the 20th Maine, would take pains not to have their fair fame, won in the service, and on many battle fields, to be thus tarnished; and that I should not permit a few to disgrace the many. I reminded them that they had not been mustered out, and were still under military discipline, and that I should enforce that discipline on the way home, and until they were discharged, with absolute strictness; that there must be no whiskey drinking and no straggling and that, while everything possible would be done for their comfort, I would spare no effort to secure the return of every man and to present the regiment for discharge, without an absentee.

THE RETURN HOME

They took it in good faith, & therefore, I put them into column for the road. We had outgrown sentimentality; or it had been ground out of us, but we could not fail to contrast the return of the regiment over this bridge, with the crossing in Sept[.] of 1862. Then we were raw recruits and the war was before us.

Now we were veterans.

We marched to the old Baltimore and Ohio Depot. The train was not ready & there was a delay of several hours. I massed the regiment in an enclosure, near the station, and kept strict guard, not permitting any of the men to leave.

An Irish woman came along with what seemed to be a bucket of milk, and, with the greenness of a countryman I let her pass in. A policeman, however, advised me that the milk was doubtless well saturated with whiskey, and I ordered the sergeant of the guard to turn her out. She had the courage of her convictions and business, and borrowed fight, but the application of a couple of bayonets to her back, changed her mind and course, with expressions of great disrespect.

The train, later in the day, took us to Philadelphia, where landing on the western side, I marched through the city to a station on the east side, where the loyal and hospitable Philadelphians had established a lunch house for soldiers. Here were ample accommodations and food for all my men, water and soap and towels, (to an abundance of which they had, for some time been unaccustomed) and excellent sandwiches and coffee satisfied them fully. We had no trouble there, and thence went by rail to N.Y.[,] crossed the river and went into bivouac for the night in the Battery Barracks, comfortable quarters, and not without supplies, but some of the men were discontented and wanted to get out. The number who had cousins and sisters and aunts living in New York, was surprising. But I was obdurate, and let nobody out.

Next morning the steamer John Brooks took the regiment on board & we started for Providence, but the sea was rough and, I suspect, the old boat not very seaworthy, and, lest we drown so many veterans saved from the war, the Captain ran into New London for the night.

We reached Providence about noon. There was a train ready, and I put the men aboard at once, with the arrangement before used, the rear car for the officers, the next for the officers of the day and the guard of picket men, and the rest of the regiment in the other cars ahead. Here we were delayed, and the men began to exhibit signs of uneasiness. The more restless, enterprising, and thirsty, were evading the guards at the doors by slipping out at the windows, and as that part of Providence appeared to be plentifully supplied with saloons, and small grocers, there was a fair prospect of having a drunken squad. So I turned out the guard and deployed them as a picket line in wide sweeps around the station, with orders to put a guard on every saloon and grocery and to let no man pass, and for one hour or so that part of the town was fairly dry. That was my last picket line. We reached Boston, marched quietly through the town with an escort of police leading the way, and about five P. M. took [a] train for Portland. It was a very slow train, and late when we reached that city. They gave us a bountiful supper and with men well fed I moved over to the old camp from which we had started on the 30th day of August in 1862. It was four in the morning of the 21st of July when I arrived at the camp. That day I turned in my arms and was busy in the making out of rolls, seeing to the mustering out of the men and the disposal of the public property.

Our military career terminated on the spot where it began within a few days of the term of years for which we had enlisted. The world was all before us where to choose, but we were out of training and out of touch with everything, and as we had been able to save little, all whom I knew, without capital.

PHOTOGRAPHS

PHOTOGRAPHS

I. Ellis Spear

II. Samuel T. Keene

PHOTOGRAPHS

III. Ellis Spear

IV. Susan Wilde Spear

V. Sarah F. and Samuel T. Keene

VI. William W. Morrell

PHOTOGRAPHS

VII. Adelbert Ames

VIII. Joshua L. Chamberlain

IX. A. W. Clark

X. Walter G. Morrill

PHOTOGRAPHS

XI. Rappahannock Station in 1863

PHOTOGRAPHS

XII. Officers of the Twentieth Maine, late 1863–early 1864. Ellis Spear is shown standing in the back row, fourth from the left.

PHOTOGRAPHS

XIII. Officers and wives of the Twentieth Maine Regiment gathered behind an arbor at the entrance to the camp at Rappahannock Station, March 21, 1864. Sarah Keene is seated at the left of the photograph, with Samuel Keene standing behind her. Susan Spear is seated beneath the "20" of the arbor, with Ellis Spear standing behind her. Mrs Rufus Plummer is seated at the right, with her husband likewise standing behind her. The woman standing at the left has not been identified.

XIV. Ellis Spear, *undated, late-nineteenth-century photograph*

XV. Sarah F. Keene Spear, *undated, late-nineteenth-century photograph*

PHOTOGRAPHS

XVI. Ellis Spear, *proof copy of undated, turn-of-the-century photograph*

PHOTOGRAPHS

XVII. Ellis Spear, *undated, early twentieth-century photograph*

CIVIL WAR DIARIES, 1863 — 1865

[FREQUENTLY-OCCURING ABBREVIATED
NAMES ARE AS FOLLOWS:

COL. AMES refs to Adelbert Ames, from Rockland, first Colonel of the 20th, a brigadier general after Gettysburg and later, by brevet, a major general.

SUSIE or S refers to Susie Wilde, a daughter of the Rev. John Wilde whom Ellis Spear met when her father was pastor in Brunswick and who became Spear's wife in March, 1863.

PAULINE, HANNAH and EM (Emily) refer to Ellis Spear's sisters.

VERRILL probably refers to Charles H. Verrill, Bowdoin College, Class of 1862, a teacher who came from Dorchester, Massachusetts.

REED refers to Edwin Reed, Bowdoin College 1858, from Bath and a ship owner.

MAC refers to George R. MacIntyre from Warren, Bowdoin College, Class of 1858 and in the Civil Service in Washington, D.C.; MRS. M is Mrs. MacIntyre.

COL. C or C refers to Lt. Col. Joshua S. Chamberlain from Brewer, who was promoted to colonel on the promotion of Ames and later a brigadier general by brevet. During the war, he was on leave from Bowdoin College where he was a professor.

HUBBARD refers to Wales Hubbard, of Wiscasset.

HILL refers to Lysander Hill from Cushing, Bowdoin College, class of 1858. He resigned his captaincy in the 20th Maine in February of 1862, and during the war was a lawyer in Washington, D.C.

Major Charles D. Gilmore, from Bangor, is sometimes referred to as MAJOR and sometimes as M.

MR. ROBINSON, sometimes R, first name not now known, refers to a Wiscasset resident who provided Spear with a uniform "on credit."

CIVIL WAR DIARIES, 1863 — 1865

[1863 DIARY]

Friday, Jan. 1 Fair.

Friday, Jan. 16 Turned over to quartermaster Eight Guns & seven sets of Equipment of men viz =
> West
> Corp Bailey
> Sergt Moody.
> Meserve.
> Barnes.
> Tibbetts.
> Buker.

Saturday, Jan. 17 Battalion drill in morning. Col. Ames came in aft. Wrote Susie, Verrill & Pauline. Under marching orders.

Sunday, Jan. 18 Slept poorly. Cold. Flagg reported dead at hospital. His father is Davis Flagg of Jefferson. Still under marching orders.

Monday, Jan. 19 Date of marching deferred 24 hours. Troops have been passing up river. Letter from Susie. Slept alone but comfortably.

Tuesday, Jan. 20 Struck tents at 10 A.M. Sent ordnance Report. Marched about 3 P.M not more than 3 miles Broke to rear by Right of Div. & marched into woods. Encamped. Slept in shelter tent with

Cap. Fitch. Lieuts. Chamberlain & Keene. Very comfortable spite of rain. Left in camp Bailey, West, Meserve, Barnes, Moody, Smith, Dodge, Tibbetts, Williams, & Buker with teams. Letter from Susie came in Eve.

Wednesday, Jan. 21 Fell in Early and stood in the mud under showers of rain. Several hours, while the artillery went slowly by. Marched through terrible mud 2 or three miles Bivouaced in column by regiments in oak woods. Cold & drizzly. Procured oak slats for bed. Put up Shelter tent. Took a little whiskey & slept soundly.

Thursday, Jan. 22 Reveille at Sunrise [*indecipherable word*] my blankets dried. Have my servant & sergeant in my tent. Cold & drizzling still. Officer of the day beginning at night. <u>Whittled</u> a bone spoon.

Friday, Jan. 23 Regiment out on fatigue duty building roads. Clouds broke away in aft. Rumors of a return. Troops receiving back Rations forthwith. 2 days of bread 1 of pork & 1 of fresh meat.

Saturday, Jan. 24 Returned to Camp.

Sunday, Jan. 25 Raining. Letters Recd letters from Reed, Mac & Verrill Wrote Mac, Verrill Pauline and Susie.

Monday, Jan. 26 Raining. Officer of the day. Letter from Susie.

Tuesday, Jan. 27 At work upon cook house & fixing up quarters Letter from Susie.

Wednesday, Jan. 28 Storm of rain & Snow. In Evening men signed pay Rolls.

Thursday, Jan. 29 Regiment was paid. Hodgdon, Kennedy, Dodge, Pease & Carter were not on list, but paid upon my certificate that they had recd no pay while in hospital. Due on Pay Roll to absentees on said Roll.

        W. H. Cushman   22.10
        L. D. Carter   20.80
        A. F. Flagg   24.70
        Orlando Flagg   17.35
        W. E. Hill   24.70

Friday, Feb. 6 Capts. Bangs & Clark with Col. C. gone on leave of 15 days. Sent $40 to Hubbard by Clark. Played Euchre in Quartermasters tent.

Saturday, Feb. 7 Col. on detached service. [indecipherable name] left in command of Regiment.

Sunday, Feb. 8 1 Cap. to [indecipherable word] are do to Carr—do Wright Inspection by Col. Ames. No service. R

Monday, Feb. 9 Col. away. In command of Reg. Still Extremely muddy. Of the four men Hiscock, Cushman, [indecipherable name] & Winslow, the two last named are on the sick list. Letter from Susie No. 39. Bought Les Miserables

Tuesday, Feb. 10 In command as yesterday. Had grounds policed thoroughly. At dress Parade men looked unusually well. Bought beans of Sutler. Conducted dress parade.

Wednesday, Feb. 11 Snowing with rain. Had my tent fixed & surrounded by a fence of wicker. Letter from Susie in the Evening. Wrote her. Ordered on picket tomorrow. Chamberlain came into mess.

Thursday, Feb. 12 Came on picket in command. 218 men. Col. Bertram of 17 N.Y. in command. Very muddy, but we came out at moderate pace Holding the reg. in reserve.

Friday, Feb. 13 Relieved 17th N.Y. Sent off my reliefs & held balance in reserve in pine woods. The country rather woody with occasional openings. The men built bough huts & were comfortable Col Ames came along & Adjutant afterwards. Sent Sergt & three men to guard reb. house outside our line.

Saturday, Feb. 14 In reserve again. Read Les Miserables & lounged stupidly. Monotonous business. Slept comfortably before a good fire.

Sunday, Feb. 15 Came in with Regt Very muddy & raining Found a letter from—one from Susie came at night.

Wednesday, Feb. 18 A. F. Flagg paid to Dec. 31st by Maj Eaton. Notified by Maj. A. D. Robinson.

Thursday, Feb. 19 Work on Returns.

Friday, Feb. 20 Work on Returns.

Saturday, Feb. 21 Working on Returns a little. Officer of the day & busy most of the time policing Regimental grounds.

Sunday, Feb. 22 Snow Storm Finished Returns.

Monday, Feb. 23 Snow Storm hardly over Sent Returns.

Tuesday, Feb. 24 Cool. Snow with letters.

Wednesday, Feb. 25 Visited camps of 4th & 17th Maine. Snow melting & weather warm.

Thursday, Feb. 26 Finished Muster & Pay Rolls & made Quarterly Returns. Letter from Susie No 45— Application for Leave of absence went with [indecipherable word] morning. Officer of the Day. Letter from Susie.

Friday, Feb. 27 Letter from Tibbetts Answered. Policed grounds in afternoon. Done nothing of importance. Noticed balloon in different places at the South apparently drifting in a South East direction.

Saturday, Feb. 28 Regiment inspection & [two indecipherable words] camp by Col. Chamberlain. Capt. Fitch & Lieut Chamberlain left in morning. No letters. Rain in Evening.

Sunday, Mar. 1 Raining in morning. Cleared off at noon. No inspection. Completed rolls.

Monday, Mar. 2   Policed grounds in morning. Battalion drill in afternoon.

Tuesday, Mar. 3   Drill in manual. Nichols papers came approved in afternoon. Litchfields & mine in Evening from Division Hd.Quarters disapproved. Put mine in again immediately. Col is going up with them tomorrow. Letter from Susie.

Wednesday, Mar. 4   Company drill in morning.

Sunday, Mar. 8   Leave of absence came in morning. Started on the 11 o'clock train. Reached Washington at five. Stopped at National. Spent Evening with Mac. Moody was paid by Maj Sabin 4 mos $504.

Monday, Mar. 9   Paid by Maj Sabin $504. Spent day with Mac & Hill very pleasantly. In Eve at 6½ took train for N.Y. Took Sleeping car & slept till we reached Philadelphia

Tuesday, Mar. 10   In N.Y. City. Went across to No 11 Dutch Street & remained till nearly ten. Then took cars. Reached Catskill about 3 P.M. Hired a team & rode to the top of the mountain. Then stopped for the night. Supper & sound sleep, spite of the noise, refreshed me. Snowing slightly.

Wednesday, Mar 11   Started Early for Stamford. Day pleasant & sleighing Excellent. Reached S. about one & was greeted as only those dear people could greet me.

Thursday, Mar. 12   Very cold. Mr Wilde not looking very well. I remained in the house perfectly happy, of course.

Friday, Mar. 13   Married—after so long delay—to the dearest, best girl in the world. So I think after more than four years acquaintance, I cannot tell how happy I am in making her my wife.—Rode with her in stage to Catskill, thence by cars to Hudson where we stayed all night.

Saturday, Mar. 14   Breakfasted & took cars for Boston. Reached B. in aft. & went to Marlboro. Went out in Eve to bookstore & purchased Carlyle's Essays & a volume of Holmes poems.

Sunday, Mar. 15   Visited Susie's Aunt at Neponset.

Monday, Mar. 16   Started for Warren. Failed to see Verrill. Left Susie at Brunswick & went on to Wiscasset. Went to [*indecipherable word*] school & saw the young people. Called at the Dr's & Hubbards & the Robinsons.

Tuesday, Mar. 17   Rode home which reached about 3 P.M. The dear old place. I regretted that I could not stay on longer. Called about. All well.

Wednesday, Mar. 18   Started at 3 A.M. for Wiscasset. Took breakfast at Mrs. Cliffords (Lands Sister) Took stage for Bath. Saw Reed again. Found Susie in Brunswick & our friends whom I was delighted to see Mrs Smith & Mrs. Doughty met us in Portland. Reached Boston in Eve & went to American House.

Thursday, Mar. 19 Remained in Boston. Sat for picture at Whipples. Went shopping with Susie. Saw Abbott. Took Norwich south for N.Y. at night. Saw Susies relation at depot. Reached N.Y in morning & went out

Friday, Mar. 20 Went out to Bloomfield.

Saturday Mar. 21 Rode with Mr Wilde to Newark. Then took cars for Washington. Off the tracks & one man hurt near Baltimore. Stopped in Washington at National. Spent Evening with Mac & wife & Hill Hill went with me to hotel.

Sunday, Mar 22 Came to camp in boat & by cars. Reached camp about noon.

Monday, Mar. 23 Drill. Officer of the Day.

Tuesday, Mar. 24 Drill—

Wednesday, Mar. 25 Drill

Thursday, Mar. 26 Brigade officer of the Day. Went out in afternoon with company on Review. Division reviewed by Gens Meade & Griffin.

Thursday, April 9 I was told that M will certainly resign being [*indecipherable word*]. Have already written Land & K.

Friday, April 10   Regiment still on picket Wrote Susie & Mac this morning with reference to my private affair.

Saturday, April 11   Regt returned from Picket. Walked with Clark to the hill near 2d Wisconsin. In afternoon held meeting of Line Officers to take action in regard to the death of Lieu. Lincoln. Drew up resolutions for the committee. Met & arranged the matter in the Evening.

Sunday, April 12   Inspection in morning by Col Ames. Review of Div. at 11 A.M. by a Swiss Gen. On sick list. In the afternoon a letter from Susie wonderful, & with photographs. Wrote her in Evening.

Monday, April 13   Expecting to move. No drill. Sent letter to Susie.

Tuesday, April 14   Under orders to be ready to move. Men with five days rations of hardbread in knapsack & three days bread & meat in haversacks. Instructions in afternoon by Col. Ames. Letter from Hill.

Wednesday, Apr. 15   Rain began in the night & continued with little intermission all day. Wrote Hill Mac & Miss C.

Thursday, Apr. 16   Sent letter to Susie. Clear. Company drill morning & afternoon. Maj Hamlin called. Visited earthworks. Letter from Susie, one fr Ross

Wednesday, Apr. 22   Left our old camp & pitched tents on a run over a mile distant—leaving our Small Pox patients in hospital.

Thursday, Apr. 23   Rain came on in the night. Slept among barrels, valises, [*indecipherable word*] and all sorts of rubbish. Rain all day. Exceedingly cold & uncomfortable.

Friday, Apr. 24   Raining Cool & uncomfortable.

Saturday, Apr. 25   Cleared off. Building tents. Refixed my own. Policed grounds. Letter from Susie.

Sunday, Apr. 26   Instruction in Duty by company officer. Regt visited by Gov Coburn & one member of his council, Mr French & Mr. Rice. The Gov went through the reg. [*deleted*: Letter from Susie] Package from Susie for Lieutenant.

Monday, Apr. 27   Warm & pleasant. Troops moving in all directions. Our brigade started about 11 A.M. the corps moving up river. There was a review out on the front with Salute of 13 guns. No teams went only pack mules. Col Ames left us to go on Meade's staff. Letter from Susie.

Tuesday, Apr. 28   Rain set in about 10 A.M. Only one regt moving. Two batteries left near us.

Thursday, Apr. 30   Third corps passed with 17, 3 & 4 Maine Regt.

Friday, May 1   Reviewed by Gov Coburn. Reg. addressed by Gov Mr French & Rice. Some cannonading.

APR. 22, 1863 — MAY 5, 1863

Our troops 6th Corps across the river below the city.

Saturday, May 2 Cannonading on the right. Col C. went to Hd Qurs. to offer the services of our regiment. Camp nearby with brigade qts. Played Euchre with Col. C. Major & Mr French.

Sunday, May 3 Woke by Col. C about 4 A.M. Ordered to be at Banks ford at daylight. My Co B & C with Major went to Meades Hd Qurs. & hence to post guards along the telegraph. Other of cos. out to Banks ford & came down leaving guards. At right witnessed the battle. Our troops drive [*indecipherable word*] out of their works. Later [*indecipherable word*] stormed their works. At night the firing was distant. [*three indecipherable words*]

Monday, May 4 Firing commenced on the 2d range of hills. Sharp & irregular volleys of musketry & heavy shelling. Our guns on this side throwing shells over into the woods. During the day it was still & sultry. At night the battle commenced again the Enemy driving ours into the woods. There was sharp [*indecipherable word*] & cannonading all night in the woods. Paper from Susie

Tuesday, May 5 The Enemy repossessed the heights & the city. Ours driven back. The Sixth corps almost ruined. Troops returning & stragglers—These showed in afternoon, rain poured torrents. Shelling occurring in the night out along the line. All cols.of corps in corps headquarters at the right. Letters from Verrill [*two indecipherable words*]

Wednesday, May 6   Rainy & cold. The army moving back. Went out with men & got the tents & axes—Fixed camp & made us more comfortable. Got dry & warm by noon. Letters from [*indecipherable word*] & [*indecipherable word*]. Came into camp in the Evening. Reached camp about nine, having marched under torrents of rain through mud & across brooks. It was a wonder that I found the way. Linscott had tent all warmed.

Thursday, May 7   Went down to 4th & 17. 17th suffered considerably. 4th very little. Rollins lost a finger. Made requisition for clothing & ammunition. Two nice letters from Susie.

Friday, May 8   Letters from Verrill & Mr R. one from Edgecomb in relation to Royal Dodge. Wrote Mr R & Verrill & Susie.

Saturday, May 9   Letter from Hannah bringing tidings of the death of Guilford. Poor, poor boy. He has given his life for the country. That is a consolation, but it is hard to have him, the youngest, die away from home amongst strangers. Quiescent. Letter from Reed.

Sunday, May 10   Instructions in morning—Very hot. Trees in full leaf & grass all green. Chamberlain held forth in aft Letter from Susie. Wrote Reed in Evening.

MAY 6, 1863 — MAY 19, 1863

Monday, May 11 Appointed on board to investigate the matter of short rations Drilled by Col. C. Weather Exceedingly warm Drill in afternoon. In Evening Land B Morrill & Capt. Keene in my tent. Sent letters to Reed & Susie.

Tuesday, May 12 No drill. Warm—

Wednesday, May 13 Burrows called. Letter from Susie. Box came. Also letter from Pauline announcing the sickness of Jason in Pensacola.

Thursday, May 14 Regiment on picket Letter from Verrill & one from Susie

Friday, May 15 Walked with Capt Keene to 4th & 17th In Evening played Euchre. Letter from Mac.

Saturday, May 16 Warm & windy. Letter from Dr Cushman relative to Sheldon. Spent a lazy listless day doing nothing & uncomfortable. Col. sent for Keene & myself. Everything favorable. Revelations of the Major.

Sunday, May 17 Regiment returned from picket. A long letter from Susie with case for Bible.

Monday, May 18 Escorted the 17 N.Y. to cars. Col. Stockins resigned. No drill. In evening walked to camp of 2d Maine. Letter from Susie with stamps.

Tuesday, May 19 Ordered out on Review for the Entertainment of Lord Somebody from England.

Wednesday, May 20   Field Officer of Day.

Thursday, May 21   Moved camp about three miles to a very pleasant ground northward of railroad.

Friday, May 22   Warm as usual. Wrote letters to Maine having been informed of the promotion of Col C. Shall secure French, Reed, Hubbard, Foote & Farwell.

Saturday, May 23   Brigade officer of the Day. Very warm. Attended to duties. Letter from Susie & wrote her. Gen Ames called in Evening.

Sunday, May 24   Hot & sultry as usual. No instructions. Made Report & attended Brigade guard mounting Letter from Hannah. Wrote the Robinsons & the Surgeons. Brigade dress parade. In Evening walked with Litchfield. Second Maine men came in 40 under guard.

Monday, May 25   No drill. [*deleted*: Warm & pleasant] Cold & cloudy. Reports around of Grants victories. Nine men assigned me Letter from Susie.

Tuesday, May 26   Brigade drill. Cloudy. Grant presses the Enemy closely in Vicksburg. Sergeant Jordan assigned to my company.

Wednesday, May 27   Warm & pleasant. Company & battalion drills.

Thursday, May 28   Brigade moved suddenly to the ford above. Bivouaced at night near U.S. Ford. Slept under an apple tree. Recd a letter from Pauline.

Friday, May 29   Moved & pitched camp about ½ mile from the ford. On fatigue duty with detachment sinking rifle pits near the ford & felling the trees. Letter from Reed & one from Susie.

Saturday, May 30   In camp & all quiet. Negotiations for a horse.

Sunday, May 31   Nothing unusual. Warm & pleasant & windy at times. Walked about half of the time.

Wednesday, June 3   All quiet in camp.

Thursday, June 4   Broke camp & marched with men about Eight miles. Bivouacked within two miles of ford. Weather very warm. Rest of the brigade rejoined us.

Friday, June 5   Moved two or three miles. Encamped in afternoon near Ellis ford in a wood. We relieved the 9th Mass. of 1st brigade. 16th Mich. near us. Enemy pickets on other side of the river. Letter from Emily. Reports of the army in motion.

Saturday, June 6   Walked down to the river. The river very low—bank high on other side. Rumors of movements below. Cannonading heard by day & night. All quiet here. Letter from Susie No 23. Inspection ordered in morning. Showers with thunder.

Sunday, June 7   Pleasant but cool. Inspection countermanded. Under marching orders. Had fifty-two (52) rifles. Turned over two, those of markers, leaving fifty.

Monday, June 8 Cool and clear. Nothing unusual. We sent out three companies alternately with the 16th & picketed along the river.

Tuesday, June 9 Warmer. Chaplain shot yesterday morning by guerillas or citizens lurking about. Rebel pickets withdrawn after the firing of yesterday at river. It is reported that ours have driven the Enemy several miles. Officer of the day. My Co. on picket.

Wednesday, June 10 Warm

Thursday, June 11 Nothing unusual Warmer—

Friday, June 12 Nothing unusual. Reported that the army is moving across to Orange & Alexandria R.R. The 3d Corps along that road. Our force to return down river.

Saturday, June 13 Warm & pleasant—Gen. Ames & Brown came. Went with Morrill of B. & picked cherries. Ordered to move tonight. Moved about 7. P.M. Marched until Eleven P.M. very rapidly. Bivouacked near Morrisville.

Sunday, June 14 Roused Early. Moved about noon. Marched until after sunset. Bivouacked in open field near railroad.

Monday, June 15 Marched about five A.M. Exceedingly hot. About noon men fell out. Halted near Manassas Junction. Geo Preble & D. A. Bailey sun struck. Lay in shade in the fork of the two roads until nearly dark. Then the regiment went down the Brentsville road towards Leesburg picketing. Marching up & down. Had those companies farthest down. Lay down about

Tuesday, June 16   Were relieved in the morning by the 16th Mich. Returned to our former place of bivouac where we remained all night. Started in the morning at six. The corps moving towards Centerville. Then turning northward on the Leesburg road. Day very hot. Marched very well, resting often. Bivouacked little before sunset near Gum Springs having crossed Broad Run.

Wednesday, June 17   Marched to Gum Springs. Heard firing in front apparently towards Leesburg or Aldie

Thursday, June 18   Lay in woods in same place as yesterday. Col Chamberlain quite sick & sent to a neighboring house. Rained with thunder & lightning in aft & Eve. Reports of fight of yesterday. Our cavalry drove infantry of Enemy. Col. Doughty killed.

Friday, June 19   Regiment moved out on picket. Left wing in reserve. In afternoon corps moved to Aldie. Formed Division & bivouacked. Ordered by Major to act as field officer. Rain & thunder during the Evening.

Saturday, June 20   Cloudy still. Rained most of the night. Few rebel prisoners brought in. Col C brought up. No better rather worse.

Sunday, June 21   In night we were wakened by an orderly with orders to be ready to march at 3 A.M. 1st Div. marched beyond Middleburg. Went south of the village & turned to the west. Soon met the Enemy. I threw forward a line of skirmishers. My own com. Drove the Enemy a half mile or so. Enemy shelled our advancing line. West killed near me. Robinson & others wounded. Robinson taken to hosp. Buried

Monday, June 22   In camp near Aldie. Col & Major still sick John Chamberlain came. On return to camp detoured on the way to bury West. He lies near the stream above the stone bridge about two miles beyond Middleburg.

Tuesday, June 23   Sent Bailey to act as Corps mail agent

Friday, June 26   Broke camp Early & marched on the Leesburg road. Light rain & road muddy. Marched through Leesburg crossed the Potomac on pontoons. Marched till late in the Evening & bivouacked.

Saturday, June 27   Marched Early. Cloudy. Crossed the Monocacy at ford. Marched through Buck co. Encamped about six within 2 two miles of Frederick.

Sunday, June 28   In camp near Frederick. Sick & weak. Recd large mail three letters from Susie. Col. C. & Major got app. No others

Monday, June 29   Marched through Frederick & bivouacked for the night.

JUNE 21, 1863 — JULY 3, 1863

Tuesday, June 30   Marched bivouacked near Unionville. Rebel cavalry had gone through.

Wednesday, July 1   Marched to Hanover & rested there two hours Firing heard Westward. Moved about Sunset towards Gettysburg & having marched Eight miles bivouacked at Eleven. Report that McClellan has replaced Hooker Fight at G. with out decided success.

Thursday, July 2   Moved Early Cannonading began in front. Brigade went into the fight at 4 P.M. Marching by the flank we filed to the left & under fire of shells went to the Extreme left. Our Reg. held the left of the brigade. We Expected an attempt to turn our left. The Enemy soon made his appearance. We fought at close quarters more than 2 hours. They flanked us & hurt us severely. Our men fell rapidly. At last we charged drove them & took many prisoners. Then we took the crest of the next hill. Sent out skirmishers & took about 20 more prisoners. Alabama brigade, 15 & 47 & 4 & 5 Texas. Regiment behaved nobly.

Friday, July 3   Were relieved in the morning & moved towards the center & lay there all day. There was occasional shelling during the morning & about midday there opened the most tremendous cannonading. The shells flew chiefly to right & left. Some over & amongst us— Nobody hurt. Gen Meade rode past. Reported Gen Longstreet taken & 2500 prisoners. About sunset a portion of the 6th drove the Enemy in front & took a battery.

Saturday, July 4 We lay in the same place. All quiet. Wrote Susie. Letter went by citizen. In afternoon rain came on & continued till night.

Sunday, July 5 Sent letter to Hill. Brigade moved out on picket. Occupied the field held on 3d inst. by rebel battery. A terrible sight. dead horses & men all about. Sixth corps gone past to the front. Towards night went back, rejoined the corps & marched south west in thick darkness & through deep mud. Bivouacked near midnight. All Exceedingly tired. Kendall died.

Monday, July 6 Moved about one mile. halted a while then went back a short distance & bivouacked for the night

Tuesday, July 7 Marched Early Cloudy & rainy with deep sticky mud. Bivouacked about 7 miles above Frederick. Went to house for provisions. Read mail—3 letters from Susie, one from Verrill, one from home, one from Ordnance Dept. Rain came on in night.—The march very hard.

Wednesday, July 8 Marched Early—Extremely muddy Rain falling heavily during the first part of the day. Bivouacked Early near Middletown.

Thursday, July 9 Moved over the mountain & bivouacked near the foot about the middle of the afternoon. The day rather hot.

JULY 4, 1863 — JULY 13, 1863

Friday, July 10   Reveiller Early but we did not move until the sun was high. We marched out until we came upon the Sharpsburg pike then turned westward & came upon our cavalry pickets we threw out Skirmishers from our brigade & moved forward with part for support. Skirmishers engaged the Enemy two or three hours in the aft. Lost several killed wounded & prisoners. Place near Tilghmantown on map Fair Play Letter from Susie Jul 3. Bivouacked with the reserves of the regiment in wood in rear of the pike. Picketed on the pike.

Saturday, July 11   Moved northward on the pike. The 2d on our left & 12th on left of that Halted near the stream of Antietam. 3d corps came up in our rear. Bathed in stream & felt better. Corps moved northward in line with regiments in double column. Moved by left flank. Halted & other troops moved forward. Wrote Susie.

Sunday, July 12   We went on as yesterday sometimes moving by the front & sometimes moving by flank to the left. We must be I judge nearly between Hagerstown & Williamsport. In the aft a heavy shower came on. We moved into the wood. Recd a mail Letters from Susie Pauline Em & Mother. Slight skirmishing in front. Moved back into field & bivouacked about sunset.

Monday, July 13   Struck tents in the afternoon & moved out towards the front. Found the 6th Corps on the right throwing up breastworks of logs & Earth. Bivouacked in the wood in front of the works

& sent out pickets about 200 under Col Conner. Our surgeon came. Raining at night. [*deleted*: Light rain in morning. Reveiller about 7] Prisoners coming in from picket line report Lee across the river. Picket firing heard. Wrote Susie Reed & Verrill. Bivouacked in same place. [*written on side of page*: Error]

Tuesday, July 14 Moved forward. Rebs over the river. brigade moved by right flank. Found Earthworks of enemy on prominent places & obstructing the road to Wmport Went back for Sutler, Neal Page. Bivouacked for the night in an open field. Rained. Prisoners taken from the Enemy. 200 in all went past. Sutler furnished us with Eatables.

Wednesday, July 15 Reveiller about 2 A.M. Marched about light. Raining at first, but soon cleared off warm. Marched rapidly Eastward across South Mountain towards Harpers Ferry. Saw Herson & Capt Carr on the way. Hard match. Not above 125 men came in. Capt Clark left gone to Sharpsburg. Bivouacked in wood about 5 P.M.

Thursday, July 16 Marched Early Bivouacked before noon near Barkerville. Sent for [*indecipherable word*], put up tents, made reports, etc. About came [*two indecipherable words*] Mrs Fogg came up. Camp commanders began rolls. Bathed in brook. Sent letter to Susie.

Friday, July 17 Recd. letters. one from Susie & one from father. Moved Early in the forenoon in rain.

Crossed the river on pontoons & marched three or four miles southward on the pike. Bivouacked in field. Trouble about straw. Slept well with Dr Baker.

Saturday, July 18 Broke camp Early & marched down the pike through Lovetsville? Halted about 11 A.M.

Sunday, July 19 Moved about 5 miles.

Monday, July 20 Moved Early 14 miles to Goose Creek.

Tuesday, July 21 [*deleted*: Moved from camp about 7 A.M & marched to the vicinity of Snickers Gap. Recd mail at night but no letters. Wrote the Rs, Verrill? Pauline & Susie.] Error revise

Wednesday, July 22 Moved suddenly about 11 A.M. southward across the road to Upperville & near the place of our skirmish on the 21st Aft. Bivouacked near Rectortown Early Nothing worthy of note.

Thursday, July 23 Moved from camp & marched towards Manassas Gap. Evening near dusk. We have marched 12 miles at least, over bad roads & none at all. We formed double column & marched over the hills back & forth over rocks & through mud. Relieved the 3rd Corps & went to the front on the western slope of a steep hill. Rations short. Considerable skirmishing during the day by 3d Corps & some shelling from the Enemy. A battery being on hill facing us. Day was warm.

Friday, July 24 Woke before sunrise. All still near us. Cannonading further down the mountain just audible, possibly at Chester Gap. We moved Early forward. In the forenoon carried the crest of a hill thickly wooded & Exceedingly steep. Brigade went to the top of the first crest & skirmish a picket and Major [*indecipherable name*] went to second. We were recalled & quite Exhausted The Corps went on past to final object we moved back in aft. & bivouacked. Saw the 3d file past. We [*three indecipherable words*] & nice cool breeze. Wrote & sent Susie a long letter. Weather warm

Saturday, July 25 Marched about sun Went back through the Gap. Turned to the right & moved down the mountain inclining Southward. Men have no rations only fresh meat part of that stolen. They have subsisted mainly on dewberries. Bivouacked near the mountain 14 miles from Warrenton. Went with Col. C. on picket. Heavy thunder shower. were posting the pickets until near midnight. Col & I slept until after the rain subsided. Men had rations. Had plenty of [*indecipherable word*].

Sunday, July 26 Woke Early finding fire rather warm at my feet. Weather clear. Had difficulty in getting in pickets. Horse used up & I walked part of the days march. Halted in middle of the afternoon & rested. Mounted Fields horse & afterward got another. Halted near Warrenton about noon.

JULY 24, 1863 — AUG. 7, 1863

Monday, July 27 Marched at 5½ in morning through Warrenton or rather past it & Encamped about two miles southwest in afternoon.

Tuesday, July 28 In camp. Mail. 2 letters from Susie—1 from Pauline. 1 from Mr Goff (answered)

Wednesday, July 29 In Camp

Thursday, July 30 In Camp.

Sunday, Aug. 2 All quiet in camp. as usual. Ordered on fatigue duty

Monday, Aug. 3 Marched Early with one hundred men from regt—100 from [*indecipherable word*] of the others of brigade—all under Col Conner. Day Exceedingly hot. Halted for orders at Gen Meades Hd.Qrs. Thence marched with my detachment to Warrenton Junction. Began work on corduroy.

Tuesday, Aug. 4 Completed work here & moved back to next run.

Wednesday, Aug. 5 Marched to [*indecipherable word*] having fixed road on the way

Thursday, Aug. 6 Began work but afterwards ordered further down toward Junction at Warrenton. Corduroying through woods.

Friday, Aug. 7 In same place

Saturday, Aug. 8 At work still on road.—

Sunday, Aug. 9 Rested—Very warm. Wrote letters.

Monday, Aug. 10 Completed work & returned to camp reaching it in the Evening—found letter from Susie & one from [*indecipherable name*].

Tuesday, Aug. 11 Rested—Battalions drill in aft.

Wednesday, Aug. 12 Rested. Men Washing.

Thursday, Aug. 13 Cloudy in morning but cleared off—cooler Letter from Susie—Paymaster came to regiment. Sent up request to be ordered to look after absentees.

Friday, Aug. 14 Paymaster commenced paying regiment

Saturday, Aug. 15 Sent Susie Gov. Order No 227 dated Aug 14. payable to me or order for $50 Pd Land similar order No 226 for Clifford. Letter from Susie.

Sunday, Aug. 16 Wrote note for the Maine Camp Hosp. Association. Wrote Susie & Hannah. Letters from Pauline Morrill.

Sunday, Aug. 23 Services aft on our grounds. Wrote Susie, Verrill.

Monday, Aug. 24 Drill Rode to see Barnard. Col C came in aft. Recd letter from Lt. Chamberlain.

Tuesday, Aug. 25 Cloudy & cool. Col C. takes command. Capt. Clark Div. off of day. Sent Fernald for coat

Friday, Aug. 28 Col. Gilmore came.

Saturday, Aug. 29 Made out papers for muster. Took oaths & affidavits before Allen. Attended the Execution of the five men deserters. Anniversary of our first muster.

Sunday, Aug. 30 Breezy day. Mrs Fogg & Mrs Mayhew here & Col. Conner. Wrote Mr Wheeler & sent letter to I. P. Starrett. Finished Muster

Monday, Aug. 31 Letter from Susie & one from Keene. [*deleted*: Rode to 5th Battery Lt. Frichet sick. Dr. Herson leaves us—Mrs Fogg & Mrs Mayhew visit us & Col Conner.] Dr. Herson going home today.

Tuesday, Sept. 1 Worked on Rolls. Drilled regt in aft. Held parade. Letter from Coburn. Wrote [*indecipherable name*] $5.

Wednesday, Sept. 2 Cloudy, but less cool. Bought the [*indecipherable word*] for Land.

Thursday, Sept. 3 Sent Susie $20 on U. S. Treas note. Wrote Sutler. Rode up picket line with Clark.

Friday, Sept. 4 Under Resolutions. Alan letter to Keene & one for Dr. Herson. Attended recitation at Brigade Hd.Qrs. in Eve. Recd letters from [*indecipherable name*] & Verrill Wrote [*indecipherable name*] in the Evening.

Saturday, Sept. 5 Letter from Pauline—Not answered—

Sunday, Sept 6 Rode to nineteenth Maine by way of Belchertown.

Monday, Sept. 7 Study Tactics & drill. Recd letters & wrote Mac.

Tuesday, Sept. 8 Brigade drill—

Wednesday, Sept. 9 No drill or other duty.

Thursday, Sept. 10 Brigade drill.

Friday, Sept. 11 [*indecipherable word*] at Brigade HdQrs. Recd long letter from Susie Changed camp.

Saturday, Sept. 12 Mrs Fogg & Mayhew visit us. Ordered in Eve to be ready to move to support 2d=Race

Sunday, Sept. 13 Inspected the regiment & streets. Wrote Verrill. The 2d Corps making a reconnaisance Cannonading began about 10 A.M. & receding.

Monday, Sept. 14 Long letter from Susie & one from Hannah. Wrote Verrill—

Tuesday, Sept. 15 Brigade drill. Ordered to have teams up & be ready to move at once. No letters. Wrote Susie in Evening & sent picture & $5. All ready to move

SEPT. 5, 1863 — SEPT. 24, 1863

Wednesday, Sept. 16 Reveiller at 3 A.M. Moved about six across Rappahannock. Encamped about 4 P.M. within a mile of Culpepper. Bivouacked & slept comfortably.

Thursday, Sept. 17 Anniversary of the battle of Antietam. We moved at 6 A.M. through Culpepper, a village of perhaps 1500 people. Other corps in advance. L Said to be at Cedar Mountain.— We Encamp in afternoon near road, two miles out from Culpepper & put up tents. Cannonading in the distance on our left. Rain came on in Evening. Recd letters from Keene, Hill, Weston & Plummer delivered in bag. Wrote Hill & L. Hall & Surgeon.

Friday, Sept. 18 Raining heavily.

Sunday, Sept. 20 Inspected the Regt & had service. All quiet.

Monday, Sept. 21 Ordered suddenly on picket with 600 men. Col. Jenkins Gen. Field Officer of Corps. Regt Inspected by Capt. West & highly complimented.

Tuesday, Sept. 22 Letter from Col. Gilmore.

Wednesday, Sept. 23 On picket duty. Came in & got pay. $269 & sent $20 to Susie.

Thursday, Sept. 24 Came in from picket. Reported to Div. Hd.Qrs. Under orders to be ready to move. Recd valise & box of clothing. Sent letter to Susie.

Friday, Sept. 25 Sent father two $50 checks Nos. 326 & 327 dated Sep 23d Washington.

Sunday, Oct. 4 Sent Susie letter with check No 328 dated Sep 23. W city.

Thursday, Oct. 8 Letters from Pauline & Nettie Hubbard. Draft recd—

Friday, Oct. 9 Letter from Susie.

Saturday, Oct. 10 Broke camp before light and moved to the front beyond Long Mountain about 5 or 6 miles. Remained all day & returned to camp. Teams ordered to the rear. Slept in old camp. Sent letter to Susie.

Sunday, Oct. 11 Moved Early through Culpepper, picket forming with cavalry rear guard. We made a stand on the range of hills north of Brandy Station but no force of the Enemy appeared. 2 guns & a few squadrons of cavalry hung upon our rear guard. We moved to our old camp at Beverly F.

Monday, Oct. 12 2d & 3d divisions across the river. Ours moved out & massed behind old corps HdQrs. A few cavalry scouts of the Enemy appear. Our forces deploying to the left on the other side. Our brigade crossed in the afternoon & advanced to the heights, 5th on the right, 6th on the left. Cavalry & artillery drove the Enemy to Culpepper & took some prisoners. We occupy the heights & built fires in camp & on picket. Fires in front & on the left. Slept soundly.

SEPT. 25, 1863 — OCT. 16, 1863

Tuesday, Oct. 13 Roused Early. Moved without bugle call. Our brigade bringing up the rear of the whole army. With companies B & C I guarded the rear. Crossed the river in the morning about 8 Rested & then moved on & encamped between Belchertown & Warrenton Junction. Cannonading at night in our rear, but distant. All the Army moving together comfortably.

Wednesday, Oct. 14 Moved about 3 A.M. to Manassus Junction. The Enemy presses our rear. The 2d Corps held them in check. We halted on a high hill 4 or 5 miles west from the Junction. Our Div. halted at the Junction about 4 P.M. Batteries in position. The cannonading in the rear heavier & at 5 we moved back on the double quick about 3 miles. The 2d corps driving the Enemy & took 5 pieces of artillery & several hundred prisoners. We formed line near railroad & about 8 P.M. quietly withdrew. Marched back & crossed over Bull Run & halted about 2 in the night on the heights near Centreville

Thursday, Oct. 15 Moved 7 A.M. Passed through the Centreville heights through the Earthworks. The 1st & 6th Corps in camp there & battery of heavy guns. Halted near Fairfax in the afternoon. Rain in Evening.

Friday, Oct. 16 Raining—Col. sick in Camp. In afternoon went on picket with 300 men from the brigade. Relieved 1st & 2d Brigade. Before the line was Established the General Sounded &

orders came to rejoin the brigade. Called in pickets & moved upon the column. Marched in heavy Showers to near Centreville works & bivouacked, the rain ceasing. Col. in ambulance.

Saturday, Oct. 17 Remained all day in Bivouac. Pontoons gone to the front. Sent letter to Susie. Lt. Bickford has 20 days leave.

Sunday, Oct. 18 Moved at 5 A.M. back to junction of Centreville & Little River roads near Fairfax. Enemy reported moving up their pickets on our front & right. Bivouacked & sent for teams. Bugle blew as we were unpacking. Marched by an out of the way route to "Ox Road" & went into camp with the Expectation that it would be a [*two indecipherable words*] camp. Col. C came up & slept at a house letter from Susie & one from Mr. Robinson.

Monday, Oct. 19 Bugles blew & orders came to move. The Div. going on the Centreville road. Thunder & rain in the morning, but towards noon it cleared up and was cool & pleasant Bivouac at 3½ oclock on the 2d Bull Run battlefield. Our Div on the slope occupied by the left of McDowells troops. Bones of the dead all about.

Tuesday, Oct. 20 Reveiller Early & we attempted to move at 3 but the roads were obstructed & it was daylight before we left the battlefield. Marched through across the railroad & on the Warrenton road. Crossed Broad Run & Encamped near New Baltimore. Bivouac & slept well.

Wednesday, Oct. 21 Rains came. Put up wall tent. Mail came. Two letters from Susie with picture. One from Hill & one from Verrill & one from father.

Thursday, Oct. 22 Moved camp to a neighboring hill. Wrote Hill & Tenny in regard to Henry Brown &c. Sent Recommendation for Strout

Friday, Oct. 23 Brigade moved across the road to new camping ground. Cold rain came on. Recd letters from Susie Pauline, Keene—Wrote S. Mr R. Hubbard & Keene.

Saturday, Oct. 24 Cold & rainy but quite comfortable with pleasant fire in front. General Sounded about 3 P.M. & we marched about five toward Auburn. A slow & tedious march at first hindered by bad crossings and too rapid at last. Bivouacked about eight

Sunday, Oct. 25 Cool & clear. Got up about 8 well rested. Changed camp. Moving about 50 rods to rear Cold. Col. went to Ambulance. Col. Chamberlain on picket HdQrs. at Auburn.

Monday, Oct. 26 Very cold. Mail but not letter for me. All quiet. Signalling last night.

Tuesday, Oct. 27 Cold

Wednesday, Oct. 28 Cold. Put up tent.

Thursday, Oct. 29 Cool. Squad drill

Friday, Oct. 30 Moved about 8 A.M. & Encamped near Three Mile Station.

Saturday, Oct. 31 Mustered the Reg.

Sunday, Nov. 1 Worked on Rolls & in the aft. went with teams on Errand. Cannot do much because tent not fixed.

Wednesday, Nov. 4 Visited 3d corps & had many pleasant calls. Letter from Sue at night with pictures. Indications of a move Reserve artillery going to Warrenton Junction & Manassas.

Thursday, Nov. 5 Drilled regt in aft. In forenoon attended to lessons Letter from Nettie Hubbard.

Friday, Nov. 6 <u>Blank</u> [*Ellis Spear's entry*]

Saturday, Nov. 7 Moved Early towards Belcherton & Rap. Station. Encountered the Enemy about 3 P.M. drove them in by Our skirmish line. shift our brigade with part of the 6th corps. The Sixth occupying the chief part of the line took the works with bayonet. 8 Stands of colors, 4 guns, cassions horses & everything & 1200 prisoners. <u>Col. Gilmore in rear in Ambulance</u>. Bivouacked in wood near the works.

Sunday, Nov. 8 Moved down to Kelly Ford & crossed & went two miles & bivouacked. My regt as flankers. Cold.

OCT. 29, 1863 — NOV. 22, 1863

Monday, Nov. 9 Drilled regt. The whole div. under Arms for shouting Hardtack to Gen Bartlett. Moved back with rest of Div. recrossed the river. Bivouacked near ford Exceedingly cold.

Tuesday, Nov. 10 Moved into wood and Encamped.

Thursday, Nov. 12 Rode to R. Station. Letter from Susie—Wrote her. much warmer

Saturday, Nov. 14 Division Reviewed. Major Cilley called. 1st Maine near Morrisville. At Div. HdQrs. Rain Letters from Susie & one from Pauline.

Sunday, Nov. 15 Rainy but clear in aft. Wrote letters. Verrill, Susie, Pauline, Hill.

Tuesday, Nov. 17 Nothing of importance

Wednesday, Nov. 18 Col. Gilmore left & Col. Chamberlain on sick leave. Attended to rations. Letter from Susie. Sent letter to Mr. Robinson.

Thursday, Nov. 19 Moved at Eight A.M. Crossed the Rappahannock & Encamped with corps two miles from the ford. Regt. rear guard today. Poor George died. It shall be a sad anniversary to me.

Sunday, Nov. 22 Sent by letter (B) [*indecipherable name*] to Washington a 50 check payable by asst. Treas. of N.Y. (No. 557) dated Washington Nov 22d to my wife. Also to Edwin Reed one of same date & amt. No. 556. Sent letters to the Rs. one to Pauline with $5 for presents.

Monday, Nov. 23 On Board of Survey to investigate bread deficiency. In the afternoon drilled battalion. In Eve attended to the Dv muster. Rewrote Report of Board. Recd letters from Susie & Pauline. Poor Mac is dead, a grevious blow. Wrote Susie & Mrs M. Ordered to move. Our corps are to cross the Rapidan at Culpepper Ford & that only promises a long march. Threatens rain.

Tuesday, Nov. 24 Reveiller about 4 A.M. Moved about 6 A.M. in the rain about a mile when the order was countermanded & we returned to camp.

Wednesday, Nov. 25 Cleared off. We remain in camp. Letter from Susie.

Thursday, Nov. 26 Moved Early & crossed the Rapidan & crossed at Culpepper Ford. With 20th and 44th flanked the Division & at night picketed the Div. Encamping between 2d Div. & 2d Corps near the house where Stonewall Jackson died.

Friday, Nov. 27 Moved to [blank space] near the unfinished Railroad. The cavalry were fighting one brigade of Greggs, 1st Maine there. Met Cilley. Bivouacked

Saturday, Nov. 28 Moved to the right in heavy rain. Bivouacked near Cross Roads at Robertsons tavern. Rain ceased & cooler. Skirmish firing on the left as we moved up & some cannonading. Cold & cloudy.

NOV. 23, 1863 — DEC. 4, 1863

Sunday, Nov. 29 Moved early to the front. Sixth Corps troops returning on same road. Very muddy. Our Brigade relieved the corps on picket. My regiment on Extreme left. Had one man severely wounded while relieving Enemy strongly fortified Clear & cool. Gen Sykes came to my HdQrs. & reconnoitered

Monday, Nov. 30 Sent out the women & children negroes & whites Artillery opened at night on the right center and left. Enemy replied on the right. Silent on the left & center. In the afternoon Gen Rice advanced a line twice. I kept up a fire on the pickets in front of me. They afterward threw several shells at our men & batteries. All quiet at night

Tuesday, Dec. 1 Quiet. Indications of falling back. The house which I occupy pretty thoroughly searched. Two pistols & a bowie knife found. Desks & other things disturbed in my absence. At night orders came to fall back at three in the morning.

Wednesday, Dec. 2 Pickets of all corps fell back at 3 A.M. Reached the Rapidan at 8 A.M. having marched 12 miles in 5 hours Marched three or four miles north of the river & bivouacked

Thursday, Dec. 3 Moved at 8 A.M. Reached the Rappahannock at 2 P.M. Men Exceedingly tired & hungry. Bivouacked for the night.

Friday, Dec. 4 Moved to Encampment near bridge. Orders to be ready to move. Mails came up.

Saturday, Dec. 5 Cold—Fixing quarters. Letter from Susie.

Sunday, Dec. 6 Exceedingly cool. Cake from Susie. Capt Flynn of the 9th Mass. breakfasted with me Orders countermanded & we build our tents.

Monday, Dec. 7 Cool. Forwarded the leave requests for Clark & Morrill

Tuesday, Dec. 15 Work on quarters.

Wednesday, Dec. 16 Cool. Letter from N. Hubbard. Wrote Mrs. MacIntyre

Thursday, Dec. 17 Cold & rainy. Letter from Col. Chamberlain. Sent letters to Clark Mr. Scott, Mrs Mac & Susie.

Saturday, Dec. 19 Letter from Susie.

Sunday, Dec. 20 Litchfield left for Maine. Cold. Instructed Regt.

Tuesday, Dec. 22 Capt. [*indecipherable name*] called. Rode to Army HdQrs with him on a fools Errand. Letter from Verrill.

Wednesday, Dec. 23 Recd letter from Susie.

Tuesday, Dec. 29 Put up application for leave & pay for self & Land.

Wednesday, Dec. 30 No trains. Lands leave came back.

Thursday, Dec. 31 Cold & rainy. Busy with muster rolls. Leave returned disapproved.

Friday, Jan 1, 1864 Rep Sta. Va. 2½ A.M. The old year has just gone out. It has been Eventful. I have much to be thankful for. Carried safely through what dangers! God help me to be wiser & better in the year to come
[*final entry in 1863 diary*]

[1864 DIARY]

Friday, Jan. 1 In camp.

Saturday, Jan. 2 In camp. Land left camp for home.

Sunday, Jan. 3 In camp. Sidelinger gone home.

Monday, Jan. 4 Orders to be ready to move. Leave of absence came down.

Tuesday, Jan. 5 Left camp at nine A.M. reached Washington at 2½ P.M. found wife & Litchfields wife.

Wednesday, Jan. 6 Visited Capitol with wife, Litchfield & wife & Mrs Gilmore & Fitch.

Thursday, Jan. 7 At American House. (Dyer's.)

Friday, Jan. 8 Friday night Missed morning train. Left W—in Evening—

Saturday, Jan. 9 Reached NY City about one (1) P.M. Called at Wilders. Left on the Boston R.R. at 3 P.M.

Sunday, Jan. 10 Reached Boston at 5 A.M. after tedious ride. Slept till 9—Attended Old South Church with Chaplain Adams. Wrote in Evening in my room.

Monday, Jan. 11 Started from Bo. for Portland & Bath. Crossed the river in a boat & reached Wiscasset at 9 P.M. Visited Mr Robinson—

Tuesday, Jan. 12 Made calls & in aft. rode to fathers—

Wednesday, Jan. 13 Made calls

Thursday, Jan. 14 Returned to Wiscasset. Called to see all the girls—that is went to Hubbards. Susies companions

Friday, Jan. 15 Started for Boston with Land & took night train for N.Y.

Saturday, Jan. 16 Breakfasted at the Astor & took train for W. Arriving at 6 P.M. Met Hill

Sunday, Jan. 17 Called on Andrews

Monday, Jan. 18 Paid & shopped.

Tuesday, Jan. 19 Came to the Army with Susie.

Wednesday, Jan. 20 Sent off Report to Hodsdon.

Thursday, Jan. 21 Wrote the Gov. in reg and to commissions Sent up paper for having a detail of officers & men sent home to recruit.

Sunday, Jan. 24 Rode over to Sixth Maine with Capt Clark.

Tuesday, Jan. 26 Rode out with the Ladies as far as J M. Botts.

Thursday, Jan. 28 On court martial. Notified that my history of operations &c. had been recd at Augusta.

Sunday, Jan. 31 no service—

Monday, Feb. 1 Orders to send names of men to be detailed for recruiting leave On court martial

Tuesday, Feb. 2 "Swapped" horses—

Wednesday, Feb. 3 Windy & cool—

Sunday, Mar. 20 Cool cloudy

Monday, Mar. 21 Cool & Snowing heavily

Tuesday, Mar. 22 Court martial. Snow one foot in depth

Wednesday, Mar. 23 Wife went home

Thursday, Mar. 24 On Court Martial Target firing commenced.

Friday, Mar. 25 On Court Martial Orders recd consolidating corps.

Friday, Apr. 1 Drills.

Saturday, Apr. 2 Cool & windy. Gen Griffin returned. Recitation of Company Commanders.

Sunday, Apr. 3   Cool. Walked a while. Two letters from my wife.

Monday, Apr. 4   Rode to Gen. Bartlett in A.M. returning in Evening. Ordered to draw coats for the men. Called upon Col. Hazen in the Morning. Brigade HdQrs. changed.

Thursday, Apr. 7   Court Martial. Visitors. Mrs. Mayhew, Mrs Dr Ripley Capt Livingston & wife of the 7th N.J. & a Quaker Doctoress.

Friday, Apr. 8   Court Martial. Two letters from S. Q.M. returned. Held round.

Saturday, Apr. 9   On Court Martial. Had two cases from 44th. Heavy rain. Letter from Col. C. asking the No. of rifles the brigade took at the battle of Gettysburg. Letter from S.

Thursday, Apr. 14   Check to Susie 75$ 700. Washington Apr 12th

Saturday, Apr. 23   Rode to 5th & 6th Maine. Letter from Susie.

Sunday, Apr. 24   Pleasant & warm during the day. Rainy in the night.

Sunday, May 1   Moved from camp at 9 A.M. Bivouacked near Ingalls Station—Men. Sent for pocket compass by Fitch. Recd letter from H—

Monday, May 2   Pleasant till night. Severe showers with wind. Letters from Susie, IPS & Adj Gen P.M.

APR. 3, 1864 — MAY 7, 1864

Tuesday, May 3 Marched at 1 P.M. & bivouacked at 4 three miles north of Culpepper.

Wednesday, May 4 Marched at Midnight. crossed the Rapidan at Germanna Ford little past sunrise & bivouacked on the pike a short distance beyond the crossing of the plank road. Went into line of battle the right of the regiment on that road.

Thursday, May 5 In the morning reported that the Enemy was advancing upon us. Threw up breastworks & levelled the trees in front. In the aft (half past twelve) the Div. & other parts of corps advanced—about a mile & a half during the Evening until flanked & then fell back to works. Lost five (5) killed & 53 wounded 32 missing.

53
5
32
90

Friday, May 6 Fell in regiment at 3 A.M. Brigade relieved troops on front line—formed line on right of the pike & awaited the attack on the right. The right failing finally to force the Enemy back. Brigade lay all day & at dark fell back to works.

Saturday, May 7 Ordered out with 118th & 2 regular regiments (Col. Herring [*indecipherable word*] while) to the Enemy it having been reported that they were falling back on the right. Drove them to the Edge of the woods where they opened on us with artillery & musketry. Fell back out of reach of artillery & held the line.

Sunday, May 8 At one oclock in the morning fell back quietly & marched on the Spotsylvania road. Our advance met the Enemy 3 miles from Spotsylvania & drove them two miles—Part of our brigade (44th, 8 & 18th & others attacked the Enemy & were after a while repulsed with heavy loss. We were sent to the front & became Engaged. Fought in woods. Took about 100 prisoners & lost several men. Capt Morrell killed. Lieuts Prince Melcher wounded. Fought under Crawford Supported Pa. Reserves. Lay under heavy shelling before charging. Lost one man

Monday, May 9 Fell back in rear of lines at 3 A.M. & lay all day. The 6th corps went to the left & the 2d to the right. Earthworks thrown up for infantry in the front & for artillery in different positions Enemy made an attack on our lines but were driven back by our infantry & artillery. Recd. Mail. Letter from S. dated April 29th. [*deleted*: Lay under shelling in the woods]

Tuesday, May 10 Ordered before daybreak to be ready to move against the Enemy or repel attack. Reported in Richmond papers that Butler is within ten (10) miles of Richmond on the South side. Reported that Butler has beaten the Enemy & Sherman driven Johnston at Dalton Laurel Hill Brigade moved in front of the works. 16th Mich as skirmishers—formed in three lines on Extreme left regular brigade on right to charge across the opening on works of Enemy. 2d corps to charge on right. Charge on right failing did not move fell back without loss. Bivouack on hill rear of batteries of Div. 6th corps said to have broken the right of the Enemy & taken 2000 prisoners & 12 guns.

Wednesday, May 11 Some firing in night. slightly cloudy in morning but warm. Continuous skirmish firing. Our artillery commenced shelling & Enemy replied. Sergt. Overlock wounded. Sent letter to Susie. Moved my regiment back to avoid the Enemys shell & lay all the afternoon. The shot thrown by them were spherical case from at least 20 pounders. Rainy at night with thunder & lightning.

Thursday, May 12 Moved to the right with brigade at 3 P.M. Occupied works with one line of battle. open field in front. Burnside & Hancock to assault the right of the Enemy at 5 A.M.—7 A.M cannonade & musketry heavy on the left; gradually receding. Artillery on the center firing occasionally. About 7 moved back & occupied works vacated the right of 6th Corps. Our left advancing. Moved to works again at 10 4 P.M. moved back to the left to 2d corps with Div. & massed in col of regts in woods.

Friday, May 13 Night March Marched back before daybreak to old place. Raining Division formed line & Entrenched. Shelled by the Enemy & Leu Griffin slightly hurt. Congratulatory order from Gen. Meade. Artillery firing on our side

& some musketry at 5 P.M. Wrote Susie this morn & the father of Capt Morrell. Bivouacked in rain. Moved suddenly with corps left in front to the left & after a severe march through woods & over terribly muddy roads reached the works on the left directly East of Spotsylvania. Passed through the 9th Army corps to the left

Saturday, May 14 Heavy showers in the morning but gradually grew clearer. Corps facing west & Southwest. Part at West of 6th Corps in view moving to left. Enemy about a mile distant in works. At 5½ PM one movement. A brigade of our Div. (1st) took a house on the left & were relieved by a Div of the 6th Corps. The Div. was driven back & the 1st Brigade advanced & retook the house. Battery D 5th US Co. in front of us. Relieved pickets. Got cold. Frequent showers till night.

Sunday, May 15 Some rain in the night. Cloudy & wind Eastward. Corps in same place—3 days ration of bread issued Early. Lay all day. No fire of either army. At night under arms & 1st & 2d Brigades moved out anticipating an attack from the Enemy—Col. Chamberlain came & Gen. Bartlett being ill, took command of the brigade. At night reported officially that Averill had cut the E. Ten. R.R. and destroyed a depot of supplies at Dalton & Butler has carried the outer work of Ft. Darling. Merriam, son of my old friend Artemus, came to see me now Sgt. Major 31st 2d Brs. 2d Div. [*indecipherable word*]

MAY 14, 1864 — MAY 21, 1864

Monday, May 16 Got up at 5½ oclock. Foggy Gradually cleared & became warm. Lay all day quietly. At night preparations made for an attack or show of preparations. Shower at night. Reported that reinforcements have come up. Col. C. took command.

Tuesday, May 17 Foggy Lieu Howe of the 14th N.Y. Heavy artillery called. Gradually clearing up. Wrote Susie & sent letter by Butler. Went out with Gen B & other regtl commanders to look out ground for advance. Moved with Div. at dark & took position on left of it Lay down.

Wednesday, May 18 Not very well. Cloudy Threw up works. Artillery opened at 5. Some musketry on right. Enemy replied with few pieces. Brisk artillery fire but slackened gradually & quite subsided by noon. Clear & warm. Mail in afternoon Letters from Susie one from Pauline & from Nettie.

Thursday, May 19 Quiet until night when a corps of the enemy attempted to break through the right & get possession of the road & trains. Tylers Div & Kildeas brigade of heavy artillery drove them back capturing 1000 prisoners.

Friday, May 20 No movement Col. on Court Martial at Corps HdQrs Very warm.

Saturday, May 21 Orders in the night to be ready to repel Attack Mail. 2 letters from Susie One from Col. G. one from Land. Fell back about midday the

Enemy Evidently withdrawing at the same time. Some skirmishing. Marched about 12 miles & bivouaced in woods, having crossed the R.R. & Ny river towards the West. Slight shower with thunder. Cannonading on the right

Sunday, May 22   Orders to march at 4. Moved a short distance & took up position in line of battle. Moved at 10¼ on road leading South—having crossed the "Ta" early in morning. Encountered the rear guard of the Enemy about midday & 1st Mich, 20th & 118 advanced & drove them out, artillery & cavalry. Bivouacked about six oclock. Took several prisoners during the day, one at night. Straggler from the 38th Va. reported that his brigade came up the night before from Richmond. Reported Butler driven back.

Monday, May 23   Bugle call. Reveiller at 4½. Marched leisurely S.W. & S. & crossed the North Anna 3¼ oclock. Some firing in advance. Cavalry above ford. Firing commenced suddenly. The Enemy threw forward having [*indecipherable word*] batteries & met a sudden advance Brigade formed quickly I led up the regiment on double quick. Hit by shrapnel in groin & bruised. I went to rear & lay down. No further firing. Held the enemy in check. Shelling came in from enemy. Our batteries replying with speed Corps picked up stragglers all the way.

Tuesday, May 24   [*written on side*: Should have been entered in April]

MAY 22, 1864 — MAY 27, 1864

[*circled in pencil*: 50 rounds on person
　40 in boxes
　10 not issued till <u>marching</u> orders recd.
　3 days full rations in havasacks not issued till orders recd.
　(coffee sugar & salt & bread 3 days in knap sack)]

Went back to the tent & lay down. Leg sore. Corps taken about 500 prisoners. Advanced two miles to R.R. Heavy firing on the left [*indecipherable word*] & I report a [*indecipherable word*]

Wednesday, May 25　Slept pretty late with Doctor near Div Amb which moved about 9 A.M. to river. Div advanced to front on left two or three miles. Sixth corps on right. Fifth made common line with Burnside Negro troops reported coming up. Chaplain came. Hospital moved down river a half mile behind Army HdQrs. 500 of the Enemy came in & laid down their arms.

Thursday, May 26　Some firing on the line. Our corps thrown across the R.R. & fortified. The road thoroughly destroyed. Remained with the Dr. Ordered at night to move. Corps Evidently to recross. Rain with thunder. Packed up about dark & moved out a hundred rods to the road. Corps passed us—straggling badly.

Friday, May 27　Did not get the road till morning & moved about one mile & found the corps resting. Marched all day. Hot—very hot—Sick with cold & leg sore. Rode my horse in rear. Made a hard march. Bivouacked near ambulances.

Saturday, May 28 Rose Early & rode forward to rejoin the regiment. Leg sore & Suffer from cold & feverishness. Corps crossed the river on pontoons. One Div of Sixth across. Bivouaced in aft. about one mile from river. Recd mail. Letter from Susie & Col. Gilmore. From Susie dated 17th.

Sunday, May 29 Reveiller at 5 A.M. Moved at 6½. Burnside forces form line. 2d corp on right 5th on left Afterwards moved to right & front. Col. heard that the Enemy had fallen back across the Chickahominy. Went back with the Dr. to rest. Saw Brown on way. Reported afterwards that there was skirmishing in front.

Monday, May 30 Rose at sunrise & came to the regiment. The Div in advance on Extreme left occupying a high hill. Moved forward. Sweitzer driving in the skirmishers of the Enemy. Having advanced about two miles formed line of battle & lay until nearly night when we moved to the left—44, 83d & 16th skirmishing. Maj. Elliot wounded supposedly mortally. Capt. Nash severely. Threw up works. Letters from Susie Pauline, Mrs. Morrell & Col G & Hill

Tuesday, May 31 Moved to the left having been relieved by Burnsides troop. Lay all day. Some skirmishing in front & right. Corps now advancing & heavy musketry towards night on left & front.

MAY 28, 1864 — JUNE 4, 1864

Wednesday, June 1   Moved to the front & took position & threw up works on a slight rise of land. Enemy move heavy & protracted assault in the right & center of the brigade but were repulsed with musketry. Enemy used some artillery Heavy firing on the left & front. 2 corps went to the left lengthening it Reported 18th corps was left having orders to White House. Gen. B & Col. Throop took upper bridges

Thursday, June 2   Quiet in morning. Moved corps about 2 P.M. Enemy advancing drove in Burnsides pickets as it retired & while the brigade halted pushed well forward & attacked the head of our column. They fell upon Burnside on the right— retarded the proposed movement. We took up position behind old works fronting North & remained for the night. Heavy shower & rain during the night.

Friday, June 3   Bethesda Church Woke Early. Enemy enfiladed our line from the left. The line faced north & west making a right angle. The right of our brigade. Sweitzer's swung around to the left & connected with Burnside. Lost heavily. Placed in charge of Brigade picket. Enemy advanced & pushed back the line slightly but I sent for reinforcements & regained the line

Saturday, June 4   Bethesda Ch Up nearly all night making connection on the right. Reported in morning that the Enemy had fallen back. Evidently swung back to our old works. Advanced the right of my line beyond their works & sent our scouts who found the Enemy. Rainy & heavy firing on the left—at night

Sunday, June 5 Bethesda Ch Quiet with occasional firing during the day. A small body of troops was advanced along our right by Gen Sweitzer line reconnoitering. The Enemy threw two or three shells. My line undisturbed. Ordered in Eve. to report to Gen. Griffin & being Senior of the Div. Picket off. to report to corps. Waited till daybreak for the column to pass. Corps moving to the left. Got orders to withdraw at daybreak & moved back without accident.

Monday, June 6 Rear of Cold Harbor Came into camp with picket of Div. which I withdrew at daylight Corps in bivouac in rear of 18th corps. Teams came up & I got clean clothes & supplies. Letters from Nettie, Verrill. Yesterday from Susie. Col. Chamberlain placed in command of 1st Brigade.

Tuesday, June 7 Chicahominy Orders at 2 AM to move at 3½. Moved about 4 miles to left & formed line in woods near Chickahominy. Threw forward pickets to river. Mail but no letters. Enemy shelled us but no casualties.

Wednesday, June 8 Few shells. Sent out 100 men under Capt Land on picket. Two men came in from the Enemy deserters from the 5th Va. Dismounted cavalry.

Thursday, June 9 Quiet—Mail, but no letters—Mail again at night with Portland papers, but no letters—

JUNE 5, 1864 — JUNE 14, 1864

two sutlers wagons ordered to each brigade instead of reg. No shelling during the day Cloudy part of the day with few drops of rain Very warm at night.

Friday, June 10 Pleasant with cool wind. Enemy shelled the relief going on picket. Two letters from Susie one of 4 & other of 6th inst.

Saturday, June 11 Quiet all day. Some heavy cannonading heard along James possibly by guns of large caliber Mrs Fogg came up in Evening. Many moving back towards White House.

Sunday, June 12 Cool & pleasant. Service at 10 AM. Mrs Fogg & Mr. Sawyer of the Chris Com. dined with me. Moved at 8 P.M. Letter from Susie dated 7th. Bivouacked after marching about 9 miles having crossed the York River & Richmond R.R.

Monday, June 13 at Long Bridge Crossed the Chickahominy in morning Early & moved westward. Halted at 7½ for breakfast & remained all day. Sent out picket. Moved at dusk & after a march of about 10 miles with frequent delays halted about 2 in the morning.

Tuesday, June 14 Harrisons Landing Started at 5¼ & marched until 9½ when halted for breakfast. Washington papers of the 12th Moved again at one P.M. passed Army Hd.Qrs. at Char City C.H. & went into position in rear of 2d Corps about one mile from river & 5½ below Harrisons

249

Landing Moved to left a short distance & bivouacked in rear of 16th Mich. 2d corps crossing in Evening.

Wednesday, June 15 Pleasant & warm. 2d corps gone & teams & artillery going.

Thursday, June 16 Crossing James—Orders in the night to be ready to move at daylight. Crossed the river at [*indecipherable name*] Landing below Harrisons & rested an hour & then moved on marching towards Petersburg. Roads very dusty. Halted at 9 P.M. for supper an hour & then moved on two miles. Artillery & musketry firing in front.

Friday, June 17 Petersburg Awakened by firing in front 2d corps Engaged. 2 corps charged at daylight & took five guns & about five hundred prisoners. Reports that the colored troop took the fort, now on our front & twelve guns.

Saturday, June 18 Moved towards the front in support Rested in field. Then in woods. Some shelling. Our troops pressing the Enemy gradually back. Moved into the woods. Then forward to a ravine. In the Eve. went back to see Col Chamberlain. He is, I fear, mortally wounded. Letter from Susie & one from Keene & others. 1st & 2d Brigade assault the works of the Enemy but are repulsed, losing heavily.

Sunday, June 19 Rose at 4½ having slept well. Breakfasted & sent letter to Susie. Mail letter from Hill & papers. Col. Brown wounded. Col. C. better.

JUNE 15, 1864 — JUNE 24, 1864

Sent in aft. to City Point on stretcher. Some artillery & picket firing during the day & a dash in front on the right. Slept well. Our corps on the left of the line. Col. C's brigade suffered heavily. Col. Prescott of 32d dead. Negro troops in rear—two brigades. 125 men on picket tonight

Monday, June 20 Rose Early and breakfasted having slept soundly. Pickets relieved & brigade moved back in Evening. Lay in open field the rest of the night

Tuesday, June 21 In the morning moved to the left across the R.R. near heavy Earth works. Rested in the Edge of woods & near sunset moved forward At dusk five regts 118th, 20th 18th—1st Mich & 16th Mich formed an advanced line & strengthened it with substantial Earth works.

Wednesday, June 22 Very warm. Poor Capt. Keene killed at 3 oclock & 10 minutes dying in my tent. Struck in the breast by a stray shot or by the bullet of a sharpshooter. The ball passing through him. White of Co G killed. Monroe of Co L wounded severely.

Thursday, June 23 Quiet with some shelling right & left & musket firing over us. Near sunset Enemy drove in Gibbons Div 2d corps & took five pieces of artillery. The Sixth corps recovered the ground. Letter from Col Gilmore.

Friday, June 24 Shelled heavily in morning by batteries on the left. One man Dunbar Co G killed. Teams ordered up. Quiet during the latter part of the day with constant picket firing. Proposal to form Battalion of sharpshooters. Letters from Susie & Nettie

Saturday, June 25 Letter from Hill dated 21st.

Sunday, June 26 Quiet during the day with less than usual firing. Nothing to break the dull monotony. Indications of a shower at night but no rain. 100 men on picket. Have written to Verrill, Em, Hannah, Susie, Lt. L. Col. G., Mr. Lane, Mr Keene (W.W.) Mrs White, Mrs Keene, Capt. Morrill, Lt Melcher Some volleys of musketry on the right but no continued firing

Monday, June 27 Very little firing from Pickets. Some artillery on the right. Read newspapers & wrote letters. Cooler.

Tuesday, June 28 Quiet except occasional cannonading on the right. We get no Washington papers & small mails Letter from Susie. Reports favorable from Gen. Chamberlain.

Wednesday, June 29 Nothing worthy of note. One paper from Nettie. Cooler at night with indications of rain. Sent Fields to [*indecipherable word*] Co. Making out Rolls & returns.

Thursday, June 30 Clear & cool in the morning. Chaplain came up. Busy making out Rolls & returns.

JUNE 25, 1864 — JULY 9, 1864

Friday, July 1   Letter this m. from Susie. Worked on returns. Not well. I suffer from nausea & extreme lassitude. [*deleted*: Verrill from the 7th called.]

Saturday, July 2   Quiet with the usual firing on the right. Very warm. 19th Corps reported present. Called at Brigade Div. HdQrs.

Sunday, July 3   Pleasant. Woke with nausea. Mail in the afternoon. Chaplain gone back ill. Verrill from the 7th & Capt. More called.

Monday, July 4   Very quiet all day

Tuesday, July 5   Letter from Susie with photograph of July.

Wednesday, July 6   As usual. No letters Very warm. Looked out a place for camp in Eve. with Expectation of being relieved

Thursday, July 7   Made out returns for 2d quarter of 63. ord. [*indecipherable word*] of Co G. Shelled by the Enemy in morning. Paper from Nettie. Recd orders from QM Dept.

Friday, July 8   Heavy fire of artillery fire struck line in afternoon. In the night sent out parties to throw up new works & strengthen the line. Letters from Susie Pauline Capt Morrill & Mr. Wheeler & paper from Susie.

Saturday, July 9   Cloudy in morn. Called upon Gen Bartlett & Gen Hays. Had poles cut. Enemy commenced shelling at night but did not disturb our working parties. One man in G. slightly wounded. Letters from Susie Pauline & Verrill.

Sunday, July 10 Slow shelling from the Enemy all night. A slight clash of musketry on the left, occasioned as reported, by some deserters coming into our lines. Kennedy wounded. Capt Morrill returned. QM came up with teams. Quiet towards noon.

Monday, July 11 Went to Hosp saw Kennedy Mrs M. Dined with the doctor. Rebs in Maryland. Left of the line occupy the front works. Enemys mortars throw shells. Letters forwarded from Wiscasset.

Tuesday, July 12 Some shelling during the day. Nobody hurt.

Wednesday, July 13 Railroad communications between Baltimore & Philada reported cut. No mail—Called on Col Herring.

Thursday, July 14 Called at Brigade Hd.Qrs. No mail Except for Washington. Letter from Mr French in regard to Keene.

Saturday, July 16 Road to 17 Maine. No shelling on our front. Mortars at work on the right. Enemy reported falling back from Maryland pursued by 6th & 19th corps. Small mail in the Evening. No letters.

Sunday, July 17 Warm & pleasant & very quiet.

Monday July 18 Warm. Recd supplies from San. Com. No mail.

JULY 10, 1864 — JULY 29, 1864

Tuesday, July 19 Rainy. Ill with nausea & fever all day. Mail in Evening. Commissions of Melcher Miller Fernald. Paper gives Commission of Field. Letters (2) from Susie & one from Hannah, one from Nettie with papers

Thursday, July 21 Rode to 1st Div Hd.Qrs. Called on Gen Hayes Dined with him & Batchelder Letter from Susie afterwards.

Friday, July 22 Gens Grant, Meade passed along the line in the aft. & Warren in the morn. All quiet. Some unusual musketry on right. Letter from Col G. & Susie dated Monday at Catskill. Sent up communication regards recruiting.

Saturday, July 23 Quiet & warm. Rode to Brigade Hd.Qrs. Gen. B disapproved new regiments. Letters from Pauline & Susie. S in Portland.

Sunday, July 24 Rose Earlier than usual. Rode to City Point. Visiting Mrs. Mayhew & Q M Baker.

Tuesday, July 26 Rode to Div Hosp. Sent for Dr Shaws papers & got them in time to send before night. Note from Susie at Brunswick.

Wednesday, July 27 Second corps gone to the right. Some fighting. Under orders to be ready to move.

Thursday, July 28 Mortars brought up. [*indecipherable word*] ten inchs on the right & six on the left.

Friday, July 29 Rode to Gen Ames, calling by the way at Brig

255

Hd.Qrs. & corps. Found Gen. A. He had just recd orders for the assault tomorrow. Recd orders late in the Evening—Letter from Pauline Drilled officers & gave orders & awake until midnight.

Saturday, July 30   Works on Reservoir Hill blew up at full daylights & fire opened all along the lines. Burnside attacked. Took the hill but failed to hold it. Killed & some of the wounded left on the field. Firing kept up most of the forenoon.

Sunday, July 31   Quiet

Monday, Aug. 1   Reports of Enemy in [*indecipherable name*] & Alexandria & Burning Chambersburg. Letter from Susie at Warren.

Tuesday, Aug. 2   Regiment paid. Moved quarters to the front.

Wednesday, Aug. 3   Turned out under Arms before daylight, anticipating an attack

Thursday, Aug. 4   Field officer of outposts of Div. Advanced picket line for purposes of ascertaining if mining operations had been going on in Ravine in front.

Friday, Aug. 5   Sent Check to Susie 80$ No 878 Dated Aug 2. Letter from Susie Cannonade on the right. Enemy sent [*four indecipherable words*] & were repulsed. One deserter came in

Saturday, Aug. 6   Ten deserters came in last night.

Sunday, Aug. 7   Reported at Brigade Hd.Qrs. & carried paper to Gen. Visited Div. hospital.

Monday, Aug. 8   Letters from Mr Hall & from Susie.

Tuesday, Aug. 9   Rode at night to Gen Ames with Col Throop.

Wednesday, Aug. 10   Ill in the morning. Sent rifle to Welch. Rode in Eve to 17th Maine. Letter from Gov. C—. No more regiments.

Friday, Aug. 12   Letter from Susie from Rockland. 2d corps gone to the right.

Saturday, Aug. 13   Bickford went home. Sent word by him.

Sunday, Aug. 14   Rose Early. Letter from Reed. Called on Col. Herring. Wrote Susie & for the Atlantic Monthly inclosing 2$. No mail. Ordered to move to rear when relieved.

Monday, Aug. 15   Relieved by portions of 9th corp at full daylight by troops of 9th corps. Moved to rear & lay awhile & then went into bivouac. Heavy shower with thunder. Letter from Susie. 2d Corps & Army operations on the right across the James. Quite cool.

Tuesday, Aug. 16   Intensely hot. Fixed quarters. Ordered on fatigue duty & marched to railroad & orders countermanded. Orders in Evening to be vigilant. Enemy having been reported & moving heavy masses to the left.

Wednesday, Aug. 17   Quiet. Regiment inspected by the Adj. Brigade. In Evening orders to be ready to move at 3 AM. tomorrow.

Thursday, Aug. 18   Tremendous cannonading all along the line from the right. about midnight. Moved this morning about 5 to the left. Our Div in advance. 1st & 2d Brig. took the railroad with little opposition & commenced to tear it up. Other troops came in & went to the right. Sharp fight in the aft. We holding ground It is said that the Maryland brigade broke & lost prisoners. Morrill left sick. Fitch went off near right. Our bridgade moved to left & beyond R.R. & threw up earthworks.

Friday, Aug. 19   Heavy cannonading in the night on our old line. Reported that the Enemy charged the line. About four P.M. Enemy made an attack on Ayers & Crawfords Divisions breaking thro 1st & getting in rear of 2d & taking 2200 prisoners. We drove them back & took about 200 of their men. Our brigade moved up in support Enemy threw some shot amongst us.

Saturday, Aug. 20   Quiet.

Sunday, Aug. 21   Enemy made heavy attack in front of 2d & 3rd Div. & threw a brigade between the 4th & 1st. They were driven back with heavy loss. Our Div took about 300.

Monday, Aug. 22   Quiet—Rain Col. Herring gone back to Hosp. Fitch said to be at City Pt.

AUG. 17, 1864 — SEPT. 15, 1864

Tuesday, Aug. 23   Letter from Susie including one from July.

Thursday, Aug. 25   Moved to the left of the brigade. The whole line Extended Location low & wet. Ill. Letter from S. & [*indecipherable name*]

Friday, Aug. 26   Col. H. going to Hosp. Chain of redoubts begun along the line.

Saturday, Aug. 27   Off duty. Called on Throop. Letter from Susie. Meade, Grant & Warren rode past. Teams ordered up.

Sunday, Aug. 28   Cool. Ordered to be ready to move at a moments notice.

Saturday, Sept. 10   Came to Div. Hosp. Morrill & Fuller returned.

Sunday, Sept. 11   Came to train. Cool & clear.

Monday, Sept. 12   Cool & clear. Rode to City Pt. Hospital & returned to train Land came.

Tuesday, Sept. 13   Rode to City Pt. with Land.

Wednesday, Sept. 14   Returned to reg. Train moved up. Letter from Susie. She still uncertain whether to go to N.Y. or not. Fuller returned to Hospital. A good many sick.

Thursday, Sept. 15   Reports of the enemy moving to the left. Reconnaissance of a brigade of cavalry & one of infantry gone the front. Some firing. Morrill gone to hospital. Throop sick. Called to see him. Order to be under arms till dark. Enemy being reported advancing in our front.

Friday, Sept. 16 Pleasant & cool. Some firing on picket line.

Saturday, Sept. 17 Rode to Brigade Hd.Qrs. Reported that Enemy captured 4500 Hd. cattle. Letter from Susie dated Sep. 9th—one week ago, announcing that she will go to N.Y.

Sunday, Sept. 18 Slight rain. Letter from S. in Rockland. Forbes called from Hd.Qrs. 9th Corps. Litchfield came. Wrote his recommendation. Read.

Monday, Sept. 19 Pleasant—Rode to Hd.Qrs. 3d Brigade with Litchfields paper.

Sunday, Sept. 25 Div officer of Outposts for three days—Notified to have unusual vigilance Exercised on the line.

Wednesday, Sept. 28 Relieved—Rode to train—Prospects of move. Col Merrill called.

Thursday, Sept. 29 Orders last night to be ready to move at 4 A.M. Unusual firing—musketry & artillery on the right during the last Evening. Cavalry moved to the left. Some musketry & artillery. A small force of infantry sent to our front. Pitched tent again.

Friday, Sept. 30 Cloudy Orders to be ready to move at eight Letters last night from Pauline Susie & Verrill. Moved at 9 AM to the front. 3d Brigade &

part of the others carried the works near the church. Col. Welsh killed. Maj. Partridge too. In aft. Col. Gwyn going back left me in charge of the brigade. Moved to the front supporting 9th corps, which, breaking the Enemy came upon us. Sustained the weight of the attack alone until 2d Bg. & art. came up. Held ground till night.

Saturday, Oct. 1 Lay in works. Rainy Gen. Bartlett takes command. Not very well.

Sunday, Oct. 2 Moved out to protect the right flank of 9th corps. Motts Div of 2d on Extreme left. Some skirmishing. Enemy threw some shells & solid shot over us, one striking very near Gens. Meade Humphrey Griffin & Bartlett. I stood near & the shot passed near my head. At night went into line & connected with 2d Div.

Monday, Oct. 3 Moved to right. Gen sent me to put brigade into position.

Tuesday, Oct. 4 All

Wednesday, Oct. 5 Quiet

Thursday, Oct. 6 Sent application for leave

Saturday, Oct. 8 Doct. Wadsworth came. Leave in the Evening. Very cool.

Sunday, Oct. 9 Rode to cars. Thence to City Pt. & boat. Reached Fortress Monroe before Evening.

Monday, Oct. 10   Reached Washington at 10 A M. Attended to business & took cars for N.Y.

Tuesday, Oct. 11   Tuesday night in Boston. Wrote Susie & Clark.

Wednesday, Oct. 12   In Portland. Found Verrill.

Thursday, Oct. 13   In Portland—Rainy.

Friday, Oct. 14   Went to Augusta in the Evening to camp to look after Lewis company but found that it had gone assigned to 19th

Saturday, Oct. 15   Saw the Gov. this morning. He professed not to have anything to do with the assignment of recruits, but promised to approve my application. Took cars for Bath. Telegraphed Reed from Brunswick & stayed with him.

Sunday, Oct. 16   Reed brought me to Wiscasset & returned. Attended meeting in Evening & called at Mr Robinson Took tea at Mr Hubbard's.

Monday, Oct. 17   Made calls & we took dinner at Mr Young's. Took chaise for Warren about 1½ PM. Called & took tea at Mrs Clarks. Reached home about Eight in Evening.

Tuesday, Oct. 18   Went to Rockland. Called on Lt. Miller

Wednesday, Oct. 19   Started for N.Y. Early, reaching W. about 8½. Stopped in Bath two hours with Reed reached Portland in afternoon. Found Land & Madam L.

OCT. 10, 1864 — DEC. 7, 1864

Thursday, Oct. 20 Took boat at night for Boston.

Friday, Oct. 21 Took cars for Albany & stopped there over night at Delaware House where I had good accommodations a shave, smoke, good nights rest.

Saturday, Oct. 22 After hearty breakfast started on the Susquehanna train for Central bridge & there took slow coach. Reached Stamford in Eve. Learned on the cars of the death of poor Mary.

Sunday, Oct. 23 At home.

Thursday, Dec. 1 Started for the Regt. in sleigh for Central Bridge.

Friday, Dec. 2 From N.Y. to Washington.

Saturday, Dec. 3 Hill & Andrews started in boat for front at 3 PM.

Sunday, Dec. 4 Reached front in Eve.

Monday, Dec. 5 Rode to 2d corps Called on Gens Bartlett & Chamberlain

Tuesday, Dec. 6 Moved out of works & bivouacked. Rode to 1st cavalry. Bot. horse of QM.

Wednesday, Dec. 7 Marched on Jerusalem road about 15 miles. Some rain—Bivouacked in Eve about 10.

Thursday, Dec. 8   Marched at two in the morn.—a heavy shower but no continuous rain & gradually became clear & cool. Struck RR in Evening & commenced tearing it up

Friday, Dec. 9   Moved on the brigade bring rear guard. Other troops destroying the road. Bivouacked at night in pine wood Cool & drizzly.

Saturday, Dec. 10   Cold the trees covered with ice. Marched at 7 A.M. over terrible roads. Bivouacked near Sussex C.H.

Sunday, Dec. 11   Moved at 7. Crossed the Nottaway & bivouacked about one oclock

Monday, Dec. 12   Cold—Moved back following teams.

Wednesday, Dec. 14   Arranged camp—cold

Thursday, Dec. 15   Still prospect of moving.

Saturday, Dec. 17   Commenced to build camp.

Sunday, Dec. 25   Field officer of outposts

Monday, Dec. 26   Rainy.

Wednesday, Dec. 28   Relieved Roade to 1st [*indecipherable word*]

Thursday, Dec. 29   Rode to 19th Corp. Attend to care of Lewis.

Saturday, Dec. 31   Letters from Susie

[*Entry on the last page of 1864 Diary (not in Ellis Spear's hand)*] Mr. E. W. Churchill presents his friendly regards to Major Ellis Spear & he desires him to accept this humble gift earnestly wishing that no evening during the year it represents will find him unable to record in it the events of the day, and that hereafter on some page within its covers may be found the record of a truth more than welcome that no traitors resist the march of the loyal armies of the North, that an honorable peace has been attained, and that the foulest stain upon the face of this nation has been forever wiped out.

[1865 DIARY]

Sunday, Jan. 1 Cold & windy Letter from Susie. Clark left on 20 day leave. Wrote recommendation for him & got it endorsed at Brig. & Div. No service

Monday, Jan. 2 Called on Gen. Bartlett at Div. to pay the compliments of the season & afterward rode to corps.

Tuesday, Jan. 3 Cold

Wednesday, Jan. 4 Cold. Had my house finished & papered. Capt. Ritchie called & Chaplain. In evening played cards with Sidelinger, Land & Donnell. Wrote Susie. No mail. Order of the Pres. assigning me to duty according to Brvt. rank.

Thursday, Jan. 5 Cool & clear. Col. G. tells me that Gen. Hodsdon wishes to send in a new company.

Wrote Clark. Called on Col. Herring. Col. Gilmore sends to company Hd.Qrs. for report of operations the past year. Wrote Susie & sent certfd. bill to Westerfield. Chamberlain cld in Eve.

Friday, Jan. 6 Warm with copious rain. Called at Col. Herring in Evening. Letters from S. & Verrill. Wrote history of reg. during the day.

Saturday, Jan. 7 Clear & cool. Looked over late Capt. S.T. Keenes accts. & read. In Evening played Euchre with Land Morrill & Col G. & read paper.

Sunday, Jan. 8 Letters from S. & V. paper & pocket testament. Read, inspected a Co. Attended service Talked with the Chaplain. Called at the Doctors. Gilmore "pretty badly off"

Monday, Jan. 9 Set detail working upon my quarters. Col. Stubins & Cilley called. Fast [*indecipherable word*] Euchre in Evening in Col's. Indications of rain

Tuesday, Jan. 10 Woke in the morning with fine rain dripping in my bed. Rain heavy & continuous.

Wednesday, Jan. 11 Cold. Orders came down allowing detail for Recrt. Service.

Thursday, Jan. 12 Detail of myself & six men ordered to Augusta. Col. G. making advances regarding his papers & proposes to resign. Called Col Herring & Col Gilmore.

JAN. 6, 1865 — JAN. 24, 1865

Sunday, Jan. 15   Started group [*indecipherable word*]. Litchfield, Wood & Bickford & Gen Chamberlain.

Monday, Jan. 16   Reached Washington about seven. Breakfasted at National Recd 441 & pay 3 mos. up to Jan. Left in the six train & took sleeping cars.

Tuesday, Jan. 17   In N.Y. Early & took cars for Boston reaching the city about 5½ PM. Went to National

Wednesday, Jan. 18   To Augusta & stopped at Augusta House.

Thursday, Jan. 19   Reported at Maj Littles. Sent off men & returned to Portland

Friday, Jan. 20   Investigated matter. Saw Capt Doughty Maj. Rawlins in camp. Called upon Col Merrill.

Saturday, Jan. 21   Saw Mr Hunt of City treasurers office. Got two men. Called upon Mrs MacIntyre in the Evening & went to bed near Eleven.

Sunday, Jan. 22   Rose at Eight & went to church at Rev Mr. Walkers in aft wrote Susie & Tab & in Eve attended Ch at the Universalist. Not feeling well warmed my feet took copious draught of cold water & went to bed

Monday, Jan. 23   Feeling better Start for Augusta. Snowing steadily. Reached Augusta about four P.M. & slept at the Stanley.

Tuesday, Jan. 24   Clear Snow fell about one foot in depth. Saw Gen Hodsdon & Maj. Little A paper went through yesterday to Maj. Clark. Saw a 15 man at the Depot. Tabot had five days from the 20th Maine.

Wednesday, Jan. 25 Saw Hines & all. Rode down with Gen Hodsdon. Letters Nos. 18. 20 & 21 from Susie, probably written in November acc. the mark. Wrote S. sending 19$ Went in Evening to hear [*indecipherable name*] in City N.Y. Saw Hutchins in the cars on his way to the Regt.

Thursday, Jan. 26 Cold—Clark came.

Friday, Jan. 27 Cold & clear.

Saturday, Jan. 28 Cold & clear. Letter from Susie She proposes to drive on & bring baby, next week, to stay at the house of a friend, C. S. D. Griffin on Congress Street.

Sunday, Jan. 29 Attended Church in the morn. Mr Walton's, in aft. Read & walked & read in Evening. Wrote Susie.

Monday, Jan. 30 Letter from True. Gov Ise. sec. Worked on Regt list. Went to cars. Two men from Regt. & Getchell of G. on way home. parolled prisoners.

Tuesday, Jan. 31 Orders to report to Augusta.

Wednesday, Feb. 1 Went to Augusta. Made report for True Stopped at Stanleys.

Thursday, Feb. 2 Returned & found Susie at Portland.

Friday, Feb. 3   Got several men. Enlisted Harding for [*indecipherable word*]. Eaton came. Advanced him $20 for coat.

Saturday, Feb. 4   One man. Made arrangements for an [*indecipherable word*] party. Snowy. Wrote Land.

Sunday, Feb. 5   Snowing.

Thursday, Feb. 9   Eight men

Friday, Feb. 10   Seven men.

Saturday, Feb. 11   24 Danforth St. Robert Brown. Three men this morning

Sunday, Feb. 12   Church Mr. Waltons

Monday, Feb. 13   One or two men—Letters from Land & others.

Tuesday, Feb. 14   Two men in the morning. No. 160 son of the Congress St. Griffin

Saturday, Mar. 18   Started for Warren

Sunday, Mar. 19   Went to church.

Monday, Mar. 20   Made calls about town.

Tuesday, Mar. 21   Rode from Warren to Wiscasset.

Wednesday, Mar. 22   Went from Wiscasset to Boston. Saw Reed.

Sunday, Mar. 26   Arrived in Washington & Col Gilmore came to see me at National & showed me the order reinstating him as Col. Left in the afternoon for the front.

Monday, Mar. 27   Reached the front at 6 P.M. Found Morrill mustered. Called at Gen. Bartletts. Wrote Susie Troops under orders to be ready to move

Tuesday, Mar. 28   Called on Gen Chamberlain & saw Gen Griffin who assures me that I shall have the colonelcy. Order of Col Gilmore came down.

Wednesday, Mar. 29   Moved about 5 AM. towards Dinwiddie & halted about noon near Hatchers Run. In afternoon moved back & up the Quaker Road toward the Boydton Plank. Engaged the Enemy & at night Established line on the Plank. Detailed on Div. staff. Fight of Lewis Farm & Quaker Road.

Thursday, Mar. 30   Pushed further to the front Enemy made an assault on our pickets line & drove it in. Rainy & very muddy. Continual skirmishing & some artillery fire. Letters from Susie, Verrill & Nettie.

Friday, Mar. 31   2d & 3d Divisions at front & broke. 3d brigade checked the Enemy. 1st & 2d Brigades advanced in aft. & drove the Enemy to their works. In Eve brigade moved toward Dinwiddie to operate against the rear of the Enemy pressing Sheridan Moved back about midnight from Dr Boisseau's. Slept on board without blanket White Oak Road.

MAR. 26, 1865 — APR. 7, 1865

Saturday, Apr. 1 Five Forks Moved at sunrise toward Dinwiddie formed junction with 2d Div & Sheridan without opposition about 8 A.M. Joined 2d Div & cavalry & massed in front of works of enemy at Five Forks in P.M. in order 2d 3 1st & swung around flanking the Enemy out of their works capturing guns & prisoners. Went with two cos towards R.R. & Skirmished in Eve.

Sunday, Apr. 2 Marched towards R.R. which crossed & turned N.E. Bivouacked near 6 P.M. Moved up mainly [*indecipherable word*]

Monday, Apr. 3 Took command of the 198th. Moved up mainly on [*indecipherable name*] Road. Our advance pushing the Enemy & captured artillery brigades & prisoners. Pushed on rapidly to cut off the enemy. Reached the Danville Road at dark & erected works. Enemy & wagon train reported in rear

Tuesday, Apr. 4 Under arms at 4 A.M. Cloudy.

Wednesday, Apr. 5 Marched at 6 AM. Entered Hamville at 2½ P.M. Marched through burnt train Found rebel flag

Thursday, Apr. 6 Passed burnt train. Long & tedious march

Friday, Apr. 7 Marched at 6 AM. Southwesterly to Prince Albert C.H. bivouacking at 9 P.M. Musketry & cannonading on the right. 24 & 2d corps up. Marched rapidly towards right. Road bad.

Saturday, Apr. 8   Ill in morning with nausea. Moved at 6 A.M. towards Lynchburg. 24th corps in advance. Halted frequently & marched until nearly 12 midnight. Report that Sheridan had captured three R.R. trains.

Sunday, Apr. 9   Appotomax C.H. Moved at 5 AM. suddenly Encountering the Enemy & formed lines of battle the cavalry moving front to right. Our lines shelled vigorously At 9½ flag of truce came in from Gen. Lee through our lines. He made propositions of surrender Time till 4 P.M. Lee surrendered the army of Nor. Vir. to Gen. Grant.

Monday, Apr. 10   Rainy. Rode into the village Saw Gens Grant & Lee & visited the House of Mr. McLains where the articles were signed. Rosser's men turning in their arms.

Tuesday, Apr. 11   Foggy. Moved into town & waited for the Enemy to turn over their arms. Troops sent into camp. Gen Chamberlain assigned to command of 3d Brig. Detailed on Gen. Cs staff.

Wednesday, Apr. 12   Our Brigade recd the arms of Gordons & Longstreets corps which included all the remains of the infantry force of the army of N. Vir All passed off quietly without demonstration Gens Ivins, Field, Wise, Bennings, Walker, & others commanding. Relieved at one by other brigade after all arms were turned over. Today the anniversary of the opening of the war saw the end of its great army.

Thursday, Apr. 13 Rainy during the night. Black mare stolen. Parties of parolled prisoners on their way through camp.

Friday, Apr. 14 Rose at 5. Clear & pleasant. Walked to regiment in aft. Letter from Susie date as Mr 2. Made document against Gilmore. Ordered to march at 12 M tomorrow. One & one half days rations. One Div 24th corp reported gone to Lynchburg. Moved forward. Wrote Reed & Susie.

Saturday, Apr. 15 Got up at six. Raining. Marched at one P.M. & halted & bivouacked in the woods near the road about 7. No rain in afternoon, but roads heavy & march severe.

Sunday, Apr. 16 Marched at six to Farmville. Halted at 3 & bivouacked. Bridges burnt. Rebel hospitals. Mail & letters from Susie Land & Furbish. Must attend to his case. News of the assassination of President Lincoln. HQ is at house of Mrs.

Monday, Apr. 17 Marched at 7 along the R.R. Bivouacked in the woods at dark on the North side of Price Station after a long march.

Tuesday, Apr. 18 Moved camp. Brigade in open fields. HdQrs at a house. Orders to move at 7 tomorrow.

Wednesday, Apr. 19 Orders suspended 24 hours. Services appropriate to the day Pres Lincoln buried. Papers recd. giving acts. of his assassination

Thursday, Apr. 20   Cloudy Moved at 6 along the S.S. R.R. as far as Nottaway. Gen. Bartlett assigned to command of a Div. 11 [*indecipherable word*] of 9th Corps. Gen. C. took comd. of 1st Div. Bivouacked near Nottoway. HdQrs. at house of Miss Fitzgerald. Bivouacked Early in aft. Showers with thunder. 9th corp going to Washington. 5 Corp train coming in our rear

Friday, Apr. 21   Moved at 6. Pleasant. Halted about 8 AM. at Jones House. Went forward to look out ground. Fixed Div. HdQrs Pitched tents at house of Mr Hobbs.

Saturday, Apr. 22   Very cold. In Evening got orders from Gen. Meade appt me Div. Inspector

Sunday, Apr. 23   Cold. Looked over reports & returns, being pressed for time.

Monday, Apr. 24   Went to 3d Brigade to inspect. Inspect 20th & remd there over night.

Tuesday, Apr. 25   Inspt. 16th & went to 1st Maine. Then orders came to move Regts below Sutherland. Retd. to Division.

Wednesday, Apr. 26   Attended to business. Rode to 185. Telegraph from Litchfield that black mare found. Wrote orders for Gen. C.

Thursday, Apr. 27   Wrote charges against Breen & Maley. Clark came with papers. Wrote order for Gen. C. in

APR. 20, 1865 — MAY 6, 1865

Evening. Pleasant. Roses in full bloom. Sent up paper concerning Gilmore.

Friday, Apr. 28 Pleasant

Saturday, Apr. 29 Raining. Showers in Eve. Gen. gone to corps.

Sunday, Apr. 30 Rode into the country. Called at house of Dr Reese, Mr Mitchell, Mr McQuade, & others. Rumors of a move. Letter from Susie. Orders to move later to Richmond via Petersburg.

Monday, May 1 Reports from 3rd Brigade. My own made up. [*deleted*: Moved near Sutherlands. Visited neighborhood of "Peebles Farm"] Tried case of [*indecipherable name*].

Tuesday, May 2 [*deleted*: Moved through Peterburg as far as the "Friend" House near Drewry's Bluff] Moved from Wilsons to near Petersburg. Visited the works near Peebles Farm.

Wednesday, May 3 Moved through Petersburg to the Friend House nine miles from Manchester & near Drewrys Bluff.

Thursday, May 4 Moved to Manchester & had HdQrs at Mr Drewrys. Rode back to Ft Drewry.

Friday, May 5 Movement postponed on acct of rain. Rode into the city visited Libby &c.

Saturday, May 6 Moved at 8½ through Richmond & bivouacked near the battlefield of Hanover CH.

Thursday, May 11   Moved at 7. Lt Wood wounded Rode ahead to get him mustered Very hot. Heavy shower at night. Bivouacked within three miles of [*indecipherable name*] Sta. [*deleted*: Moved at 6. 1st Div in advance]

Friday, May 12   Moved at 6 AM. 1st Div in advance Came in sight of the city early in the afternoon & went into camp East of the R.R.

Saturday, May 13   Rode to Washington & got our muster pay 191 + [*indecipherable word*].

Sunday, May 14   Went to Alex but cld. not find Hill. [*indecipherable word*] on return.

Tuesday, May 16   Saw Gilmore

Friday, May 19   At Alexandria. del by rain.

Saturday, May 20   Inspected property in the morning. Rainy in afternoon. Letter from Susie. Maj. Whittelsay called.

Sunday, May 21   Rainy. Attended church twice at C.C. tent. Heavy showers with thunder during the day. Read Les Miserables.

Monday, May 22   Cloudy & warm.

Tuesday, May 23   Review of A of Pa. Moved at 7. Stopped in city & purchased hat & was threatened with arrest for being in the city without leave.

MAY 11, 1865 — JUNE 2, 1865

Wednesday, May 24   Shermans army reviewed. Rode into the city & retd in aft. Saw. Gen. [*indecipherable name*] & Verrill

Thursday, May 25   Rained

Friday, May 26   Rained.

Saturday, May 27   Cleared off. Inspected Property for Capt. Carson Charges against Gilmore. Chamberlain informed him of the fact.

Sunday, May 28   Gilmore made appearance. States that in answer to his using rations the Dept call upon him to [*indecipherable word*] his muster while his resignation was pending! Troops have muster rolls nearly ready.

Monday, May 29   Pleasant. Inspected property in Sixteenth Mich. 83d Pa & 20th Maine. Sent up Rep. of Div. Work on Inspec. Reps. Commenced mustering of troops. Gilmore brought over his discharge & I was mustered as Col. of the Regt.

Tuesday, May 30   Inspected Websters property.

Wednesday, May 31   Ill. Worked up inspection reports. In Eve rode to Alexandria.

Thursday, June 1   Ill.

Friday, June 2   Not very well but rode to W in Spring wagon Saw [*indecipherable name*] & got pay for 1 month.

Tuesday, June 6   Ill & did nothing Order came relieving me from duty as Ins.

Wednesday, June 7   Retd to Rgt. Rode to Div. & wrote telegram for Records of Companies.

Thursday, June 8   Warm. Rose feeling ill. Wrote Susie. Made out records for Cos.

Friday, June 9   Ill & waiting for Records

Saturday, June 10   Found retained rolls at Div. Hd.Qrs. Telegram from Morrill to effect that Company Records had been turned over to Capt Holmes Mustering officer. Telegraphed Holmes. Taking Dr Lowes medicine & am better Rain.

Sunday, June 11   Better. Rode to Alex in afternoon & had con. with Hill. Ret 8½.

Monday, June 12   Letters from Morrill & Land & Furbish. At Div. Hd.Qrs. in Evening.

Tuesday, June 13   Sent recommendations of Chamberlain as Lt. Col. Butler Capt of B. Furbish 1st Lt. of B. &

Wednesday, June 14   Went to Washington in Evening. Bought "Life of Caesar". Sent Records & recommendations for 1st Lieut. of K.

Thursday, June 15   Warm. Walked to Brig. Hd.Qrs. in Eve.

Friday, June 16   16th & 1st Mich. left. Wrote Hodsdon, Prince,

JUNE 6, 1865 — JUNE 25, 1865

                Susie, Verrill. Invoices of Colors from Inman. Letter from Susie. Reg. Inspection.

Saturday, June 17   At Div. Hd. Qrs. orders for the 9th Co. to report on the 21st inst.

Sunday, June 18   Rode to Alexandria.

Monday, June 19   Cool & pleasant—Shower in afternoon.

Tuesday, June 20   Cool with Showers in afternoon. Made application for Roll of 9th Co. Doing Nothing.

Wednesday, June 21   Brevet Com. came. Letters from Land, Prince & Verrill. Sent to Alex. express office. No books or colors.

Thursday, June 22   Acknowledged recpt. of Com. by Brvt. Order drills. Rode to W. Found Books & colors. Bot Tristan Shanty.

Friday, June 23   Sent for Books & Colors. Got Books Pd. 6$ Express.

Saturday, June 24   Arranging & consolidating. Disturbance in Evening.

Sunday, June 25   Quiet. Cooler. <u>More flies</u>. Inspected Regt. Adj. QM & [*indecipherable word*] moved over. Letter from Gilmore relating to Sergt Owen, Fitch, Hall. Sent D. list. Finished arrangement of Cos. & assigned officers. Wrote Owen, Susie Jason & Hannah.

Monday, June 26	Have done nothing. Rain. Ordered Co. officers to take up books & papers. Notice of informality of muster. Letter from S. Rumors of consolidation of corps into Div. Doyle reports.
Tuesday, June 27	Theodore James. Q.M. [indecipherable name] "K" St. below 1st. Forwarded recommendations for his behalf.
Wednesday, June 28	Rode to the City to get my muster arranged, which acc. without difficulty. Ret. in Eve. Met. Gen. [indecipherable word] adjt. Gen. Mess. Took command of Brigade.
Thursday, June 29	32d & 83d left this morn. Men to Exchange photographs with Rodgers at Harrisburg. In comd. of brigade. Rode to Div. Hd.Qrs. Orders breaking up corps. & reassigning the troops. Letter from Pauline & bundle from Hayes. Moved Regt camp & united battalions
Friday, June 30	Warm & oppressive. Letter from Price reconsidering his app.—declined com. 2 letters from S. 12th & 27th in al. Heavy Showers in evening.
Saturday, July 1	Very warm. Wrote H & sent Brvt. Com. to [indecipherable name] at Cumberland Center. Sent Receipts for colors. Wrote Mr Robinson. Reports that old Vet. organizations are to be mustered out.
Sunday, July 2	Rode to Alexandria Street opposite U.S. Hotel. No mail. Cool & pleasant Wrote S.

JUNE 26, 1865 — JULY 11, 1865

Monday, July 3 Cool. Third Div. Provisional Corps Established. Letter from Gov. Coburn.

Tuesday, July 4 Very warm. Attended to business in morning. Gen. Chamberlain assuming command of 1st Brigade. Very quiet all day. Negro celebrations & fireworks in W. in Evening. Letter from S. Forwarded letter for Morrill. Sent thro furlough. Wrote to Gen C regarding disturbances in 2 & 6 Corps.

Wednesday, July 5 Cooler & cloudy. Made reports on Dunn. Wrote Hutchinson. Arranged papers, & made out furlough & c &c.

Thursday, July 6 Sent Documents relating to Moran & those relating to Cap Dunn. Wrote recommendations to Gen. H. Read Rolls. Wrote Susie. Recd notice of Rounds Com. [*indecipherable word*] for Litchfield.

Friday, July 7 Forwarded letters to Gen. H. Ask commissions.

Saturday, July 8 Rode to Washington & commenced business of settling accts.

Sunday, July 9 Case of Barry [*two indecipherable words*]

Monday, July 10 Rain. Rode to W. Drew pay to include May 28th. 186.10. Sent Susie 50$

Tuesday, July 11 Wrote Gov. C relating to [*indecipherable name*] &c. Sent Tyler letter. Sent Col. Breck papers relating to Verrill. Sent Capt Land documents relating to Pri. ____. Wrote Col. Tilden. Showers in Evening. Made up Records for Gen. Hodsdon. Sent through requisition for arms.

Wednesday, July 12 Raining. Wrote Recd letters from Oliver Spear. [*indecipherable name*] & Susie & wrote replies. Finished up muster & Pay Rolls. Got requisitions approved, & sent them to Washington by Sawyer.

Thursday, July 13 Warm. Attended to office business. Made application for Donnell.

Saturday, July 15 Made up old records.

Sunday, July 16 Worked upon rolls & old Records & in eve rode to Alexandria. Returning called to see Gen. C.

Monday, July 17 Moved at 9 AM. & waited in W with regiment until 7½ then moved with 45 Pa. Reached Baltimore about 12.

Tuesday, July 18 Reached Philada. about noon. Got dinner for the men & reached N.Y. 6 P.M. Put men in Battery Barracks. Slept at Washington House. Mr Connell of the New England Room gave us all necessary information. Saw Lewis & W Sent him papers & rifles

Wednesday, July 19 Moved on board the John Brooks at Eleven (11½) for Providence. Rainy at night. Ran in to New London, it being too rough to continue.

JULY 12, 1865 — AUG. 2, 1865

Thursday, July 20   Cloudy with some rain Moved about 5 A.M. & reached Providence at noon. Whence proceeded at once to Boston by rail. Reached Boston in the Eve 5 oclock & took train for Portland. Reached about one. Turned over papers.

Friday, July 21   Moved out to camp after giving the men Supper provided by the city. Reached camp 4½ A.M. Turned in arms.

Saturday, July 22   In camp

Sunday, July 23   In camp

Monday, July 24   Brought out Rolls of seven companies & had them signed.

Tuesday, July 25   Men paid Except Co. K.

Friday, July 28   Sent horses to Portland & Rockland. Telegraphed Abbott

Saturday, July 29   Went to Bath.

Sunday, July 30   To Wiscasset. Called at Hubbards & Robinsons & went to meeting in Eve.

Monday, July 31   Returned to Portland & took boat for Boston. Left box &c at American House.

Tuesday, Aug. 1   From Boston to Albany.

Wednesday, Aug. 2   From Albany to Stamford.

Sunday, Aug. 6 Went to Church at Hackersfield.

Monday, Aug. 7 To Bloomville. Put advertisement in paper. Wrote Hill.

Tuesday, Aug. 8 Sick

Wednesday, Aug. 9 Wrote Pauline & Land. Sent McEvans papers.

Sunday, Aug. 13 Went to Church at Hackersfield.

Monday, Aug. 14 Rode to Richmondville in Eve. with the Churchills.

Tuesday, Aug. 15 Rode from R in AM to caves. Visit Explored Cave.

Wednesday, Aug. 16 Cool. Wrote McCray. Sent photograph & Edwin B[*indecipherable name*] paper for copies. Recd letters from Hill & Land. Returned from caves

Thursday, Aug. 17 Pleasant. Wrote Em. Saw Mr. Stephenson regarding project. (By error shld be 18th)

Friday, Aug. 18 Pleasant. Anniversary of battle of Weldon R.R.

Monday, Aug. 21 5 P.M left for Deposit. [New York]

Tuesday, Aug. 22 Reached Deposit.

[*End of Ellis Spear's daily entries*]

AUG. 6, 1865 — FINAL ENTRY

[*Entry on the last three pages of the 1865 Diary*]

Peter Breen Cattle guard.
1st Division
James Maley Amb. Corp.
Both of 16th Michigan

Using threats against family of Jas. H. Clay and taking pistol from him. Reported that _____ had orders from Gen. Chamberlain act as scout &c at house of Richard D. Wales took his horse (he having taken oath of allegiance & having protective papers nailed on the door & their attention being called to them.) Also seven negro girls Anna & Ele Servants of R. D. Wales. Witnessed Mr & Mrs W. negro girls Anna & Eliza. Negro men. Isaac & Andersen. All servants of Mr. Wales. Also using threats to family of R. E. Clay to obtain brandy & took brandy from house of said Clay threatening to burn his house.

THE PERSONAL MEMORANDA
OF THE WAR OF THE REBELLION
(1896)

[*written by the author on the front endleaf*]

Personal Memoranda of the War of the Rebellion
by Ellis Spear
Col[.] 20th Maine Vol. Inf.
Brevet Brig. Gen. U.S. Vol.

Commissioned —
Capt. Co. G. 20 Maine Vol. Inf. Aug. 1862
Major 20 Maine Vol. Inf. Aug. 1863
Brevet Lt. Col. U.S. Vol. Sept. 30 [18]64 for "gallant & distinguished service" at the Battle of Peeble[']s Farm
Lt. Col. 20th Maine Vol. Inf. 1864
Brvt[.] Col. U.S. Vol. 1864
Col. 20 Maine Vol. 1864
(Issued 1865)
Brevet Brig. Gen. April 9, 1865

THE PERSONAL MEMORANDA OF THE WAR OF THE REBELLION

[INTRODUCTION]

I propose herein, at odd times, and as occasion may offer, to put into effect a long cherished plan, of writing my own personal recollections of the War of the Rebellion. I do not for a moment suppose that there will be any public interest, but may possibly be of interest to some of my descendants.

As I have not the time to make searches or verify statements as to times or dates, I wish it to be understood that I set down only my personal recollections, and I shall write as truthfully as I am able, and as fully as my time & a memory dim perhaps by the lapse of more than thirty years will permit.

[FROM WISCASSET TO WASHINGTON]

During the first year of the war I was teaching school in Wiscasset[,] Maine. I remember well the strain of the war, in that first year, upon those who remained at home. The eager interest for news from the front, the hopes fondly cherished & too often as insufficient foundation: the reverses (& these were serious.) The jealousy with which we watched the Copperheads, and all the dull & constant pain of anxiety for the fate of the country. It was as if the sky was always clouded. I had, for my own part, a feeling which I could not always suppress, that the Confederates, (Rebels we then called them) were better commanded & probably better fitted for war, & I feared they were, over the whole, superior soldiers. We had known them as fighting men, quarrelsome, with a trait of domineering & overbearing insolence, bred of a slaveholding state of society. I rather feared disaster than hoped for success before the battle of Bull Run. And when the news came of other riots, it seemed, for a little while, like the beginning of the End. The disaster at Balls Bluff, was a severe blow also. Fort Donelson lightened the darkness, & gave us a firm ground of hope. Here was not only victory, certain to remember, but, what was of more acc[oun]t a man, at last discovered, who could win victory. And, I remember too, what was encouraging, he appeared to be modest. There was no putting on of airs, only plain business. Very inadequately however, did we then, in all the fervor of our hopes, foresee the coming Grant. My school dragged on, & I have noticed memoranda which I made in the old copy of Virgil (the Aeneid) one of the few of the old school books which I have kept, & which memoranda related to incidents of the war, then occurring.

At the close of the first year, it seemed easier to go than to stay. There was a call which followed the disastrous Peninsula & Richmond Campaigns, "300[,]000 more" troops were required to take part in the struggle. It was a relief after the bitter disappointment & grief, which that great & bitter failure caused; but to my mind, there was an added pang of want of confidence, not only in the ability, but in the honesty of the leaders. At first reports came of success, & Genl. McClellan reported under the euphonious title of "change of base," what we afterwards knew was utter defeat & failure. It is true he saved the bulk of the army.

However, there was nothing to be done, but to put more men into the war, & we must all go who could. I think it was early in July when I began to raise a company. I procured the necessary authority from the State Government, the blanks & other papers, & started in the business which was altogether new and as unlike anything I had ever done, as could well be imagined. It was slow work. I had little money, and was at many disadvantages. For a while it seemed as if I should make a failure, & I contemplated enlisting myself. Fortunately however, there were two others in neighboring towns in the same business & as yet unassigned to any regiment or company. One of these was in Edgecomb across the river, J. F. Land, and the other, J. J. A. Hoffses, in Jefferson.

No one of us alone had men enough to make up a company. The other regiments, under the call, were full & we and our men were consolidated, or rather we consolidated ourselves, and formed a company which was assigned to the 20th regiment. We collected our men, & took them to Portland, the rendezvous [o]f the regiment. The understanding was that I should be captain, Land 1st Lieutenant and Hoffses 2[n]d Lieutenant.

The regiment was the last to be collected & organized of Maine[']s quota under the call for 300[,]000, men, made in the summer of 1862. It was collected from widely separated parts of the state, & had little material from the larger centers. But the men were almost wholly of New England stock and sturdy reliable men, self respecting and as good as any before organized into regiments. The same may be said of the officers. Most of them were educated men. Very few however, had any military experience, or military training.

One captain had served in the Mexican War, & was supposed therefore to know all that was necessary to be known. He proved afterwards to be of no account. I believe now that his age impaired his usefulness. There was another captain, who had served in another Maine regiment, as lieutenant, whose experience was of value, in organizing the regiment. Of the field officers[,] the Major had served in the Sixth Maine, and had procured his transfer & promotion for a captaincy in that regiment to the majority in this. He appeared to have had political influence, but I do not remember that he rendered any material aid in the organization or instruction of the regiment, and I do remember that afterward he proved to be the most untrustworthy, worthless skulker, the worst I ever knew.

The Lt. Col. (Chamberlain), was fresh from a professorship in Bowdoin, where I had before known him—a gentleman, though without military experience or knowledge.

Ames the Col., a young man, was a West Pointer, & had served in a battery from the beginning of the war. He proved to be an excellent officer, but was inexperienced in dealing with men & very little understood volunteers.

The camp was provided with comfortable quarters & plain camp rations, cooked for each company. But there was a scramble for everything. The clothing was dumped down & practically each helped himself. An inexperienced captain acted as quartermaster. Company books were provided, but few knew how to use them. Before we had time to drill or even learn the first rudiments of the military art, & almost before we were fairly organized we were ordered to Washington. My recollection of the time spent in that camp is rather dim. Like many others, it was some time before my commission came. At first we had no uniforms. I remember distinctly that I had no money. I had spent every cent in raising the company. I had not even funds to buy food & (as did others I believe) sponged upon the common supply. (Officers were not supposed to be supplied with rations.)

Fortunately a kind friend loaned me ten dollars (Wales Hubbard of Wiscasset, of grateful memory.) Another friend furnished a suit of clothing, uniform & undergarments complete on credit. I don[']t know how I obtained sword & belt. The company presented me with a revolver. Most of the officers, I believe, were better off than I, but in experience & military knowledge there was small difference with the few exceptions mentioned. Two companies had arms. Thus, partially armed, partially organized, wholly undrilled, not even in the manual of arms, able only to form line, & go into columns, we were rushed by train to Boston & from Boston by steamer, in company with the 36th Mass. to Washington. The ship, though large, was crowded, & we had a very uncomfortable time. On the way Ames kept a school of officers, & we studied tactics [in] the manual of arms & company movements. It was a very laborious voyage, but we reached Alexandria, just in time to see the wharves & river near the wharves crowded with craft, principally river steamers, occupied largely by wounded men, & there we heard first of the disastrous battles of the 2[n]d Bull Run.

We had been mustered on the 29th of Aug. & had left Portland at once. The ghastly sights at Alexandria were not at all cheering, nor was the news which accompanied these sights. We were transferred to another steamer & landed in Washington & the next day moved down to the arsenal & were armed. My first night in Washington was spent in an open lot near the arsenal grounds.

After arming the remaining eight companies, we started near nightfall with the purpose of joining the Army of the Potomac at or near Arlington Heights. The distance, I now know, must have been about six miles, but it seemed much longer then. The evening was warm, early in September, and the men were just disembarked from the steamer, after a wearisome voyage, in which they had been cramped & without exercise, and many of them weakened by seasickness. In addition they were utterly unaccustomed to marching & unused to the burden of the knapsack, ammunition & guns, which under the most favorable circumstances annoy the soldier, and impede his movements. Ames, I think, had never moved an infantry column before and had no idea of the nature of the business. He rushed the regiment, without halt, the whole distance at a quick pace. Nothing could have been more injudicious. With such new troops, & under the circumstances he should have halted frequently, and by steps made the men accustomed to their load, & to the gait. In consequence of the hot haste the men were strung out, & straggled badly. I had been accustomed to take long walks, about daily, for exercise, & was not so loaded. So I kept up without difficulty. But when, in the dark, we reached the camping ground, Ames, unwisely angry, upbraided, in terms calculated to humiliate the men: & unfortunately only those who had kept up, & therefore deserved praise rather than censure, heard the condemnation. The men, every one of them, sore, chaffed, heated & exhausted, by a march which they knew had been made unnecessarily hard, & who had done their best, listened in angry mood to this angry lecture from a man who had ridden all the way on horseback.

I saw these same men afterwards & I had them follow me many times on harder marches, more prolonged & painful without a murmur—but this rankled in their minds a long time.

We lay down on the ground, unsheltered & supperless. We had no tents, but blankets only. My recollection of the time spent at that place [is] very dim. I believe I had not enough to eat, even of bad rations, & the work of studying, drilling, perfecting the organization, was incessant. I cannot tell with certainty how long we were there. We had joined the 3[r]d brigade of the 1st Div. of the 5th Army Corps. There were rumors of attack on our front, all false, but the recent & utter defeat, & the presence of the enemy in the country near, were basis enough for any sensational story & camp is always a hotbed of stories. One day—it must have been only a few days after we joined, suddenly to us—we started. Ames had taken so little pains to inform us & prepare us, that, for my part, I thought we were only changing camp, when, in fact we were going on a long hard march.

I made no preparations, but my men had the rations delivered to them.

We crossed the Potomac by the Aqueduct bridge. The column moving in the canal aqueduct underneath the wagon way, the water having been let out. We moved through Georgetown and climbing the hill, turned into the Tenalley town road, & moved towards Rockville.

I think we must have haltered before reaching Rockville, but my memory of that march is almost a blank. I remember the heat by day, the chill & dew by night.

I remember passing through Rockville, & seeing some peaches, which my hungry soul longed for. I remember Frederick City, & the cattle killed & half dressed by the Confederates, hastily withdrawn.

[SHEPHERDSTOWN AND FREDERICKSBURG
SEPTEMBER—DECEMBER, 1862]

Thence, the army moved to South Mountain after delays. I kept no diary then. My whole energy & thought were absorbed & expended in keeping up with the column & in urging the men of my company to keep up. Sometimes I carried a gun of one of the men, to give him a rest. I remember one night, only twelve men of the 87 (the whole number of the company) came into bivouac with the regiment. I suppose it was as well as any of the companies did.

At the South Mountain we saw the first battle field with the dead lying upon it & to our unaccustomed eyes it was a ghastly sight. We came to the field of Antietam on the eve of the 16th of Sept. All the world knows about that battle. The fifth corps lay in the rear in reserve, & did not fire a gun. The 20th lay in the rear of a battery & had the experience of a "few shells," but nobody was hurt, & we did not hurt anybody. Our innocence was rewarded, with safety, but not with praise.

After that battle we advanced to the river, slowly, & on the 20th of Sept. a part of the brigade, (I am not now certain that more than the 20th crossed, wading at the ford.) Another brigade of the Div. was crossing on the dam a few hundred yards above us. There was the noise of battle there, but none on our front. After crossing we filed to the left & formed line under the bank & had scarcely formed, when we faced to the right & began to move back.

Somebody, it appeared, had blundered. The enemy opened fire with musketry upon us, as we returned, inflicting however, but slight damage. A battery on our side, on the hill above, by sniper firing, held back the enemy & saved us, as returning waist deep in the water, & slowly wading, we were as helpless as unarmed men, & worse, could not even run. The troops above, not thus protected, fared ill, & were badly cut up. We moved up to their position & lay all that day & the next night, on picket, firing at long range, upon the enemy on the other side, & receiving their compliments in return. When off duty in the night, we slept, or tried to sleep in the drained (imperfectly) bed of the canal, (slipps) the only unexposed place. Next day, it seemed to occur to one of our batteries to shell the enemy out of their shelter on the other side, & when the country there had become safe, we left.

We moved down the river to Antietam Creek, near the mouth,

on low malarial ground, & a raw regiment without tents unacclimated slept in that malarial air, during September & October nights, exposed as no acclimated man would dare to expose himself. I do not wonder that we lost by sickness, at that place, about one third (300) of our men. I now wonder that we did not lose more—that anyone escaped sickness. For the sick the only shelter was found in some old houses nearby, dirty & without furniture, deserted houses, & the sick lay on the bare floors, & layed with heads up against the walls. There was no food except camp rations, & not even candles for light & I do not now remember seeing any medicines. Although we were within 70 miles of Washington, the sick were exposed to deadly malarial air, without proper food, care or medicines.

How many died I do not know, but many, & no wonder. I remember one young fellow of my company, named Heath, (I think). He was not more than 18 or 19 years old, & had come to Portland with a younger brother, two sons of a widowed mother. I sent the younger back, & would not let him be mustered in. The other died in one of those shanties, lying on the bare floor, & for lack of the ordinary sanitary means of rescue.

At Antietam Creek we worked hard. The line officers studied tactics & the manual of arms, & company & regimental drill, reciting to Ames, & were drilled by him, & then in turn drilled the men. I never worked harder or faced worse. I had, as shelter a fly, which formed a cover open at both ends, & lay on the ground. I ate chiefly hardtack. Only a good constitution carried me through. One captain died & one was so seriously ill that he never returned to the regiment. Very many of the men lay in the hospital & we could do nothing for them, & the army was idle, as it had so often been before. On the whole our first experience in the army was miserable—nothing was done, & there was much sickness & suffering & loss to no purpose. I did not know then, but I did know afterwards that there was wretched management, & the loss & suffering was in great part unnecessary.

SHEPHERDSTOWN AND FREDERICKSBURG

Early in November we moved, tramping on foot, as a captain must, my outlook was scant. I do not remember, if I knew at the time, by what routes the other corps moved. The Fifth went down the river, on the left bank, crossing the hills, generally wooded, & passing the old rendezvous of John Brown, where he held his men, preparing to invade Va.

At Harpers Ferry we crossed on pontoons. The railroad bridge was in ruins, as usual. As we filed down the wooded hill slopes, & the gateway of mountains with the river flowing between, the thread of a pontoon stretched across the river, & men like flies, walking across, the ruined bridge and ruins of arsenal, all came into view. They presented a picture quite remarkable, & to me altogether new—picturesque mountains, the wrecks of war, & a moving army. Mixed with my remembrance of this unusual scenery, & act, is another quite as distinctly impressed on my memory, and showing how near the heart is to the stomach. I was in perpetual hunger, & by some accident at that time became possessed of a tin can of lobster, & I remember eating from the can, as we marched down the road.

Our corps crossed the Shenandoah, & moved down east of the ridge, & encamped near Warrenton, where McLellan was relieved. Our men had not become attached to that army commander; had no high opinion of his military abilities. We looked on with indifference as he made his last military flourish, & I do not recollect that there was anywhere, more than a slight & temporary ripple in the army.

There was some expectation of battle, but none came. Burnside took command, & we looked on that with indifference. There was no enthusiasm & no occasion for any. We moved on to (I think now) White Plains, a snow storm coming on as we marched, & when we encamped there was snow in the woods three inches deep, light & cold. I had left my blankets in the company wagon, & we had no ration—neither I nor my lieutenants. The prospect was dismal, cold, hunger & a snowbank for bed, for the wagons had not come up. But after a long tramp, I found the wagon. As both Lieutenants had first tried in vain, it was late, but when I got back the scene had brightened somewhat. Some of the men had kindled a fire for us, & another had brought me a part of the hind quarter of a captured sheep. We brushed away the snow, down to the leaves and spread our blankets before the fire. Soon there was mutton frying, and we dined sumptuously, and slept comfortably. I remember some hard marching on the way to Fredericksburg, and three days['] bivouac in a clay field, in the mud and rain. That was dismal, but fortunately we had procured shelter tents, and although a shelter six feet by five, and not high enough to stand in, and open at one end is poor shelter, against a November storm, it was much better than none.

Finally we came down to Fredericksburg, and the Fifth corps encamped near Stoneman Switch, in the railroad to Acquia Creek.

There we resumed drilling & were busy till the battle of Fredericksburg. On the morning of the eleventh of Dec. 1862, the sound of cannons broke the stillness of a clear & pleasant winter morning. We moved out towards the town of which we had before had but a glimpse.

The battle had begun before we came fairly in sight of the field, which was between the town & the hills beyond. The town itself was of brick and extended up & down along the river. The hill curved towards the town, on the right above, approaching the river, near the cluster of houses called Falmouth. On the left the hills receded again from the river. The general plan of the battle, is a matter of history, and so is the utter incompetence of Burnside.

As we stood on the hills north of the river & looked across at the fortified hills, crowded with artillery & lined with rifles pits, & upon the broad & clear level to be advanced over, against an almost semicicle of fire, I think few had any hope of success.

For my part, I went in simply to do my duty without enthusiasm or even hope. I saw the line engaged, halted in front of the works of the enemy & firing. Along it, & along that of the enemy extended the thin angry smoke of musketry, wreathing up &

drifting away, & constantly renewed. This was on the center, & to our right. I could not see on the left, but all up and down the enemy[']s line were smoking batteries, and everywhere in the air white puffs of bursting shells.

On our side, north of the river, on the high ground our battery was replying, and on the plains beyond the town the field batteries. In the afternoon we crossed. The clayey road was muddy and slippery. Field batteries were hurrying up, & running their horses down one muddy slope to gain momentum enough to carry them up the opposite. A horse on one gun slipped & went down, & the whole team, horses[,] men & guns, were piled up together, & rolled in the mud. We were moving in column, down the river, to the head of the pontoon. A battery of the enemy had the range of the pontoon, & just as my company turned to enter upon the bridge, a shot dropped plump down into the mud, by our side. We laughed to see [William] Rankin—an underwitted fellow in the company—jump as the shot struck, but generally there was not much hilarity or little occasion for it. We got across without loss, filed to the right, on the first street & moved westward. The town was utterly deserted of inhabitants. I remember how the brick walls were shattered, where solid shot had crashed through, & there was a bank building on the right hand side of the street, in ruins. There were troops, at random, in the streets, & men on the other sidewalk were passing freely about bills from the wrecked bank. One handed me a roll, & supposing them worthless I passed them along to the men. I afterwards saw these bills quoted at 30 cents on the dollar. But I was not at the time thinking much of bills. We filed rapidly to the left, & moved obliquely to the front, through the town. Beyond we halted on a road leading southwest, with a haystack near the center of our regiment. Our corps, was in the center grand division, but whether the whole was put in, I do not know, I do not think our whole corps was in.

We sat down & rested, the men sitting & lying. About us was incessant roar, & the scream of shells, & much smoke. On the right I saw a battery galloping through the smoke, half hidden. It seemed to me like a great storm, such as I had seen in the woods in Maine, when the oak trees roared in the wind, & clashed their branches, & creaked where limbs crossed. The men were sitting or lying down all quiet. I remember, when they were ordered to lie down, one of my company, Dodge, in squatting or in some way, exploded his gun cartridge & shot himself in the hand.

It was a curious effect of the uproar & danger, that, feeling the wound, he dropped his gun & ran, his impression being, I suspect, that he had been struck by a missile from the enemy. It was our first severe battle, and I suppose I noticed little things, or took a different view of things. I walked to the center where Ames & Chamberlain were & Ames said, "This is earnest work." That struck me as a remark very appropriate to the occasion. I went back to the company, & sat down on a rock, in front of the men.

While I sat there a little dog came along. It was, as I remember now, a small dog of the rat terrier breed, & evidently somebody[']s pet, probably left behind by some family, in their flight. The little fellow was shivering with terror, and I took him in my arms & held him, & soothed him as well as I could. The poor little fellow seemed to have intelligence enough to understand the danger. Perhaps, like raw troops, the noise most alarmed him. But he knew more than some cows that we passed, which were feeding in spite of the uproar. But to return. How long we waited, I can not now tell, if I ever knew, I do not think I looked at my watch. At last however, I heard the brigade bugle blow the charge, or "forward," & we moved by the front. After we had advanced a hundred yards, or so[,] it occurred to me to see whether or not my company was coming on all right & keeping closed up. So I drifted to the rear. It seemed "all right" & I plunged through to the front again. I do not remember thinking of any danger. The uproar was immense, & the air was full of the shriek of shells. Soon we reached fences, & I broke my company to the front, & went through by the flank, & then came forward into line. We soon thereafter reached a ridge, where a line of troops were lying, pretty well sheltered, but in musket range of the enemy. Here we halted, & lay down. It appeared that we were put in simply to reinforce the line first sent in, & if there were any intentions to renew the assault on that day, it was abandoned—this was the 11th day of Dec. 1862—(I am writing from memory alone). We had lost but a few men, in the advance, I remember only one in my company, but I saw some of our dead covered with a blanket.

The enemy kept up a steady but scattering fire on us, mostly with musketry, but, as we were fairly well sheltered when lying down, we suffered little excepting in discomfort.

It was unsafe to stand, & only comparatively safe to move around while it was light. Soon however, night came, not unwelcome. Exposure & discomfort in a hopeless adventure: defeat & humiliation, the loss we knew not how many of good men, discouragement and increased distrust in the commanding General, all this was worse than all the danger a thousand times, and covered us with gloom. But weariness overcame our despondency and I, for my part, was soon asleep, [in] spite of the surroundings. I had left my blanket with Vinal, my man, and he had not appeared. He was a man of no enterprise & had kept out of danger. I had been suffering from billiousness and jaundice & was yellow from a saturation of bile, but I had no thought or anxiety on this acc[oun]t. I found a piece of board, which I interposed between my body & the mud and lay down. Some one near me loaned me the use of one side of his blanket. I remember waking in the night & witnessed that phantasm, in the sky, always strange, but at that time & with the surroundings, well calculated to strike the imagination. The northern sky was red with the Aurora Borealis and blood red flushes ran from near the horizon upward. Lying on the field, in the stillness of the night, with the bodies of the dead about me, with heaps of them a little to the front where the center had been cut down or driven from the stone walls, I might well imagine it the reflection of the thirteen thousand killed or wounded that day; or perhaps it was the flush of shame on the face of the north; or did it portend worse. We were a defeated army, weakened by loss, & dispirited, and with the river behind us, & a veteran & victorious army in our front. But a kindly weariness, like death, dissipated foreboding & regrets. We lay in the same place the next day, & there was no change. Next night our brigade moved back into the city, and the 3[r]d night came again to the front. We understood that the army was to withdraw that night. A captain in a regiment does not know much of the general movements of an army, until the battle is over, & he hears it in camp, or sees the account in the newspapers. What had occurred on the left we did not know, but only that there was failure there, as on our front, in the Center-Grand Division, for the enemy were unshaken. During our advance from the front[,] trenches had been dug, & these we occupied. There was no sleep, & we were on the alert. With another officer I crawled out to the front, as far as we thought it prudent to go, and we could hear the voices of the enemy, & what seemed to be the sound of picks or spades. After midnight the clouds were scudding across the sky & I saw glimpses of the waning moon.

About two o'clock we began to move to the rear, silently withdrawing from the disastrous field, thirteen thousand less, & more than thirteen thousand worse. Only one pontoon bridge remained, and the men of the engineer corps were waiting to take this up. As we crossed it began to rain. Stumbling and waiting through the dense darkness, we moved up the bank, & apparently away from the river, and wet & tired our regiment turned aside into a stumpy field, where the tree[s] had been cut away by the soldiers.

Here in the dark & rain we halted for the remainder of the night. The men had their blankets & shelter tents with them, & by using their muskets, contrived to brace them up so as to form some shelter, and cover from the rain, although their only bed was the wet ground. But my lieutenant, Land, and myself were in more uncomfortable plight. We had had little to eat, were hungry, wet, tired, & without shelter in the night & darkness. We sat on a stump & held council of war. I suggested to Land that it seemed to me the place or near the place, where we had rested the day before the battle, & that if that were so[,] Vinal might be near, that he would be likely to return to the place he knew. So Land, having a prodigious voice, got upon a stump & roared into the stillness of the night, "Vinal!" There was a pause, & in the stillness we heard the squeaking voice of Vinal, not fifty yards away. Him we found carefully housed in a shelter tent, dry & with some straw for bed, & something to eat. Him also we displaced & having eaten a few of the delectable crackers, we slept soundly.

[WINTER QUARTERS—"THE MUD MARCH" JANUARY—APRIL, 1863]

As for the details of the battle of Fredericksburg I have after all, little personal knowledge. I know that we moved into camp, opposite the town with the river between, several weeks before the attack. We gave constructive notice of intended attack & then waited for the enemy to fortify & prepare for us; & we gave them ample time. They used it well, & to a natural[l]y strong position they added works almost impregnable. In front of these we were dashed. Nobody had any enthusiasm for Burnside at the best, & he proved worse than McClellan, for McClellan had more sense & prudence. After Fredericksburg there could be no doubt of his incompetence, but he was not then relieved. We lay in camp in an uneventful way, always studying and drilling, with little spare time. Army life grew pleasanter, as we became better accustomed to it. Ames was less intolerant & we had all the natural advantages of better acquaintance with him, & with each other. I had reason to be satisfied, as he complemented me "for the handsome manner in which I brought my company up" in the battle. Excessively spurred by defeat, and I suppose by crying from Washington, Burnside made another attempt. Of the general place of the movement, I was not aware, & never since have taken trouble to learn, except that it was an attempt, to turn the left flank of the enemy, by crossing at (I think) U.S. Ford, a little above Falmouth. I think it was the 1st day of January, when we moved. A threatening day, which before evening[,] developed a winter storm. The roads must have been soft when we started. I write what I now remember, for part is dim & part vivid. As to the number of days I was not certain. I distinctly remember that cold winter storm. We were moving on a road, which ran along by the side of a wood, of oak trees. Somewhere ahead, the column was blocked. Near us doubled teams were struggling particularly to pull a single gun, the wheels of which were in mud to the hub. The starting rain struck us in the face, & wet us through. Under foot there was only mud, & no dry place where we could sit; yet it was miserable to stand with boots in the cold mud. Standing was more tiresome than marching, yet we were halting most of the afternoon (I believe). Near dark the order came to bivouac for the night, & we moved into the wood. I wrapped myself as well as I could in a blanket & sat at the foot of a tree leaning against the trunk. After the miserable night, we moved on a few miles, & went into camp in a forest of oaks, where we lay that night & part of the next day. The rain ceased, but there was fog. The men built fires of the green split oak which caused a pungent smoke, very painful to the eyes, & tolerable only when we wrapped our heads in our blankets & lay down on the ground. The whole affair was a failure, and the confederates jeered at us from the other side of the river. We moved back to our old camp, more dejected than ever, and with even less confidence in the commanding officer. We returned to camp life, to which we had now become accustomed.

I put up a rude shelter, partly excavated in the sandy soil,— partly made of poles laid one upon the other, log house fashion. The width was about six feet, & length about 10, I think. The bed was across the rear end, and at the front there was a fireplace of mud, stones & sticks, & by the side of it a door. It was my first house. Prior to that the only shelter had been a "fly", a piece of canvas about 7 feet by 12 or 14 feet, which formed a shelter, when

WINTER QUARTERS—"THE MUD MARCH"

laid over a ridge pole, but had the disadvantage of being open at both ends, & required adjustment according to the direction of the wind. For this new house I had obtained some shreds of cloth. The plan of the house was something like this—[diagram from Spear's manuscript] A=bed of poles covered with pine boughs, B=fire place, C=door, D=chair made by cutting a barrel thus & filling the lower part with boughs.

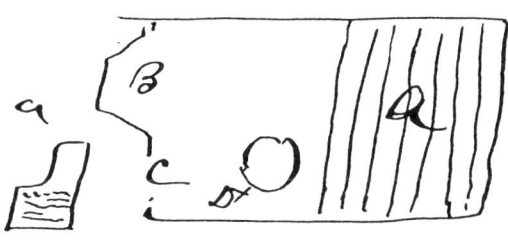

This house was occupied by my lieutenant & myself. Snow drove through freely, & neither in bottom, top or sides, was it water tight. Fire wood was scarce & green pine at that, nearly incombustible. In bad weather we either both went to bed, or took turns, one lying in the bed, & the other sitting in the barrel. How it snowed on the 22[n]d of Feb. (1863)—our bed was supplied with an extra white coverlet of snow. When possible we drilled. We had many sick in the regiment, mainly, I think, from lack of care. There were many deaths, but none in my company.

I looked after the diet of my men, & gave them flour porridge, when sick. The ordinary army rations of "hardtack" and salt pork was abominable, and for a man sick of malarial fever & diarrhea, almost deadly. I have no doubt the flour [o]f which I was fortunate enough to save the barrel delivered at one time in lieu of bread, saved lives. We had this winter some camp rationing, & once I procured soft bread, an immense luxury, though without butter.

I remember well the 22[n]d day of Febr[uar]y 33 years ago today. My lieutenant at that time was [Thomas D.] Chamberlain & we woke in the morning to find a snow storm blustering outside, & a considerable snow bank on our bed. The cracks between the small logs which formed our walls, had admitted plenty of snow on bed & dirt floor. As the floor was below grade sweeping would have been difficult even if we had had a broom. We built a feeble fire out of the green pine wood & made the best we could of the uncomfortable circumstances. It was cold & damp outside and cold & damp within. However, the snow ceased, & in a few days melted and we were again comfortable. I had a rather severe sickness as a result or culmination of the jaundice with which I was afflicted prior to & during the battle of Fredericksburg, but I did not go to the hospital & by careful dieting, (I lived on flour gruel) I recovered, & before spring had gained in flesh to 130 lbs. Nothing unusual occurred in camp. The usual routine was in drill, & study, & keeping the men in good condition. We were becoming acquainted with the business, & were feeling more at home.

About the 8th of March in this spring, (1863) I obtained leave of absence (of 14 days) and left for Stamford, N.Y. where, on the 13th of the same month, I was married to Susie M. Wilde to whom I had long been engaged. It was much more than a year since I had seen her and there had been no time in the press of raising men in the summer of 1862, & too much hot haste to get to the front, when the regiment had been raised. There was not much time, & to many, it might have seemed an improvident scheme at that time. But the dear girl herself desired it, and in case of my death in the service, it seemed to me better that she should be left a widow. We were married at her father[']s house by him, in Stamford, Delaware Co. N.Y. on the 13th day of March 1863, & afterward left for Maine. In our mutual happiness we forgot the slenderness of our outfit, the extreme plainness of our wedding, absence of presents, and all that. I left her at Sara Wilde (her cousin) in N.J. & with a heavy heart started for the front again. The pleasure had been short, only a few days, & there were many chances that I should never see her again. I was with the regiment again within the limit of my leave.

The routine of camp went on as usual. While at Stoneman[']s switch the small pox appeared & the disease broke out amongst our men. This was towards spring, & the regiment was detached from the brigade and moved across the railroad to a piece of high ground where it was isolated. Those having the disease were removed to the hospital and we were soon rid of it. It somewhat interrupted our drill, but by that time our men, (what remained of them,) were well drilled. I do not now remember the number of men remaining. We had brought into the field about 900 men or more, but not quite a full regiment. When the campaign of 1863 opened, we suffered small loss in battle, but I think we had left not fully four hundred (400) men. The campaign opened while we were in quarantine. The Army left us in the same camp. But before a few days, Ames had his promotion as Brig. Genl. which left a vacancy. I had not thought of promotion. I was a junior captain, without political influence, and ambitions only to do the duty assigned to me. Chamberlain was Lt. Col. & Gilmore Major. The former had faithfully & ably attended to his duties, & stood well. Gilmore had skulked in every action in which we had been engaged, & had taken no part. But he was, (as we did not so well know then,) a schemer, and with some political influence. We, Keene, myself, my Lt. Chamberlain, & others, [were] in Land[']s tent, in the evening of the day Ames['s] promotion had been announced, & Gilmore was there also. It was after dark, and our orderly came saying that Col. Ames wished to see Capts[.] Keene & Spear. We went directly to his tent & found him alone.

To be brief he told us of his promotion, & that Chamberlain would succeed him as Col. Further that Gilmore was not fit for the service, but that, to let him down easily, he was to be promoted to be Lt. Col. & then retire by resignation. I was to be made Major, & as soon as Gilmore resigned, (which was to be immediately after receiving the promotion) Keene should be major & I Lt. Col. This was highly satisfactory to us, as it was unexpected & unsolicited. Soon Gilmore came in looking foolish, & we took our leave. As we went out, Chamberlain (Tom) met us & told us that Gilmore had followed us & while we were talking with Ames he (G.) had been listening with his ear to the canvas of the tent. I wonder now how we could have been so stupid as not to see that he could not be trusted & why we did not at once proceed against him, or at least inform Ames of the sneaking act. But we did not & let the matter drift.

[THE BATTLE OF CHANCELLORSVILLE MAY—JUNE, 1863]

Soon, on the first of May, came the battle of Chancellorsville. As we were in quarantine we could not join the brigade, but on request to be assigned to some duty, we were sent to guard the telegraph line from the right at C. to Falmouth. As my company was the left Co. my station fell at Falmouth & from the hill I could see the charge of the 6th Corps on the Heights. From the hill opposite Falmouth, I could see the town, the line of the Rebel works against which we had charged in December, & the slopes between the works & the town, & the fields nearer the town. I saw the sixth corps form on the green field, the batteries go into position, and then of the enemy open fire, & then the steady forward movement of the line. The hill was soon covered with smoke, and as the line got nearer there was a mingled crash of artillery and musketry, & the blue line dashed into the smoke, with fixed bayonets. Instantly the canon ceased, & evidently the stillness denoted that the bayonets were at work. Soon the enemy appeared running to the rear, & the batteries limbered up & galloped forward [i.e., hitched horses to carriages to move artillery]. I could see the rebel infantry rally & endeavor to make a stand, but ran again, as the shells began to burst over them.

But the works were taken, & the 6th moved out of sight. Meantime the noise of battle had been audible far [to] the right. The sad result is well known, but we waited there in ignorance.

There was no very great confidence in Hooker. After a day or two, (My memory is not clear as to the time,) orders came down to go back into camp. It was near night & threatening rain. I determined to risk the attempt to take my company directly across the country to our old camp. There was no direct road & the intervening country was full of stumps where the troops had cut the timber during the winter, and all about, were wagon tracks in all directions, where the wood had been hauled out. Night & rain & utter darkness soon came on, but not before I had pretty well secured the direction, as near as I could guess, for the camp was several miles distant & there was no guide, or land mark. However, my experience in the woods in my boyhood, served me good purpose, & I led the company directly to the camp. Chamberlain came by the circuiting road & did not reach the camp till midnight, & then only with [f]ew, the rest straggling. Soon after we moved to a camp farther up the river, & then still further, and bivouaced in the woods in the river vall[e]y, picketing along the river.

[THE BATTLE OF GETTYSBURG JULY, 1863]

It was a malarious country. I do not now remember how long we lay there, but in June we moved again, & thereafter began the Gettysburg campaign. A night march brought us to a well, soon drained dry & we were tortured with thirst. Next day fortunately we crossed Cub Run (I think) and we moved in to Manassas Junction or near, & after a day or two moved across near the outposts of the defenses of Washington, towards the Potomac. I well remember the painful marches. The heat was excessive and the roads of clay, trodden & ground by thousands of feet & hundreds of wheels, sent up clouds of dust of unpalpable fineness, & so dense as to render it impossible to see twenty feet ahead. So[,] wet with perspiration and dried with dust that penetrated mouth, nose[,] ears & every part of the clothing, we dragged on. The features of no man were distinguishable. One night however, or rather early in the evening, we came to Goose Creek, a clear abundant stream, amongst green banks & slopes, & shaded by great oak trees. It seemed a Paradise, & we bathed & rested, & had our underclothing washed. Thence we moved to near Aldie, where the cavalry preceding us, had a sharp fight. (Where Col. Doty was killed.) Here Chamberlain was absent, as I distinctly remember. I am not certain where he was, & he soon returned. His absence, however, had left Gilmore in command, and the manifest approach to the enemy, soon determined the state of his health. He at once became sick & left for the hospital. Our commissions had not come, & Keene & I were still on foot. In the absence of all field officers[,] Clark of Co. E was senior & would have commanded the regiment. However, the brigade commander sent Lt. Col. Conner of the 44 N.Y. to us, temporarily. We (the 3[r]d brigade) moved out from Aldie, towards Snickers Gap supporting the calvary. A little beyond Middletown we encountered a small body of the enemy posted behind walls, & there we drove across the creek, & the cavalry followed them. As we approached the creek in the woods, the enemy began shelling us. Here a solid shot or unexploded shell struck one of my men John P. West, a non commissioned officer, and tore his leg from his body. I was near him but nothing could be done for him, for although he seemed to be breathing faintly he was not conscious, and the leg was torn off close to the body, & appeared to be connected only by a single tendon on one side. I went in with the Co. & sent men back after the fight was over, who found him dead & buried him. Whether his remains still lie there or not I do not know. The enemy was driven back though Upperville & we returned—as I now remember—through Aldie & after some days moved to the Potomac. I had been about this time, appointed as acting Major, although my commission had not come. I had been recommended, but Clark was making a fight for the place, and had some friend or relative on the Governing Council. This temporary appointment, however, gave me one privilege, most fortunate, as it happened, of riding a horse. The horse was a very poor one, but I am not sure that he did not save my life, for on the way I fell sick. I suppose the malarial poisoning of the Rappahannock valley, feeling the heat & improper food, brought on malarial fever and this was accompanied by diarrhea. I was barely able to ride, and after dismounting at the rests, it sometimes seemed impossible to remount. I would not think of going to the hospital in such a time as active campaign, with so much at stake. Lee was known to have crossed the Potomac and with a powerful & confident army, he might strike anywhere. Unless met & checked the north would be in his power.

There had never been a time of greater anxiety, or one where every man was more urgently needed. It was no small element, too, in the anxiety, that right in the midst of the movement, we had changed commanders. The greater part of the army did not know Genl. Meade, and felt no special confidence in him. Indeed I remember well the night march of the 1st day of July, when we were hurrying forward to the front at Gettysburg. A report was spread along the column, that McClellan was in command of the army. The men cheered as if a great victory had been won. Certainly McClellan had never done much to inspire confidence, but even McClellan, compared with any body unknown to the army, was or appeared to be welcome.

I do not recall very distinctly my own feelings. I believe what little vitality I had was consumed with keeping up with the column. I remember only weakness, utter fatigue, no food except pork & hardbread, which my soul loathed. We rested in a field on the afternoon or evening of the first & then moved rapidly to the front, & a very hard march brought us to the battle field, where we rested some hours. I think there I slept. I fancy everybody did, who could. But in the afternoon we moved to the left, towards the "Wheatfield." I remember that shells broke in our columns, as we moved to the left.

Turning towards the front, with Little Round Top just at our left, we were near entering the wheatfield, when the head of our brigade was turned to the left, and we moved back & around, in rear of Little Round Top. I did not notice the front of that rocky ridge, but the rear or east side was wooded, a rather open wood of oak mostly, and the slopes were strewn with boulders. We went into line facing the left. The 16th Michigan at first was on our left, but was at once moved to the right of the brigade & we remained on the extreme left, and "refused," on facing directly to the left, towards Big Round Top. The uproar of battle was going on, but now wholly out of our sight, & not near. I remember hearing the sound of artillery on the right, which seemed to be in the rear. It must have been on the extreme right. We had then no knowledge of how the battle was going, except that we seemed to be holding up our own. I do not remember hearing then anything after of the engagement of the first day. I did not know where the original line of battle was, nor of the "Sickles Angle," so much discussed afterwards. The uproar of battle was loud in the Wheatfield in or near which our line of battle seemed to be, when we turned aside from the movement we were marching towards it. But from the shot[s] which were coming over while we were then moving to the Wheatfield, we were sheltered when passed in rear of Little Round Top. I found it difficult when on this ground a few years ago, to determine exactly the position we occupied during the battle of the Second Day. I know that it was on the southern slope of the Top & that the right faced about squarely to the left. There were oak trees in abundance, but the view was open to the front, for there was no underbrush that way, nor where the center & left of the regiment stood. I remember that on the right there were some pine or similar small trees which hid that part of the line from view. When I visited the field, after the war, and again more recently, I could not perceive any marked change in the forest, except as must have been, the trees were larger. But even these had apparently grown very slowly. We selected the spot some years ago, (may be 10) [October, 1882] a party of officers of the 20th choosing that line on which we could all agree, and more particularly determining it by a large boulder, on which, or near which, some said our colors stood, during the battle until the charge was made. I was on the left, in my position as acting major. I saw a line of battle of the enemy moving down the hill, on the other side of the vall[e]y. I remember distinctly now, the appearance. It was the first intimation of their approach, as they came on in solid line, without skirmishing & the woods on Big Round Top hid them until they nearly reached the level between the two hills. The trees, I think on that further slope were smaller, & thicker. My recollection is that I first saw their gray legs & that they seemed to be extending beyond our left, & to be coming in a direction to strike our left. I went quickly to the right & found Col. Chamberlain & told him & suggested that it would be well to bend back two companies to face Slightly to the left & with his approval, I did this. From this, & my recollection of the appearance of the confederate line, I knew that they disclosed the line more than musket range distance. It must however, have been only [a f]ew minutes before they opened fire.

But I should here say that, on taking position Chamberlain had thrown forward, as skirmishers, Co. B (Capt. Morrill[']s) and these men had disappeared in the woods in front. I do not know what the instructions to Morrill were, but evidently he had inclined to the left, or that the enemy, in advancing, had inclined to his right, (or both) as Morrill was not driven in, & I have no recollection of hearing a shot, indeed I am certain that there had not been a shot fired, when the enemy appeared coming down the slope.

Soon enough[,] however, the firing began. I don[']t remember, if I noticed, who fired first. I doubt if there was appreciable difference in time. Our line, weakened by the absence of Morrill, numbered about 300 men, & officers. We had some advantage perhaps of higher ground, but no shelter.

The battle was hot at once, and wholly musketry. The enemy did not charge us, but stood up & fired. Their line scattered out somewhat, there men taking advantage of the boulders, which afforded them some shelter, & so they probably got nearer than otherwise they would. It was hot indeed and the men were falling. At one time in the early part of the fight, but not at the first, the line on or near the left swayed back a little. I remember that Land & I were, in the excitement of the moment, holding our swords in both hands, by hilt & top, against the backs of the men to keep them up. But the movement was only slight—some stayed. But the movement was from the color company toward the left. The colors did not move. It seems to me now that there was a lull at one time in the fight. I remember going to the center, at the colors, & seeing Knight, a corporal of my company, detailed in the color guard & down. I asked him where he was shot. "Right through me" he feebly said.

I remember these incidents: the rest was uproar & earnest hot work. I smelt the hot smoke, the faces of the men were set. How they worked. One fellow fell out. I went to him & he said that his gun was clogged.

I saw Kennedy limping to the rear, wounded as I supposed & knew afterwards. But there was no skulking on my part of the line I know, at least after the battle began, & I believe there was none before, or at anytime during or before the battle.

After the slight lull[,] the firing grew hot again. Suddenly, on the right, I heard the shout "advance," "forward." I saw the line begin to move, I had rec[eive]d no orders to charge, & there was no time to deliberate on the result. The whole line, as far as I could see it, was moving & shouting, or appeared to be, and if any were going forward, all must & I shouted "forward," & down the slope we plunged, in not very orderly line, but with a good deal of momentum, & with no small noise. The enemy did not seem to resist much. For my part[,] I did not expect them to. It seemed as if we must go over them.

We did run over some, the men scattered & lying behind the low boulders. There were two behind one rock on which I leaped. It was lower uphill. Two men rose up behind it, surrendering at once. The rest ran—for awhile we were busy picking them up. We captured about 300 men. After, or rather during the last of the fight, Morrill appeared, & I will now tell his story. Advancing perhaps too far & too much to the left, he had been cut off by the confederate line, interfaced between him & us. He seems to have expected the

THE BATTLE OF GETTYSBURG

flanking attack around the east side of the mountain. The enemy did not discover him—taking his men, & some sharpshooters from another organization who were there—about 50 men in all, he moved up, unobserved, & took position behind a stone wall, in rear of the position occupied by the enemy. The stone wall bounded that part of the wood & separated it from a field in the rear. Behind that it seems, Morrill had been keeping up a fire on the enemy, from the rear, during the fight & when we charged & the enemy fell back he had them in nearer range, & gave them the impression that they were surrounded, an impression the more easily entertained for the reason that they knew they had no support on their right, & must also have known that they were in rear of our main line. This made their surrender more easy & complete.

[*The writing is interrupted here by the following passage added to the blank recto sides of several manuscript pages. This passage is placed where Spear marked it (with an X) to be inserted.*]

Of the 300 captured many were taken in a lane bordered by high "worm" [wooden zig-zag] fences, between which, in their flight, they had corralled themselves. A few were shot attempting to escape over the fences, & the others surrendered.

In explanation of the charge I add here the story told by the men at the time, for it seemed strange that I did not get orders or notice, seeing that I was in my duty as Acting Major in command of the left of the line & the extreme flank.

We had gone into position on the slope of the hill facing to left & rear. The line on the left bending back from the colors. On the first appearance of the enemy, coming down the opposite hill, Big Round Top, & scattering themselves through the trees & bushes, I went to Col. Chamberlain & told him that they seemed to overlap us, & asked him if I should not bend back the left a little more to meet this flanking movement[.] He assented. As the sharp fire continued [I adjusted] the ranks & turned & the men readjusted themselves amongst the rocks, thus drawing back the line about the center, and the men wounded by the earlier fire, were lying in front, [their] side exposed and calling to their comrades to take them back out of the fire. Some men in Co. K suggested that they "advance & cover them" & therefore started the shout to advance. The shout & corresponding movement immediately spread to the left, (and I suppose to the right also.) But the cause & nature of the movement was not also transmitted with the shout, it was understood to be an order to charge—I repeated the order, which came "in the air," though I had received none directly, as it seemed to be the only thing to be done—Fortunately it resulted well. [*end of added passage*]

The wounded & dead of the enemy lay scattered along our front on the ground we had passed over in charging. One little fellow I remember calling to me for water. His arm was broken above the elbow. I called one of the men & we gave him water, I had none. After the rush & rout of the enemy & capture was over, I sat down on the ground utterly exhausted. How long we waited there I can[']t remember, but not long, for soon orders came for the 20th Maine to advance to the summit of Big Round Top.

What this was for I never knew. The movement would separate us, less than two hundred men, from the left of the Army, by half an hour[']s march over this difficult ground. However, there was no choice & laboriously we climbed that steep & rough hill. It was dusk when we reached the top, a wild rocky place, inaccessible except on foot. Down the further (western) slope, in the dark we encountered some Texas troops & by stratagem captured between 30 & 40 with a lieutenant Christian. We lay on the hill, unsupported, all night.

Feeling weak, and not daring to lie down, as I had no blanket, (my man servant had gone to the rear, during the battle,) I sat down at the foot of a tree and leaned my back against it. I suppose I fell asleep at once, as our sleep had been greatly curtailed during the forced marches of the past few days. When I awoke it was quite dark, & still about us, & I was shivering, & my teeth were chattering. I concluded that I had a chill,—crawled to a man lying near me. He shared his blanket with me,—that & the warmth of his body after a while warmed me, & I slept. The next morning the hospital steward gave me some whiskey—quinine, & I continued taking that with a great benefit, & soon recovered.

I should add one other point in this story of the Second day['] s battle at Gettysburg.

It was an extraordinary act, to charge as we did leaving our place in the line of battle without orders from the brigade commander or some higher officer. Writing for myself I can say that I had no orders, & did not see Chamberlain during the fight. What I did see & hear, relating to the advance, I have hereinbefore told. The story told by the men was as follows: The line on the left of the colors, as I have stated, either to get better footing in the rocks or to straighten, or to close up the gaps, fell back a few feet. This left the men wounded by the first fire of the enemy, lying in front of the line, exposed to the battery. They naturally called to their comrades to get them back out of the fire. This was not easy, as the men so doing, would be compelled to leave the ranks, & to break & disturb the ranks in bringing back the wounded men. Besides the fire of that part of the line would be checked. The easiest—quickest way would be to advance beyond the position on where the men were lying. Some one proposed to do this, some man in the company next on the left of the colors. He & others called out "Advance," & those next seeing the movement, & perhaps hearing the cry, also advanced, & so the whole line started. But, whatever those beginning the movement intended[,] the rest supposed it was a charge upon the enemy which was intended, & all rushed promptly. This Accords with what I saw, but I have heard that Chamberlain says he ordered the charge.

We had advanced to the summit of Big Round Top unsupported, the 20th alone. Later some of the Pennsylvania Reserves (our 3[r]d Div.) who had not joined us in the fight on the Little R.T. came up in our rear, after the skirmish on the B.R.T. but did not remain. The next morning however, (July 3[r]d) other troops came up on our right and, as I understood, completed the line of battle to the right on Little Round Top. But we were relieved and rejoined our brigade, and on the 3[r]d day were massed on the left of the center, & in the rear, where we remained during the heavy cannonading which proceeded the charge on the center. So much has been said & written of that cannonade that the subject seems worn out. Undoubtedly it was the heaviest we had seen or heard up to that time. We however, were pretty well out of its reach, and, while we were near enough to hear the whole uproar, an intervening hillock hid the combatants from our view. The "Pickett Charge" is a matter of history. I heard it but did not see it. We lay there all that day, & the night of the 3[r]d of July. It rained during the night—a heavy shower.—Capt. Clark & I had picked up a soldier[']s blanket, and lay down upon that, on a spot free from boulders, but it was a low spot, and we were flooded. We sat upon the wall near us, during the remainder of the night. Whether the battle was over or not we did not then know. I do not now remember that it gave us any very great concern. We knew we had beaten back the enemy, and we were too tired & sleepy for much reflection. But on the morning of the 4th we advanced. There was no enemy in sight. We crossed the Emmitsburg Pike, & moved, in column. The field bore ample evidence of the severity of the battle. Between our lines & the Emmitsburg Pike the ground was strewn with dead horses & dead men. In one place, huddled, were 19 dead horses. The heat & moisture had made all the dead bodies very offensive. Horses & men were swollen & the men were black. The swelling of the bodies of the horses had caused their legs to rise & this gave them [a] peculiar appearance, always noticed on the fields of battle in warm weather. A sickening odor pervaded the whole field. We halted on the Pike & remained during the greater part of the day. I remember at least eating my dinner there, not very savory, in that corpse infected air. At a barn near us, the shells had struck frequently. The ground was plowed in many places, & dead men of the enemy lay thick, & dead horses. The barn had caught fire and burned down to the mass of charred hay, on which were the burned remains of men—outside were half roasted remains of horses & men.

We buried the men about us, in the soft field. On the left, the sixth Corp was moving to the front. But the sound of musketry & cannon had ceased utterly—the enemy had escaped. Yet I remember how slow our movements were. Many miles (60 or more) lay between that defeated army—the river. What were we doing? It was only near night of the 4th of July that we moved, & then southward along the eastern base of the Allegheny range, while Lee had crossed to the western side.

[FOLLOWING LEE'S RETREAT
JULY—OCTOBER, 1863]

On the second day[']s march, the 5th corps crossed a span of the Allegheny range, extending eastward north of the village of Middletown. As our brigade came over the crest there appeared in front of us a charming view.

The broad vall[e]y lay at our feet, bounded on the west & north by the mountains & on the east by hills, mostly open fields with clumps of trees here & there. The farms were in view as upon a map. The farm houses in their groves, with other farm buildings, fields divided by fences and green with grass freshened by the recent rains, or yellow with grain field stubble. Over all this map, thus lying before us was a moving panorama, long columns of infantry & artillery & trains of wagons, on different roads, & in the distance white tents. No sound came up to us from that body of men & horses & mules & on the sweet rural landscape lying still in the July sun, we saw grim war moving without a sound.

I was not much inclined to sentiment in those days. Rough work, & slender fare, & (what was worse) malarial fever had knocked out of me all enthusiasm, yet that scene left impressions upon my mind, which I can[']t well describe. However, there was more hard marching. We crossed Maryland & the South Mountain & on the 10th of July were on the Sharpsburg Pike, with the enemy in our front,—skirmishing. We lost eight (8) men out of

Co. E. captured. Next day we advanced, but not fast enough to bring on a fight, & on the night of the eleventh the enemy escaped across the Potomac. Why did we not push them earlier? I don[']t know. We were in fighting direction, & ready.

Our corps returned in the sweltering heat of July, over the South Mountain. The march was exceedingly hard & men & battery struggled. Halting a day or two we then crossed the Potomac on pontoons,—moved down the eastern Slope of the mountains. The necessity of keeping in touch with the enemy on the other side turned our corps up through Manassas Gap. This was a march of ten or fifteen miles through ravines in the mountain slopes & depressions.

There was some fighting at Wapping Heights, in advance of us but we did not meet the enemy—our division at least did not. At our farthest advance [*deleted:* we] our brigade formed [a] line of battle and advanced through the woods up a not difficult slope. Fortunately it was not difficult for we were weak from lack of food, our rations not having kept up with the column, which occupied the single road. There was expectation, founded on I don[']t know what, that we should soon meet the enemy, & we kept sharp watch through the woods. That did not prevent hungry men snatching at the blueberries. After a while meeting no enemy we halted, & subsequently were recalled. I remember that my cook & general purveyor somewhere procured the fragments of a duck which he boiled with a few stray leaves of beet tops, found in a much trampled & plundered garden. It was served in a tin kettle[,] the beet tops floating, with a few scarcely distinguishable globules of fat, on the top of the unsalted water in which the bird had been boiled. We fished up the dismembered fowl, & tried to eat it, but without success. I could not get it down—one other member of the mess could not retain it. We moved down the vall[e]y, in the same famished condition, and, after two days past[,] moved into old fields overgrown with the common low black berry. The brigade nearly broke up. The men could not resist the temptation to gather berries. We went early into bivouac and a steer was shot, cut up & distributed before the beef had time to cool. I was fortunate enough to secure a small piece hastily broiled, before going on picket, & ate it on horse back. We made haste to establish the picket line, as a tempest was threatening in the northwest, & the line was to be established across fields & through woods in country[,] of course[,] unknown to us. One especial difficulty in establishing picket lines arose from the necessity of connection with the lines of other divisions on the right & left, the flanks of which must be discovered. The matter was not so difficult of course, in daylight. In this case however, darkness & a furious storm came upon us before the task was completed, and we were compelled to feel our way. I rode with Chamberlain, who was especially charged with the duty, & was in command of the division picket. Finally after much groping about we established the lines & made the required connections, & C [and] I rode back down the line. He selected one place & I rode to another part of the line, hoping to find my man & blanket, but not expecting to find any provisions. I found my way by the flashes of lightning, disclosing enough of the ground in front, to ride through in the utter darkness between the flashes. After awhile I saw in front a dim light, & feeling my way along, I found some of our men who had put up their shelter tent, & had a bit of candle.

The drenching rain had nearly ceased when I reached this little shelter, & on my call the men came out & brought me a piece of honey comb. During the rain they had procured a hive of honey, the rain beating down the bees, & of this they gave me a generous piece. In the rage of my hunger I devoured it, sitting on my horse, in the darkness. I ate the whole comb & all, & then it occurred to me that bees wax might not be digestible! However, there was no remedy, & I left the matter to be cared for by a good constitution & healthy stomach, not at all pampered by luxuries in those days. Further down the line I found Capt[.] Land, who had a fire by the side of a fence, where I partly dried myself, & lay down & slept soundly the remainder of the night.

I heard no more of the bees wax, & the next day we procured rations of that abominable stuff—hard bread.

That movement through Mannassas Gap never appeared to me to be a very sensible or brilliant affair. We marched up & then marched down.

I do not distinctly recall the other marches on the way towards the Rappahanock. We were a few days at the White Sulfur Springs, then moved to Beverly Ford on the Rappanhanock River, & there we went into camps & for the first time in three months, obtained camp rations—a change from the vile saltpork (fat) and if possible still more vile hard bread. My commission as Major had not yet come, & Clark, (Senior captain) had command, I acting also as field officer, when we first encamped at the Ford. It seems now very trivial that our minds should be occupied with such small affairs. The ordinary occupations of war are commonplace & camp life especially so. The dull routine of march changes to the dull routine of camp. The opportunity for anything very heroic, comes, (or did in those years before [18]64,) only now & then.

First we established the camp, & left the men, the position & order having been arranged—to make themselves comfortable. Then a detail was made to put up the headquarter tents.

This is in the suppositions that the encampment is for some days & the wagons are up. For some days the men are allowed to rest, put themselves & clothing & equipments, in proper condition, as far as possible, & if the quartermasters have supplies of shoes & clothing, & there be need, to supply any need. At this time, as usual, the first need was of "camp rations." These included fresh beef, and beans principally.

We had sometimes what the men called "desecrated" (desiccated) vegetables. The blunder of the men was near the truth. There were other items, salt[,] sugar, coffee, & very rarely soft bread. On this occasion I remember well the addition to the usual marching ration was the bean ration.

For cooking this the men used the big sheet iron kettles, which were carried in the wagons. The beans were put into the kettle and thoroughly boiled. Meantime a hole was dug in the ground and the earth about it heated by a fire kindled therein. Then the kettle, with the beans & a piece of fat pork, all closely covered, was put into the hole, & covered with the hot ashes & earth, & left to the action of the heat. Such a kettle of beans I had prepared and buried near my tent, under the eyes of the guard,—left to cook during the night. There was a violent tempest with rain during the night. The morning was chilly, and I did not rise on waking, but waited basely thinking of the beans, with watering mouth. All my patriotism, all zeal to put down the rebellion, all thought even of care of the regiment, discipline & drill, or sweetheart & friends was swallowed up in anticipation of those beans. Every pore & all the interior surfaces of my body, clogged for months with the fat of rusty pork and the uncooked plugs of still more rusty "hard tack," cried out for beans. No drunkard, recovering from a fit of delirium tremors ever wanted whiskey more than my stomach hankered for beans. And when the cook put his ungainly head into the tent, and dolefully announced that "somebody has stole them beans," I felt as if we had lost a battle. All my visions vanished & we breakfasted again on fried pork & the detestable unwholesome bread, some called bread, but really dried dough.

While at the camp my commission as Major came, and I assumed command of the regiment, Chamberlain absent, & his former Major, [*added between lines:* Lt.Col. before I was commissioned—then got his assignment at once & easily having friends at court,] whom I do not now name, (I believe I have before in this record) being also absent, skulking as usual, while there was danger of fighting. He was using his cheek & political pull to the utmost to save his worthless skin.

We remained some days at the Ford. Thence we moved out beyond Culpeper C. H. & went into camp, in a pleasant field, in that agreeable season of the year, September. The nights were cool & the warm days pleasant. We obtained some fresh vegetable from the surrounding country. My quartermaster, whose activity was great & his scruples small, had obtained, I believe from N.Y. a supply of counterfeit Confederate paper money, & with this he purchased eggs & sweet potatoes, most grateful additions to the scant bill of fare. I did not know of the Kind of money he used until afterward. He assumed generosity, I think. However, I suppose the money was the same to the vendors, & if it hurt appreciably the Confederate finances that was fair in war.

["PLAYING FOR POSITION"
OCTOBER — NOVEMBER, 1863]

As to [the] exact date at this encampment, I am at a loss, nor does it much matter. After a few weeks but some time early in October, (1863) I think, we moved one day, suddenly, towards the Rapidan, beyond our former picket lines. The encampment near Culpeper was a pleasant one. I drilled the regiment, the labor was light, & we were free from care. Our picket lines, which we passed had extended through wood & field, looking towards Madison C. H. It included one old plantation, with comfortable looking houses. I was in command of the Division pickets & in riding around I came upon this house. It looked pleasant, while neater than the ordinary Southern house, & with locust trees about it. The owners or white occupants did not appear. I saw only the colored domestics. The colored men had deserted. Some came through the lines at other points. On the picket line, stolen from some house in the neighborhood, I suppose, & dropped as useless to the thief, I found an old Donnegary Greek Lexicon, & it seemed like an old friend met unexpectedly in a strange place. It was indeed a strange place, there in the woods, for a Greek Lexicon.

To return to our movement, the fifth corps had, (I do not know if others were with us), advanced towards Madison C. H. & there we lay most of the day, waiting listlessly[.] Then suddenly we moved back, halted near our old camp for the night, & then moved through Culpeper towards the Rappahanock. Evidently there was general movement,—the two armies were maneuvering for advantage. After we crossed the river, part of the troops moved back & drove back the enemy advancing to follow us. This must have been only a part of the main body, that, as we afterwards knew, was then crossing the river above us. After some little delay we moved rapidly back on the line of the Orange & Alexandria R.R. It was reported that the enemy was moving on our left flank, & that a battle was imminent. Late in the afternoon the enemy struck Warren at Reams['] Station, but was resisted and a battery captured from him.

During the fight our brigade was hurried back to support Warren, but the engagement was over, & we met the captured battery. We continued our march, & fell back to Centerville, crossing the Bull Run. The last day was a long one & it was near midnight when we went into bivouac. There had been much straggling & the men were gathered by bugle calls from brigade Hd. Qrs. Thence we moved back to a point north of Fairfax C. H. & thence moved to the right to Ox Bow Creek, where we went into line of battle, in the woods. Then we bivouaced, & there were camp rumors that we were to go into Winter Quarters. Such stories will circulate in camp. However, there was doubtless some expectation that we should encamp there for awhile, & this belief had some ground of credence.

Chamberlain, then commanding this brigade, came over, after I had put my men into bivouac and suggested that he would give me more room to camp on, the next day. So we crawled into our shelters, rather discouraged by the fruitless movements, almost aimless movements of the week, but glad of a chance to rest. Next morning however I heard the bugle sounding the signal to "strike tents," & soon we were off again. What the movements of the enemy were we could scarcely guess. We moved down to the pike leading to Fairfax.

I established the brigade pickets [on] the right. This was towards night, & rain was threatening. After hard riding and much trouble to place the pickets in the wood, I had established them, and was riding along the line, when I met a staff officer, with orders to call the pickets in & to join the brigade, & follow it to Centerville. It was dark before we joined the brigade, & the march was in mud & heavy rain. About midnight however, we reached the neighborhood of Centerville. The rain had ceased,—we filed to the right into an open field, & lay down on the wet ground, for we were utterly tired out.

I have never learned the object of those moves back & forth, but they were probably more in view of real or supposed moves of the enemy. The next day we moved forward, Custer clearing the way, & the infantry of the enemy having fallen back beyond the Rappahanock. Our corps encamped near Three Mile Station on the Warrenton branch of the R.R. There we lay a week or more perhaps more than two weeks. Gilmore who had been skulking in the hospital or under pretense of being in the hospital, returned to the regiment, while we lay here. He had been absent 59 days, & under the general orders relating to such cases, would have been liable to be mustered out had he remained away 60 days.

As we were in camp he was safe for awhile at least, & so ventured back. His first care was to look after his personal property. Two fine blankets, claimed by him, said to have been obtained from the Sanitary stores, had disappeared, and he found them on the Quartermaster[']s horses. He therefore put the Q. M. under arrest, the first instance of discipline I ever knew him to show[.] In the advancing & retreating & rapid movements rendered necessary by the advance of the enemy[,] all the roads were required for the use of troops and trains, & sutlers had been sent to the rear. There was however, a hanger on about our Hd. Qrs. a sutler clerk, or some such character, and a friend of Gilmore[']s. Him[,] G. contrived to utilize in an ingenious manner. He (G.) wrote to the Hd. Qrs., or to the Dept. at W. representing that his men were suffering from lack of tobacco, & requesting permission to have a "package" for this need, transported on the Govt. train from Washington. So humane & thoughtful a request was granted, though probably there may have been some political influence. The package came down, & appeared as a big dry goods box, 500 cwt. as I remember, & this, in utter disregard of all decency, went into Gilmore[']s Hd. Qr. tent, which was for the occasion, converted into a sutler[']s shop. The tobacco was sold only for cash, & to anybody having cash. I remonstrated, but in vain, Gilmore had not a particle of soldierly spirit. However, after two or three days & before half of the tobacco had been sold, orders came to move. I had expected it the night of the 6th, & the order came early on the morning of the 7th—We struck tents early, the box of tobacco was put into the Hd. Qrs. wagon.

[RAPPAHANNOCK STATION NOVEMBER, 1863]

I formed the regiment, as usual. Gilmore knew enough only to ride in the column. We turned toward the enemy, & the river. As I moved the regiment by the right flank to the Hd. Qrs. where Gilmore sat upon his horse, I turned to go to my place in the rear of the column. Gilmore asked me to ride with him at the head. I knew perfectly well that he could not handle the regiment, & that he knew he could not, & I had lately seen him skulk. But of course I rode with him. We had not ridden far before he began to complain of pains in his hip, & this he kept up at intervals, growing more emphatic. I told him he would better go back, if he felt so badly, & get into the ambulance, for I was anxious to be rid of him. After a little[,] we came to a fence of which the men threw off the upper rails. I jumped my horse over, & looking back saw Gilmore on the other side, & that was the last I saw of him for a week. We moved down to Rappahannock Station where [there] was a brigade of the enemy on our side of the river, intrenched & with artillery.

The railway ran at nearly right angles to the river. The works were on a hill near the river & near also to the road & remains of

PERSONAL MEMORANDA

the bridge. The sixth Corps was on the right, of the R.R. & ours (the 5th) on the left. We moved in line of columns of regiments; doubled in the center. The works were on the right & more directly in front of the Sixth, & an embankment of considerable height intervened between the works & us.

Russell[']s brigade was in advance—& was to storm, but our skirmishes were well out, & on the left of the sixth, but separated from them by the embankment. Co. B from my regiment, Morrill in command, was on the right of the skirmish line, & finding that the sixth Maine was on the other side of the embankment, he with his company went over & joined them to give them aid, volunteering for the charge. We brought up considerable artillery, to which the enemy responded from batteries on both sides of the river, & there was a lively cannonade, until the charge. This was spirited, Russell charging in this line through dense fire, but over the works, the line grappling with the enemy, artillery & infantry.

Excepting my Co. B there was nothing of our corps in the charge, we standing back & watching the fight, but ready to join if necessary. It was not. The sixth corps troops supported Russell by charge in the left of the enemy line, & they broke for the river.

Then battery men cut the traces & spurred to the pontoon bridge. Horses & men crowded this narrow railless pass, & subjected the while to our fire, crowded each other off, into the stream, & some fell by the musketry.

I think all the guns & many of the infantry were captured, & the dead & wounded lay where they fell. The explanation of the actions of Co. B was made after the fight. They had volunteered; Morrill, the captain, had discovered that the Sixth Maine, (In which he had formally been an enlisted man) was on the other side of the embankment, & were going to charge. So he called this to his men & invited them [to] the neighborly entertainment of getting over & charging with them. Co. B did excellent service & we never carried our discipline to such Roman extremes as to punish a man for overzeal in getting into a fight.

RAPPAHANNOCK STATION

We lay that night in the woods guarding prisoners. The dead confederates were buried in the trenches, as well as could be done, & our dead on the west of the works. For so small an affair there were many. The charge was over an open field & in the face of musketry & artillery.

Next day our division moved down the river a few miles, & crossed, where we lay in the cold & snow. We were also short of rations. In view of the possibility of failure to connect with our horses, the men had been supplied with several days['] rations of bread when we left Culpeper, but in the mean time rations had been issued every three days, as usual. Bread carried so long is wasted, & after awhile, the waste accumulating, so to speak, the men were three days short. But the Commissary had no authority placed to duplicate an issue, & when hunger pressed the men there was resort to subterfuge. A large quantity of bread in boxes was laid out and submitted for condemnation, alleged to be spoiled. I was on the board whether as sole inspector or with others. I do not now remember, but I examined the boxes. They were open & full of bread. The top layers were mouldy, all of them. I did not examine underneath, but condemned the whole, & gave certificate for [a] new supply. I do not know that the bread was not destroyed, but I suppose & do not doubt that it was used to make up the deficiency. The regulations made such personal frauds necessary, The fact in this case was, I doubt not, we condemned bread, (mostly good) to supply a deficiency unavoidably occurring, nobody profited by it, or could possibly, & the men were kept from starving.

To resume the narrative. There was a considerable fall of snow. We recrossed the river, (what we went over there for I don[']t know,) & moved up on the left bank & went into bivouac. There we got up our wagons & I pitched the Hd. Qrs. tents, & had a bed of boughs made & my blankets opened. We were tired & hungry.

While I was busy in getting the regiment into bivouac, Gilmore came up. I found him on my bed. He pretended not to know that there had been a battle, & with cool impudence took command of the regiment.

There seemed to be something which had gone wrong, & soon I found that the Hd. Qrs. wagon of the 20th Maine had been raided, & all of Gilmore[']s tobacco stolen. Gilmore was in as much of a rage as his cold blood permitted. The cowardly sneaking out of the fight, of which he had been guilty did not appear to affect his conscience at all, but the loss of the tobacco, that was grievous. He suspected the teamsters of complicity in the plundering and directed that they be ordered back to their companies. I protested, & said that if they were, I should send them back to the teams, on the occasion of the next fight we got into. He evidently understood the suggestion, & withdrew the order. I have no doubt that Litchfield was at the bottom of the affair. Nothing was done about it, & G. did not dare to have it inquired into. In fact he had himself detailed to Washington, very soon after this. He had influence sufficient to keep himself out of the Army: and although I was left with only the rank & pay of major, ($149.50 per month), the only field officer, & with all the labor and care, & expense of keeping up the command[,] I was glad to be rid of him.

[MINE RUN
NOVEMBER—DECEMBER, 1863]

We were quiet until the 26th day of November. I was in the meantime saddened by news of the death of my classmate & near friend, the playmate of my boyhood, George R. MacIntyre. He died of consumption, in Warren, in November of 1863.

On the 26th day of November we moved across the Rapidan, crossing at German Ford. There was a small cotton field near the crossing, & I remember a battery of Light-Twelves in the field. After crossing we passed some rusty machinery near an old gold mine, & then took the road through the woods, which were dense on each side, and continuing all the march of that afternoon [and] evening. There was occasionally a cross road, & the column was exposed to dashes of the enemy cavalry. The wagons were in the column of infantry, at intervals. Flankers were thrown out on each side. With my own regiment and part of the 44th N.Y. I flanked the right of the brigade. The task was no easy one. The wood was a dense thicket of small pines & scrub oak, & I could not see ten yards. I kept at proper distance from the road by means of a line skirmishing near enough abreast to see each other, the line extending from the head of the brigade to the head of my flanking column, which consisted of a single file. I succeeded in keeping a closed column, and suffered no attack. On the right the enemy cavalry found a gap, at a cross road, & turned the head mules & ran off a few wagons, among others, Bartlett[']s Hd. Qrs. (brigade) wagon[.] We reached the Chancellorville House about midnight. It was a crisp frosty night, and the moon shone in [a] clear sky.

The flankers, weary with the long pull through the wood, doubly weary, were ordered to picket on the right, & after I had extended the line, connecting with the left, I rode back to where C[.] Clark had established my Hd.Qrs. Spruce pine boughs covered by the "A" tent carried on my span house, afforded an excellent bed, & there was a bright fire at our feet. We slept soundly, sleep interrupted only by the bed catching fire. Next morning we moved to the left, & I found the cavalry on our front engaged with the enemy. Some shells dropped our way, but otherwise we were quiet. I found Prince Cilley in the woods, & we lunched together i.e. munched our hard tack & fried pork. That day it rained, & we moved to the right, & I lay in the rain all night. Roused the next morning before light, I found my regiment as best I could & followed rather by sound than sight. The wind had shifted to the north west & blew bitterly cold, as we faced it toward Mine Run. It was full light when we came out into the open & found ourselves in front of the enemy intrenched on the further side of the run. I relieved a part of the 6th corp & went on the picket line with the 44th N.Y. & 83[r]d Pa. [and] covered the 5th corps front.

We were on the western slope of a low hill. Higher up, in the rear was the corps artillery[,] some of it in position. The corps was concealed in the woods, but the ground on our front was open from the artillery positions to the enemy. On the right the woods extended forward to the stream which ran in the low grounds, & from this stream (a small one & fordable) the ground rose gradually to the works of the enemy about 1000 yards distant from the stream (more or less)[.] A few lateral ravines extended from the hill sides to the stream, & there [we] had low bushes [for] firing cover. But our line of pickets was in the open, & the men put up slight cover by throwing up a bank from a ditch.

The defense of the enemy seemed formidable & elaborate. It was understood that the 2[n]d Corps (Warren[']s then) was to attack on the right of the enemy, and that the sound of his battle was to be the signal for attack on the front, to be made by our corps & the Sixth on our right. This was to be the place on the next morning at 8 o[']clock. The day was occupied in reconnoitering (I suppose) and getting into position. I should have related earlier, in proper order, the conditions, when I occupied the line. I relieved a portion of the sixth corps, in front of a house. This house was a respectable, but not pretentious house, evidently of a man of the better class, with slaves['] quarters & granaries about it. After I had put my regiment into position, I went into the house and found there a middle aged man and young woman, in what appeared to be a sitting room. They were troubled by the excitement & movement about them, but more immediately by an artillery man who was boldly plundering[.]

I found him when I went in, in the act of searching the drawers of a bureau, in the room. He did not promptly move when I ordered him out and I put my revolver to his head & so drove him out.

Encouraged by this the man asked me to go down into the basement & reassure the people there. The basement was open on the west side, towards the enemy (The house stood on the hillside).

The room, apparently a dining room was a large one, and in it had the people of all the neighborhood, who suddenly caught as in a net, between two Armies, had fled to the basement room, as more secure. As many as 40 people, all women—children[,] excepting two very stout elderly men. One of the women was quite bed ridden and appeared to be very aged, quite deaf. I reassured them as well as I could, & put a sentinel at the door. A battery officer during the day advised me that he had orders to open fire at 8 A.M. the next morning, & we knew that the people would be in peril if they remained in the house the next day. But it seemed better to let them stay during the night, & in order that they might not be in additional disturbance[,] we said nothing to them of the intention. There was skirmishing & picket firing during the day. The weather was bitterly cold, & temperature all day, below the melting point. Water froze during the first night in canteens. Our picket lines were rather more than easy musket shot from those of the enemy, but a scattering & desultory fire was kept up. Sometime in the evening I had orders to advance some trusty men across the stream, to ascertain the nature of the ground. I sent three men of Co. B who went during the night through the picket line of the enemy, and reported that the ground was marshy, which information I sent to Hd. Qrs. of the corps. I slept in the house, but getting up frequently & going out on the line I caught a serious cold. The next morning after our occupation of the line in front of the enemy, very early I called out the man of the house, & told him of the impending battle, & that the people must be moved out before 8 A.M. Of course there was great excitement & more wailing amongst those frightened women & children. They turned out in the bitter cold of the early morning. I sent the old lady on a stretcher, & the sad procession moved out to the rear though the woods, to I know not what distant shelter. At 8 o[']clock the artillery opened. The enemy replied slowly & to small extent. I was on the picket line, during this time. The plan of battle was this: The 2[n]d Corps, under Warren, had been sent around the left, to endeavor to turn the right of the enemy. If from the noise of his battle it appeared that he was making any headway, the sixth corps on the right, the fifth next to the left, & the 1st on the left of the 5th were to advance. On these fronts there were formidable works, of the enemy,—the advance, from crossing the stream, was over a level & unprotected plain. We waited, & the forenoon wasted away, without action.

If I recollect rightly there was some slight musketry fire on the left, where Warren was supposed to be, but nothing to show any serious battle. Then came report, afterwards confirmed, that Warren finding the enemy so strongly intrenched—guarded on his right, that no advantage could be gained by attack, had taken the responsibility to decline the fight. So the whole planned attack failed. I believe it would have failed if attempted, & that we could not have carried such works,—further that a repulse, ten mile[s] south of the Rapidan, with poor and few roads, in such a wooded country, would have been disastrous in the highest degree.

We remained in the front of the enemy two more days. But when, at night I went back to the house I had occupied, (It was a little in rear of my line), I found that it had been thoroughly sacked by some stragglers. Of course everything eatable had been taken, for man or beast. We remained there, I now think, two days after the failure of the battle. This must have been the last day of November or the 1st of December, when we fell back. I was still on the skirmish or picket line. Our orders were to remain on that until two o[']clock in the morning. The army began to move soon after dark. As the roads were so hard, being frozen solid, it seemed to me that the enemy must be aware of the movement. I kept up the fires on my part of the line, which was in the open, &, as there was a bright moon plainly in view. About one o[']clock I was awakened, & went along the line. I could hear the bugles of the enemy blowing. Nothing of our army seemed to be left excepting the picket line, so far as our part of the line was concerned. It looked as if they intended to come over and take us in. The full light of the moon was favorable for the purpose. I went along my line & had the usual fires renewed, so that they should continue to burn after our departure. I directed the men to wrap their blankets or tent pieces around their gun barrels to prevent glitter in the moonlight, & cautioned them to make no noise, but to creep back at the given signal, along the ravines, which extended to the rear. I remained on the center of the line, & those on the right & left were to guide on me. Precisely at 2 A.M. by my watch, I moved. The men crept up the ravine & emerged over the hill in rear of which they reformed. Other picket regiments came in & there was also a section of a battery.

Without much delay we moved. The ground was frozen, the northwest wind blew bitterly, and I was sick of a severe cold, & weary with lack of sleep. Moving slowly, with an infantry column, on horseback, is not very active exercise. We were not distributed & about nine (9) o[']clock in the morning we crossed the Rapidan & reformed the corps. Nothing had been gained, certainly no confidence, but it was better than Fredericksburg & Chancellorville. We had no material loss. The army went into Camp about Culpeper C. H. between the Rappahanock & Rapidan rivers.

[WINTER QUARTERS
DECEMBER, 1863—APRIL, 1864]

I was sent to guard the bridge at Rappahanock station. I leveled down the old earth works on the low hill near the bridge, on the north side of the river, and established there my camp. At first we suffered from the severe cold, being still in tents. On the first day of January the cold was extreme. Ice formed on the river to the thickness of three inches. But gradually we improved our shelter.

The men built comfortable quarters of split logs, which they covered with their pieces of tent buttoned together. Inside were bunks, for four men, & a fireplace of bricks or stone & clay. I established a kitchen for each company, and the food was cooked for each company separately. I also had prepared a hospital, and a substantial guard house of logs with a big fire place, where the relief off duty could be comfortably housed.

My own tent was an ordinary "Wall" tent, against the side of which I had built a chimney, with a fire place flush with the wall of the tent. This wall was cut on each side of the fireplace & rolled up so as to uncover the fireplace. In the rear I had an "A" or wedge tent joined to the wall, & with an opening between. This formed the bedroom. Some boards acquired by borrowing, I suppose, in the absence of the owner, furnished a floor. The furniture was of the scantiest, but the shelter was comfortable, and compared with that in the field, was palatial. So with the table. We had a table & soft bread, cooked meats. The frying pan was no longer sole cooking utensil.

On the first of January, for example, Col. Hayes, who was then temporarily in command of the brigade and had his Hd. Qrs. in the edge of a forest, about a half mile distant from my camp, invited the other regimental commanders & some of the division staff to dine with him.

We had the amazing luxuries of oysters & roast turkey. It did not so much matter that we shivered at the table. Consuming hunger & appetite long cherished occupied our attention. In the evening we sat by the fire & smoked. But the ride home was cold, as I remember well, & that night Capt[.] Clark & I put our blankets together & with the double covering, & mutual warmth, managed to get through the night without freezing. I had my tent afterwards protected by pine boughs interwoven with stakes driven near the wall.

The winter passed pleasantly. Permission was given to ladies to visit camp, and, in Feb[ruar]y, I think, Susie came with Sace Keene, the wife of Captain Keene, who was there, in the absence of Clark, senior captain. There were also several other ladies, wife of Capt[.] Plummer, & wife of Lt. Stanwood. I was for a considerable part of the time, Pres[iden]t of a Court Martial, of which Keene was Judge Advocate.

Capt. K. & wife were much at my Hd.Qrs. in the winter & we were in happy ignorance of the future & enjoyed the passing days, without apprehension of the future. As I now look back, I wonder that we could all be so unconcerned & cheerful. It was the first time, since our marriage[,] that Susie and I had lived together. (A few days in journeying hardly equalled [*illegible word*] an affair) and the presence of dear [*illegible word*] Keenes added greatly to the enjoyment. It was a sad day however, when they [Susie and Sarah] left us. We could not even obtain leave to accompany them to Washington. Parting gave more to apprehensions for them, & for us there remained only hard duty, for the time for active service was near, & there was prospect of hard fighting—plenty of it. Chamberlain had been absent all winter, and Gilmore always was, if he could, almost always was, in practice. My men were in excellent condition. They had been well fed & well sheltered, and there had been almost no sickness. I had as well as I can now remember, 350 men, & I think there were 21 officers. [*no paragraph break in manuscript*]

[THE WILDERNESS
MAY, 1864]

On the first day of May I moved forward & joined the brigade, bivouacing near Culpepper C. H. We attempted a brigade dress parade, but a tempest interrupted it. On the fourth we crossed the Rapidan at Germania Ford, & marched in the plank road, through the wilderness woods. I recollect well the incidents of that first day[']s hard march. It was hot, and in the narrow road, the sun had no mitigation of heat. Men threw away their blankets. They were overloaded, as men usually are from winter camp, and were not yet hardened to the march. I have no direct remembrance of the bivouac of that night. In the morning we were in line of battle in woods country, on a slight ridge, across the [*space left for road name*] Plank road. Our brigade was on the left of the road. In my front was the 83[r]d Penn[sylvani]a, and I formed the 2[n]d line.

The remainder of the brigade, excepting the 44th N.Y., held in reserve & was on our left, but not visible to me, in the woods.

After awhile the men began to lie down, resting. No appearance of the enemy, & no orders, excepting to be ready & in line.

I am writing this as nearly as I can from the standpoint of that time, & not from what I learned afterwards. After another interval, & I think towards the middle of the day, Bartlett, (the brigade commander), rode along and told me that the enemy was in our front, he smiling, and speaking, as it seemed to me, as if he regarded it as a joke. I called to my adjutant to have the men at attention, & [by] myself rode forward, to get a view of the enemy. I saw dust in the road, a half mile or so to the front. Soon after, we advanced. The wood in our front was so thick that it was impracticable to ride, and all the field officers dismounted. We moved forward steadily, & emerged into an opening, when the enemy opened fire on us with musketry. This caused the line to move forward more quickly, and we speedily broke through the enemy, who were forted in the edge of the woods on the opposite side of the open field. We had to cross a considerable ditch in the center of the field—which broke up our formation, but did not materially check our progress. I went on however, through this second wood. I remember a confederate officer captured, but was too much engrossed to pay any attention to him. We soon emerged into a second open place in the woods, not so large as the field & not, like the first, extending across the road to the right. I could not see much of the line on my left, none to the right, & not far to the front. In this opening, perceiving that the 83[r]d was greatly broken up, & seeing no field officer, I shouted to the 83[r]d captain to let me move my regiment to the front, I was in better shape. I also caught the sound of musketry on my right & rear, & that indicated that the line on the right had not kept pace with us. I therefore directed my right company to deploy into the woods on the north side of the road, & to observe & report the condition on that flank. [*The following sentence was inserted here, between the lines:* The captain reported none of our troops up, but skirmishing of the enemy in our rear.]

At the same time, (none of the field officers of the 83[r]d appearing[)], I had wheeled that regiment, (now in my rear,) & faced it along the road, towards the right. At that Col. Hays, commanding a regiment of our brigade (18th Mass.) on my left, walked up through the bushes to me, & I gave him the situation & asked what he thought best to do. He approved what I had done, & my suggestion to hold on, as we were; and left me to go back to his command. He had scarcely left me, when the firing on my left broke open & more violently, in heavy volleys, & looking that way I saw the line breaking to the rear rapidly. Knowing that there was nothing of support on my right, something of the enemy in my right rear, & seeing the left break, I was not long in deciding that this was not a good place to stay in. I shouted to face by the rear rank, & moved back in line. Not far back, in the woods, I met McCoy[,] Major of the 83[r]d & learned that Col. Woodward had been severely wounded in the advance. I suggested to McCoy that we endeavor to reform our lines & hold on awhile to see if we could not obtain part of the ground gained. We attempted this, but in vain. We could not be seen or heard far, & got only a short line. Then I directed what of my men remained to get to the rear as soon as possible, especially I cautioned the color bearer.

I believe I was the last man in. The line had all gone back to the original position, & we had gained nothing. I had lost ninety men, & four or five officers, a heavy loss. What the other parts of the line had accomplished, we did not then know, but we were rather disheartened, at this first attempt & failure. It was said that the sixth corps, on our right, was delayed by the dense thickets, & could not keep pace with us. I think we charged without sufficiently knowing our ground, we did not have prompt reserves to fill gaps, & there were no general officers on hand.

We lay behind some slight works, that evening, & the night of May 5, 1864. It is my recollection that we had some slight works, but where they were put up, I can[']t now remember.

The next morning we moved out again, this time on the right of the plank road, & nearer the 6th corps. My recollection is that we lay in three lines, there was some skirmishing on our front, which at no time assumed the proportions of a battle, but on the right, in the front of the Sixth, there was at intervals, heavy musketry & artillery. There was much also of "rebel yells," extending down to their line in front of us. At one time it seemed diagonally, for their artillery was so advanced that it seemed to be enfilading our line, and the yells appeared to come from points where the sixth corps line should have been. During this spasm our rear line was faced to the rear. Soon however the noise subsided & the broken line restored, & the enemy forced back again on the right.

We accomplished nothing, but lost little, & we moved back & lay in the same place approximately, as the night before.

I slept so soundly that I did not hear new troops marching in, in the night. Some rascal stole the hat from my head, as I lay on the ground asleep. I suspected a new regiment, I knew that none of our troops would do such a thing. I sent a sergeant & two men to search that regiment, & they found the hat in the possession of some scallion [i.e., scoundrel], & took it from him. The loss of a hat at that time was a serious matter. There was not a hat store in a hundred miles: & I was right glad to recover the hat & [for] my head. I mention an incident illustrating not common, but occasional conditions. The evening of the 2[n]d day, after we had moved back, the 155th Pa. Col. Pearson[']s regiment, moved back & bivouaced in rear of us. He belonged in Ayers['] brigade. In the morning, Genl. A rode up & roughly reproached him for deserting his brigade (as he said) the night before. Pearson was very angry & retorted that he did not desert the brigade but that the brigade deserted him: that he (Pearson) had not been notified when we moved back, the night before, but had been left there, & in danger of capture if he had not hurriedly discovered the mistake "made" he continued—growing warmer. "If it had not been for a drunken Brigade Genl. I should not have lost so many men yesterday." That ended the conversation. I don[']t know whether Ayer[s] was drunk "yesterday" or not. Sometime after the war another brigade General told me he always took a drink of brandy before going into battle. I wondered that any man having such responsibility, should dare to stimulate himself artificially in that manner.

So far as I saw[,] matters on our front were the same as at first, only I apprehend that we had lost more than the enemy. I should have mentioned that on the first day, in falling back, I caught some of the enemy[']s skirmishers, who had got into our rear, and captured them, some 30 or more. I did not hear of any other captures in our division. We lost one gun, which was run out on the road.

On the third day four regiments were ordered forward to feel the enemy, & ascertain if they were still in our front, viz. the 118th Pa.[,] 20th Maine & 11th & 12th regulars. We moved forward[,] my regiment on the right, and my right on the left of the road. We made some noise, drove in a few skirmishing of the enemy, and, as we emerged into the open field met a fire of artillery & musketry. Col. Herring (of the 118th) and I were together, leading the advance. We had drawn a heavy fire, and concluded, that as we were unsupported, it was useless to charge into the enemy[']s works. We had ascertained what we were sent to ascertain. So we fell back, out of range of the musketry & reported. We remained on the line all the remainder of the day & night following. During the night, the corps moved. The orders came around after dark. I remember well with what interest I lighted my bit of candle to read the orders. We had on our part gained nothing, on the left, it was reported, there was some gain. What should we do? Our former experience in the Army of the Potomac had led us to expect, that for two or three days of fighting, there would be a lull of weeks. Were we going forward or back[?] Our direction, when the enemy appeared in our front, on the morning of the fifth, had been by the left flank, towards Spotsylvania Court House. Were we to go back or forward: move by the left flank towards Richmond or by the right flank in retreat? When the order came this question was uppermost in my mind. By the dim light I read the words, "left in front."

The order designated the hour, and as usual the order of the march, & added the significant words "left in front"—That told the whole story. No going back.

With face towards the enemy, or ready to halt & face instantly at any moment, we were to move further into the enemy[']s country.

We moved early in the morning of the 8th of May, following the corps. The road was fair, but mostly through woods country, & occasionally crossed muddy streams. We made strenuous efforts to keep the men closed up, and to get them across muddy places promptly. We reached the open field where the corps was, as nearly as I can now remember, about the middle of the forenoon. We met our brigade,—what of it had gone ahead, coming back, in some confusion. The first man I saw was Col. Conner of the 44th N.Y. wounded in the shoulder. He told me that the brigade had assaulted the line of the enemy & been repulsed, that the enemy were in force & were constantly receiving reinforcements. It was clear that they had anticipated our movement, & had gotten ahead of us, & were across the road leading towards Richmond, & no advantage could be obtained there, by the way of compelling them to come out & fight us on equal terms in a favorable field for us. Conner told me that the advance had expected to find nothing but calvary in their front, that Maj. Knox was wounded, & that his regiment had suffered serious loss.

Genl. Sedgwick of the 6th corps had been killed there. It looked like more earnest work. Our detachment just came up, was sent to report to Crawford, [which was] not to our liking for we had not much confidence in Crawford, & besides did not like to leave our brigade. However, there was nothing to do but obey orders, except to grumble a little. We moved forward, & a little to the left & advanced in to an oak wood, of large trees. There were other troops massed in the wood.—We had been ordered as I said, to report to Crawford but he was[,] however[,] not to be seen. The men had marched seven or eight miles, & starting early, and not time to make coffee, & had eaten nothing except to nibble a little dry "hard tack." Col. Herring was senior officer of our detachment & he w[oul]d not take the responsibility of moving the men back to allow them to get coffee. So I took the responsibility myself. Afterward I moved up again—massed the men amongst the oaks. The enemy commenced shelling & exploded shell after shell about us & over us. A piece struck an officer near me, but not many were hurt. Only as usual, it was very trying to the nerves to lie there & take the pounding with no opportunity to strike back. Soon however, one of our batteries moved to the front, & got the range of the enemy, & gave them something to think about. But we lay there all day or the remainder of the day, waiting, but not all the time under fire. This was the fourth day in which we had been under fire.

Towards night—it must have been near sunset, too late anyway, we advanced.

We were in the 2[n]d line, supporting the Penn[sylvani]a Reserves, (Crawford[']s Brigade)—and, as I understood the orders, (none were officially given) we were to support this line. We advanced across some low ground, through bushes, & into [a] second growth of pine, a fairly thick forest but passable, & of small & of thick shade. Advancing a considerable distance & closely following the Reserves, we perceived that they halted—there was some musketry pretty sharp. We halted, awaiting their further movement, when suddenly they broke—came rapidly back upon us. Capt. Keene & myself were together, (He was acting as field officer) & we exerted ourselves, not to rally our own men, for they stood firm, but to rally the other men form[ing] Crawford[']s line. I caught the colors of the 11th Penn[sylvani]a & compelled the bearer to stand on my line, & endeavored to get as many as possible of their men to stay with us. Almost instantly the enemy were upon us. It was so dusky in the woods that colors were not discernible but we could distinguish the enemy by their short jackets. We had a rough & tumble fight, hand to hand in a brief struggle in which bayoneting[,] clubbing & shooting were mixed in about equal proportions. But we drove them back, capturing some prisoners & one regimental color.

Then we waited to see if the attack would be renewed, & to gather up our wounded. I do not remember the number I lost, but Capt[.] Morrell was killed, instantly[,] & Lieutenants Melcher & Prince severely wounded. By the time we had attempted to move, it had become quite dark. We examined the right & left & found that we were certainly unsupported on either flank. We got no orders. Genl. Crawford had either forgotten us, or had adopted the remarkable theory that we had deserted him. We were there by orders, & unless driven back could not move without orders. We were not running like the rest. After consultation we agreed (Herring and I) to send some one to find Crawford, or any one who might be in our rear. Jacklin, adjutant of the 16th Michigan volunteered. He did not return it seems, and we sent out other men. They delaying[,] I took Sergeant Greenwood of Co. G and undertook the task myself, of finding either friend or foe. I felt my way along followed by the sergeant. After proceeding several hundred yards I felt a soft mossy covering of the low ground we had crossed, and the sergeant calling to be sure that he was following, some one answered in front. Proceeding I came upon a captain in the 6th Maine (6th Corps), whom I knew. He told me that Gen[.] Neale was in command & to him I reported & got orders to bring back our line to his rear. He did not know that we were in his front, & might have fired into us—We fell back to his rear, and next morning rejoined our brigade. [*The following sentence is added here, between previously written lines. The words after the second ampersand are crossed out:* As we did so Crawford appeared & complained that we did not support him & took the flag we had captured.]

[*The following paragraph is also crossed out:* I regret very much the loss of my memoranda of this time. I kept a diary, but have lost it I fear. I have therefore the more difficult task to give an orderly account of the succeeding actions.]

This last engagement was on Sunday evening, on the 8th day of

May 1864, and we had been fighting four days, during which time we had been on picket one night. It was a matter of great satisfaction to be returned to our brigade, where we could be certain of fair treatment.

[SPOTSYLVANIA COURT HOUSE MAY, 1864]

This was on the morning of the 9th of May. We lay that day close in front of the enemy under some fire of musketry & artillery, but not actually engaged. On the 10th or 11th, I think it was the 10th[,] the fifth Corps was drawn up in line of battle in front of the works of the enemy at a place, according to my present recollection, called Laurel Hill. The right of the corps was in the woods, but the regular brigade, on our right, was in the open, and visible. I was on the extreme left. We lay in a slight hollow, & protected thusly from the fire of the enemy. A battery in my rear was throwing solid shot over our heads. We had had no breakfast, and were weary & the outlook was for a determined charge. Bartlett, (or one of his staff) came down & directed me to the wheel, where we should advance, slightly to the left, & direct my charge towards a clump of tall pines. There was an orchard in our front, & by reason of the formation of the ground, we could not see the enemy. We had no doubt that they had works & were behind them in force. While we lay waiting Old Fields came up with his usual grin and a tin pail of coffee & some hard tack. I confess that the very probable prospect of being shot in the next fifteen or twenty minutes had not improved my appetite, never very eager for hardtack. But for the sake of appearing cheerful I took some coffee & chewed awhile on the abominable bread. I had taken the precaution to have my men lay aside their knapsacks, and had detailed Alvin Miller to stay with them—As he was from Warren, I thought I would save his life. Orders came to guide on the regulars & it appeared to be the plan that the right of the corps, in the woods &

able to get nearer to the enemy, should charge first & if they succeeded, should be followed by the rest of the line in succession. We were ready, but lying down, when watching the right, I saw the line rise.

I ordered my men up. There was a tremendous crash of musketry on the right[.] The regular brigade advanced a few paces, we were about moving, when those on our right halted & we also. The affair was evidently a failure. We knew afterward that the right of the line in charging, had come up to the enemy[']s breastworks & been met by a voll[e]y at close range, which cut the line down.

No further attack was made that day, but we remained in front of the enemy, on the 10th & 11th, but on the evening of the 11th or morning of the 12[th], we moved to the left, & were in line of battle early on the 12th[,] on the right of the troops about to attack the enemy[']s lines at the "Bloody Angle," as it was afterwards called. We knew the attack was to be made at 5 in the morning & we stood in the woods awaiting the sound, for we could not see the line to right or left.

There was continually a patter of picket fire, and, all at once, this quickened into a volley fired irregularly, and almost instantly, deepened into a roar, as the pattering drops of a summer shower merge into an indistinguishable uproar in which no single drop is heard. Indeed it seemed to me that the tearing sharp tempest of musketry drowned the artillery, which I seemed to hear throbbing faintly through the overwhelming whirlwind of musketry. We knew well what that meant. I listened utterly unconscious of anything but the sound that filled the woods. Would they, could they[,] take the works, through such fire?

In a few moments, which might have been an hour, the musketry partially subsided, And we heard—not the "rebel yell", but a "hurrah," & we knew that our men had succeeded. Soon a staff officer, hatless & breathless, came riding through the woods, announcing that Hancock had captured the enemy[']s line of works & a division of his infantry & over Several officers—We moved, later in the day, in rear of the troops holding these captured works, & lay all night, under fire, in slight rain.

The scattering & desultory fire of the enemy was kept up through the night, ours replying. I heard the dint of the bullets in the trees, before I went to sleep, and after I awoke.

But sleep, when it could be procured, was of the first consequence, & was not to be declined by reason [o]f risk of being shot. The wet & drizzle & lack of proper food made things uncomfortable; for we could not have fires to make coffee and the abominable fat pork & quite as abominable dry "hard-tack" were not a nourishing diet. They were not so unpalatable to me, but I could not eat much of this fare, & was not nourished. In the midst of the hardship & care occasional merriment was not wanting. As we lay in the woods near the Bloody Angle stragglers of the 56th Mass. passed us.

About the first of May this regiment had relieved me at Rappahannock Station, those troops forming a part of the Ninth corps, which took the place of the Fifth on the railroad. The story got about among the men, who foresaw little of the plan of campaign, & assumed that that road would continue to be our line of communication, that the Ninth Corps were not to go into the fighting, but were to hold the line of communication. They were mostly new troops, the 56th Mass. being a new regiment. It was with no little reluctance therefore, that my men relinquished their comfortable quarters, the log houses or rather plank houses, which they had built with so much care & labor.

I had difficulty in preventing them from setting the huts on fire: in fact they did in one place, but I ordered the fire extinguished & we left the raw recruits of the Fifty sixth in our houses, to remain, as they supposed, & as our men believed, during the campaign. As therefore my men saw the forlorn stragglers pass in squads, with "56 Mass" on their knapsacks, a yell of derision went up, & hearty laughs at the practical joke.

The Massachusetts men had probably not occupied our quarters more than two days.

Leaving the Angle the brigade moved back to the right, & built works, under fire of artillery. It was on the morning of the 12th I think, that we moved to the right, & later in the day to the left again, all the while with in canon range of the enemy.

My recollection of these days is indistinct as to specific details. We were moving about & usually under fire, either of musketry at a distance & scattering, or of artillery, of like character. On the evening of the 13th or 14th, we were occupying the ground in open field, about some earth works, & at or near dusk, had bivouaced. It was starting to rain, in fact had rained somewhat. I had my shelter tent put up, & quite tired out had crawled in, for sleep, when suddenly came an order to be ready to move at once. I directed my adjutant to send the order to the company & to see to the formation, & send for my horses which had been moved to the rear out of range of the enemy[']s artillery. It was growing dark, & the forward line stood ready to move. I waited anxiously & was greatly relieved when I saw the white face of my black [horse], coming through the gloom.

We moved very soon, & were on the road all night, plodding in the mud and darkness. I think I never passed a more uncomfortable night.

It was cloudy, and so dark that [the] form of a man could not be distinguished ten feet distant. The column was often blocked & we stood in the mud waiting. It was impossible for the men to sit down, & once I dismounted and sank so deep in the mud that I could hardly extricate my boots therefrom to movement again. As usual after such halts, the column would start suddenly and move quickly, and when halting or in motion, it was necessary to keep close watch of the next regiment ahead. I was in constant apprehension lest on the one hand I should ride too rapidly & leave my own regiment, toiling in the mud, and on the other[,] lest I should miss the way, losing sight of the regiment ahead of me. For we were crossing the country and did not appear to be on any road. A break in the column, causing divergence, would have been disastrous. But the column held together. For men weary when they started, it was a long weary, sleepless night, pulling through the mud & in the darkness. [*On the blank manuscript page opposite this passage, Spear wrote following sentence:* Insertion: It was a painful anxious march, in which the physical weariness was forgotten in the mental anxiety, though we were without rest 24 hours and with little time for food.] With the dawn we came around in front of Spotsylvania C. H. which was in sight, a few houses & court house, on a high ground to the west. The enemy opened up on us with artillery, & under salutes of that, we had our coffee. Shells exploded over us as we drank, & a battery (I think it was D. of the 5th) artillery, went into position near us, to return the compliments. This must have been the 14th of May. We lay here all day, and, under cover of the darkness, leaving our horses, we silently moved forward to take up position nearer the enemy. I was in the advance. We came upon one of the branches of the Mattapony River. This was a rocky stream, & in the very dim light I could discern the stones in the stream[,] crossed, or attempted to cross, stepping on them, unfortunately I slipped & fell in, but recovered myself & got out, wet & with boots full of water, and long legged riding boots hold a large quantity. Beyond the stream we advanced four or five hundred yards, and took up a position directly in front of the hill on which the enemy were occupying, & here we began at once to intrench. In the morning at dawn the enemy opened upon us, with artillery—killed one or two of my men, but they made no effort to dislodge us. My impression is [*illegible word*] while [*illegible word*] was not in line. We lay in the works built here several days, as nearly as I can remember, but it may have been not more than two. I distinctly recall that a mail was brought up, & the carrier, finding some nook, sheltered from the fire of the enemy, distributed the very welcomed letters & papers. The mail carrier delivered the bundles in a little hollow behind the slight breastwork, sheltered from the fire of the enemy. There were letters and papers. One I remember sent me from Wiscasset by Nettie

Hubbard, one of my Wiscasset scholars. It amused us greatly. There was a picture of Bartlett[']s brigade charging in the Wilderness. Evidently the artist was not there, & drew mainly upon his imagination. The lines were "dressed" as if on parade—in the picture. Those of us who were there remembered well the rush & the lines disordered by the woods & ditches.

   I lost but few men here. One poor fellow I remember whose head was pierced by a splinter of a shell, so driven into his head that the asst. surgeon had difficulty in pulling it out. I thought it impossible that he should live an hour, but I saw, after the close of the war, his grave at Arlington, so that he must have lived long enough to be brought to the hospital here in Washington. I remember now a sergeant, a fine fellow, who was "falling in" his company, & was shot in the leg—which seemed a comparatively slight wound. "It was good" he said, "for sixty days"—meaning that he would have a furlough of that length. Alas he died, from the wound. I can[']t now recall how many days we occupied these works, one or two, or three—but suddenly, at mid-day, or thereabouts, we moved back, & the enemy appeared to be doing the same thing. We hurriedly marched to the left, & soon came upon their rear guard, & pressed them, capturing some prisoners.

   Only cavalry & a light battery opposed us on the road we were following, but a battery on a road on our left fired upon us.

   The brigade formed line, when we struck this guard, & advanced, but they did not resist stoutly. For the greater part[,] this march gave us a rest. For several days I did not lose a man. I believe.

ENDNOTES

ENDNOTES

1. Copperheads (after the poisonous snake) was the derisive name given to those northerners who advocated a negotiated peace even if it meant the dissolution of the Union.

2. Ball's Bluff (October 21, 1861) was a poorly-managed skirmish that cost 921 Union casualties.

3. Fort Donelson on the Tennessee River was captured by Union forces under Ulysses S. Grant (the "man at last discovered") on February 16, 1862.

4. The legal structure under which the Union government assembled its armies was a call up of the states' militias. Lincoln's first call to the states in the wake of Fort Sumter was for 75,000 men. The call up referred to here for 300,000 additional men was issued on July 1, 1862.

5. Joseph F. Land of Edgecomb was later promoted to captain of Company H, and breveted major on March 26, 1863. Joseph J. A. Hoffses (Company G) of Jefferson resigned on November 20, 1862.

6. All three of these captains resigned in 1862: Isaac W. Haskell (Company D) of Garland and Phineas M. Jeffards (Company B) of Foxcroft on November 29, and Isaac H. McDonald (Company C) of Buckfield on December 10.

7. Joshua Lawrence Chamberlain was born in Brewer, Maine, on September 8, 1828, and was therefore 34 years old at this time. A Professor of Rhetoric at Bowdoin College, Chamberlain secured a sabbatical in order to join the army.

8. Adelbert Ames of Rockland graduated fifth in the West Point class of 1861 and commanded a battery at the Battle of Bull Run where he

was wounded. Breveted to major for gallantry at Bull Run, and to lieutenant colonel for his role in defending Malvern Hill during the Seven Days campaign, he was appointed colonel of the 20th Maine on August 20, 1862.

9. This carefully-phrased passage seems to be a reference to an officer who was particularly flatulent.

10. The 36th Massachusetts regiment was organized at Worcester in August 1862, and left Boston on September 2.

11. On shipboard Spear studied Silas Casey, *Infantry Tactics, for the Instruction, Exercise, and Maneuvers of the Soldier, a Company, Line of Skirmishers, Battalion, Brigade and Corps d'Armee* [New York: D. Van Nostrand, 1862]. Casey's book was adopted by the U. S. War Department as the standard manual for U. S. troops.

12. The Battle of Second Bull Run, or Second Manassas (August 30, 1862) was another rout of Union forces in Virginia. Major General John Pope, in command of what was called the Army of Virginia, was driven from the field by Lee's Army of Northern Virginia while much of McClellan's army was still en route back to the Potomac from the Virginia peninsula.

13. The Long Bridge was a wooden structure, barely wide enough for wagons, that crossed the Potomac into Virginia from the foot of Maryland Avenue.

14. South Mountain is the continuation of the Blue Ridge in Maryland and Pennsylvania. It effectively screened the advance of Confederate forces under Robert E. Lee from Union forces under McClellan. Aware that McClellan's superior army was moving west toward him, and that his own forces were scattered, Lee ordered the passes through South Mountain defended in order to buy time to concentrate his army.

15. Salt pork and hardtack was standard fare in the army. Hardtack, the "cracker" referred to here, was a quarter-inch thick hard biscuit, four to five inches square, which was made of unleavened flour and which had very little taste. A notion of its character may be gained by the fact that it was occasionally used to line the floors and fireplaces of winter quarters.

16. Confederate Major General Thomas (Stonewall) Jackson captured Harpers Ferry on September 15, 1862, two days before the battle at Antietam. In addition to the town, its arsenal, and 73 cannon, Jackson also captured some 12,000 Union soldiers.

17. Having run out of patience with George B. McClellan, President Lincoln ordered him relieved in the first week of November.

18. Ambrose Burnside accepted command on November 7, 1862.

19. Burnside was determined to demonstrate his aggressiveness despite the lateness of the season. His swift march to the north bank of the Rappahannock across from Fredericksburg was designed to steal a march on the Confederate army and get around Lee's flank.

20. Euchre was a popular game of the time.

21. Though Burnside had planned to cross the Rappahannock immediately upon his arrival, the pontoon bridging equipment he had ordered had not arrived. Rather than attempt to cross by fording or rafting, he sat down and waited for the pontoons to arrive, thus losing the advantage he had won by the hard marching of his troops, and giving Lee's army the opportunity to get in position to contest the crossing.

22. To "refuse" a line meant that the flank was turned back at an angle to prevent the enemy from rolling up the line with a flanking maneuver.

23. The high ground north of Fredericksburg, which gave Spear such a good view of the Union assault on Marye's Heights, was Stafford Heights.

24. The town of Fredericksburg was badly damaged by Union artillery fire ordered by Burnside because snipers in the buildings close to the river had harried the efforts of his engineers to bridge the river. At this point in the war, there were still some who viewed shelling a city as beyond accepted military practice.

25. The wounded soldier was Royal Dodge (Company G) of Edgecomb. He later recovered and returned to the army in the Veterans Reserve Corps.

26. Spear included this subheading in his original manuscript. It is the only subheading in the document.

27. English General Sir John Moore (1761-1809) was in command at Corunna, Spain, during the Napoleonic Wars. After Moore ordered a 250 mile retreat to Corunna, he was killed in action as his forces finally advanced to victory. Moore was buried in a somber ceremony on January 17, 1809.

28. Federal losses at Fredericksburg were 12,653 killed, wounded, and missing. Confederate losses were only 5,309. The 20th Maine lost four killed and 32 wounded.

29. The night of December 17, Burnside made plans to renew the attack on Marye's Heights the next day. The attack would be spearheaded by the Ninth Corps, his old command, which he planned to lead personally. On the morning of the 14th, however, Major General Edwin V. Sumner talked him out of making the attempt, telling Burnside that every general in the army opposed it.

30. The reference here is to John Vinal (Company G) of Jefferson, Maine, who was Spear's cook and orderly. He had remained on the north bank of the river during the attack.

31. Spear is about three weeks off here. The infamous "mud march" actually began on January 19.

32. Burnside's march upstream was a complete fiasco. Though the weather was clear when the march began, it soon began to rain heavily and far from taking the enemy by surprise, his troops struggled hopelessly through deep mud, provoking jeers from the enemy who mocked the whole effort and held up signs pointing the way to Richmond. Burnside cancelled the movement on January 23, and the army struggled back to its campsite. Burnside was relieved from command two days later.

33. Adelbert Ames served as an aide to Major General George G. Meade until Ames was promoted to brigadier general on May 20, 1863.

34. Though Lincoln professed continued confidence in Burnside after Fredericksburg, negative reaction to the "mud march" helped convince him that a change in command would improve morale in the army. He therefore appointed Joseph Hooker to replace Burnside on January 26, 1863. Hooker's plan for the spring campaign was not significantly different from what Burnside had attempted in January: a westward move to cross the Rappahannock upstream and thereby threaten Lee's left flank. The Sixth Corps under John Sedgwick was to remain opposite Fredericksburg to hold in place as much of the Rebel army as possible while the move was underway. Once the battle was joined near Chancellorsville, however, Hooker ordered Sedgwick to seize Marye's Heights and advance on Lee's rear. Though he had numerical superiority, Sedgwick's men were driven back several times with heavy losses before they finally seized the high ground. This was the charge that Spear witnessed.

35. The "comparatively small body" defending Marye's Heights consisted of William Barksdale's brigade of Mississippi troops.

36. Sedgwick's corps advanced westward as far as Salem Church, but Hooker's defeat near Chancellorsville enabled Lee to send two divisions to support Barksdale and repel this probe as well.

37. Lieutenant Thomas D. Chamberlain, Company I, of Brewer, was the younger brother of Joshua L. Chamberlain.

38. Spear was in the tent of his good friend, Captain Samuel T. Keene of Thomaston.

39. The cavalry battle at Brandy Station was fought on June 9 about ten miles west of the position of the 20th Maine.

40. These northward marches shadowed the movements of Lee's army which had moved westward across the Blue Ridge, then northward through the Shenandoah Valley.

41. The firing "in direction of Leesburg" was from one or more of a series of cavalry skirmishes at Aldie and Middleburg on June 17.

42. These skirmishes, though successful in driving the dismounted Rebel cavalry, did not succeed in uncovering either Ashby's Gap or Snicker's Gap to expose the disposition of Lee's forces in the Valley. Hooker therefore had little choice but to continue his parallel movement northward.

43. During the army's northward march, Hooker had requested that the Harpers Ferry garrison be withdrawn. When Lincoln rejected this advice, Hooker submitted his resignation, no doubt expecting Lincoln to back down. Instead, the president accepted it. Lincoln then put Major General George Gordon Meade in command.

44. "Unionville" here probably refers to the village of Union Mills through which three brigades of Stuart's cavalry had passed on June 29. Stuart was conducting a raid—subsequently very controversial—behind (that is, eastward of) the Federal main body. While Stuart did capture a valuable wagon-train near Rockville, Maryland, his absence from Lee's main body hindered Lee's operations.

45. The Battle of Gettysburg began on the morning of July 1. Since Sedgwick's corps was a dozen or so miles east of Gettysburg, the men of the 20th Maine had to march westward to the sound of the guns.

46. Meade ordered Major General Daniel Sickles, commander of the Federal Third Corps, to occupy a modest ridgeline (Cemetery Ridge) in order to extend the Federal left. Seeing what he believed was a stronger position to his front, Sickles moved his corps forward at about three o'clock in the afternoon of July 2 as the 20th Maine was marching to the battlefield. The positions occupied by Sickles (the Devil's Den, the Wheatfield, and the Peach Orchard) became the target of the Confederate attack that began at about four o'clock.

47. Major General Gouverneur Warren recognized the importance of Little Round Top, still unoccupied at three p.m., and ordered that a brigade be sent there at once. Colonel Strong Vincent accepted the duty and ordered his brigade, consisting of the 16th Michigan, the 44th New York, the 83rd Pennsylvania, and the 20th Maine, to occupy the hill. Vincent led his four regiments around the reverse (eastern) side of the hill, and took up a position facing west and south on a rocky outcropping known ever since as Vincent's Spur.

48. Rather than take up positions in front of the main line—the normal duty of skirmishers—Chamberlain ordered Company B, under Captain Walter G. Morrill, to deploy beyond the left, behind a low stone wall southeast of Little Round Top, in order to provide warning of any Confederate attempt to get completely around the Federal flank.

49. The attacking Confederates consisted of two Alabama regiments—the 15th and 47th—under Colonel William Calvin Oates.

50. Chamberlain does not credit Spear with this suggestion. In his memoirs, Chamberlain notes only that "I called the captains and told them my tactics. . . . Then I took the colors with their guard and placed them at our extreme left, where a great boulder gave token and support; thence bending back at a right angle the whole body. . ." (Joshua L.

Chamberlain, *"Forward! Bayonet": My Civil War Reminiscences* [reprint: Gettysburg: Stan Clark, 1994], 26-27).

51. James A. Knight, of Edgecomb, later died in a Fifth Corps hospital.

52. The limping soldier was Private John M. Kennedy, Company G, of Richmond, who survived his wound in the groin.

53. In his memoir, published in 1905, Oates acknowledges that "There never were harder fighters than the Twentieth Maine men...." He also notes that "Federal infantry were reported to be coming down on my right and certainly were closing in on my rear...." (William Calvin Oates, *The War between the Union and the Confederacy and its lost opportunities*, [reprint: Dayton, Ohio: Morningside Bookshop, 1974], 219).

54. Balaklava is a seaport village in the Crimea, Ukraine, where an indecisive battle of the Crimean War was fought on October 25, 1854; the battle is best remembered for the "charge of the light brigade."

55. Spear's testimony here differs from the traditional account of this famous charge which portrays Chamberlain as making a deliberate decision to attack out of a concern that, without ammunition, his men would be unable to resist another enemy assault. In his memoir, Chamberlain asserts that he suggested to Spear the possibility of a "forlorn hope" when Lieutenant Melcher "asked if he might take his company and go forward and pick up one or two of his men left wounded on the field." Chamberlain agreed, and ordered "BAYONETS!" But he admits that the charge went forward spontaneously: "It was vain to order 'Forward.' No mortal would have heard it. . ." (Chamberlain, *"Bayonets! Forward,"* 32-33). Melcher's testimony is in an 1885 article that he wrote for his local newspaper. Melcher writes: "Colonel Chamberlain gave the order to 'fix bayonets' and almost before he could say 'charge!' the regiment leaped down the hill." (H. S. Melcher, "The 20th Maine at Little Round Top," printed originally in the *Lincoln County News,* Waldoboro, Maine, March 13, 1885, reprinted in *Battles & Leaders of the Civil War* [New York: The Century Co., 1884-8], 1:314-15).

56. Of 358 men engaged, the 20th Maine lost 40 killed and mortally wounded, and 80 wounded—losses of just over 33%—leaving 238.

57. The Confederate attack on the left, which included the assault on Little Round Top, was only a partial success. Southern troops captured the important ground in the Devil's Den, the Wheatfield, and the Peach Orchard, and inflicted more casualties on the Union defenders than they suffered themselves (a rarity in Civil War combat), but they had failed to achieve a decisive breakthrough. On the right, on Culp's Hill, they had opened a gap in the Union defenses, but failed to exploit it.

58. This shelling, from 140 Confederate guns under the supervision of Colonel E. Porter Alexander, was intended to prepare the way for the grand infantry assault subsequently known as Pickett's Charge.

59. Spear quotes Book XI, line 1 from Alexander Pope's early eighteenth-century translation of Homer's *Iliad*.

60. Samuel T. Keene, Spear's close friend, recorded similar images when he wrote his wife that same day: "Heaven save you from the distress of such scenes—blackened and mangled corpses—dead horses—guns and equipment broken and strewn—trees cut and mangled—fences demolished—the grounds trodden, muddy, and messy—and an almost intolerable stench—confusion all about—burying dead—hauling away wounded etc. etc. Oh, what scenes!" [unpublished letter, Keene family papers].

61. The speed and route of Meade's pursuit of Lee's retreating army became a major issue both at the time and subsequently. Lincoln believed that Meade could have brought an early end to the war by a more aggressive pursuit. Meade's defenders (then and later) pointed out that he had been in command of the army for only a week, and that his army had suffered heavy casualties at Gettysburg.

62. Spear was probably remembering Catoctin Mountain.

63. Lee planned to cross the Potomac back into Virginia at Williamsport, but found the rain-swollen river too high to ford. While his engineers built a pontoon bridge at Falling Waters, he deployed his army to protect the bridgehead. The skirmish at Tilghmanville on July 10 was one of several probes by Meade to test Lee's defensive lines.

64. Major General George Sykes, an 1842 graduate of West Point, replaced Meade in command of the Fifth Corps when Meade accepted command of the army.

65. Lee's plan was to draw Meade's army westward through Chester Gap into the Shenandoah Valley. Meade followed as far as the mountains, but then moved south rather than west. Since this threatened to cut Lee off from Richmond, the Confederate commander returned east of the Blue Ridge and fell back south of the Rappahannock to Culpeper.

66. To corduroy a road, in order to make a roadway passable for wagons, the troops cut standing timber and laid the stripped logs side-to-side perpendicular to the direction of the road, covering them with a thin layer of earth.

67. Chamberlain contracted malaria in the second week of August and left the army for two week's convalescent leave, returning, as Spear notes, on August 24.

68. In early September, two divisions of the Confederate army (those of John Bell Hood and Lafayette McLaws), both under the command of James Longstreet, were detached from Lee's command and sent to the western theater. Learning of this, Meade ordered his own army to advance on Lee's weakened force at Culpeper. Lee reacted by falling back behind the Rapidan River. (Spear here makes the common error of spelling Culpeper with an extra "p.")

69. The typed portion of Spear's manuscript ends here. The rest of the manuscript is hand-written.

70. In the wake of the Confederate victory at Chickamauga (September 19-20, 1863), two of Meade's corps (the Eleventh and Twelfth) were detached from the Army of the Potomac and sent to reinforce the Federal armies under siege at Chattanooga. Now it was Lee's turn to advance against Meade's reduced army at Culpeper. Lee moved on October 9, provoking the action described here.

71. The tactic of retreat and attack can be found in the *Anabasis* by the Greek historian Xenophon (c. 430-357 b.c.). The "ten thousand" also refers to a passage in the the same author's *Symposium*.

72. Spear's instinct was correct. Lee was deliberately attempting to replicate his successful maneuvering at the Battle of Second Manassas (Bull Run) by sending the corps of A. P. Hill on a wide flanking march designed to cut Meade's rail communications. Perceiving Lee's intent, Meade withdrew northward, marching along the line of the railroad.

73. Hill arrived on the Federal line of communications five miles north of Warrenton and, instead of the Federal rear, he found the Union army marching northward. Unwisely, he attacked anyway, precipitating the action described by Spear.

74. When Chamberlain returned to the army from sick leave on August 24, he was elevated to command of the brigade. This left Lieutenant Colonel Charles D. Gilmore in command of the regiment.

75. The impetuous assault by A. P. Hill at Bristoe Station (October 14, 1863) was unsuccessful and ended Lee's effort to turn the Federal right.

76. However confusing, Meade's maneuvers allowed the Federal army to consolidate its position at Centreville and convinced Lee to begin a withdrawal two days later on October 17.

77. Meade broke camp on October 19 to pursue Lee's now retiring columns. The quotation is from Milton's *Paradise Lost*, Book XI, line 269.

78. The Latin phrase *Jove non probante* literally means "Jove not approving"—that is, God would not approve.

79. The quotation is from Virgil (70 b.c.-19 a.d.), *Aeneid*, Book I, line 203; literally translated, it means: "Perhaps some day these things will gratify you to recall." At this early point in the *Aeneid*, Aeneas addresses his men after they have been shipwrecked on an island off the coast of Carthage. This speech is the first indication of Aeneas' great leadership ability in the face of adversity.

80. The quotation referring to Auburn, the "loveliest village of the plain" is from the first line of the 1770 poem, *The Deserted Village,* by English poet and essayist Oliver Goldsmith.

81. Lee's decision to leave a fortified bridgehead north of the river at Rappahannock Station was designed to encourage Meade to cross upriver at Kelley's Ford, which would allow Lee to assail Meade's flank. The strength of the Confederate salient at Rappahannock Station was about 1,500 men.

82. After the death of Strong Vincent at Gettysburg, Colonel James Clay Rice (44th New York) commanded the brigade. When Rice assumed command of another brigade in the First Corps, Chamberlain took over the brigade, though he remained a colonel. Chamberlain, however, had a relapse of malaria immediately following the fight at Rappahannock Station, and as a result, he left the army for Washington where he spent the rest of the winter. Brigadier General Joseph J. Bartlett then assumed command of the brigade.

83. After the annihilation of his bridgehead at Rappahannock Station, Lee gave up on his plan to contest the land between the Rappahannock and the Rapidan, and he fell back behind the latter river.

84. Gilmore's letter appeared in the November, 1864, "appendices" to the *Bangor Daily Whig and Courier*. His departure left Spear in command of the regiment *de jure* as well as *de facto*.

85. Jonathan Prince Cilley graduated from Bowdoin with Spear in the class of 1858. He was wounded and captured at Middleton on May 24, 1862, but subsequently released.

86. This ruin was possibly the remains of the Chancellor Mansion; all that was left of it after the battle there in May, 1863, was the cellar.

87. The "Six Hundred" is a reference to the charge of the light brigade in the Crimean War.

88. A literal translation of *sub Jove frigide is* "under the frigid Jove"—that is, under the cold sky.

89. The Robertson Tavern on the Old Turnpike was ten miles west of Chancellorsville and less than two miles east of Lee's defensive lines behind Mine Run.

90. Meade's movement on Thanksgiving was an effort to turn Lee's right flank. The difficult terrain slowed the march sufficiently to allow Lee to bring up reinforcements and entrench along the banks of Mine Run where he invited attack.

91. The 44th New York was on Spear's right, and the 83rd Pennsylvania on his left.

92. On November 29, Sedgwick (commanding the Sixth Corps on Spear's right) reported to Meade that Lee's left was unentrenched and vulnerable to an attack by the Fifth and Sixth Corps. Meade thereupon ordered both the preliminary bombardment described by Spear and a follow-up infantry attack. Sykes' visit to Spear's portion of the line was to select a route for this attack.

93. Rice, formerly the colonel of the 44th New York, had been promoted to brigadier general after Gettysburg and now commanded a brigade in Lysander Cutler's Division of the First Corps. The partial assault against Lee's lines along Mine Run was a feint designed to hold him

in place while Major General Gouveneur Warren's Second Corps moved into position to assault the Confederate right. Lee adjusted his lines overnight to foil this gambit. It is noteworthy that, as a major commanding a regiment, Spear was aware of Meade's tactical plan.

94. This hungry soldier was probably Captain Atherton W. Clark, Company E commander, and the senior captain in the regiment.

95. Since Warren's flanking movement had been discovered, Warren reported to Meade that his chances of success had become very slim, and recommended calling off the attack. Meade agreed, and ordered a general withdrawal.

96. Actually, Lee was quite anxious to bring on a fight, and he had already determined to attack the next day. When he learned that Meade's army had withdrawn, he remarked, "We should never have permitted those people to get away."

97. "Fabian strategy" involves a delaying action. Quintus Fabius Verrucussus (d. 203 b.c.) was famous for his strategy of slowly retreating while waiting for the enemy to come forward. The idea was that the enemy would become overextended and eventually cut off. During the Second Punic War this strategy did not turn out well, and the Romans were badly defeated at Cannae by Hannibal in 216 b.c.

98. *Alum* [potash] *igniferious* [of the fire], or fire ash. Soldiers mixed fire ash and water into a mortar-like compound used to chink their fireplaces.

99. The Pyramid of Cheops (or Khufu) is the largest of the three true pyramids located near Cairo, Egypt. The Renaissance architect Vitruvius Pollio was author of a seminal work in architectural history entitled *De Architectura libri dece traducti de latino in vulgqare affigurati*.

100. Spear's reference is to the explorer, Frederick A. Cook, who claimed that on April 21, 1908, he had reached the site of the North Pole. In December, 1909, a committee of scientists at the University of

Copenhegan rejected the conclusion that Cook's data constituted proof that he had in fact reached the Pole.

101. The "A" tent was standard issue used primarily for officers in fixed circumstances. Wall tents were used on the march. Enlisted men carried shelter halves, called "dog tents" during the Civil War.

102. *Mala in se* means "evil in itself."

103. The literal meaning of *Vade mecum* is "come with me" or "go with me"—that is, it is equipment you routinely carry.

104. In July 1862 the U.S. government passed the Legal Tender Act, authorizing paper currency. The bills (called greenbacks) soon began to depreciate in value relative to gold.

105. Presumably this was Colonel W. S. Tilton (22nd Mass.) who had brigade command through the winter months (November 1863 to March 1864).

106. Sibley tents were standard issue and could be used to shelter twenty men and their goods. Raised on an iron tripod with a center pole, they were circular tents, eighteen and a half feet in diameter and twelve feet high.

107. This is a reference to powdered potatoes, an early use of dehydrated rations.

108. Each regiment was authorized one sutler, a civilian entrepreneur, who was licensed to sell a long list of non-rationed goods to those who could pay—or to whom he extended credit. Popular items included tobacco, newspapers, razors, and cutlery. Though alcohol was forbidden, occasionally sutlers sold it, too.

109. The correct line (from Milton's *Paradise Lost*, Book I, line 346) is "'Twixt upper, nether, and surrounding Fires."

110. Spear's references to oleomargarine and microbes in this paragraph are anachronistic. Oleomargarine was not invented until 1869, and the role of microbes in human health—indeed the whole germ theory of disease—was the product of post-Civil War work by Louis Pasteur in France and Robert Koch in Germany.

111. The correct line (from Shakespeare's *Richard the Third*, Act I, scene 1, line 9) is: "Grim-visaged war hath smooth'd his wrinkled front."

112. Lincoln called Grant to Washington in February, 1864, to endow him with the command of all Union armies. Promoted to three-star rank in March, he attached himself to the Army of the Potomac. Though Meade retained titular command of the army, he was subject to Grant's supervision.

113. The Fourth Division of the Fifth Corps was organized on March 25, 1864. That same date, Brigadier General Romeyn Ayers took command of the First Brigade in the First Division, to which the 20th Maine belonged.

114. Both officers spent the winter in Washington: Chamberlain recovering from malaria; Gilmore indulging a variety of complaints.

115. Because it proved easier to recruit volunteers for new regiments—allowing friends and kinsmen to join together—than it was to induce new recruits to join established regiments, older regiments grew smaller with attrition while new regiments came to the war full-sized. By 1864 a veteran regiment might number only a few hundred, while some new units could approach the regulation size of a thousand men.

116. Deciding that the dense thickets of the Wilderness minimized his numerical inferiority, Lee launched a full-scale attack against the Army of the Potomac on May 5, thus inaugurating what became known as the Battle of the Wilderness.

117. Colonel Orpheus Woodward was shot in the right knee; Lieutenant Colonel DeWitt McCoy took over command of the regiment.

118. Spear's experience in this fight was typical of many small unit commanders in the Battle of the Wilderness. The dense forestation made visibility difficult and effective coordination impossible. The result was a battle characterized by scores of small-unit confrontations.

119. Hayes was among those wounded in this fusillade. A bullet creased his skull and literally knocked him out. He was replaced by Captain Benjamin F. Meservey.

120. In his official report, Spear wrote that his command brought off "35 prisoners, with the loss of 10 killed, 58 wounded, and 16 missing." (O.R., I, 36[1]:573).

121. The Confederate attack on the Union right was executed by the brigade of Major General John B. Gordon whose goal, as Spear suspected, was to seize the Germanna Plank Road, the Union army's main line of communications with its base. While partially successful, Gordon's assault was undermanned and came too late in the afternoon to be decisive.

122. The commander of the 155th Pennsylvania, Colonel Alfred L. Pearson, claimed in his official report that "the regiment received orders to fall back." (O.R., I, 36[1]:557).

123. One of the nightmarish qualities of the Battle of the Wilderness was that the flash of powder started a number of brushfires, and many wounded men burnt to death in the spreading flames.

124. Hancock's Second Corps faced a furious assault by two Confederate corps (those of A. P. Hill and James Longstreet). Hancock's line bent, but did not break, though he sustained very heavy casualties.

125. Once he appreciated that the Union army was advancing southward rather than retreating, Lee, too, sent his infantry marching to the south. The Confederate infantry reached the vicinity of Spotsylvania only minutes ahead of the vanguard of Warren's Corps, and threw back the initial Federal assault.

126. Samuel W. Crawford was a medical doctor from Pennsylvania who served as an army surgeon in the decade before the war. He commanded a battery at Fort Sumter, and was promoted to brigadier general in 1862 after the Shenandoah Valley campaign.

127. Crawford's Pennsylvania Reserve Brigade was composed of soldiers who had originally been part of the 13th (and later the 42nd) Pennsylvania Volunteers. Because they wore deer's tails on their caps, they came to be known as the "Bucktails." Officially disbanded in June 1864, many of the original members of the Bucktails joined the 190th and 191st Pennsylvania, and were designated a Reserve brigade.

128. Despite Spear's critical assessment, Crawford was breveted for gallantry in the Battles of the Wilderness and Spotsylvania, and later at Five Forks. Crawford did not file a report on this battle, or at least one is not included in the *Official Records*. Captain William W. Morrell, who was killed here, should not be confused with Captain Walter G. Morrill who survived the war and briefly commanded the regiment.

129. The key element of Grant's grand strategic plan was for all Union armies to advance more-or-less simultaneously. As Meade's Army of the Potomac moved into the Wilderness, Benjamin Butler's Army of the James was to move up its namesake river to Petersburg (Richmond's "back door"), and William T. Sherman was to assail Joseph E. Johnston's Confederate army in north Georgia. Sherman flanked Johnston out of his defensive lines near Dalton in early May, but Butler's campaign bogged down almost at once.

130. This attack plan was the inspiration of Colonel Emory Upton who convinced the new Sixth Corps commander, Horatio Wright, that a

charge in column, as opposed to the conventional line-abreast, could break through the Confederate defenses. The forces on Spear's right—a division under Gersham Mott—were to have supported Upton's anticipated breakthrough. Upton's twelve regiments did indeed break the Rebel line, but Mott's Division was itself broken by concentrated Confederate artillery fire and Upton had to fall back. Despite reports, Hancock's attack that evening was not successful.

131. Burnside's Ninth Corps and Hancock's Second Corps, supported by Wright's Sixth Corps, were to assault a Confederate salient called "the muleshoe" in this all-out attack. As part of Warren's Fifth Corps, Spear's 20th Maine was to assault the Confederate salient further to the right.

132. According to official reports, Hancock and Burnside attacked at 4:30 a.m. and Wright's Corps at 6:00 a.m.

133. Edward Johnson ("Old Allegheny"), commanding Stonewall Jackson's old division, was captured along with most of his men, more than 3,000, in this impetuous assault.

134. Hancock's attack broke the Confederate salient, and the Rebels had to fall back to a secondary line across the base of the "muleshoe." The heavy fighting there gave this salient the nickname Spear applies: the "Bloody Angle."

135. This night march by the Fifth and Sixth Corps (Warren and Wright) was supposed to culminate in a dawn attack on Spotsylvania from the east.

136. The slowness of the march of May 13-14 ruined any chance of a successful assault. Possessing interior lines, Lee could shift reinforcements across the chord of the arc much faster than the Federals could move around the outside perimeter. As a result, Grant called off the scheduled attack.

137. Spear alludes here to the Roman poet Horace (65-8 b.c.). Horace's doctrine of a "full cup" is found throughout his *Odes*.

138. Chamberlain's command of the brigade was temporary. When Bartlett recovered, Chamberlain reverted to command of the 20th Maine, bumping Spear back to second in command.

139. The fighting on the 19th was the result of a reconnaissance in force by the Confederate corps of Richard Ewell, ordered by Lee to discover what he could about Federal movements. Ewell ran into Warren's flank and a severe fight erupted before Ewell withdrew.

140. The Mat, Ta, Po and Ni streams in eastern Virginia are collectively known as the Mattaponi River.

141. Butler's campaign on the James started off well enough as he led 39,000 men against Petersburg, south of Richmond. Attacked by a scratch force under General Pierre Gustave Beauregard on May 16, however, Butler lost his nerve and retreated into defensive lines where he was, in effect, neutralized.

142. The correct lines (from Oliver Goldsmith's "An Elegy on the Glory of her Sex, Mrs. Mary Blaize," lines 19-20) are:

> The King himself has follow'd her,—
> When she has walk'd before.

143. Henry C. Corbin served as adjutant general during the Spanish-American War and acted as President McKinley's chief of staff. After the war, photos of him in full dress uniform were common in the newspapers.

144. Jericho Ford is more commonly known as Jericho's Mills.

145. By this time the "Iron Brigade," formed originally from midwestern troops, was only a memory. They were decimated at Gettysburg, and

regiments were added to the former force, which retained only its name.

146. Lee laid an elegant trap for Grant on the North Anna River. By allowing the corps of Wright and Warren to cross the river upstream of Ox Ford, which Lee held, and allowing Hancock's to cross downstream, Lee put himself in a position to strike first one, then the other, of Grant's corps. The trap never closed because Lee was too ill to exercise effective command. When Grant realized his peril, he ordered a swift withdrawal.

147. At about 3:00 p.m. on June 2, Lee sent two divisions forward to secure a piece of high ground from which he could dominate the Chickahominy bottoms. The artillery that harassed the 20th Maine fired from this high ground. The rest of the army spent June 2 preparing for an all-out assault by three corps the next day.

148. The 20th Maine was not involved in the Battle of Cold Harbor on June 3, one of the great disasters of the war. In a massive frontal assault, the Union army lost nearly 7,000 casualties, most of them in a period of twenty minutes.

149. Grant, moving again to the left, was now determined to swing south of Richmond and assail that city's rail connections southward through Petersburg.

150. The pontoon bridge crossed the Appomattox River, a tributary of the James, at Point of Rocks. The 14th and 15th of June were critical; Grant's forces were now in strength south and east of Petersburg which was the key to Richmond. Spear's reference to Xerxes is from Milton's *Paradise Lost* (Book X, lines 307-11):

> *Xerxes*, the Libertie of *Greece* to yoke,
> From *Susa* his *Memnonian* Palace high
> Came to the Sea, and, over *Hellespont*
> Bridging his way, *Europe* with *Asia* joyn'd,
> And scourg'd with many a stroak th' indignant waves.

151. The Confederate defenses around Petersburg had been laid out in 1862 by Captain Charles H. Dimmock and were therefore known as the Dimmock Line. Until June 18, when the lead elements of A. P. Hill's veterans arrived, however, those lines were very lightly defended.

152. The brigade of black soldiers under Brigadier General Edward Hincks was among the first to encounter the Rebel defenses. These black soldiers, who had relatively few opportunities to see combat, took 300 prisoners and twelve guns.

153. Chamberlain's wounds were believed to be mortal and the thought of Chamberlain's imminent death probably provoked Grant to promote him, finally, to brigadier general effective June 19. Chamberlain, however, survived his wounds and lived until 1914.

154. City Point on the James River just below the confluence of the Appomattox, was the site of Grant's headquarters. A new hospital, with a capacity to care for 6,000 patients, had recently been erected there, and this was where Chamberlain was to be treated.

155. The president referred to here as temperamentally "spoiling for a fight" was Theodore Roosevelt.

156. The quotation is from Milton, *Samson Agonistes*, line 1721. Spear quotes the poem more fully on page 128. Quoted with Milton's punctuation, the passage (lines 1721-4) reads as follows:

> Nothing is here for tears, nothing to wail
> Or knock the breast, no weakness, no contempt,
> Dispraise, or blame, nothing but well and fair,
> And what may quiet us in a death so noble.

157. Spear's manuscript includes the following paragraph just before the four-line quotation beginning "Nothing is here for tears." Spear obviously had second thoughts as he wrote the paragraph, and he crossed it out. It is printed here in order to present a complete transcription of the manuscript while attempting to honor the explicit intentions

of the author. Although at this point Spear felt that these "ugly facts" involving Lieutenant Colonel Gilmore belonged in "oblivion," he recalled the same situation on page 28. Of course, Spear's remembrance coming at this juncture carries enormous emotional weight.

> One circumstance came about with his [Keene's] death unfortunately left an indelible bitterness against one man—who held the commission of Lt. Colonel, and who, by some means always kept out of battle, and [spent] most of the time in Washington. When Col. Ames was promoted in May of 1863, and before he left the regiment, he had sent for Keene and myself, then captains, and assured us that he would recommend us for promotion. Chamberlain, then a Lt. Col. should be Colonel. Of that there could be no question. The [*indecipherable word*] of whom I have mentioned, then Major, (and as we were in camp presently) was to be made Lt. Colonel, (out of compliment) and immediately to resign, on the allegation that he was physically unfit for the service— Then according to the plan, I was to be Lt. Col. and Keene Major. The plan miscarried by reason of the failure of the Lt. Col to resign. The promotion of Col. Chamberlain, on the 19th of June, to be Brigadier General, left another vacancy, but too late for Captain Keene. The absentee, instead of resigning, sought the Colonelcy: but at that time the regiment was reduced by the casualties of the campaign, below the numbers where the muster of a Colonel could, under the Regulations, be permitted. But perhaps this were better omitted, and the small ugly details of this was concealed from posterity, and left to oblivion.

158. In four days of heavy fighting (June 15-18) the Union army lost some 11,000 casualties attempting to break through the Confederate defenses around Petersburg. After June 18, both sides settled into a siege that lasted until the following spring.

159. In military parlance, vidette means a mounted sentry or picket.

160. The coehorn mortar was a relatively small (4.5 inch) field mortar that

threw a fused shell in a high arc to explode over enemy lines. Union forces generally used much larger mortars—up to thirteen inches.

161. The Sanitary Commission was a civilian volunteer organization, funded by donations, that provided care for the wounded and often brought luxuries such as fresh food and writing paper to troops in the front lines.

162. Fort Hill was a strong point in the Confederate lines named for the corps commander Ambrose Powell Hill.

163. Even before the two armies had settled into a siege, Lee had dispatched Jubal Early, with 9,000 men, to join with other Confederate forces in the Shenandoah Valley in order to mount a credible threat to Washington. Lee hoped this threat would compel Grant to fall back to protect the national capital.

164. Early's forces reached the outskirts of Washington on July 10, but the substantial fortifications and the arrival of reinforcements from Grant's army, compelled them to withdraw.

165. The tunnel under the Confederate lines was the idea of Lieutenant Colonel Henry Pleasants of the 48th Pennsylvania whose members came from the coal mining region of Schuylkill County. The tunnel was 586 feet long, and its terminus was packed with 8,000 pounds of black powder. The idea was that after blowing a huge hole in the Confederate line, Union troops would rush through the breach.

166. Ambrose Burnside, whose Ninth Corps occupied the portion of the Union lines where the explosion occurred, had assigned a division of black troops under Brigadier General Edward Ferraro to make the charge. At the last minute, however, Grant ordered him to use a white division out of a concern that, in the event of a failure, critics would charge either that the black troops had been sacrificed, or that they were incapable of an effective offensive. This last-minute substitution contributed significantly to the confusion evident in the attack and

probably doomed it to failure. The Union lost 3,798 casualties, many of them taken prisoner.

167. In July, 1861, Congress (at the request of Treasury Secretary Chase) authorized a loan of $250 million funded by twenty-year bonds in denominations of not less than fifty dollars, and at a rate of 7.30 percent. Called "seven thirties" for the interest rate, the government used them to pay salaries or other debts. In addition to their face value (ostensibly redeemable in coin), the notes had coupons attached that could be removed periodically to redeem the interest payments.

168. Chambersburg, Pennsylvania, was burned by 2,600 Confederate cavalry under the command of Brigadier General John McCausland on July 30-31, 1864. McCausland demanded a payment of $100,000 in gold (or $500,000 in paper) to compensate for the destruction of homes in the Shenandoah Valley by Union Major General David Hunter. When the townspeople refused to pay, McCausland burned the town.

169. Horatio Wright's Sixth Corps was the force Grant sent to Washington to help repel Early's raid.

170. The brigade of Joseph Finegan (note correct spelling) suffered more than most from desertion that fall and winter, so much so, that in the spring the unit was disbanded and Finegan himself returned to Florida a few weeks before Appomattox.

171. Grant's gradual move leftward not only threatened the roads and rail lines connecting Petersburg (and therefore Richmond) to the rest of the Confederacy, it also forced Lee to stretch his outnumbered forces even thinner. The movement Spear describes here, which began on August 18, was intended to cut the Weldon Railroad, the last (save one) out of Petersburg. It was executed by four divisions of Major General Gouveneur Warren's Fifth Corps, including the Third Brigade (Colonel James Gwyn) of the First Division (Brigadier General Charles Griffin), which contained the 20th Maine.

172. The Second Division (Brigadier General Romeyn Ayres), on the Federal right, was the target of a furious counter-attack by the Confederate Division of Major General Henry Heth. In the ensuing fight, Ayres's Second Brigade—four Maryland regiments under Colonel Samuel Graham—was routed. Warren had to pull back to Glode Tavern having lost 382 killed and wounded and 2,518 missing—most of them taken prisoner.

173. The North Carolina troops that attacked on August 21 were part of A. P. Hill's Confederate Corps. This time, Hill was driven back, ending what is known as the Battle of Globe Tavern. The Federal occupation of a segment of the Weldon Railroad did not block that route for the Confederates, however. Trains bound for Petersburg merely offloaded south of the Federal enclave and transferred their cargo to wagons which detoured around the salient.

174. The raid, led by Confederate Major General Wade Hampton on September 16, 1864, netted the attackers 2,486 head of beef cattle and more than 200 Federal prisoners at a cost of 61 casualties. Abraham Lincoln called it "the slickest piece of cattle stealing I ever heard of."

175. The weapon described here is the Lindsay Musket which was supposed to fire two bullets—one at a time—from the same barrel. The Lindsay Musket had a tendency, after repeated use, to fire both bullets at once, thus causing the breech to explode. The Spencer carbine fired seven copper cartridges from a long metal tube loaded through the stock, and the Henry rifle carried fifteen rounds of cartridges in a magazine under the barrel. Though available in 1861, these rifles were not issued in quantity until late in the war, and then mostly to cavalry units.

176. Grant appointed Major General Philip Sheridan to command the Army of the Shenandoah in August. Sheridan defeated the forces of Jubal Early at Third Winchester (September 19) and Fisher's Hill (September 22) thus effectively reclaiming the Shenandoah Valley for the Union.

177. Grant ordered Major General Benjamin Butler's Army of the James to attack Confederate lines north of Petersburg. Expecting Lee to respond to that attack by sending his reserves there, Grant also ordered Warren's Fifth Corps to feel for the Confederate right flank. It is possible that the orders for the band to play while marching may have been designed to deter Lee from sending even more reinforcements from his right to combat Butler's attack.

178. Weston H. Keene of Bremen died instantly; Joseph W. Libby of Warren died of his wounds on November 8.

179. Probably this was General Bartlett's younger brother, Chester.

180. Spear turned thirty on October 15, 1864.

181. This procedure for wrecking railroads was standard practice for both armies and in all theaters during the war. Troops often gave colorful names to the resulting twisted rails such as Jefferson Davis neckties or Mrs. Lincoln's hairpins.

182. During Spear's sojourn to Maine on recruiting duty, the Fifth Corps participated in the Battle of Hatcher's Run (February 5-7, 1864), an attempt to secure the Boydton Plank Road. Union troops briefly seized the road, but could not hold it. Captain Walter G. Morrill is listed as the commanding officer of the 20th Maine in this engagement. Spear joined the staff of the division commander, Brigadier General Joseph J. Bartlett.

183. Lee's assault on Fort Stedman was indeed desperate. His plan was to effect a temporary breakthrough east of Petersburg thereby forcing Grant to recall some of his forces from the left, south of the city. The plan was meant to enable Lee's army to regain some freedom of movement. The gambit failed, and Grant recognized that Lee must have weakened his defenses south of the city to mount the attack, as indeed he had. Grant therefore ordered Warren and Sheridan to undertake the movement which Spear describes here.

184. In this Battle of Dinwiddie Court House (or the Battle of Gravelly Run), Warren's infantry (with the 20th Maine) fought off a counterattack by Major General George E. Pickett.

185. Spear's reference here is to Confederate Brigadier General Eppa Hunton who commanded a brigade at Dinwiddie Court House and who, after the war, served eight years as a U.S. Congressman and three years as a U.S. Senator from Virginia.

186. The volume to which Spear refers here is A. A. Humphreys, *The Virginia Campaign of 1864 and 1865* [New York: Charles Scribners Sons, 1883].

187. The ladies may never have seen Spear again, but they soon saw a great many more Yankees, for the next day Major General Sheridan made the Boisseau House his headquarters.

188. Spear here refers to *Paradise Lost,* Book I, line 392. Moloch was a god of fire of the Ammonites, to whom children were sacrificed. Spear's quotation of the following line is somewhat inaccurate. With Milton's original spelling and punctuation, the quoted passage (lines 392-6) reads as follows:

> First *Moloch*, horrid King besmear'd with blood
> Of human sacrifice, and parents tears,
> Though for the noyse of Drums and Timbrels loud
> Thir childrens cries unheard, that past through fire
> To his grim Idol.

189. Sheridan's plan was for the Second Corps (Hancock) and his own three cavalry divisions to attack frontally, while Warren's Fifth Corps (including the 20th Maine) rolled up the enemy flank.

190. Ayres' Division was driven by 5,000 men of Bushrod Johnson's Confederate Division. The Confederate drive stalled, however, when it reached Griffin's Division in reserve. It was the Confederacy's last gasp.

191. Warren had overestimated the length of the Confederate defensive line to such an extent that he sent two of his three divisions attacking into a void. Sheridan was so infuriated that he obtained permission from Grant to relieve him on the spot. After the war, Warren demanded a court martial to clear his name. Spear testified at the November, 1882, hearings that exonerated Warren—three months after his death.

192. The Union army captured 5,200 Confederate prisoners and four cannon at the Battle of Five Forks. The large number of prisoners evidenced the deterioration of Confederate morale, and convinced Grant to order a general assault all along the line.

193. Here Spear recalls *Paradise Lost*, Book II, lines 44-5. In this passage, Moloch, addressing Satan, advocates open warfare against God in order to recover Heaven. The passage (lines 43-50) reads (with original spelling) as follows:

> He [Satan] ceas'd, and next to him *Moloc*, Scepter'd King
> Stood up, the strongest and the fiercest Spirit
> That fought in Heav'n; now fiercer by dispair:
> His trust was with th'Eternal to be deem'd
> Equal in strength, and rather then be less
> Car'd not to be at all; with that care lost
> Went all his fear: of God, or Hell, or worse
> He reck'd not . . .

194. Lee realized that the defeat at Five Forks made a continued defense of Petersburg impossible—and if Petersburg had to be evacuated, so did Richmond. He notified the government, and prepared to fall back westward with his army, still hoping to effect a junction with Joseph E. Johnston's Confederate army in North Carolina.

195. The "ancient German women" were described in *Germaniae* by the Roman historian Tacitus (c. 55-c. 117 a.d.).

196. Due to a shortage of iron, many southern railroads were built in what was known as "strap and stringer" fashion: thin strips of iron were affixed to wooden rails.

197. The skirmish at Sailor's (or Sayler's) Creek on April 6 was known as "Black Thursday" in the Confederate army. Lee's rear guard, outnumbered and outgunned, was devastated by the attacking Federals who took over 8,000 prisoners. Lee was shocked by the apparent collapse of his army and cried out: "My God! Has the army been dissolved?"

198. On April 7, Grant sent Lee a message inviting him to surrender. Still hopeful of making an escape, Lee responded noncommittally. But on April 9, accepting the inevitable, he agreed to meet with Grant to discuss the surrender of his army. It was this agreement to meet, rather than the actual surrender (which took place that afternoon), that provoked the cries of "Lee surrendered" overheard by Spear.

199. A hoecake is a thin, fried cake made with cornmeal.

200. This statement on the use of airplanes in warfare dates Spear's work on his manuscript to 1914 or later.

201. Fort Darling (which Spear refers to as Fort Drury) on Drewry's Bluff on the James River south of Richmond, had resisted repeated Federal attacks since 1862, and was evacuated by its defenders only when Richmond was abandoned.

202. During the Civil War, Libby Prison was used for the incarceration of Federal officers.

203. Spear wrote the date "May 7" at this point in the manuscript.

204. The capitol dome was re-built during the war. An older, iron dome was replaced by a higher, white marble dome, the one that adorns the building today.

205. Although Moses was forbidden from entering the Promised Land, he could view the Promised Land from Mount Nebo. In addition to the Biblical reference, Spear is again referring to *Paradise Lost* (Book I, line 407).

206. "Old members" of the regiment were mustered out on June 4; the regiment itself was dismissed from service on July 16 to begin the trek back to Maine.

INDEX

NOTE: Page numbers appearing in italic type refer to plate numbers. Page numbers for endnotes are followed by the letter "n" and the endnote number. Page numbers in parentheses indicate contextual references where the name itself does not occur on the page.

A

Abbott, George R., 191
Abbott, William, 204, 283
Acquia Creek, 24, 298
Aeneid, 364n79
African Americans, 50, 123, 178, 184, 251, 324, 374n152, 376n166
airplanes, 186, 382n200
Alabama Troops, 35, 215, 359n49
alcohol, 80–82, 143, 160–162, 340–341
Aldie, 30, 213, 214, 310, 358n41
Alexander, E. Porter, (38n58), 361n58
Alexandria, 10, 137, 276, 292
Amelia Court House, 179
Ames, Adelbert
  appointed Colonel, 7, 291, 353n8
  Chancellorsville, 27, 210
  Fredericksburg, 20, 300, 303
  as Meade's aide, 357n33
  Petersburg, 134, 255, 256
  photograph, *VII*
  and Spear, 15, 47, 294, 303
  training officers, 10, 296
  training troops, 8–9, 11, 197, 291, 293
  winter quarters, 200, 205, 307
Andersonville prison, 42
  See also Libby prison
Andrews, Timothy F., 263
Antietam, 11, 12, 295

Antietam Creek, 14, 42, 295–296
applejack, 162
Appomattox, 175–184, 272
Aqueduct Bridge, 12, 294
Army of the Potomac
  Appomattox, 183
  Fredericksburg, 18
  joining, 293
  McClellan command, 16
  return home, 188–194
  Wilderness, 99
  See also individual battles; commanders
Ayres, Romeyn B., 172, 258, 340–341, 368n113, 380n190

B

Bailey, David A., 197, 198, 212
Baker, (Doctor) (first name unknown), 219
Balaklava, 36, 360n54
Ball's Bluff, 4, 290, 353n2
Baltimore and Ohio Depot, 193
Bangs, Isaac, 199
Banks Ford, 207
Barksdale's Brigade, (27n35), 357n35
Barnes, (first name unknown), 197, 198
Bartlett, Chester "Chet," 154, 167, 379n179
Bartlett, Joseph Jackson
  after war, 274
  Bethesda Church, 119, 247
  Gravelly Run, 167
  "Hardtack drill," 63–64
  illness, 109, 151
  muskets, 146
  Peebles/Pegram's Farm, 151, 153, 154, 155, 261

Bartlett, Joseph Jackson *(continued)*
  Petersburg, 125, 253
  Spotsylvania, 103, 109, 110, 242, 243, 345, 350
  Wilderness, 93, 242, 338
Batchelder, R. N., 255
Bealton, 53
beanholes, 77–78
Beauregard, Pierre Gustave T., 372n141
Benning, Henry T., 272
Bethesda Church, 116–123, 246–250
Beverly Ford, 322
Bickford, William, 228, 257, 267
Big Round Top, 33, 37–39, 315, 316–317
  See also Gettysburg
Bloody Angle, 106, 346–348, 371n133, 371n134
  See also Spotsylvania Court House
Boisseau, Dr. (House), 169–170, 270, 380n187
Boston, 194, 236, 262, 283
Bracket, (first name unknown), 161–162
Brandy Station, 53, 358n39
Breck, (Col.) (first name unknown), 281
Breen, Peter, 274, 285
Brent, (first name unknown), 152
Broad Run Creek, 29, 59, 229
Brock Road, 99
Brown, John Marshall, 124, 246, 250
Brown, Moses W., 7–8
Buckeystown, 31
Buker, William G., 197, 198
Bull Run, 4, 54, 58
  Second Battle of, 10, 292, 354n12, 363n72
Burksville, 43
Burnham, Hiram, 150
Burnside, Ambrose E.
  Bethesda Church, 116, 246–247
  Fredericksburg, 22–23, 298, 356n29
  Head Quarters, 188
  incompetence of, 18, 135, 298, 303, 355n21
  Mud March, 25, 357n32
  Petersburg mine assault, 135, 256, 376n166
  replacing McClellan, 17, 297, 303, 355n18, 355n19
  Spotsylvania Court House, 106, 241, 245, 371n131, 371n132
Butler, Benjamin F., 104, 111, 187, 240, 242, 244, 372n141, 379n177
Butler, John, 278

C

"call up," 5, 353n4
camp conditions
  Antietam Creek, 14, 296
  Centreville, 55, 57
  Gettysburg, 38
  Petersburg, 130–131
  Rappahannock, 48
  Rappahannock Station, 66–67
  White Plains, 17, 297–298
  winter quarters, 23–24, 76–91, 198–205, 303–307
Carr, Almon, 199
Carr, (Capt.) (first name unknown), 218
Carter, Lewis D., 199
Casey's *Tactics,* 10, 142, 354n11
casualties
  Fredericksburg, 21, 302, 356n28

casualties *(continued)*
  Gettysburg, 40
  Little Round Top, 37, 361n56
  Pegram's Farm, 153
  Petersburg, 375n158, 377n166
  Wilderness, 96, 239, 339, 369n120
Catoctin Mountain, (42n62), 361n62
cattle, 145–146, 260, 294
Cemetery Ridge, 38
  See also Gettysburg
Centreville, 29, 52, 54–57, 213, 227, 228, 325–326, 363n76
Chamberlain, Joshua L.
  absenteeism, 92, 213, 231, 310, 337, 368n114
  appointment to Lt. Col., 7, 214, 291, 353n7
  Bethesda Church, 120, 248
  Chancellorsville, 27, 30, 309
  and Col. Ames, 9
  commanding ability, 7, 156
  Fredericksburg, 20, 300
  illness, 47, 362n67, 364n82
  leave, 199
  Lee's retreat, 44, 45, 222, 321, 323
  Lewis Farm, 167, 270
  Little Round Top, (33n48), 34, 313, 315, 317, 359n48, 359n50, 360n55
  Mud March, 198
  Ox Bow Creek, 325
  photograph, *VIII*
  promotion, 28, 209, 210, 272, 281, 363n74
  Rappahannock Station, 62
  Spotsylvania, 109, 114, 372n138
  Weldon Railroad, 164, 263, 266
  winter quarters, 200, 201, 209, 337
  wounded, 123, 250, 252, 374n153

Chamberlain, Thomas D., 28, 191, 278, 305, 358n37
Chambersburg, 137, 377n168
Chancellor Mansion, (69n86), 365n86
Chancellorsville, 27–32, 68, 308
chaplain, 117, 212, 252, 253
Chester Gap, 44, 220
Chickahominy River, 120–121, 246, 248, 249, 373n147
Christian, (Lt.) (first name unknown), 37, 316
Churchill, E.W., 265
Cilley, Jonathan Prince, 65, 69, 231, 232, 266, 331, 365n85
City Point, 124, 131, 255, 259, 374n154
civilians
  after the war, 184, 187, 193
  Confederate, 53, 164, 170, 176
  Gettysburg, 32
  Mine Run, 70–71, 72, 332–333
  stealing from, 115, 155, 163
Clark, Atherton W.
  Gettysburg, 39, 318
  leave, 199
  Lee's retreat, 218, 223, 322
  Mine Run, 71, 331, 366n94
  photograph, *IX*
  promotion, 28, 47, 310
  recruiting, 90, 92
  and turkey, 163
  winter quarters, 84, 237
Clay, James H., 285
clothing, 9, 46, 79, 94, 136, 292
Coburn, Abner, 27, 206, 223, 257, 262, 281
Cold Harbor, 116, 373n148
Colors Company, 34–37, 36, 314
Columbia Pike, 187, 189

commissary, 46, 85–86, 136
Confederate
  cavalry, 31
  civilians, 32, 164, 169–170, 176
  deserters, 137, 178
  money, 19, 49, 183, 299, 324
  See also Lee's Army
Connecticut Troops, 52
Conner, Freeman, 43, 100, 218, 221, 223, 310, 342
Cook, Dr. Frederick A., 78, 366n100
cooks, 7, 49, 320
  See also Old Fields
Copperheads, 4, 5, 289, 353n1
Corbin, Henry C., 113, 372n143
corduroy wagon roads, 45, 221, 362n66
coupon notes, 136
court martial, 82, 83, 237, 238
Crawford, Samuel W., 370n126, 370n127
  Five Forks, 172
  Spotsylvania, 240
  Weldon Railroad, 258
  Wilderness, 100, 103, 342, 343, 344, 370n128
Cub Run, 309
Culpeper, 48, 53, 76, 93, 225, 226, 324–325, 362n65
Culpeper Court House, 48, 323, 335, 337
Cushman, Wales H., 199
Custer, George A., 171, 326
Cutler, Lysander, 365n93

D

Dalton, 104, 240
Danville Road, 271

deserters, 48, 137, 178, 248, 256
Devin, Thomas, C., 171
Dimmock, Charles H., 374n151
Dinwiddie Court House, 166, 168, 270, 271, 380n184
discipline. *See under* soldiers
disease, 24
  malaria, 13–14, 30, 132, 296, 305
  small pox, 26, 28, 306–307
doctor, 24, 43, 51–52
Dodge, Royal, (20n25), 198, 199, 208, 300, 356n25
dog, 20, 300
Donnell, William E., 265
Doty, (Col.) (first name unknown), 310
Doughty, Calvin S., 213, 267
dress parades, 9, 79, 84, 199
Drum Corps, 8
Dunn, (Capt.) (first name unknown), 281
Dutch ovens, 86–87

E

Eagan, Father, 114
Early, Jubal A., 132, 137, 138, 166, 376n163, 376n164, 378n176
Eighteenth Corps, 120
Elliot, Robert F., 246
Ellis Ford, 29, 211
Emmitsburg Pike, 40, 318
euchre, 17, 199, 208, 209, 266, 355n20
Ewell, Richard, 372n139
executions, 48

F

"Fabian strategy," 76, 366n97
Fairfax, 55, 227, 228, 325

Falmouth, 298, 308
Farmville, 184, 273
Fernald, John Q., 223
Ferraro, Edward, 376n166
Field, Charles W., 272
Fifth Corps
  Antietam, 12, 295
  Appomattox, 181
  Centreville, 55
  Five Forks, 168, 171
  following Lee's retreat, 226
  Fredericksburg, 17, 298
  and Grant, 113
  Laurel Hill, 345
  Mine Run, 331, 334
  Rappahannock Station, 328
  Washington, DC, 10
  Weldon Railroad, 157
  See also battles
Finegan, Joseph, 137, 377n170
fireplaces, 66–67, 79
First Corps, 55, 334
Fitch, Joseph B.
  Mud March, 198
  Petersburg, 127, 134–135
  Weldon Railroad, 141, 258
  Winter quarters, 201, 235, 238
Five Forks, 168, 171–174, 271, 381n192
Flagg, Alexis F., 199, 200
Flagg, Orlando, 197, 199
Florida Brigade, 137, 377n170
Fogg, Isabella, 48, 120, 218, 223, 224, 249
Fogler, Prentiss M., 126
food
  alcohol, 80–82, 143, 160–162
  beans, 46, 57, 77–78, 84, 200, 323
  biscuits, 86–87

food *(continued)*
  oleomargarine (butter), 87, 368n110
  chestnuts, 57
  coffee, 49, 58, 136
  condemned bread, 65–66, 329
  cooking, 77–78, 86–88, 163, 320
  dew berries, 44
  doughnuts, 67
  hardtack, 14, 17, 46, 49, 63, 84, 136, 305, 355n15
  hoecakes, 184, 382n199
  honey, 45, 321
  hunger, 11, 16–17, 55, 73, 297, 320, 323, 329
  lobster, 16, 297
  meat, 17, 44, 73, 84, 321, 322
  peaches, 126
  peanuts, 153
  purchasing, 84–86, 324
  rations, 11, 14, 46, 49, 65–66, 85, 136, 322
  salt pork, 46, 48, 86, 136, 163, 305, 355n15
  scavenging for, 44, 57, 115, 153, 321
  soft bread, 24, 84
  sugar, 136
  turkey, 163, 336
Fort Darling (Drury), 187, 275, 382n201
Fort Donelson, 4, 290, 353n3
Fort Hill, 131, 376n162
Fort Stedman, 166, 379n183
Frederick, 31, 41–42, 214, 215
Frederick City, 12, 294
Fredericksburg, 18–23, 207, 299–303, 355n23, 356n24
French, E. B., 127, 128
French, Luther P., 117, 206, 208, 210
Friend House, 186, 275
Furbish, George W., 273, 278

G

Georgetown, 294
Germanna Ford, 91, 93, 239, 330, 337
Germanna Plank Road, 94, 369n121
Getchell, Henry W., 268
Gettysburg, 32–41, 215–216, 309–319, 359n45, 360n55, 361n57
Gibbons Corps, 183, 251
Gilmore, Charles D.,
    absenteeism, 30, 48, 55, 60, 92, 214, 229, 231, 337, 364n84, 368n114
    character, 54, 56, 65, 307
    charges against, 189, 270, 273, 277
    Gettysburg, 310
    promotion, 28, 47, 151, 156, 166, 363n74
    Rappahannock Station, 62, 329–330
    Spear's opinion of, 164, 323, 374n157
    tobacco incident, 61, 64, 326-327, 330
Globe Tavern, (142n173), 378n172, 378n173
Goldsmith, Oliver, 364n80, 372n142
Goose Creek, 30, 44, 219, 309
Gordon, John B., 272, 369n121
Grand Review, 189–190
Grant, Ulysses S.
    Appomattox, 182, 272
    character, 147
    on Confederacy, 185
    Five Forks, 175
    Fort Donelson, (4n3), 353n3
    as leader, 39, 89, 290, 368n112, 370n129
    Petersburg, 132, 134, 140, 255
    physical appearance, 113
    Weldon Railroad, 140, 145, 259
Gravelly Run, 167–168, 380n184
    See also Dinwiddie Court House
Greek lexicon, 51, 324
Greenwood, William B., 102, 344
Griffin, Simon G., 150, 153–154, 172, 174, 175, 248, 261, 270
Griffin, William, 107, 241
Griffin's Corps, 183, 380n190
Gum Springs, 29, 213
Gwyn, James A., 151, 261, 377n171

H

Hagerstown, 217
Hampton, Wade, (146n174), 378n174
Hancock, Winfield Scott
    Spotsylvania, 106, 241, 346, 371n131, 371n132, 371n134
    Wilderness, 94, 97, 369n124
Hanover, 31, 215
Hanover Court House, 187, 275
Harpers Ferry, 15, 16, 297, 355n16
Harrison's Landing, 122, 249
Haskell, Isaac W., (7n6), 353n6
Hatcher's Run, 166, 173, 270, 379n182
Hayes, Joseph, 95–96, 253, 255, 336, 339, 369n119
Heath, Xenophon, 15, 296
Herring, Charles P., 254
    Weldon Railroad, 145, 258, 259, 266
    Wilderness, 98, 100, 101, 341, 343
Herson, Nahum A., 218, 223
Hill, A. P.
    Bristoe Station, 363n75
    Globe Tavern, 378n173
    Manassas Junction, (54n72, 54n73), 363n72, 363n73
    Petersburg, 374n151
    Wilderness, 369n124
Hill, Lysander, 202, 204, 205, 225, 229, 236, 246, 250, 252, 263, 284

Hill, William E., 199
Hincks, Edward, 374n152
Hiscock, Abner S., 199
Hodgdon, (first name unknown), 199
Hodsdon, John L., 236, 265, 267
Hoffses, Joseph J. A., 5–6, 290–291, 353n5
Hood, John Bell, (48n68), 362n68
Hooker, Joseph, 27, 68, 308, 357n34, 358n42, 358n43
Hopper, I. Harris, 152–153
Horace, 372n137
horses, 46, 51–52, 82–83, 273, 274
Howe, (Lt.) (first name unknown), 243
Hubbard, Nettie, 226, 230, 243, 248, 252, 255, 270, 350
Hubbard, Wales, 9, 199, 203, 210
Humphreys, Andrew A., 154, 168, 261, 380n186
hunger, 16, 17, 55, 233, 268, 297, 320, 323
Hunter, David, 377n168
Hunton, Eppa, 168, 380n185
Hutchins, Alvah L., 268
Hutchinson, (first name unknown), 281

I

Ingalls Station, 93, 238
insects, 24, 123, 130, 279
Irish soldiers, 80–82, 161–162
Iron Brigade, 114, 372n145

J

Jacklin, Rufus W., 102, 344
Jackson, Daniel A., 73
Jackson, Thomas (Stonewall), (15n16), 355n16

James, Theodore, 280
James River, 121, 132
Jeffards, Phineas M., (7n6), 353n6
Jenkins, (Col.) (first name unknown), 225
Jericho Ford, 113, 372n144
Jerusalem Plank Road, 158, 263
Jetersville, 177–178, 178, 179
Johnson, Bushrod Rust, 176, 380n190
Johnson, Dr. Samuel, 192
Johnson, Edward, 106, 371n133
Johnston, Joseph E., 104, 240, 381n194
Jordan, William S., 210

K

Keene, Samuel T.
 court martial, 82
 death of, 125, 127–128, 251
 detail as Major, 92
 Gettysburg, 310, 361n60
 letter to wife, 361n60
 Little Round Top, 37
 Mud March, 198
 Petersburg, 124–126
 photographs, *II, V, XIII*
 promotion, 28, 209, 307, 358n38
 recruiting, 88
 Wilderness, 343
Keene, Sarah F. (Sace), *V, XIII, XV,* x, 88–89, 90, 336
Keene, Weston H., 153, 379n178
Kendall, Warren L., 28, 216
Kennedy, John M., 34, 199, 254, 314, 360n52
kitchens, 77, 78, 87, 88
Knight, James A., 34, 314, 360n51
Knox, (Maj.) (first name unknown), 342

L

Land, Joseph F.
  Bethesda Church, 248
  creation of 20th Maine, 5, 6, 290–291
  Fredericksburg, 22, 302
  leave, 235
  Lee's retreat, 222, 321
  Little Round Top, 313
  promotion, 28, 307, 353n5
  sister (Mrs. Clifford), 203
  Weldon Railroad, 250, 266
Laurel Hill Brigade, 240, 345
Lee, Robert E., 30, 61, 74–75, 182–183, 215
  Mine Run, 366n96
  See also Lee's Army; military strategy; battles
Lee's Army
  Bethesda, 116
  Chancellorsville, 27, 30–32
  Five Forks, 381n194
  Gettysburg, 311
  retreat, 41–52, 176–180, 216, 319–323, 362n63, 382n197
  Spotsylvania, 112, 115, 370n125
  surrender, 181–183, 272, 382n198
  Weldon Railroad, 141
  winter quarters, 93
Leesburg, 29, 213, 214, 358n41
leisure activities, 17, 48, 59, 84, 89, 131
Lewis, Addison, 264
Lewis Farm, 166–167, 270
Libbey tent, 73
Libby, Joseph W., 153, 379n178
Libby prison, 187, 275, 382n202
lice, 24
Lincoln, Abraham, 185, 273, 353n4, 355n17, 357n34, 358n43, 361n61

Linscott, Joseph, 208
Litchfield, Alden, 46, 51–52, 210, 234, 235, 260, 267, 274, 330
  See also quartermaster
Little Round Top, 33–37, 215, 216, 217–221, 311–317, 360n55
  memorial, x, 312
  See also Gettysburg
Long Bridge, 10, 121, 249, 354n13
Longstreet, James, (48n68), 74, 182, 215, 272, 362n68, 369n124
lumbermen, 143–144

M

MacIntyre, George R., 198, 202, 204, 231, 232, 234, 267, 330
Madison, 93
Madison Court House, 324
mail. *See friends and relatives of Ellis Spear*
Maine Troops
  First Cavalry, 64, 69
  militia before 1861, 4
  sharpshooters, 189, 190, 191
  11th and 12th Infantry Regiment, 341
  6th Infantry Regiment, 62, 103, 328, 344
  20th Infantry Regiment
    Company B, 33–35, 62, 129, 313, 328
    Company E, 73
    Company K, 316
    creation of, 6, 7, 290–291
    first battle, 12–13
    mustered out, 189–190, 190, 383n206
    photograph of officers, *XII, XIII*
    reporting to Washington, 10, 292

Maine Troops *(continued)*
  training of, 8, 9, 293
  trip home, 191–194, 282
  See also battles; soldier's names
malaria, 14, 28, 30, 132, 296, 310
Maley, James, 274, 285
Manassas. *See* Bull Run
Manassas Gap, 44, 219, 320, 322
Manassas Junction, 29, 54, 212, 227, 309
Manchester, 187
Marshall, Charles, 182
Martin, Augustus P., 53
Marye's Heights, (18), 27, 308, 357n34, 357n35
  See also Chancellorsville; Fredericksburg
Massachusetts Troops
  22nd Infantry Regiment, 91, 100
  32nd Infantry Regiment, 123
  18th Infantry Regiment, 91, 95, 100, 124, 152, 251, 339
  36th Infantry Regiment, 10, 292, 354n10
  56th Infantry Regiment, 347
  57th Infantry Regiment, 92, 93, 107, 368n115
Mattaponi River, 110, 111, 349, 372n140
Mayhew, Ruth, 48, 223, 224, 238, 255
McCausland, John, 377n168
McClellan, George B., 32, 215, 297, 303, 311
  relieved of command, 16, 355n17
McCoy, DeWitt, (95n117), 339, 369n117
McCray, (first name unknown), 284
McDonald, Isaac H., (7n6), 353n6
McLaws, Lafayette, (48n68), 362n68

McLean House, 182, 272
  See also Appomattox
Meade, George G., 204, 221, 358n43
  Appomattox, 182, 274
  Centreville, 363n76, 363n77
  Gettysburg, 39, 311, 359n46, 361n61
  Mine Run, 365n90, 365n92
  Pegram's Farm, 154, 261
  Petersburg, 134, 255
  soldiers attitude towards, 31
  Weldon Railroad, 145, 259
medicine, 24, 38, 142–143, 278
  See also doctor; disease
Melcher, Holman S., 36, 103, 240, 255, 344, 360n55
Merriam, Henry C., 242
Meserve, Elisha, 197, 198
Meservey, Benjamin F., 369n119
Michigan Troops
  1st Infantry Regiment, 124, 244, 251
  16th Infantry Regiment, 277
    Chancellorsville, 29, 211, 213
    Gravelly Run, 167
    Peebles Farm, 149
    Petersburg, 124, 251
    reorganization, 91
    Shepherdstown, 12
    Spotsylvania, 104, 111, 240
    Wheatfield, 312
    Wilderness, 98, 100, 344
Middleburg, 30, 214, 358n41
Middletown, 216, 310
military strategy
  Appomattox, 181
  Culpeper, 53, 362n65, 362n68, 363n70
  Five Forks, 380n189
  Fort Stedman, 379n183
  Fredericksburg, 18

military strategy *(continued)*
  Jetersville, 177
  Little Round Top-Gettysburg, 359n47, 359n48, 361n57
  Mine Run, 68, 74, 365n90
  North Anna River, 115, 373n146
  Petersburg, 373n149, 373n150, 374n151
  Rappahannock Station, 62, 364n81, 364n83
  shadowing Lee's army near Centreville, 29, 358n40, 358n42
  Sickles at Gettysburg, 359n46
  Spotsylvania, 371n136
  Weldon Railroad, 140, 377n171
  Wilderness, 98–99, 370n129
Miller, Alden Jr., 255, 345
Milton, John, 363n77, 367n109, 373n150, 374n156, 380n188, 381n193, 383n205
Mine Run, 67–76, 233, 330–335, 365n90, 365n93, 366n95, 366n96
Mink, Charles E., 152
Moloch, 171, 380n188, 381n193
Monacacy River, 31, 214
money, 49, 136, 299, 367n104, 377n167
Monroe, (first name unknown), 251
Moody, (first name unknown), 197, 198, 202
Moore, Sir John, 22, 356n27
Morrell, William W., *VI,* 103, 107, 240, 344, 370n128
Morrill, Walter G.
  Little Round Top, 33–35, 313–315, 359n48
  mustering out, 190, 270, 278
  Petersburg, 254
  photograph, *X*
  promotion, 166, 370n128

Morrill, Walter G. *(continued)*
  Rappahannock Station, 62–63, 328
  Weldon Railroad, 141, 258, 259, 266, 379n182
Morrill's Neck bridge, 166
Morrisville, 212
Mott, Gersham, 371n130
Mount Cassod Church, 112
Mud March, 25–26, 197–198, 304–308, 356n31, 357n32
Munrow, Nathum P., 24

N

Nash, E.A., 246
New London, 194, 282
New York Troops
  5th Cavalry, 173
  17th Infantry, 200
  44th Infantry Regiment, 94, 331
    Lee's retreat, 42–43
    Mine Run, 68, 365n91
    reorganization, 91
    Shepherdstown, 12
    Spotsylvania, 108, 240
    Wilderness, 94, 100, 338, 342
  Ninth Corps
    Bethesda Church, 116
    Peebles Farm, 151, 261
    Pegram's Farm, 152, 155
    Petersburg, 128, 138
    Spotsylvania, 107, 109
    Weldon Railroad, 257
    Wilderness, 92
Norfolk and Petersburg Railroad, 124
North Anna River, 113, 115, 132, 244, 373n146
North Carolina Troops, 142, 378n173
Ny River, 111, 244

O

Oates, William C., 35, 359n49, 360n53
officers
  incompetence, 12, 18, 22, 53, 135, 139, 298, 303
  lack of experience, 6–7
  pay, 46, 92, 136, 156, 330
  rations, 46, 85
  See also individual names
Old Fields, 104, 109, 220, 252, 345
Orange and Alexandria Railroad, 29, 45, 76, 212, 325
Orange Turnpike, 94
Overlock, David N., 105, 241
Owen, William H., 279
Ox Bow Creek, 56, 325
Ox Road, 228

P

Page, Neal, 218
Pamunkey River, 115
Partridge, Benjamin F., 167, 168
pay, 46, 92, 136
Pearson, Alfred L., (97n122), 340, 369n122
Peebles Farm, 148–151, 186, 260, 275
Pegram's Farm, 152–157
Peninsula Campaign, 5, 290
Pennsylvania Troops, 134
  83rd Infantry Regiment
    Little Round Top, 33
    Mine Run, 331, 365n91
    Peebles Farm, 151
    reorganization, 91
    Shepherdstown, 12
    Wilderness, 94–95, 337–339
  reserves, 57, 101, 240, 317, 343, 370n127
  11th Infantry Regiment, 97, 149, 343
  118th Infantry Regiment
    Pegram's Farm, 152
    Petersburg, 124, 251
    reorganization, 91
    Spotsylvania, 111, 240, 244
    Weldon Railroad, 141, 145
    Wilderness, 97, 98, 100, 341
  155th Infantry Regiment, 97, 340
  198th Infantry Regiment, 179
Pero, Henry, 25
Petersburg, 123–140, 186, 250–257, 373n149, 374n151, 374n152, 375n158
  Mine Assault, 134–136, 256, 376n165, 376n166
Philadelphia, 193, 282
Phillips, Charles A., 117
Pickett's Charge, 39, 318, 361n58
Pickett's Division, 176, 380n184
Plummer, Rufus B., *XIII*, 336
plundering, 73, 155, 164, 170, 177, 332
pontoon bridges, 16, 302
Pope, Alexander, 39, 361n59
Portland, 194, 283
Preble, George, 212
Prescott, Hiram L., 123
Price Station, 273
Prince, Howard L., 35, 103, 152, 240, 248, 344
prisoners
  after war, 273
  Five Forks, 381n192
  Gettysburg, 43, 215, 314, 316
  Peeble's Farm, 151
  Petersburg, 250
  Rappahannock Station, 63

prisoners *(continued)*
  Spotsylvania, 115, 241, 243, 244
  Weldon Railroad, 142, 258
  Wilderness, 101, 245, 341
Providence, 194, 283

Q

Quaker Road, 166, 270
quartermaster
  arrest of, 326
  counterfeit money, 49, 324
  euchre, 199
  hay incident, 82
  horses, 46, 51–52
  inexperience of, 7
  peaches, 126
  tobacco incident, 64, 330

R

Railroads. *See individual Railroad names*
Rankin, William, 299
Rapidan River, 67, 68, 93, 330, 335, 337
Rappahannock River, 28, 47, 61, 225, 322, 325, 335
Rappahannock Station, *XI,* 61–67, 230–232, 235, 327–330, 335
Rawlins, John A., 172, 267
Reams' Station, 147, 325
Rectorville, 44, 219
Reed, Edwin, 198, 203, 208, 209, 210, 211, 231, 257, 262, 273
"refusing" a line, 18, 355n22
"Reservoir" Hill, 134, 256
Rice, (first name unknown), 206
Rice, James Clay, 72, 364n82, 365n93
Richmond, 187

Richmond and Danville Railroad, 179, 249, 382n196
Richmond Campaign, 194
rifles. *See* weapons
Ripley, (first name unknown), 238
Ritchie, (Capt.) (first name unknown), 265
Robertson Tavern, 70, 232, 365n89
Robinson, Albert D., 200, 214, 228
Robinson, (first name unknown), 203, 208, 236, 262
Rockville, 294
Rodes, Robert E., 116
Roosevelt, Theodore, (125n155), 374n155
Ross, Ezekial, 205
Rosser, Thomas L., 272
Russel's Brigade, 328

S

Sabin, (Maj.) (first name unknown), 202
Sailors' Creek, 179–180, 382n197
Sanitary Commission, 130, 254, 376n161
Sawyer, (Capt.) (first name unknown), 173, 191
Sawyer, (Christian Commission) (first name unknown), 249
Second Corps
  Culpeper Court House, 48
  Harrison's Landing, 249
  Jetersville, 178
  Manassas Junction, 54
  Mine Run, 332–333
  Pegram's Farm, 155
  Petersburg, 122, 123, 132, 138
  Weldon Railroad, 140, 257
  Wilderness, 94

Sedgwick, John, 27, 94, 342, 357n34, 357n36, 365n92
seven thirties (coupon notes), 136–137, 377n167
Shady Grove Church, 149
Sharpsburg Pike, 42, 319
sharpshooters, 35, 128, 189, 190, 191
Shaw, Abner O., 43
Sheldon, Warren, 209
shelter, 14, 15, 17, 59–60, 66–67, 132, 298, 304–305, 331, 335
   1863 winter quarters, 23–24, 303–307
   1864 winter quarters, 77–79, 335–337
Shenandoah River, 16, 297
Shepherdstown, 12–13, 294–296
Shepherdstown Ford, 12
Sheridan, Philip Henry
   Appomattox, 182, 272
   Five Forks, 166, 168, 171–172, 174, 175, 271, 381n191
   halting Lee's Right, 166
   Sailor's Creek, 180
   Spear's account of, 174, 181
   Weldon Railroad, 146, 147
   Winchester, 148, 378n176
Sherman, William T., 104, 190, 277
Sibley tent, 84, 89, 367n106
Sickles, Daniel E., 33, 359n46
Sickles' Angle, 312
Sidelinger, Henry F., 235, 265
Sixth Corps
   Antietam Creek, 43
   Centreville, 55
   Five Forks, 166
   Jetersville, 178
   Marye's Heights, 27, 308
   Mine Run, 70, 73, 331–332, 334
   Petersburg, 137
   Petersburg, 251, 138

Sixth Corps *(continued)*
   Rappahannock Station, 62–63, 328
   Spotsylvania, 103, 112, 116, 242, 245
   Wilderness, 94, 340, 342, 344
small pox, 26, 28, 306–307
Smith, James H., 198
Snicker's Gap, 16, 219, 310, 358n42
Snickersville, 30
soldiers
   character, 13, 25, 180, 192
   discipline, 63–64, 80–82, 160–162
   Irish, 80–82, 161–162
   leisure activities, 84, 130
   morale, 56, 58, 63–64, 75, 90, 92, 125, 180, 347
   recruitment, 6, 165
South Mountain, 12, 43, 294–295, 319–320, 354n14
South Side Railroad, 155, 174, 175, 185, 274
South Side Road, 148, 172
Spear, Ellis
   arrest of, 15
   birth of daughter, 157
   Chamberlain, opinion of, 307
   civilian life, ix, x
   command of PA regiment, ix, 179
   commission, ix
   diaries of, xi
   as Division Inspector, 65–66
   later years, x
   leave of absence, 157, 202–203, 235–237, 262–263
   Lee, opinion of, 170, 182
   Little Round Top testimony, 36, 360n55
   marriage, x, 203–204, 306
   Northern soldiers, opinion of, 5, 191–192

Spear, Ellis *(continued)*
  photographs, *ii, I, III, XII, XIII, XIV, XVI, XVII*
  promotion, 28, 46, 153, 189, 307
  recruiting, 5, 165, 266–269
  sickness, 30, 37, 156, 306, 310, 317
  Southerners, opinion of, 170
  teaching, 4, 290
  wounded, 114
Spear, Emily, 217, 252, 284
Spear, Guilford, 208
Spear, Hannah, 208, 210, 222, 224, 252, 255, 279
Spear, Jason, 209, 279
Spear, Julia, 157
Spear, Pauline, 197, 198, 209, 210, 217, 219, 221, 224, 226, 229, 231, 232, 243, 246, 253, 254, 256, 260, 280, 284
Spear, Samuel Perkins, 149
Spear, Susan Wilde (wife), x, 88, 89, 90, 116, 165, 196, 197, 198, 199, 200, 201, 202, 203, 204, 205, 206, 208, 209, 210, 211, 216, 217, 218, 219, 220, 221, 222, 223, 224, 225, 226, 228, 229, 230, 231, 232, 234, 235, 236, 238, 243, 246, 248, 250, 252, 253, 254, 255, 256, 257, 259, 260, 262, 264, 265, 266, 267, 268, 270, 273, 275, 276, 278, 279, 280, 281, 282, 306, 336, 337
  photographs, *IV, XIII*
"spiders," 87
Spotsylvania Court House, 99, 103–116, 240–246, 341, 345–350, 371n131, 371n132, 371n134, 371n135
Squirrel Level Road, 149
Stafford Heights, (18n23), 355n23
Stamford, 157, 165, 202, 283
Stanwood, James E., 336
Starrett, Isaac P., 223
Stoneman's Switch, 18, 298, 306
Stuart, J.E.B., 31, 358n44
Stubins, (first name unknown), 266
Sumner, Edwin V., 356n29
supplies, 92–93
sutler, 61, 84, 200, 367n108
Sweitzer, Jacob B., 246, 247, 248
Sykes, George, 43, 71, 233, 362n64, 365n92

T

tactics. *See* military strategy
Ta River, 111, 244
Tenalley Town Road, 294
tents, 59, 73, 84, 89, 93, 331, 367n101, 367n106
Texas Troops, 37, 215, 316
Thomas, Ruel, 36
Three Mile Station, 60, 230, 326
Throop, William A., 247, 259
Tibbetts, Jotham D., 197, 198, 200
Tilghmanville, 42, 362n63
Tilton, W. S., (84n105), 367n105
tobacco, 61, 64, 85, 93, 136, 184, 326–327, 330
Tozier, Andrew J., 34
truce, 138
Tyler, (first name unknown), 281

U

uniforms, 9, 46, 79, 94, 292
Unionville, 31, 215, 358n44
Upperville, 44, 219, 310
Upton, Emory, 370n130

V

Verrill, Charles H., 197, 198, 208, 209, 215, 216, 219, 222, 224, 229, 234, 248, 252, 254, 260, 262, 270, 277, 279, 281
videttes, 129, 130, 132, 133, 375n159
Vinal, John, 23, 37, 301, 303, 356n30
Vincent, Strong, (33n47), 359n47, 364n82
Virginia Troops, 111, 272
Vitruvius, 77, 366n99

W

Wales, Richard D., 285
Walker, James A., 272
Wapping Heights, 320
war, first reports of, 4, 289
Warren, Gouverneur Kemble, 359n47
  Bethesda Church, 118–119
  displacement of, 175
  Five Forks, 173–174, 381n191
  Mine Run, 72, 75, 332–333, 334, 366n93, 366n95
  Petersburg, 134, 255
  Reams Station, 325
  Spotsylvania, 370n125, 371n135
  Weldon Railroad, 145, 259, 377n171
Warrenton, 16, 45, 46, 220, 297
Warrenton Junction, 53, 221, 227
Warrenton Road, 59
Washington, DC, 188, 296
weapons, 73, 93, 129, 146, 211, 330, 375n160, 378n175
Welch, Norval E., 146, 149–151, 167, 257, 261
Weldon Railroad, 140–148, 158–166, 257–260, 263, 378n173, 379n181
West, John, 30, 197, 198, 214, 225, 310
Wheatfield battle, 311–312
  See also Gettysburg
whiskey, 38, 142–143, 161–162
White, (first name unknown), 251
White, Sylvanus R., 251
White Oak Road, 171, 270
White Plains, 17, 297
White's Ford, 30
White Sulfur Springs, 322
Wilde, John (Susan Spear's father), 203
Wilde, Sara, 306
Wilde, Susie M. *See* Spear, Susan Wilde
Wilderness, Battle of the, 68, 92–103, 239, 337–345, 368n116, 369n118, 369n123
Williams, Jotham D., 198
Williamsport, 217
Wilson's Station, 186
Winchester, 148, 378n176
Winslow, Allison, 199
winter quarters
  of *1863,* 23–24, 198–205, 303–307
  of *1864,* 76–92, 234–238, 335–337
Wiscasset, 4–5
Wise, Henry A., 167, 272
women
  at Dr. Boisseau's house, 169–170
  visiting camp, 88–89, 90, 91, 336–337
Wood, George H., 267
Woodward, Orpheus, (95n117), 339, 369n117
Wright, Fred Roscoe, 127, 199
Wright, Horatio G., 106, 370n130, 371n131, 371n132, 377n169

X

Xenophon, 53, 363n71